# George Orwell's
# Perverse Humanity

# George Orwell's Perverse Humanity

## Socialism and Free Speech

*Glenn Burgess*

BLOOMSBURY ACADEMIC
NEW YORK • LONDON • OXFORD • NEW DELHI • SYDNEY

BLOOMSBURY ACADEMIC
Bloomsbury Publishing Inc
1385 Broadway, New York, NY 10018, USA
50 Bedford Square, London, WC1B 3DP, UK
29 Earlsfort Terrace, Dublin 2, Ireland

BLOOMSBURY, BLOOMSBURY ACADEMIC and the Diana logo are
trademarks of Bloomsbury Publishing Plc

First published in the United States of America 2023

Cover design: Eleanor Rose
Cover image: Lion and Unicorn from linocut prints by Edward Bawden CBE RA
(1903–1989) © World History Archive / Alamy

Library of Congress Cataloging-in-Publication Data
Names: Burgess, Glenn, 1961- author.
Title: George Orwell's perverse humanity : socialism and free speech / Glenn Burgess.
Description: New York : Bloomsbury Academic, 2023. |
Includes bibliographical references and index. |
Summary: "A portrait of George Orwell that gives centre-stage to his deep commitment to
freedom of speech and thought, and to speaking truth to power"– Provided by publisher.
Identifiers: LCCN 2022045298 (print) | LCCN 2022045299 (ebook) | ISBN 9781501394669
(hardback) | ISBN 9781501394652 (paperback) | ISBN 9781501394676 (ebook) |
ISBN 9781501394683 (pdf) | ISBN 9781501394690 (ebook other)
Subjects: LCSH: Orwell, George, 1903–1950–Political and social views. |
Socialism. | Freedom of speech. | Politics and literature–Great Britain–History–20th century.
Classification: LCC PR6029.R8 Z595 2023 (print) | LCC PR6029.R8 (ebook) |
DDC 823/.912–dc23/eng/20220928
LC record available at https://lccn.loc.gov/2022045298
LC ebook record available at https://lccn.loc.gov/2022045299

ISBN:   HB:    978-1-5013-9466-9
        PB:    978-1-5013-9465-2
        ePDF:  978-1-5013-9468-3
        eBook: 978-1-5013-9467-6

Typeset by Integra Software Services Pvt. Ltd.

To find out more about our authors and books visit www.bloomsbury.com
and sign up for our newsletters.

*In memory of Colin Davis (1940–2021)*
*Teacher, Mentor, Friend*

# CONTENTS

# PREFACE

Writing this book has taken me far from my usual patch as an historian of early modern British political thought. It was begun while I worked in university senior management and was unable to continue with substantial archive-based research, and was finished as a Covid lockdown project. But it takes me back to a teenage obsession with the writing of George Orwell. The state of the world over the last few years seemed to demand a re-engagement with this early interest. I began the book working almost entirely from primary sources – Orwell's books, essays, journalism, diaries, notebooks and letters. Only gradually in the course of the project did I come to grips with the vast scholarly literature on Orwell. That has been an enormous pleasure: Orwell has been the subject of much excellent work. I owe a particular debt to Bernard Crick's biography – not because it is the best, though it may be, but because it is the one of most use to someone interested in Orwell as a political thinker – and to John Newsinger's work on Orwell's political ideas. The book has benefited enormously from the supportive but challenging comments of the four anonymous readers of the proposal and/or typescript commissioned by Bloomsbury, and from the advice and support of Amy Martin and Hali Han of Bloomsbury Academic. It has been a pleasure working with them and with this publisher. I am most grateful also to Shamli Priya of Integra Software Services for her superb project management of the technical production of the book.

Like everyone who works on Orwell today, my debt to Peter Davison, editor of Orwell's complete works, is beyond measure. Davison, whom I never met or corresponded with, died only a couple of weeks before I write this. Having lived with the fruits of his editorial work for several years, I can only say that it is difficult to find sufficient praise. Davison's edition is more than it claims: meticulously annotated, it builds into a vast compendium of information about Orwell and his life. I know of nothing else quite like it. I would like to thank Ariane Bankes for providing me with material from the diary of her mother, Celia Goodman, as well as the many kind and helpful archivists who facilitated my research in the Orwell Archive (University College London), the National Archives at Kew, the Liberty Archive at the Hull History Centre and the papers of Arthur Koestler at the Edinburgh University Library. Researchers rely heavily on librarians and archivists, and all of those whom I have encountered have been unfailingly knowledgeable and generous in the help they provided. In addition to those whom I actually met, archivists at the Modern Records Centre, University of Warwick, scanned some material for me from Victor Gollancz's papers, without charge.

The last year of my work on this project has been a melancholy one. Three people with whom I have talked about my work on Orwell died, and I deeply regret that I shall not have the opportunity to discuss this book with them. My father, who died in February 2022, shared Orwell's deep sense of social justice, dedicating much of his life to the Labour movement in New Zealand. My Hull colleague and friend, Howell Lloyd, who died in May 2022, demanded monthly updates on my progress over a pint or two at Larkin's Bar. But I dedicate the book to Colin Davis (J.C. Davis to those who know him only from his writing). Colin taught me many years ago, at Victoria University in Wellington, New Zealand. He inspired my interests in the seventeenth century and in the history of political thought, and has been a mentor and friend for my entire adult life. Colin guided me towards the Prince of Wales Scholarship that took me to Cambridge and a PhD. Without Colin, I would not have had the career of an academic historian. He opened up possibilities that I did not know existed. Colin, too, had a lifelong interest in Orwell, who has always attracted the dissident Left. My debt to Colin, and to his widow, Sandra, is incalculable.

**A Note on References:** All references to Orwell's works (including diaries, notebooks and letters) are to Peter Davison's edition of the *Collected Works* (abbreviated throughout as CW). For Orwell's books (and his *Diaries*), I have also provided references to the current editions in Penguin Classics, as these may be more accessible to many readers. For most of the books, the pagination is the same in CW and Penguin, but not in all. These are the only editions of the books that reflect Peter Davison's editorial work.

Peter Davison (ed.), *The Complete Works of George Orwell* (London: Secker & Warburg, 20 vols. 1986–98; revised paperback edition of vols X–XX, 2001). There is also a volume of supplementary material: Davison (ed.), *The Lost Orwell* (London: Timewell Press, 2006). The last eleven volumes (X–XX) and *The Lost Orwell* (i.e. everything except Orwell's full-length published books) have been published in a well-organized, searchable (and cheap) Kindle edition from Penguin Books, *The Collected Non-Fiction: Essays, Articles, Diaries and Letters, 1903–1950* (London: Penguin, Kindle edition, 2017).

Glenn Burgess
September 2022

# Prologue: *'Ownlife,* it was called, meaning individualism and eccentricity'

'We hold that the most perverse human being is more interesting than the most orthodox gramophone record.'[1] Perverse humanity: the phrase today may have connotations alien to George Orwell. It was his way of aligning himself with heresy rather than orthodoxy, with nonconformity rather than conformity, with plain-spokenness not ideological evasiveness, with direct speech not circumlocution, with speaking truth (as you see it) not hiding it in a 'good' cause, with fearlessness not timidity, with eccentricity not conventionality. Orwell lived his perversity.[2] He developed in his own life a reputation for unbending integrity and eccentricity, but also for cussedness and wrong-headedness. He was a ferocious and fearless debater in print, not always fair to his opponents, and seldom inclined to give ground. He sought to experience life among the poor of Paris and London, among hop-pickers and tramps, among the miners of northern England, to escape the limitations of his own class. The world needed to be made safe for perverse people of Orwell's kind. It could be made safe by a sort of liberal Socialism, one that both cherished the intellectual freedoms that gave perverse people the space to speak their minds, and ensured an equality that empowered everyone with the resources to exercise their own particular form of perversity.

---

[1]George Orwell, 'Books and the People: A New Year Message', January 1945, CW, XVII, p. 11.
[2]See also William E. Cain, 'Orwell's Perversity: An Approach to the Collected Essays', in Thomas Cushman & John Rodden (eds), *George Orwell into the Twenty-First Century* (London: Routledge, 2004), ch. 15.

# 1. Orwell and the Culture Wars

In November 2017 George Orwell appeared outside Broadcasting House, the BBC's London home. Orwell had worked for the BBC during the Second World War, producing propaganda broadcasts for India. His former employer had (eventually and with some reluctance) accepted an offer to have a sculpture of him placed outside their headquarters. Martin Jennings, the sculptor, delighted in the opportunity to capture in bronze Orwell's body and mind: 'to express both his mental and physical angularity. Orwell was forever a member of the awkward squad and his tall bony frame was almost purpose-built to express this'.[3] Three years later, another member of the awkward squad, musician and activist Billy Bragg, declared that 'whenever I walk past this effigy of the English writer that I most admire, it makes me cringe'.[4]

This was not a judgement on the artistic quality of Jennings' work (even though *Private Eye* awarded it – with Orwellian linguistic precision – its 2017 prize for the ugliest new building).[5] No, what made Billy Bragg cringe was the quotation from Orwell that was engraved on the wall adjacent to the sculpture. 'If liberty means anything at all, it means the right to tell people what they do not want to hear.' Orwell wrote these words in 1945 as a preface to *Animal Farm*. Frustrated by the difficulty he had in finding a publisher for the first book that would make him famous, Orwell was furious. No one wanted to hear his attack on Britain's Soviet allies while they were winning the war against Hitler. His book had been turned down by four publishers and Orwell wrote his preface to denounce the cowardice and bad faith of 'liberals who fear liberty and the intellectuals who want to do dirt on the intellect'. By the time *Animal Farm* was published in August 1945, he had calmed down and his fiery defence of freedom of the press was not used. It would not be published until 1972.[6]

There is much in Orwell that might strike the modern reader as cringe-worthy. His scorn for artificial contraception, aspirin, tinned foods, 'the pansy left', vegetarians, feminists, pacifists, sandal-wearers, health-food cranks; his persistent misogyny; even his struggles to free himself from

---

[3]About the BBC Blog, 7 November 2017, https://www.bbc.co.uk/blogs/aboutthebbc/entries/41a0eedb-c435-479d-aa63-a89ad81daf01 (accessed 3 February 2021).

[4]Billy Bragg, '"Cancel culture" Doesn't Stifle Debate but It Does Challenge the Old Order', *The Guardian*, 10 July 2020, https://www.theguardian.com/commentisfree/2020/jul/10/free-speech-young-people (accessed 3 February 2021).

[5]'Statue of George Orwell', *Wikipedia*, https://en.wikipedia.org/wiki/Statue_of_George_Orwell (accessed 3 February 2021).

[6]George Orwell, *Animal Farm: A Fairy Story* [CW, VIII] (London: Secker & Warburg, 1986), pp. 97–108. The quotations are from p. 108. The first publication of this essay was in *The Times Literary Supplement*, no 3680 (15 September 1972), pp. 1037–9.

ingrained anti-semitism – none of this has dated well (possibly excluding the bit about sandal-wearers). A good deal (but not all) of his vituperation was aimed at the emergence of an artificial, mechanistic, industrial mass society. He raged against a collectivist modernity the triumph of which he thought inevitable. Even so, it's surprising, given the range of Orwell's eccentric, trenchantly expressed and intransigently held prejudices, that he has so far escaped the worst that our contemporary cancel culture can do. In the face of all of this, his resounding defence of free speech seems an odd thing before which to cringe.

But free speech is having a hard time in our culture wars. Weaponized by those on the Right who want protection for their racism, transphobia and misogyny, and repudiated by elements on the Left who think that liberalism has failed to make progress in tackling precisely these matters,[7] freedom of speech has become a toxic issue. 'Surely,' asks an uneasy Billy Bragg, 'the author of *Nineteen Eighty-Four* would understand that people don't want to hear that 2+2=5?' (*Yes, we might respond, but he also understood the danger in arrogating to yourself the final judgement about what people do and don't want to hear. Who decides?*) 'Orwell's quote is not a defence of liberty; it's a demand for licence, and has become a foundational slogan for those who wilfully misconstrue one for the other.' (*And, we might continue: dismissing liberty as licence is a lazy way of claiming just this power to judge what other people can hear – or say.*)

Hear or say: Orwell's statement was about people's freedom to *say*. (It was more than that, as we shall see, involving also a *duty* to speak the truth as one sees it.) Being able to say something doesn't amount to a right to demand that anyone else must listen to you. Nor does it require others to refrain from condemning, criticizing, refuting, ridiculing or reviling what you have said. Orwell has become a free speech icon,[8] his name invoked globally in causes and campaigns of all description. Some random examples: Brad Polumbo invoked Orwell to defend Bari Weiss, forced to resign her role as columnist for the *New York Times* by 'the outright harassment and cruelty she faced at the hands of her colleagues';[9] attendees at the Bristol Festival of Ideas 2019, on the other hand, had the opportunity to hear

---

[7]For the Left disavowal of liberalism, see for example Mark Bray, *Antifa: The Anti-Fascist Handbook* (Brooklyn, NY: Melville House, 2017), ch. 5; and Natasha Lennard, *Being Numerous: Essays on Non-Fascist Life* (London: Verso, 2019), ch. 9. One could argue for a much longer tradition of this stretching from the illiberal Stalinist-sympathetic Left of Orwell's day, via Marcuse (et al.), to contemporary Antifa intellectuals. See Robert Paul Wolff, Barrington Moore Jnr & Herbert Marcuse, *A Critique of Pure Tolerance* (Boston, MA: Beacon Press, 1969).

[8]A Google search for Orwell + free speech generates over 3.3 million results.

[9]Brad Polumbo, 'How "Self-Censorship" Hurts Free Speech: Why George Orwell's Warning about Being Silenced Is More Relevant than Ever', https://catalyst.independent.org/2020/07/20/free-speech-self-censorship-hurts-orwell/ (accessed 7 February 2021).

how those 'who wish to continue to have racist, misogynist, homophobic thoughts' took Orwell's name in vain,[10] while the *Wall Street Journal* ran in 2017 an opinion piece on political correctness in universities under the title 'Censorship Is Free Speech? It Must Be the Class of 1984'.[11] Everyone thinks they know George Orwell. Yet his faith in freedom of thought, freedom of expression and a free press had features that have been lost to public memory. He can be more at odds with some of our own values than he might initially appear.

Orwell often enjoyed the company of people with whom he disagreed. Public debate, however, was another matter. He was neither gentle nor benign in argument. He was not above lashing out with personal abuse. He was unfair in debate, attributing to people caricatured versions of the thoughts they had expressed, and much inclined to doubting people's motives as a way of undermining their ideas. His was an *adversarial* world of ideas. He even took steps to avoid the sort of human feeling that might compromise his intellectual brutality, as he told Stephen Spender (one of his 'pansy poets'):

> Even if when I met you I had not happened to like you, I should still have been bound to change my attitude, because when you meet anyone in the flesh you realise immediately that he is a human being and not a sort of a caricature embodying certain ideas. It is partly for this reason that I don't mix much in literary circles, because I know from experience that once I have met & spoken to someone I shall never again be able to show any intellectual brutality towards him, even when I feel that I ought to …[12]

Spender quickly forgave Orwell his personal insults, and became a staunch defender of his integrity. He later recorded in his diary a response to Michael Ayton's disparaging remarks on Orwell's writing about Spain: 'I said angrily that George Orwell was able to judge matters by the standards of his own life which in politics were as exacting as those of a saint.'[13] Even being already a friend of Orwell's was no protection against a roughing-up. Arthur Koestler complained to Orwell about his unsparing review of Koestler's play

---

[10]https://www.ideasfestival.co.uk/blog/festival-of-the-future-city/thought-police-and-freedom-of-speech/ (accessed 7 February 2021).

[11]Jillian Kay Melchior, 'Censorship Is Free Speech? It Must Be the Class of 1984', *Wall Street Journal*, 27 January 2017, https://www.wsj.com/articles/censorship-is-free-speech-it-must-be-the-class-of-1984-1485478244 (accessed 7 February 2021).

[12]Orwell to Stephen Spender, 15 April 1938, CW, XI, p. 132.

[13]Stephen Spender, *New Selected Journals 1939–1994*, ed. Lara Feigel & John Sutherland, with Natasha Spender (London: Faber & Faber, 2012), p. 256.

*Twilight Bar.* '"It was a bloody review you wrote, wasn't it?" He said, "Yes, it's a bloody bad play, isn't it?"'[14]

Apart from wartime security, Orwell identified few boundaries to debate. One of his more noteworthy skirmishes was about pacifism and took place in the pages of *Partisan Review* in 1941. (It is discussed later in this book.) When George Woodcock one of the combatants wrote a year later to take issue on another matter, Orwell replied, 'I am afraid I answered rather roughly in the "Partisan Review" controversy. I always do when I'm attacked – however, no malice either side, I hope.'[15] Orwell and Woodcock became good friends.[16] Giving offence was part of the fun. Orwell *enjoyed* combat with the typewriter; he relished putting his enemies to the verbal sword. He would have had little time for modern sensitivities and our marked (if selective) reluctance to upset others.

In other ways, though, Orwell hardly needed the lecture he got from Billy Bragg, who scolded:

Although free speech remains the fundamental bedrock of a free society, for everyone to enjoy the benefits of freedom, liberty needs to be tempered by two further dimensions: equality and accountability. Without equality, those in power will use their freedom of expression to abuse and marginalise others. Without accountability, liberty can mutate into the most dangerous of all freedoms – impunity.

Let's consider for a moment these things that might temper freedom of speech.

---

[14]Arthur Koestler, Interview with Iain Hamilton, 5 March 1974, pp. 28–9, Edinburgh University Library, Koestler Papers, MS 2436/5. There is a softer version of the story in 'Koestler on His Friend', in Audrey Coppard & Bernard Crick (eds), *Orwell Remembered* (London: Ariel Books / BBC, 1984), p. 168.

[15]Orwell to George Woodcock, 2 December 1942, CW, XIV, p. 214.

[16]Another example of the enemy-turned friend also emerged from the *Partisan Review* episode, Alex Comfort: see Eric Laursen, *The Duty to Stand Aside: Nineteen Eighty-Four and the Wartime Quarrel of George Orwell and Alex Comfort* (Chico, CA: AK Press, 2018). Notwithstanding the outbreak of better relations between them, Orwell included Comfort in the notorious list of names that he gave Celia Kirwan for the Information Research Department in 1949. Those named were considered by Orwell to be too sympathetic to Communism to be asked to write anti-Soviet propaganda. He said of Comfort: 'Potential only. Is pacifist-anarchist. Main emphasis anti-British. Subjectively pro-German during war, appears temperamentally pro-totalitarian. Not morally courageous. Has crippled hand, Very talented.' Though in Part Two of this book I offer a defence of Orwell's list in general, nonetheless this particular entry is disgraceful. George Orwell, 'List of Names of Crypto-Communists and Fellow-Travellers Sent to Information Research Department 2 May 1949', in Peter Davison (ed.), *The Lost Orwell* (London: Timewell Press, 2006), p. 142.

*Accountability* – For Orwell, the greatest thing about the idea of free speech was that accountability was built in. Where freedom really existed, it included the freedom to hold others to account – to demand reasons and explanations, to ask for evidence, to expose mendacity. Freedom imposed responsibilities to the truth and to honesty. If intellectuals abandoned those responsibilities, a culture of freedom would crumble. The lie would be indistinguishable from the truth. Much of his writing was a reminder of the importance of holding people accountable to the truth. Or, rather, accountable to the principle of truthfulness, to the acceptance that there was in principle a truth to be found, however difficult the hunt. People were often wrong, of course. Those who were prepared to say $2+2=5$ might be liars or might be brain-washed, but they might be just innumerate. The innumerate, though, were open to correction. They knew there was a right answer even if they didn't know what it was. So long as they lived in a society in which others could point out their mistake, all would be well. Their error didn't matter. So Orwell defended not simply an individual right to say what you pleased. That was important, but so too was exercising this right in a society with a flourishing culture of frank speech. A society of truth-tellers and truth-seekers. He did not seek to censor. Orwell's reminders of the value of free speech, even when addressed to those who were its enemies, were demands for more not less free speech. They were also demands for truthfulness and plain-speaking. He almost always opposed the temptation to censor, regardless of whether that censorship was aimed at his enemies (Left and Right) or his friends. Free speech was, in Orwell's eyes, the willingness to speak frankly, to speak one's mind, to refuse orthodoxy of any sort. When this honesty of speech was characteristic of a culture, accountability would follow. The lie could not escape exposure.[17]

*Equality* – Orwell shared the view that inequality undermined freedom. That didn't mean that the freedoms enjoyed in a liberal capitalist society were worthless; it did mean that they were compromised. It was better to live in a liberal democratic society than an illiberal or totalitarian one, but it would be better still to live in a democratic Socialist society.[18] Only there would liberal freedoms deliver their full promise. This promise could be

---

[17]My use of the term 'frank speech' is a gesture towards aligning Orwell with an approach to freedom of speech that has its roots in ancient Athens and the Greek concept of *parrhēsia*: for an introduction to this, see Teresa M. Bejan, 'The Two Clashing Meanings of "Free Speech"', *The Atlantic*, 2 December 2017, https://www.theatlantic.com/politics/archive/2017/12/two-concepts-of-freedom-of-speech/546791/ (accessed 7 February 2021).
[18]Orwell always gave an initial capital to 'Socialist' and 'Socialism'. I have followed his lead throughout this book.

redeemed by all and not only by capitalists and oligarchs. There would be no Rupert Murdoch, no Robert Maxwell. This combination of freedom and equality is what mattered to Orwell. He wished to see social privileges obliterated, and a real equality (not an equality of opportunity) established. This meant a society in which extreme disparities of wealth did not exist. Ideally, he thought, everyone should be paid the same amount, provided that it was a reasonably generous amount.[19] Only in such a society could freedom be fully enjoyed. You could not have a proper culture of free speech and thought if all the means of public speech were in the hands of a capitalist class. This is why it matters so much that Orwell looked beyond an individual *right* of free speech to a broader *culture* of freedom. Individual rights were hard to exercise in conditions of inequality (though they were still valuable to have).

Equality and accountability were essential features of a culture of free speech. Orwell didn't need Billy Bragg to tell him any of this.

This book starts with Orwell the eccentric who valued individuality, human cussedness, heresy, unorthodoxy, nonconformity; it starts with the Orwell who valued a society in which these qualities could flourish. His appreciation of them was even-handed: he cherished them in others as much as in himself. It was also a deep-rooted appreciation, shared by Eric Arthur Blair and his later creation, George Orwell. Yet Orwell, unlike Blair, was a Socialist; as well, he became convinced that the world was being fundamentally transformed. Collectivist planned societies would inevitably replace liberal capitalist societies because they were economically more efficient and powerful (or so he and many others thought). Was individualism therefore doomed? Was individual freedom of thought and expression therefore soon to be rubbed out by history's eraser? Orwell's answer was: not inevitably. Not if you did something to avert this outcome. For Orwell that something was often writing. The pen, it has been said, can be a mighty sword,[20] and Orwell was very much an activist journalist, as Ricard Lance Keeble has so thoroughly demonstrated.[21] But, as we shall see, he was also an *activist for freedom* in the more direct sense of involving himself in organizations and campaigns that were dedicated to the protection of freedom, at least in so far as time and his declining health allowed. It was, he thought, possible to create democratic, liberal and humane Socialist societies. For Orwell, the

---

[19]George Orwell, 'The Cost of Letters', September 1946, CW, XVIII, p. 383.

[20]James Tully, 'The Pen Is a Mighty Sword: Quentin Skinner's Analysis of Politics', *British Journal of Politics*, 13 (1983), pp. 489–509.

[21]Richard Lance Keeble, *Journalism beyond Orwell: A Collection of Essays* (London: Routledge, 2020), Part One.

original vision for Socialism was to fulfil the hitherto empty promises of liberal individualism and ensure that freedom existed for the many and not just the few. That vision was fading more rapidly than the Cheshire cat, but a smile still remained. Certainly, Socialism had been perverted by the Soviet example and by those Western supporters of Communism who said that the future lay in Stalin's ruthless embrace. For Orwell, though, Soviet Communism was a betrayal of liberalism and Socialism alike. It was a betrayal of Socialism *because* it was a betrayal of liberalism. True Socialism came to enhance liberalism not to destroy it. There was the smile. It was worth fighting for.

The remainder of this Prologue will explore the nature of Orwell's (liberal) individualism. There was nothing more important to Orwell than living in a society in which individuals were free to express themselves. This was the bedrock both of his political ideals and of his identity as a writer. Literature as we know it could not exist on any other foundation. Once we have established our bedrock, the bulk of the book will explore two things. First, the way in which Orwell's Socialism was layered *on top of* a liberal individualism. He built a Socialism for liberals. Second, on this foundation we will explore Orwell's work as a writer and activist for intellectual freedom. The nature of his Socialism helps us to understand why, by the final years of the Second World War, his central pre-occupation was defending liberal individualist values. He had not lost his commitment to Socialism, even if the hope of its imminent arrival that he felt in 1940–1 had reduced; nor had he ever repudiated his willingness to embrace violent revolution. Not at all: defending liberal values like freedom of thought was a necessary part of ensuring victory for any Socialism worth having.

Orwell brooded: how would free speech and free thought survive the inevitable victory of collectivism? His final book, *Nineteen Eighty-Four*, was the last answer he was able to give: people needed to be so frightened of an illiberal and totalitarian future that they would prevent it from ever coming into being. Perhaps they still do.

* * * * * *

The remainder of this Prologue establishes a foundation for the rest of the book: Orwell's early and abiding interest in human individuality. Long before he was a Socialist, Orwell was a liberal individualist. He remained one, forging a Socialism that didn't just accommodate this individualism, but served to further it. When, from the mid-1940s, his work focused more than anything else on the defence of intellectual freedom, this implied no diminution of his Socialist commitments. It showed just the sort of Socialist that he had always been.

# 2. How to Be Yourself (or Not): Orwell's Early Novels

Imagine that you were a lover of fiction in the 1930s. You read the first novel of a new writer, George Orwell and quite liked it. The novel was *Burmese Days* so you made sure you read each of his new novels when they appeared. By the outbreak of war in September 1939 you could have read four novels by this not especially prominent author. What would you have made of them and of the man who had written them? One of Orwell's contemporaries at Eton, author of one of the first books about him, suggests a starting point: 'The Orwellian man ... is always a solitary – a member of a society which is uncongenial to him – standing out alone in front of it.' Writing specifically of *To Keep the Aspidistra Flying*, he added that 'as in all Orwell's novels, there is really only one character – one character who stands out in loneliness'.[22] You can recognize the early novels in this, but is it quite right? It makes it sound as if the characters in these novels were loner rebels, fighting against their societies. To some degree they may have been – especially Gordon Comstock in *Keep the Aspidistra Flying* – but more generally they were people desperate to find a community of which they could be a part. The books explored Orwell's most fundamental concern in the face of modernity. They posed the question 'how can man find some kind of workable truce with an inevitably demanding community?'[23] How could we develop human communities, infused by the spirit of fraternity, that nurtured and protected free and fractious individuals? However assertive his characters might appear, they were all fragile, mostly unable to reconcile the spirit of individuality with the world around them. In the end, they conformed. As Terry Eagleton has put it, in an important critique of the early fiction, Orwell's characters had an 'incapacity either to accept or transcend the texture of "normal" society'. Each makes some sort of attempt to live a free life, but 'the movement to freedom and renewal ... ends in failure'.[24]

Orwell's fiction before *Animal Farm* was unsure of itself, of what it wanted to say and what the best way of saying it might be. Much would change as his writing matured, but not the importance of individuality. *Animal Farm* was his most perfectly formed work because it was able to evade the abiding weakness of all his fiction: he struggled to give his

---

[22]Christopher Hollis, *A Study of George Orwell: The Man and His Works* (New York: Racehorse Publishing, 2017, orig. ed. 1956), pp. 1, 73.
[23]Robert A. Lee, *Orwell's Fiction* (Notre Dame, IN: University of Notre Dame Press, 1969), p. xiii.
[24]Terry Eagleton, 'George Orwell and the Lower Middle-Class Novel', in Eagleton, *Exiles and Émigrés* (London: Chatto & Windus: 1970), ch. 3, pp. 87, 89.

characters deep and convincing interiority. As Hollis noted, there is usually only one character who is present in any depth, and even then there are limitations to the way in which that depth is conveyed. Given the importance of individuality as a theme, this might be thought a disabling weakness. But Orwell's early fiction is better than is often allowed.[25] *Burmese Days* is a well-shaped book in a conventional sort of way, but the next two novels were much more experimental. *A Clergyman's Daughter*, though the plot lurches unconvincingly from one set of unlikely episodes to another, contains some powerful scenes, notably Orwell's reconstruction of the language of those living rough on the streets of London and his cutting satire of private schools, anticipating the later memoir of his schooldays 'Such, Such Were the Joys'. *Keep the Aspidistra Flying* is a very amusing book and it shares with *A Clergyman's Daughter* a tone of heightened reality. Gordon Comstock is a caricature, and at times a tiresome one, but his rage at the world of advertising hits its target. Both of these novels extended Orwell's range as a writer, and reflected his reading of other contemporary authors (notably Joyce). If *A Clergyman's Daughter* looks forward most of all to his later non-fiction and his innovative journalism, the caricature of *Keep the Aspidistra Flying* honed some of the skills used in writing *Animal Farm*. Both of these books also reflect Orwell's abiding love for Swift's *Gulliver's Travels* and its approach to satirical writing. Orwell's final novel of the thirties, *Coming Up for Air*, which he wrote after his transformative experiences in Spain, is dealt with in the next part of this book, but it is perhaps the most successful of his early novels. Interestingly its success as a novel lies in part in its being the least didactic of his books. There is often a temptation to read these novels as straightforward expressions of Orwell's opinions, usually through the voice of their central character. But this does not do them justice, and the temptation should be resisted. *Coming Up for Air* is the only Orwell novel written in the first person, and is as a result able (though in a different way from *Animal Farm*) to overcome better than most Orwell's difficulties in creating characters with rich internal lives. By the time Orwell created George Bowling, though, he was a thoroughly committed Socialist not the politically undefined character of his novel, though Bowling nonetheless shared many of his author's fears for the future.

---

[25]See especially the defence in Loraine Saunders, *The Unsung Artistry of George Orwell: The Novels from* Burmese Days *to* Nineteen Eighty-Four (Aldershot: Ashgate, 2008). There are aspects of the defence that I don't agree with (e.g. the section on 'Prole *vs* Intellectual', pp. 13–16), but Saunders makes a strong case for the artistic quality of the early books in relation to the way that in each 'frame is vigorously foregrounded' (p. 129); Orwell can make 'the episodic cohere through the foregrounding of frame' (p. 131). The books thus 'help make sense of a disturbing world' (p. 131). From this perspective, conventional weaknesses of characterization may not matter, and the books cohere more than a plot summary might suggest.

It is, though, the three novels of the earlier thirties that help us to understand the mind of George Orwell as he moved towards the Socialist commitments that were fully confirmed by what he would witness in Barcelona. The novels reveal Orwell's deepest concerns and help us to understand his intertwined commitments to liberal individualism and to Socialist fraternity.

The central character of *Burmese Days*, John Flory commits suicide after his rejection by Elizabeth Lackersteen, following a humiliating scene created by his Burmese mistress, Ma Hla May. Flory throughout the book is an outsider to the community of Englishmen in Kyauktada. He rejects, or at least tempers, its racism, as signalled by his friendship with Dr Veraswami and his interest in Burmese culture; he loathes its hypocrisy. It is, though, in conversation with Veraswami that Flory first indicates the limits to his nonconformity.

'Seditious?' Flory said. '*I'm* not seditious. *I* don't want the Burmans to drive us out of this country. God forbid! I'm here to make money, like everyone else. All I object to is the slimy white man's burden humbug.'[26]

Nonetheless, Flory feels alone in this society – 'If he had one person, just one, to halve his loneliness!'[27] – and pins his hopes on Elizabeth to end this.

Things start off well enough. At their first meeting, Elizabeth declares, 'I simply adore reading', which induces Flory to reply, 'What it means to meet somebody who cares for books! I mean books worth reading, not the garbage in the Club libraries. I do hope you'll forgive me if I overwhelm you with talk. When I met someone who has heard that books exist, I'm afraid I go off like a bottle of warm beer.'[28] But in this, as in many things, Flory has comically misjudged Elizabeth. Her taste ran to *The Tatler*, horses and country life. She admired those 'who did not go in for this nonsense of writing books and footling with paintbrushes; and all these highbrow ideas – Socialism and all that. "Highbrow" was a bitter word in her vocabulary'. She wanted to lead the life of the rich – but cheaply. So she appreciated India, where 'it was almost as nice as being really rich, the way people lived in India'.[29] Flory never seemed to notice that his aspirations were focused on someone who wished to share the conventional cut-price luxury of the English in India. Flory tries to interest her in the culture around her, such as Burmese dance. She is disgusted by the 'hideous and savage spectacle'.[30]

---

[26]George Orwell, *Burmese Days* [CW, II] (London: Secker & Warburg, 1986), p. 37. The CW edition of *Burmese Days* has the same pagination as the Penguin Classics edition.
[27]Orwell, *Burmese Days*, p. 57.
[28]Orwell, *Burmese Days*, pp. 86–7.
[29]Orwell, *Burmese Days*, pp. 96–8.
[30]Orwell, *Burmese Days*, pp. 107–8.

Flory's delusion is quickly apparent to the reader, if not to himself. He saw himself as a man who lived 'in bitter loneliness, among people to whom your true opinion on every subject on earth is blasphemy'. For such a person, 'the need to talk is the greatest of all needs'. But he was puzzled that with Elizabeth this seemed 'impossible'. They talked freely only when they talked of 'trivialities'. All their conversation ended in banality. 'Her taste in books appalled him.' But still he maintained his illusions. 'Later, no doubt, she would understand him and give him the companionship he needed. Perhaps it was not only that he had not won her confidence yet.'[31]

In time, Elizabeth understands her distaste for Flory. 'She understood why it was that he had so often bored her and irritated her. He was a highbrow – her deadliest word – a highbrow, to be classed with Lenin, A.J. Cook and the dirty little poets in the Montparnasse cafés.'[32] But this is to misjudge him. All that Flory wanted was the life of a respectable middle-class Englishman. At one point he was able to recognize that what he could see in Elizabeth was that she brought the air of England with her, 'dear England where thought is free and one is not condemned forever to dance the *danse du pukka sahib* for the edification of the lower races. Where is the life that late I led?'[33]

In spite of her irritation and distaste, expressed in just about every meeting they have, Elizabeth's options are limited, and she is on the verge of becoming engaged to Flory before the scene with Ma Hla May produces a level of disgust (racial as well as sexual) from which there is no return for either party. It is not Flory's rebelliousness or his rejection of the norms of his social class that destroys him – or rather, precipitates his self-destruction. His problem is the utter conventionality of his wish to belong. There is little substance to his highbrow reputation, which is why he is unable to see Elizabeth for what she really is. He has no resources to protect himself from the community before which he is humiliated, however much he might think he rejects its values. Just before Ma Hla May intervenes, Flory imagines his future in terms of utter bourgeois conventionality:

Twenty years ago on winter Sundays in his pew in the parish church at Home, he used to watch the yellow leaves, as at this moment, drifting and fluttering against leaden skies. Was it not possible, now, to begin over again as though those grimy years had never touched him? ...When they were married, when they were married! What fun they would have together in this alien yet kindly land! He saw Elizabeth in his camp, greeting him as he came home tired from work and Ko S'la [his servant] hurried from the tent with a bottle of beer; he saw her walking in the forest

---

[31] Orwell, *Burmese Days*, p. 120.
[32] Orwell, *Burmese Days*, p. 207.
[33] Orwell, *Burmese Days*, p. 156.

with him, watching the hornbills in the peepul trees and picking nameless flowers, and in the marshy grazing grounds, tramping through the cold-weather mist after snipe and teal. He saw his home as he would remake it. He saw his drawing-room, sluttish and bachelor-like no longer, with new furniture from Rangoon, and a bowl of pink balsams like rosebuds on the table, and books and watercolours and a black piano. Above all the piano! His mind lingered upon the piano – symbol, perhaps because he was so unmusical, of civilised and settled life. He was delivered for ever from the sub-life of the past decade – the debaucheries, the lies, the pain of exile and solitude, the dealings with whores and money-lenders and pukka sahibs.[34]

John Flory was certainly an individual at odds with the world in which he lived. But his tragedy is that he reproduced many of its values, failing to escape his own conventionality. He was not much of a rebel, consumed instead by nostalgia. It destroyed him in the end, not because he was a remarkable man but because he was a decent one, uncomfortable with the hypocrisy needed to maintain the veneer of Englishness in a place it did not belong. All he wanted was to create a better simulacrum of a remembered England than the men and women at the Club represented.

It is hard not to believe that Flory's nostalgia had led him astray. He would no more have belonged in respectable England than he did in respectable Burma. The problems that *Burmese Days* explores are not simple. The white society generated by imperialism was not fit for human habitation; it denied human individuality, forcing a small white elite to band together in artificial solidarity. The pressure to conform was great.

Criticism of *Burmese Days* has understandably given much attention to the book's anti-imperialism,[35] but many have noted the degree to which this is compromised by Flory, who provides 'the voice of the imperial in an anti-imperialist tone'.[36] Some critics have suggested that the theme of the book 'is not anticolonialism, but the failure of community';[37] *Burmese Days* is 'less a considered critique of imperialism than an exploration of private guilt,

---

[34]Orwell, *Burmese Days*, pp. 283–4.
[35]A key work relating the book to Orwell's own colonial experience is Maung Htin Aung, 'George Orwell and Burma', *Journal of Asian Affairs*, 1 (1970), pp. 19–28; Rosinka Chaudhuri's introduction to the Oxford World's Classics edition of the book gives an excellent and nuanced overview of its relationship to anti-imperialism and to racism, noting that it is a book 'from the critical perspective of a British insider', with a central character whose 'objection to empire are, in the end, personal ones': George Orwell, *Burmese Days*, ed. Rosinka Chaudhuri (Oxford: Oxford University Press, World's Classics edition, 2021), Introduction, pp. xv, xvii.
[36]Başak Ağin Dönmez, 'The Voice of the Imperial in an Anti-Imperialist Tone', *Cross-Cultural Studies Journal*, 28 (2012), pp. 5–16.
[37]Lee, *Orwell's Fiction*, p. 19.

incommunicable loneliness and loss of identity'.[38] However, these features of the book could be understood as contributing to the anti-imperialist message. One of the consequences of imperialism was to corrupt its agents so that their critique of it was always compromised by their complicity with it. Flory railed, but he had no coherent vision of an alternative to the colonial oppression to which he contributed. Though Flory might have had an unusual love of the natural world that he lived amongst, he was still 'an Englishman in colonial Burma. He is not his own man.'[39] There was a shallowness even in Flory's own self. His individuality was partly a sham; certainly, it was deformed by the world that formed him both in England and in Burma. He was without a sustaining vision of a better society than the one he lived in. Orwell's struggle to create a rich interior life for his characters here served an artistic purpose.

Dorothy Hare, the eponymous clergyman's daughter, is another of Orwell's characters with a limited inner or emotional life, though she has some remarkable adventures. She dramatizes one of Orwell's central concerns: the social and political consequences of the loss of religious faith.[40] Dorothy charts a course almost the opposite of Flory's, returning to the community that she left with a new appreciation of what it gave her. Dorothy's life as we first see it is grim. She is trapped in a relentless round of parish work, little of which her father, the Rector, has much taste for. She looks after him, including dealing with the tradesmen whose bills she is unable to pay, thanks to her father's tightfistedness. She also attracts the unwanted attention of Mr Warburton, an ageing 48-year-old bohemian, who subjects her to repeated sexual assault and attempted rape (the latter more explicitly indicated in Orwell's original manuscript than in the published version of the book). Dorothy, partly as a result of this and partly as a result of having, as a nine-year-old girl, seen 'certain dreadful scenes between her father and her mother', had a deep and persistent revulsion from sex.[41] In a remarkably contrived series of plot developments, Dorothy, following Warburton's latest onslaught, loses her memory, embarks on a hop-picking expedition to Kent, lives homeless on the streets of London[42] and then works in a dismal private school for girls, run by Mrs Creevy. Throughout

[38]Eagleton, 'George Orwell and the Lower Middle-Class Novel', pp. 85–6.

[39]Douglas Kerr, *George Orwell* (Tavistock: Northcote House / British Council, 2003), p. 14.

[40]For fuller discussion of this theme, see Gordon Beadle, 'George Orwell and the Death of God', *Colorado Quarterly*, 23 (1974), pp. 51–63; and Michael G. Brennan, *George Orwell and Religion* (London: Bloomsbury, 2017), esp. pp. 41–6 on *A Clergyman's Daughter*.

[41]George Orwell, *A Clergyman's Daughter* [CW, III] (London: Secker & Warburg, 1986), p. 82. The Penguin Classics edition has the same pagination.

[42]Orwell was particularly pleased with this section, his most experimental piece of writing. See Kerr, *George Orwell*, pp. 27–8; Martha C. Carpentier, 'Orwell's Joyce and *Coming Up for Air*', *Joyce Studies Annual*, (2012), pp. 131–53.

she firmly maintains her virginity, in spite of some 'furtive fondling of the women' sleeping on London's streets.[43]

At first, Dorothy has success as a teacher in Mrs Creevy's school. She takes to the job, realizing that what the children needed, but had never had, was 'individual attention'. With this they flourish and develop 'the habit of thinking for themselves', until Mrs Creevy and the parents conspire to end an approach that might actually educate the girls.[44] Nonetheless, this is a sort of turning point for Dorothy. More or less simultaneously, she loses her faith and builds a selfless sense of vocation, returning to her father's vicarage and a life ostensibly much like the one that she had left. Mr Warburton's final proposal of marriage is firmly and definitively rejected.

Orwell's account of Dorothy's development is often seen as satirical and negative, but there is more to be said about it than this.[45] When she is teaching, Mrs Creevy requires Dorothy to attend church, though she is not herself religious. The parents would expect it. Dorothy was happy to comply, but 'in a state of completest abstraction'.

> There was never a moment when the power of worship returned to her. Indeed, the whole concept of worship was meaningless to her now; her faith had vanished, utterly and irrevocably. It is a mysterious thing, the loss of faith – as mysterious as faith itself. Like faith, it is ultimately not rooted in logic; it is a change in the climate of the mind. But however little the church services might mean to her, she did not regret the hour she spent in church.[46]

Dorothy can still take comfort from the rituals of religion, even without any faith; but what came to matter to her was a sense of community. Even when still hop-picking, after she became aware of the scandal attached to her name from the assumption that she had eloped with Warburton, Dorothy mused that there were those who would 'know her and trusted her', like the Mothers' Union and the girl guides. And her father. 'Almost any situation is bearable if you have a home to go back to and a family who will stand by you.'[47] Her trust is not altogether misplaced. Though her father is slow, ineffectual and lukewarm in supporting her, he does indirectly enable her to escape from life

---

[43] Orwell, *A Clergyman's Daughter*, p. 178.

[44] Orwell, *A Clergyman's Daughter*, pp. 219–20.

[45] One strength of this book (and of its immediate successor) lies in their quality as portraits of poverty and its consequences, a theme they shared with Orwell's early non-fiction. One critic has appositely drawn comparisons with the works of Orwell's literary heroes Samuel Butler and George Gissing: Gordon Beadle, 'George Orwell's Literary Studies of Poverty in England', *Twentieth-Century Literature*, 24 (1978), pp. 188–201.

[46] Orwell, *A Clergyman's Daughter*, pp. 248–9.

[47] Orwell, *A Clergyman's Daughter*, p. 133.

on the street and become a teacher. A little after writing to her father and getting no response, Dorothy hears church bells, and is hit by nostalgia:

> The sound planted a spear of homesickness in Dorothy's heart, bringing back to her with momentary vividness a medley of remembered things – the smell of the glue-pot in the conservatory when she was making costumes for the school play, and the chatter of starlings outside her bedroom window, interrupting her prayers before Holy Communion, and Mrs Pither's doleful voice chronicling the pains in the backs of her legs, and the worries of the collapsing belfry and the shop-debts and the bindweed in the peas – all the multitudinous, urgent details of a life that had alternated between work and prayer.[48]

Work and prayer: the latter, she almost immediately finds, is now lost to her, meaningless, but work persists, initially in the pleasure of teaching, finally in her return to a dutiful life.

This return was not really a return to her old life. When Warburton comes to rescue her from Mrs Creevy and to take her back to her father's house, Dorothy recognizes that though she has been through much, this was not important: 'it's the things that happen inside you that matter.' Once things inside your head change, 'the whole world changes, because you look at it differently'.[49] Her loss of faith transformed Dorothy's world. Indeed, she thinks 'I've got to begin my life all over again'.[50] The world had become empty and meaningless. Warburton draws at some length a picture of Dorothy's likely future – a future full of 'sameness and futility', 'a poor, disappointed old maid', 'all the time withering, drying up, growing more sour and more angular and more friendless'.[51] She does not dispute this, but her physical disgust at Warburton leads her to reject his proposed alternative, marriage. She will return to her old life, now no longer dignified by her faith, and in full knowledge of her likely future. Warburton wonders whether she might be dismayed at this prospect. 'I expect it'll be all right once I'm back at work', Dorothy replies. 'I've got the habit you see.'[52] Habit is important, but it is not all there is to the matter. She would change her habits, notably by abandoning the infliction of pain on herself, necessary in the past to keep her mind on the ways of God. The justification of her life lay no longer with God, but with a repudiation of 'hedonism' (represented by the sybaritic Warburton) and the embrace of usefulness:

---

[48]Orwell, *A Clergyman's Daughter*, pp. 136–7.
[49]Orwell, *A Clergyman's Daughter*, pp. 272–3.
[50]Orwell, *A Clergyman's Daughter*, p. 275.
[51]Orwell, *A Clergyman's Daughter*, pp. 280–3.
[52]Orwell, *A Clergyman's Daughter*, p. 285.

Because, you see, I do feel that that kind of work, even if it means saying prayers that one doesn't believe in, and even if it means teaching children things that one doesn't always think are true – I do feel that in a way it's useful.

As well, though, she did not want to change 'the spiritual background of her mind'. For Dorothy, 'the Christian way of life was still the way that must come naturally to her'.[53] She prefigures in this two central features of Orwell's later thinking – his rejection of hedonism,[54] and his recognition that the decline in religious faith threatened to destroy the foundations of human fraternity and community. Dorothy's solution was not one to be treated lightly, to continue a Christian community on secular grounds. This was a community of habit and custom, but a community that had its uses in sustaining and giving purpose to the lives of those within it. 'Faith vanishes', Dorothy reflected, 'but the need for faith remains the same as before'. Orwell, or the books' narrative voice, rendered this verdict:

> She did not reflect, consciously, that the solution to her difficulty lay in accepting the fact that there was no solution; that if one gets on with the job that lies to hand, the ultimate purpose of the job fades into insignificance; that faith and no faith are very much the same provided that one is doing what is customary, useful and acceptable. She could not formulate these thoughts as yet, she could only live them. Much later, perhaps, she would formulate them and draw comfort from them.[55]

This humane and compassionate verdict on Dorothy's life should be given the respect it deserves. Orwell himself would soon wonder where the fraternity necessary for Socialist community might come from in a Godless world. A new grounding for human morality was necessary if genuine Socialism were to be achieved. A part of Orwell shared Dorothy's attachment to a life of customary observance. But there was a price. Such a life could not accommodate the heretic and the perverse. It came at a painful cost to individuality of spirit. And, in any case, Orwell would come to think that the conditions that made it possible to live such a life were disappearing.

Though a good case has been made for the 'oblique' political engagement of *A Clergyman's Daughter*,[56] there is truth still in Eagleton's downbeat

---

[53]Orwell, *A Clergyman's Daughter*, pp. 285–6.
[54]See also Gregory Claeys, 'Industrialism and Hedonism in Orwell's Literary and Political Development', *Albion*, 18 (1986), pp. 219–45.
[55]Orwell, *A Clergyman's Daughter*, pp. 292, 295.
[56]Nathan Waddell's introduction to the Oxford World Classics edition: George Orwell, *A Clergyman's Daughter*, ed. Nathan Waddell (Oxford: Oxford University Press, 2021), Introduction, pp. xxii–xxv.

verdict that a core message of the book is that 'life is hopeless and sterile, but the worst false consciousness is to think you can change it'. Dorothy's conformity 'is ultimately affirmed as superior to a radical criticism of contemporary life'.[57] Truth but not the whole truth: the criticism of poverty and of bourgeois sham, especially the sham of religion and of private education, is powerful and un-countered; but there is no vision of a 'realistic' alternative, and without that, there is no sustainable alternative to conformity.

John Flory could not escape the pull of the conventional in a bourgeois world; Dorothy settled for a life of quiet usefulness in which her own individual needs were firmly kept in their place. Both of these characters were shaped by the worlds in which they were enmeshed, their very individuality compromised, leaving them powerless to imagine any substantial alternative to the society in which they endured. No more was Gordon Comstock able to defy the world that trapped him, though he gave it a run for its money. Critics have certainly seen the book as coming from the same mould as its predecessors. Gordon has to learn to abandon beliefs that 'are unqualified and *unrealistic*', to escape from a 'childish petulance, [which was] ineffectual and demeaning'.[58] Like Dorothy Hare he finds a path to the 'customary, useful and acceptable'.[59] For Eagleton, Gordon Comstock endorsed and shared bourgeois values while pretending to despise them. His protest ends in capitulation not challenge.[60] More recent criticism qualifies these verdicts, perhaps, but does not eradicate them. Douglas Kerr captures Gordon neatly: 'while it lasts, his resistance to materialism has a comic magnificence that is only partly spoiled by his relentless self-pity.'[61] Though the book has little 'vision of social change', it does nonetheless convey some insight into 'the broader structures of social injustice'.[62]

Gordon Comstock has thrown over a job in advertising in order to focus on becoming a professional writer. He is supported by Philip Ravelston, editor of the magazine *Antichrist*,[63] in the pages of which Gordon has some modest success, and by his long-suffering girlfriend, Rosemary Waterlow. Gordon Comstock's main obsession is, though, not writing but money, more precisely his own lack of it. In spite of his constant 'tirading against

[57]Eagleton, 'George Orwell and the Lower Middle-Class Novel', p. 89.

[58]Lee, *Orwell's Fiction*, pp. 53, 55.

[59]Lee, *Orwell's Fiction*, p. 64, quoting, a little out of context, Orwell, *A Clergyman's Daughter*, p. 295.

[60]Eagleton, 'George Orwell and the Lower Middle-Class Novel', pp. 97–100.

[61]Kerr, *George Orwell*, p. 30.

[62]Benjamin Kohlmann in George Orwell, *Keep the Aspidistra Flying*, ed. Benjamin Kohlmann (Oxford: Oxford University Press, World's Classics edition, 2021), Introduction, p. xx.

[63]Based on Richard Rees and the *Adelphi*, a magazine at the heart of Orwell's early career as a professional writer.

Capitalism', Gordon is no Socialist. Like the author of *The Road to Wigan Pier*, he found it too middle class. Money was 'the price of optimism. Give me five quid a week and I'd be a Socialist, I dare say.' It had no appeal for the poor, consequently, 'there's only one objection to Socialism, and that is that nobody wants it'.[64] His 'tirading' can be amusing enough:

> [H]e grasped that *all* modern commerce is a swindle ... What he realised, and more clearly as time went on, was that money-worship had been elevated into a religion. Perhaps it is the only real religion – the only really *felt* religion – that is left to us. Money is what God used to be. Good and evil have no meaning any longer except failure and success.[65]

Observing an advertising poster, Gordon notes 'the imbecility, the emptiness, the desolation! You can't look at it without thinking of French letters and machine-guns.'[66] Like Dorothy's predicament in *A Clergyman's Daughter*, this gestures to a central theme in Orwell. Without traditional religion, where will our values come from? Is there no alternative to the worship of success and power? The contemporary world, the machine age, had at its heart a deep spiritual malaise. Orwell's later writing was a search for ways of repairing this.

The problem of a corrupted meaningless world was also a problem of individuality. How could Gordon live a life in this world that was worthy of his self-respect. His initial response – a distorted and caricatured version of an impulse shared by his author – was the desire 'to go down, deep down, into some world where decency no longer mattered, to cut the strings of his self-respect'. This was the place where 'tramps, beggars, criminals, prostitutes' live, 'that great sluttish underworld where failure and success have no meaning'. As Orwell would later say, though in words not to be taken quite at face value, if there is hope it lies with the proles, the people who lived 'beneath the world of money' and so were not worshipping the values of the money-god.[67] As with George Bowling in *Coming Up for Air*, and like their creator himself, Gordon expected war, and with some initial glee noted that it would 'send our civilization back to hell where it belongs'.[68]

But by the time he formulated this, something had happened to Gordon and he realized that he no longer wanted this war to happen. In a remarkably sudden and unconvincing *volte face* Gordon makes his peace with the money God and returns to advertising. Though this change is unconvincing

---

[64] George Orwell, *Keep the Aspidistra Flying* [CW, IV] (London: Secker & Warburg, 1987), pp. 94, 96–7. The Penguin Classics ed. has the same pagination as CW.
[65] Orwell, *Keep the Aspidistra Flying*, p. 46.
[66] Orwell, *Keep the Aspidistra Flying*, p. 93.
[67] Orwell, *Keep the Aspidistra Flying*, p. 227.
[68] Orwell, *Keep the Aspidistra Flying*, p. 275.

as art, it may well be that Orwell at this time took it seriously as a solution to Gordon's predicament. Like Dorothy he comes to an accommodation with a thoroughly imperfect world but on new grounds; it is him and not the world that has had to change. After some considerable attempts at persuasion, and the fiasco of their trip into the country, where Gordon was hoping for sex *en plein air*, he eventually persuaded the virgin Rosemary to sleep with him. The encounter would win no good sex award, but Rosemary gets pregnant anyway. It is the prospect of a baby that transforms Gordon's attitude. He will need to support it.

> The money-god is so cunning. If he only baited his traps with yachts and race-horses, tarts and champagne, how east it would be to dodge them. It is when he gets at you through your sense of decency that he finds you helpless.[69]

It was not that he now thought much better of advertising. It was still 'a panorama of ignorance, greed, vulgarity, snobbishness, whoredom, and disease'.[70] But you could not defy the money-god forever. The world is as it is, and you have to live on its terms if you wish to enjoy the small decencies that life, however grim in general, always has to offer.

> He had blasphemed against money, rebelled against money, tried to live with like an anchorite outside the money-world; and it had brought him not only misery, but also a frightful emptiness, an inescapable sense of futility. To abjure money is to abjure life.[71]

The book ends with Rosemary and Gordon having the first quarrel of their new married life. But then the baby moves inside Rosemary, and Gordon kneels.

> For a long time he remained kneeling there, his head pressed against the softness of her belly. She clasped her hands behind his head and pulled it closer. He could hear nothing, only the blood drumming in his own ear. But she could not have been mistaken. Somewhere in there, in the safe, warm, cushioned darkness, it was alive and stirring.
>
> Well, once again things were happening in the Comstock family.[72]

That hypothetical reader of the 1930s, the one who had read the first three novels of a new writer, might doubt that any of them fully realized

---

[69]Orwell, *Keep the Aspidistra Flying*, p. 258.

[70]Orwell, *Keep the Aspidistra Flying*, p. 262.

[71]Orwell, *Keep the Aspidistra Flying*, p. 266.

[72]Orwell, *Keep the Aspidistra Flying*, p. 277.

their author's artistic potential. However well written they were – and from the start Orwell had a perspicuous prose style – they did not cohere structurally or in terms of character development. But our reader might be struck, too, by just how interesting the concerns of this author were. He had an enviable talent for capturing the hollowness of contemporary societies and the ways in which they thwarted the human spirit. His very individualistic central characters all struggled to find a place for themselves in the society in which they lived. They were, though, all shaped by that society, which is one reason they struggled to escape from it. The struggle destroyed John Flory, but Dorothy Hare and Gordon Comstock both found ways of being themselves while accepting the need to live in the world as they found it. Their individualism is conforming not revolutionary, finding in a distasteful world a modest space for the decencies that mattered to them. For one of them, that space was Christian community without faith; for the other, family, for whose sake the money-god would need to receive obeisance.

These novels, written before Wigan and before Spain, are politically quiescent for the most part. What rebellion there is in them is highly individualized and ineffective. But two things carry forward into the mind of Orwell the Socialist – that there is something so deeply wrong with modern society that it thwarts the full development of human individuality, and that individuality matters. Our ability to enjoy our lives and the many small pleasures of the world was not trivial.[73] But Orwell the Socialist would come to think, unlike his early characters, that perhaps it would be possible to build a society that better supported the often perverse individuals of which it was composed. Terry Eagleton sees Orwell's fiction of the 1930s getting worse and worse; and none of his books, in this view, escaped a central dilemma: he was 'unable either to fully accept or fully reject the social system, and so [was] critical both of the common life and of its possible alternatives'.[74] Eagleton is here gesturing towards the interpretation presented in the *locus classicus* of left-wing Orwell criticism, Isaac Deutscher's essay on *Nineteen Eighty-Four*.[75] Orwell was never, in this view, properly of the Left. His fiction was, in the end, anti-Socialist, undermining possibilities of genuine social transformation with an ineradicable class snobbery and a willingness to undermine Socialism from within. Like his characters, he could never convince himself that it

---

[73]There is more on the small pleasures in Part One of this book, but perhaps Orwell's most pointed presentation of them was his splendid essay 'Some Thoughts on the Common Toad', published in *Tribune* in April 1946 [CW, XVIII, pp. 238–40].

[74]Eagleton, 'Orwell and the Lower Middle-Class Novel', p. 107.

[75]Isaac Deutscher, '"1984" – The Mysticism of Cruelty', in Deutscher, *Marxism, Wars and Revolutions: Essays from Four Decades* (London: Verso, 1984), pp. 60–71, originally published 1955.

was a real possibility, and it all ended in the despairing prophecy of his final novel. In Eagleton's view, the trajectory was set by 1939.

But this is not so. Orwell before Wigan and (especially) Spain does seem to have lacked any vision of social transformation, notwithstanding his deep sense of social injustice. But Spain would show him that there were alternatives to custom and convention; a better society was possible. He knew because he had seen it – a society individualist, anarchist, Socialist.[76] *Nineteen Eighty-Four* looks on the surface very much like a continuation of the novels of the 1930s, the story of yet another bid for freedom that is crushed. But there are big differences. Winston Smith did not accommodate himself willingly to the society of Oceania. He was destroyed by simple thuggery. His rebellion was buttressed by the sense that there could be something better, even if that better world was located largely off stage. This book was a warning not a prophecy, the prophetic reading being a staple of left-wing critique. But *Nineteen Eighty-Four* was a continuation of Orwell's liberal activism of the 1940s. It warned that one must act to preserve and enhance a society that was compatible with human individuality. The individual must resist, not to be crushed anew, but to have any hope of living in a better world.

# 3. The Expression on a Human Face

Orwell described the faces of his characters in some detail. They are often less than handsome, prematurely ageing, carrying the visible imprint of lives spent struggling not to be defeated by the powerful demands of social conformity.[77] John Flory's alienation from the society around him was symbolized by 'a hideous birthmark stretching in a ragged crescent down his left cheek, from the eye to the corner of the mouth'. The fact that Flory 'is quite aware of its hideousness' adds to the awkwardness of his interactions with those around him;[78] while for them, the birthmark was central to their perceptions of his oddness and perversity: 'there had always been something dubious about Flory; his age, his birthmark, his queer, perverse way of talking.'[79] The face of the woman he pursued, Elizabeth Lackersteen, was a marked contrast: 'a pale oval, like a flower'.[80] Elizabeth was 'chalk-faced', with 'delicate regular features; not beautiful, perhaps, but it seemed so there,

---

[76]The importance of this pivot is well captured in Lee, *Orwell's Fiction*, pp. xii–xiv, 65, 136.
[77]See D. J. Taylor, *Orwell: The Life* (New York: Henry Holt, 2003), pp. 57–60.
[78]Orwell, *Burmese Days*, p. 14.
[79]Orwell, *Burmese Days*, p. 181.
[80]Orwell, *Burmese Days*, p. 186. Cf. Lee, *Orwell's Fiction*, pp. 2–5.

in Burma, where all Englishwomen are yellow and thin'.[81] Lacking strong distinguishing features, she found racial and social conformity easy; in the Burmese context, Flory could mistake her for something that she was not. Dorothy Hare was described in ways comparable to Elizabeth. Her face 'was her weak point' – 'a thin, blonde, unremarkable kind of face, with pale eyes and a nose just a shade too long'. It was a face that 'in repose, looked tired' on its way to becoming a 'spinsterish face', though with an 'almost childish earnestness in her eyes'.[82] The face alone seems enough to destine Dorothy to a life of conventional but conscientious fitting-in. Gordon Comstock was described with more specificity, but his was not the face of someone likely to seize life by the throat, either. 'Not a good face. Not thirty yet, but moth-eaten already. Very pale, with bitter ineradicable lines … Hair mouse-coloured and unkempt, mouth unamiable, eyes hazel inclining to green.'[83] Orwell was to write, towards the end of his life, that 'at 50, everyone has the face he deserves'.[84] His characters seemed to get to this point rather sooner.

These were Orwell's first novels. His last, *Nineteen Eighty-Four*, is dominated from the start by the looming, inscrutable face of Big Brother. Winston Smith is destroyed by a man (O'Brien) possessing 'a coarse, humorous, brutal face'.[85] O'Brien had, in part, tricked Winston into thought crime by lending him the book of Oceania's arch-enemy, Goldstein, who is described thus:

> It was a lean Jewish face, with a great fuzzy aureole of white hair and a small goatee beard – a clever face, and yet somehow inherently despicable, with a kind of senile silliness in the long thin nose near the end of which a pair of spectacles was perched. It resembled the face of a sheep, and the voice, too, had a sheeplike quality.[86]

All of these faces appear in the first chapter of the book, as does Winston's own. He is described as 'a smallish, frail figure, the meagreness of his body merely emphasized by the blue overalls which were the uniform of the Party. His hair was very fair, his face naturally sanguine, his skin roughened by coarse soap and blunt razor blades and the cold of the winter that had just ended.'[87] The book is saturated in faces that seem to convey inner truths. Julia it is said 'was used to judging people by their faces, and it seemed

---

[81]Orwell, *Burmese Days*, pp. 81, 83.

[82]Orwell, *A Clergyman's Daughter*, pp. 3–4.

[83]Orwell, *Keep the Aspidistra Flying*, p. 4.

[84]'Notes from Orwell's Last Literary Notebook', CW, XX, Appendix 2, p. 213.

[85]George Orwell, *Nineteen Eighty-Four* [CW, IX] (London: Secker & Warburg, 1987), p. 12 (Penguin ed. p. 13).

[86]Orwell, *Nineteen Eighty-Four*, p. 14 (Penguin ed. p. 15).

[87]Orwell, *Nineteen Eighty-Four*, p. 4 (Penguin ed. p. 4).

natural to her that Winston should believe O'Brien to be trustworthy on the strength of a single flash of the eyes'.[88] This was, of course, to be deceived. Winston would carry the consequences of that deception on his own face, one of the few in Orwell's fiction that undergoes significant change. Towards the end of the book, Winston sees himself in a mirror.

> A bowed, grey-coloured, skeleton-like thing was coming towards him. Its actual appearance was frightening, and not merely the fact that he knew it to be himself. He moved closer to the glass. The creature's face seemed to be protruded, because of its bent carriage. A forlorn, jailbird's face with a nobby forehead running back into a bald scalp, a crooked nose and battered-looking cheekbones above which the eyes were fierce and watchful. The cheeks were seamed, the mouth had a drawn-in look. Certainly it was his own face, but it seemed to him that it had changed more than he had changed inside. The emotions it registered would be different from the ones he felt. He had gone partially bald. For the first moment he had thought that he had gone grey as well, but it was only the scalp that was grey. Except for his hands and a circle of his face, his body was grey all over with ancient, ingrained dirt. Here and there under the dirt there were the red scars of wounds, and near the ankle the varicose ulcer was an inflamed mass with flakes of skin peeling off it. But the truly frightening thing was the emaciation of his body. The barrel of the ribs was as narrow as that of a skeleton: the legs had shrunk so that the knees were thicker than the thighs.[89]

Was this the face he deserved by fifty?[90]

But not all of the faces in Orwell's writing are faces of defeat. *Coming Up for Air* begins with George Bowling's new false teeth. He is shaving, teeth out, and looks at himself in the mirror. 'I haven't such a bad face really,' he muses. 'It's one of those bricky-red faces that go with butter-coloured hair and pale-blue eyes, I've never gone grey or bald, thank God, and when I've got my teeth in I probably don't look my age, which is forty-five.'[91] For once, someone who looks *younger* than his age. Bowling, as we shall later see, was not without his fears for the future, or his regrets for the past, but his face was largely one of complacency, even self-satisfaction.

A characteristic feature of Orwell's non-fiction writing – and of his mind – is the sudden recognition of another person's full humanity. His ability momentarily to see the world as if he were someone else disrupts the

---

[88]Orwell, *Nineteen Eighty-Four*, p. 159 (Penguin ed. p. 175).
[89]Orwell, *Nineteen Eighty-Four*, p. 284 (Penguin ed. pp. 310–11).
[90]Winston was, in fact, only thirty-nine when the events of *Nineteen Eighty-Four* occurred.
[91]Orwell, *Coming Up for Air*, p. 3.

sometimes dogmatic reasoning to which Orwell could be prone. His thinking crystallizes around individuals, notwithstanding his frequently reiterated belief that the world was becoming less and less welcoming to human individuality. Industrialism '*must* lead to some form of collectivism'.[92] 'We live in an age in which the individual is ceasing to exist,' he said, a totalitarian age, and everywhere 'a collectivised economy is bound to come'.[93] But Orwell was fighting to ensure that not all of the freedoms of individuals would be obliterated by this coming collectivization. The individual always mattered most to Orwell, and the individual always had a human face. Even in the sort of collectivist society that Orwell most feared, individuality might never be eradicated ('the heretic ... will always be there') – but the heretic, perhaps the only sort of individual worthy of the name, existed only to be defeated and humiliated again and again. 'If you want a picture of the future, imagine a boot stamping on a human face – for ever.'[94]

Orwell's first great essay, 'A Hanging' (1931), contains a moment of human empathy that not even our over-familiarity with the piece can dull. A condemned man was being walked to the gallows when, 'in spite of the men who gripped him by each shoulder, he stepped slightly aside to avoid a puddle on the path'. Orwell reflected:

It is curious, but till that moment I had never realised what it means to destroy a healthy, conscious man. When I saw the prisoner step aside to avoid the puddle, I saw the mystery, the unspeakable wrongness, of cutting a life short when it is in full tide. This man was not dying, he was alive just as we were alive. All the organs of his body were working – bowels digesting food, skin renewing itself, nails growing tissues forming – all toiling away in solemn foolery. His nails would still be growing when he stood on the drop, when he was falling through the air with a tenth-of-a-second to live. His eyes saw the yellow gravel and the grey walls, and his brain still remembered, foresaw, reasoned – reasoned even about puddles. He and we were a party of men walking together, seeing, hearing, feeling, understanding the same world; and in two minutes, with a sudden snap, one of us would be gone – one mind less, one world less.[95]

In different circumstances, Orwell might have encountered the hanged man as one of 'the sneering yellow faces of young men that met me everywhere' in Burma.[96] On an occasion that was the subject of another of his best essays,

---

[92]George Orwell, *The Road to Wigan Pier* [CW, V] (London: Secker & Warburg, 1986), p. 175. The Penguin Classics ed. has the same pagination as CW.
[93]George Orwell, 'Literature and Totalitarianism', May 1941, CW, xii, pp. 502, 505.
[94]Orwell, *Nineteen Eighty-Four*, p. 280 (Penguin ed. p. 307).
[95]George Orwell, 'A Hanging', August 1931, CW, x, pp. 208–9.
[96]George Orwell, 'Shooting an Elephant', Autumn 1936, CW, x, p. 501.

Orwell, in front of two thousand such faces, and acutely conscious of their gaze, confronted an elephant that had just killed a man. The elephant, he knew was best left alone, but Orwell was aware that if anything went wrong he could not only be killed, but made to look ridiculous in the process. 'And if that happened it was quite probable that some of them would laugh. That would never do.' So he shot the elephant, ineptly, 'solely to avoid looking a fool'; and it died, slowly.[97] Imperial rule in Burma was a piece of theatre, in which the actors performed to meet the expectations of their audience. The hatred of imperialism that Orwell acquired in Burma came from his ability to see himself and the forces he represented through the eyes in those 'yellow' faces, the eyes of those he had been sent to oppress. Nameless the possessors of these eyes might sometimes have been, especially when encountered in crowds. But nonetheless some were encountered as individuals, and seeing them as such shattered illusions.

> The thief whom we put in prison did not think of himself as a criminal justly punished, he thought of himself as the victim of a foreign conqueror. The thing that was done to him was merely a wanton meaningless cruelty. His face, behind the stout teak bars of the lock-up and the iron bars of the jail, said so clearly. And unfortunately I had not trained myself to be indifferent to the expression of the human face.[98]

Looking back on his Burmese experience, Orwell was haunted by 'innumerable remembered faces – faces of prisoners in the dock, of men waiting in the condemned cells, of subordinates I had bullied and aged peasants I had snubbed, of servants and coolies I had hit with my fist in moments of rage'.[99]

This pattern was to be repeated in Orwell's writings. The *Road to Wigan Pier* is in part an account of how Orwell overcame his middle-class disgust at proletarian filth and manners; Orwell's hostility to the left-wing intelligentsia drew power from his ability to empathize with the miners of Wigan. He viewed capitalism – and the Socialist intelligentsia – through their eyes, just as he viewed imperialism through the eyes of its victims. These were not just generic victims of oppression (imperial or capitalist), but the individuals Orwell met. And in Wigan, as in Burma, it is the individual in whom Orwell can see the human face of oppression. Individuals like the slum woman – about twenty-five, and again nameless – whom he saw from a train. She was poking a stick into a waste pipe. Her face

---

[97] Orwell, 'Shooting an Elephant', CW, x, pp. 505, 506.
[98] Orwell, *Road to Wigan Pier*, p. 137.
[99] Orwell, *Road to Wigan Pier*, p. 138.

wore, for the second in which I saw it, the most desolate, hopeless expression I have ever seen. It struck me then that we are mistaken when we say that 'It isn't the same for them as it would be for us', and that people bred in the slums can imagine nothing but the slums. For what I saw in her face was not the ignorant suffering of an animal. She knew well enough what was happening to her – understood as well as I did how dreadful a destiny it was to be kneeling there in the bitter cold, on the slimy stones of a slum backyard, poking a stick up a foul drain-pipe.[100]

This flash of human recognition through the train window was artfully deployed. Orwell had actually seen the woman when doing the rounds with NUWM (National Unemployed Workers Movement) collectors. The more immediate account in his diary is very much about a meeting of minds, a piece of telepathic communication of the sort that fuelled Orwell's responses to many things: 'At that moment she looked up and caught my eye, and her expression was as desolate as I have ever seen; it struck me that she was thinking just the same thing as I was.' The diary, too, drew more explicitly the general point of which this was the illustration:

What chiefly struck me was the expression on some of the women's faces, especially those in the more crowded caravans. One woman had a face like a death's head. She had a look of absolutely intolerable misery and degradation. I gathered that she felt as I would feel if I were coated all over with dung. All the people however seemed to take these conditions for granted.[101]

Always faces; always windows into minds; always a connection that goes beyond mere sympathy.

Orwell was not given to sparing his enemies, but at least once in Spain he was unwilling to shoot at one of his Nationalist opponents because of that flash of empathy, reminding him of the humanity of the person in front of him.

At this moment a man, presumably carrying a message to an officer, jumped out of the trench and ran along the top of the parapet in full view. He was half-dressed and was holding up his trousers with both hands as he ran. I refrained from shooting at him. It is true that I am a poor shot and unlikely to hit a running man at a hundred yards, and also that I was thinking chiefly of getting back to our trench while the Fascists had their

---

[100]Orwell, *Road to Wigan Pier*, p. 15.
[101]George Orwell, '*The Road to Wigan Pier* Diary', 15 February 1936, CW, X, pp. 426–7; George Orwell, *The Orwell Diaries*, ed. Peter Davison (London: Penguin, 2010), pp. 34–6.

attention fixed on the aeroplanes. Still I did not shoot partly because of that detail about the trousers. I had come here to shoot at 'Fascists'; but a man who is holding up his trousers isn't a 'Fascist', he is visibly a fellow creature, similar to yourself, and you don't feel like shooting at him.[102]

His memoir of the Spanish war, *Homage to Catalonia*, had opened with Orwell's encounter with an Italian militiaman. He said later:

I remember – oh, how vividly! – his shabby uniform and fierce, pathetic, innocent face ... This man's face, which I saw only for a minute or two, remains with me as a sort of visual reminder of what the war was really about. He symbolises for me the flower of the European working class, harried by the police of all countries, the people who fill the mass graves of the Spanish battlefield and are now, to the tune of several millions, rotting in forced-labour camps.[103]

Mass graves and the loss of individuality of the concentration camp were given human scale by the memory of one face. Orwell ended his essay 'Looking Back on the Spanish War' with a poem in memory of this Italian militiaman. Its last stanzas read:

Your name and your deeds were forgotten
Before your bones were dry,
And the lie that slew you is buried
Under a deeper lie;
But the thing that I saw in your face
No power can disinherit:
No bomb that ever burst
Shatters the crystal spirit.[104]

The expression on the face was important to Orwell as the mark of human individuality, a quality to be fiercely defended. At the very end of his first published book, Orwell offered some advice for the improvement of England's lodging-houses: 'The lodging-house keepers should be compelled to provide adequate bedclothes and better mattresses, and above all to divide their dormitories into cubicles. It does not matter how small a cubicle is, the important thing is that a man should be alone when he sleeps.'[105] There is little elsewhere in the book to prepare for this last cry. But it makes

---

[102]George Orwell, 'Looking Back on the Spanish War', written 1942?, CW, XIII, p. 501.
[103]Orwell, 'Looking Back on the Spanish War', p. 509.
[104]Orwell, 'Looking Back on the Spanish War', p. 511.
[105]Orwell, *Down and Out in Paris and London* [CW, I] (London: Secker & Warburg, 1986), p. 213 (Penguin ed. p. 228).

sense that Orwell should value moments of solitude as a necessary way of preserving a sense of individuality. Winston Smith sensed as much:

> This was the second time in three weeks that he had missed an evening at the Community Centre: a rash act, since you could be certain that the number of your attendances at the Centre was carefully checked. In principle a Party member had no spare time, and was never alone except in bed. It was assumed that when he was not working, eating or sleeping he would be taking part in some kind of communal recreation: to do anything that suggested a taste for solitude, even to go for a walk by yourself, was always slightly dangerous. There was a word for it in Newspeak: *ownlife*, it was called, meaning individualism and eccentricity.[106]

Following this thought, Winston went on a walk alone amongst the proles, visiting a pub, and ending up in the junk shop in which he had bought the notebook that now formed his diary. The owner of the shop showed him an upstairs room, and it occurred to Winston that he could rent the room.

> It was a wild, impossible notion, to be abandoned as soon as thought of; but the room had awakened in him a sort of nostalgia, a sort of ancestral memory. It seemed to him that he knew exactly what it felt like to sit in a room like this, in an armchair beside an open fire with your feet in the fender and kettle on the hob; utterly alone, utterly secure, with nobody watching you, no voice pursuing you, no sound except the singing of the kettle and the friendly ticking of the clock.[107]

A moment alone, secure, and with the kettle ready to make the perfect cup of tea – these were among the small pleasures that made for a decent life. But in the world of *Nineteen Eighty-Four* they could not be taken for granted; nor could the pleasure of reading and writing, or of sex. Beneath the grander talk of equality and justice and freedom, these quotidian pleasures were markers for Orwell of a free society. He came to think that their enjoyment would only remain possible with the achievement of democratic Socialism.

# 4. Individualism, Liberty, Socialism

What Orwell called the Soviet (or Russian myth) never dies: for many, Stalinism is enough to discredit all forms of Socialism. The intimate relationship of individualism, freedom and Socialism seems to be something

---

[106]Orwell, *Nineteen Eighty-Four*, p. 85 (Penguin ed. p. 94).
[107]Orwell, *Nineteen Eighty-Four*, p. 100 (Penguin ed. pp. 110–11).

that Socialists need to keep rediscovering in the face of this myth and its portrayal of Socialism – any Socialism – as a dire threat to any sort of liberty.[108] Introducing Christopher Caudwell's posthumous *Studies in a Dying Culture* in 1938, John Strachey presented the author as 'a Communist who died for democratic freedom', remarking how odd this must look to those who blindly saw Communists as 'the dangerous enemies of democratic freedom'.[109] Caudwell himself pointed out that for many in a bourgeois society there was 'plainly lack of leisure in which to cultivate freedom'. Only Communism, in providing freedom from want and poverty, from economic oppression, could ensure that humanity 'passed from the sphere of necessity to that of freedom'.[110] Strachey, who was later to become a minister in the Labour government of Clement Attlee, was in the 1930s 'the intellectual force behind the Left Book Club', which published his *Theory and Practice of Socialism* in 1936.[111] The book devoted a chapter to Socialism and liberty. With the aid of several quotations from a freedom-loving Joseph Stalin, Strachey elaborated the argument that 'Liberty in the capitalist epoch has been conceived of more or less exclusively as the absence of restraints; it is seldom thought of as the presence of opportunity'. Ensuring that everyone could actually exercise the freedoms that they might in theory possess was a matter of resource allocation. Wealth must be shared equitably. 'Until this has been done, liberty will remain for the greater part of men an aspiration, glorious but insubstantial. In fine, liberty cannot be effectively enjoyed, outside the ranks of the capitalist class, without that general plenty and security which socialism alone can provide.' Freedom of expression was 'a very precious liberty', but it was a fraud unless the working man or woman had as ready an access to 'the Press, the wireless, and the cinema' as the capitalist did.[112]

This is scarcely an isolated view, or a new one. From the start Socialists were interested in the question of how freedom could be made real for all people. Isaiah Berlin, no friend of Socialism, could accept that 'socialist fanatics' could, perhaps not unreasonably, point out that, 'though there may have been liberty, that liberty was nothing without economic equality'.[113] Orwell

---

[108]For example David Harvey, 'Socialists Must Be the Champions of Liberty', *Jacobin* (online), 22 October 2020, https://jacobinmag.com/2020/10/david-harvey-the-anti-capitalist-chronicles-socialism-socialism-freedom; Nick French, 'Democratic Socialism Is about Freedom', *Jacobin* (online), 13 March 2020, https://jacobinmag.com/2020/03/democratic-socialism-freedom-rights-authoritarianism-capitalism.

[109]Christopher Caudwell, *Studies and Further Studies in a Dying Culture* (New York: Monthly Review Press, 2009), pp. v–vi.

[110]Caudwell, *Studies*, pp. 196, 226.

[111]John Lewis, *The Left Book Club: An Historical Record* (London: Victor Gollancz, 1970), pp. 36–7, 39, 135.

[112]John Strachey, *The Theory and Practice of Socialism* (London: Victor Gollancz, 1942), pp. 200, 207.

[113]Isaiah Berlin, *Freedom and Its Betrayal* (Princeton, NJ: Princeton University Press, 2002), pp. 120–1.

was right that from the start many Socialists were not enemies of liberty; conversely many liberals could see the merits of Socialism as something that continued and extended the liberal tradition itself. Not the least among these was that iconic figure of liberal thinking, John Stuart Mill.[114] By Orwell's own day, English liberals were deeply divided by their attitude to Socialism, but 'Socialism with a liberal face' certainly existed on the spectrum of views.[115] Another product of the Left Book Club was Stephen Spender's *Forward from Liberalism*. Though Orwell in the 1930s sneered at Spender as a 'pansy poet', the two men later became friends as we have seen already. Spender's book of 1937 captured (even in its title) his gradual realization that the ideals of liberalism would only be realized when Capitalism had been superseded by Communism. Liberal freedoms were valuable but, as they existed in capitalist societies, they were not enough.

I have explained that by political freedom in a liberal democracy I mean the right to vote, the right to a good education, the right to speak freely, rights of assembly, equality before the law, freedom from imprisonment without trial, or arrest without warrant; these freedoms all point to the freedom of an equal and classless society in which they will be fulfilled in every man's life, and not remain ironic abstractions for the poor and legal instruments of ascendancy for the rich.

Communist societies 'will produce more individuals of imagination, intelligence and creative genius'.[116] The only sensible thing for the 'liberal individualist' was to become a Communist.[117] It wasn't the falseness of its ideals that bothered these critics of liberalism; it was the hollowness of its achievements.

---

[114]There is an enormous scholarly literature on Mill but for an accessible introduction to this aspect of his thinking, see Matt McManus, 'John Stuart Mill, Socialist?', *Areo*, 12 May 2021, available online: https://areomagazine.com/2021/05/12/john-stuart-mill-socialist/#:~:text=Mill's%20 emphasis%20on%20expressive%20individualism,mature%20Enlightenment%20 conception%20of%20science (accessed 7 June 2022). There is a more substantial account in Helen McCabe, *John Stuart Mill, Socialist* (Montréal & Kingston: McGill-Queen's UP, 2021), on which see the valuable discussion in Alexander Zevin, 'Gradualism's Prophet', *New Left Review*, 135 (2022), pp. 131–42. Zevin points out the distinct limitations to Mill's Socialism. Mill himself said that one of the key developments in his later political thought was 'a greater approximation, so far as regards the ultimate prospects of humanity, to a qualified Socialism', J. S. Mill, *Autobiography* (Oxford: Oxford University Press, Worlds Classics ed. 1924), pp. 161–2.

[115]Michael Freeden, *Liberalism Divided: A Study in British Political Thought 1914–1939* (Oxford: Clarendon Press, 1986).

[116]Stephen Spender, *Forward from Liberalism* (London: Victor Gollancz, 1937), pp. 136–7.

[117]Spender, *Forward from Liberalism*, pp. 169–76. Even Spender's generally laudatory account of Soviet Russia in the 1930s, which is built on the Webbs' notorious *Soviet Communism: A New Civilisation?*, works hard to maintain some semblance of adherence to liberal values (e.g. pp. 272–5, 284–6, 288–90) and the hope that the transition to Socialism can be less traumatic in countries that are already liberal democracies.

In March 1948 Orwell approached the editor of *The Observer*, Ivor Brown, suggesting that he write a 'piece' for the paper on Oscar Wilde's 'The Soul of Man under Socialism'. It had just appeared in pamphlet form, published by his friend (and former enemy) the anarchist critic George Woodcock, who sent a copy to Orwell. Orwell loved and collected political pamphlets, and this one, he assured Brown, 'raises some quite interesting points'.[118] Brown agreed. The article was 'not actually a review but one of those articles they have on the leader page',[119] which was in keeping with Orwell's view that both he and Wilde had something important to say.

Orwell sketched sympathetically Wilde's 'Utopian and anarchistic' vision of Socialism. It was a Socialism that 'will make possible the full development of the individual', creating a 'world ... populated by artists, each striving after perfection in the way that seems best to him'.[120] Wilde did indeed argue that 'Socialism itself will be of value simply because it will lead to Individualism'.[121] He contrasted his own form of Socialism with an 'Authoritarian' brand, which if victorious would create 'Industrial Tyrannies, then the last state of man will be worse than the first'.[122] Wilde praised instead disobedience ('man's original virtue') and agitation. '[N]o Authoritarian Socialism will do.' In the present, some people were free; but under an authoritarian form of Socialism, all would be slaves. 'Every man must be left quite free to choose his own work. No form of compulsion must be exercised over him.' This was to be a society of 'free association'.

---

[118]Orwell to Ivor Brown, 27 March 1948, CW, XIX, p. 305; Orwell to George Woodcock, 23 March 1948, XIX, p. 301. Orwell had earlier told Woodcock, who was working on a book about Wilde, that 'I've always been very pro-Wilde' (Orwell to George Woodcock. 18 June 1947, CW, XIX, p. 157). He particularly liked *The Picture of Dorian Gray*, which he had described in a radio talk as 'a deeply moral book' (Orwell, 'Talk on *Lady Windermere's Fan* by Oscar Wilde', 21 November 1943, CW, XV, p. 335).

[119]Orwell to George Woodcock, 24 April 1948, CW, XIX, p. 324.

[120]Orwell, 'Review of *The Soul of Man under Socialism* by Oscar Wilde', 9 May 1948, CW, XIX, p. 333. The article, as noted already, was not a review, and was published under the title 'Wilde's Utopia' (Gillian Fenwick, *George Orwell: A Bibliography* (Winchester: St Paul's Bibliographies, 1998), p. 238).

[121]Oscar Wilde, 'The Soul of Man under Socialism' [1891], in Wilde, *The Soul of Man under Socialism and Selected Critical Prose*, ed. Linda Dowling (London: Penguin, 2001), p. 128. This edition is not unusual in treating Wilde's essay purely as a piece of literary criticism, but there is a growing body of work that takes his anarchist Socialism seriously. A pioneer was George Woodcock, *Anarchism: A History of Libertarian Ideas and Movements* (Toronto: Toronto University Press, rev. ed., 2009), pp. 379–82, which draws on Woodcock, *The Paradox of Oscar Wilde* (London: T.V. Boardman, 1949). Now see especially Matthew Beaumont, 'Reinterpreting Oscar Wilde's Concept of Utopia: "The Soul of Man Under Socialism"', *Utopian Studies*, 15 (2004), pp. 13–29; David Goodway, *Anarchist Seeds beneath the Snow: Left-Libertarian Thought and British Writers from William Morris to Colin Ward* (Oakland, CA: PM Press, 2012), ch. 4; and Kristian Williams, *Resist Everything Except Temptation: The Anarchist Philosophy of Oscar Wilde* (Chico, CA: AK Press, 2020).

[122]Wilde, 'Soul of Man under Socialism', pp. 128–9.

In a sense, this would be a community of universalized artistic freedom of expression, but the benefits would not be restricted to the few people of artistic genius. The abolition of property would unleash 'the great actual Individualism latent and potential in mankind generally'. The institution of private property resulted in 'confusing a man with what he possesses ... It made gain not growth its aim'. Socialism would enable all people, not just a wealthy and leisured few, to grow and cultivate their individuality.[123]

There is no mistaking Orwell's sympathy with this anarchist utopianism. He associated it with Morris's *News from Nowhere*, also claimed as an anarchist utopia by some.[124] Both works 'may demand the impossible' but they do at least 'remind the Socialist movement of its original, half-forgotten objective of human brotherhood'.[125] Orwell believed that this sort of thing was what Socialism was originally about, and that it had become corrupted by authoritarianism (of which Soviet Communism was the most dangerous form). It is not clear where Wilde drew his individualistic Socialism from, though we know that he was a friend and great admirer of the anarchist Peter Kropotkin.[126] George Bernard Shaw claimed that the inspiration for 'The Soul of Man under Socialism' lay in a lecture that he had given and which Wilde attended. Even if there is some truth in this (and there are doubters), Wilde's Socialism was very different from Shaw's. As Hesketh Pearson noted, 'his whole trend of thought was antagonistic to the Webbshavian deification of the state'.[127] Shaw, indeed, dismissed 'The Soul of Man under Socialism' as 'very witty and entertaining, but [it] had nothing whatever to do with socialism'.[128]

---

[123]Wilde, 'Soul of Man under Socialism', pp. 130–3.

[124]Morris's relationship to anarchism is complicated – for an analysis of the issues, see Goodway, *Anarchist Seeds beneath the Snow*, pp. 20–4. For the relationship between Morris and Wilde, see Peter van de Kamp & Patrick Leahy, 'Some Notes on Wilde's Socialism', *The Crane Bag*, 7:1 (1983), pp. 141–50; and Ben Granger, 'Wilde and Morris – Saving Socialism's Soul', *The Wildean*, no 42 (January 2013), pp. 100–22.

[125]Orwell, 'Review of *The Soul of Man under Socialism*', CW. XIX, p. 334.

[126]Goodway, *Anarchist Seeds beneath the Snow*, pp. 73–5 is a good overview. For Wilde's admiration of Kropotkin, see Oscar Wilde, *De Profundis* [1897], in *The Complete Works of Oscar Wilde*, ed. Merlin Holland (London: HarperCollins, 5th ed., 2003), p. 1038.

[127]Hesketh Pearson, *The Life of Oscar Wilde* (Harmondsworth: Penguin, 1988), p. 163. Notwithstanding the Webbshavian quip, Beatrice Webb herself soon after becoming a Socialist recorded a discussion in her diary (15 February 1890) in which she declared: 'I have become a Socialist not because I believe it would ameliorate the conditions of the masses (though I think it would do so) but because I believe that only under communal ownership of the means of production can you arrive at the most perfect form of individual development – at the greatest stimulus to individual effort; in other words complete Socialism is only consistent with absolute individualism' – Webb, *Typescript Diary*, vol 14(1), pp. 25–6, available via the LSE Digital Library at https://digital.library.lse.ac.uk/objects/lse:wip502kaf (accessed 2 April 2021).

[128]Hesketh Pearson, 'Introduction' to Oscar Wilde, *De Profundis and Other Writings* (Harmondsworth: Penguin, 1973), p. 15.

Orwell, in turn, had little time for Shaw and his 'shallow Fabian progressivism'.[129] Shaw lacked all 'respect for common decency' – Orwell was here comparing him with Thomas Mann. Mann held firm to liberal principles, and was 'a believer in the freedom of the intellect, in human brotherhood; above all, in the existence of objective truth'.[130] But Shaw was no liberal, and consequently was susceptible to the lure of totalitarianism. His work contained a 'sadistic and masochistic element', which no doubt helped to explain his 'admiration for dictators'. He worshipped power and cruelty. It should, therefore, have been no surprise that he was someone 'who, for some years at any rate, declared Communism and Fascism to be much the same thing, and was in favour of both of them'.[131] This power-worshipping version of Socialism was, as we shall see, the sort of thing that Orwell despised from the very moment he became a Socialist himself.

However little Wilde's essay had to do with Shaw's version of Socialism, it chimed with Orwell's. Wilde had said that 'I hardly think that any Socialist, nowadays, would seriously propose that an inspector should call every morning at each house to see that each citizen rose up and did manual labour for eight hours'. Orwell wryly noted that 'unfortunately, this is just the kind of thing that modern Socialists would propose'. Something was wrong. Collectivism was conquering the world but 'Utopia is no nearer'.[132] Certainly, Orwell thought that Wilde's vision was a prophecy unrealized and, as things stood, unrealizable. Wilde was mistaken, like many Socialists, in thinking that the obstacle to Socialism lay in the 'maldistribution' of goods. For Orwell, as we shall see later, Socialism would not be achieved unless there was equality for all – the workers of India or Africa as much as those of America or France. But overcoming global poverty was not just a matter of redistribution. Even within the British Empire, Orwell thought, Socialism would be likely to reduce the standard of living in the short-term. Wilde was also mistaken in attaching too much hope to mechanization as a way of relieving all men and women of the need for unpleasant labour. In fact, even if Socialism triumphed a lot of 'dull and exhausting work' would need to be done by 'unwilling human muscles'.[133]

Perhaps Wilde would have agreed that his vision was not immediately realizable. At one point he asked, 'Is this Utopian?' His answer: 'A map of the world that does not include Utopia is not worth even glancing at, for it

---

[129]Orwell, 'The Re-discovery of Europe', 10 March 1942, CW, XIII, p. 214.
[130]Orwell, 'Review of Order of the Day by Thomas Mann', 10 September 1943, CW, XV, pp. 242–4.
[131]Orwell, 'Raffles and Miss Blandish', 28 August 1944, CW, XVI, p. 354; Orwell, 'Second Thoughts on James Burnham', 3 May 1946, CW, XVIII, p. 279 n.
[132]Wilde, 'Soul of Man under Socialism', p. 132; Orwell, 'Review of The Soul of Man under Socialism', CW, XIX, p. 333.
[133]Orwell, 'Review of The Soul of Man under Socialism', CW, XIX, pp. 333–4.

leaves out the one country at which Humanity is always landing. And when Humanity lands there, it looks out, and, seeing a better country, sets sail. Progress is the realization of Utopias.'[134] The plural is important. Utopia was not a place in which to stay but a force to drive you forward. Orwell, in many ways an anti-utopian thinker and writer, could see the point of this. These matters, indeed, take us to the very heart of his thinking and the heart of what this book is about.

There were two varieties of Socialism in Orwell's view. One sought to give substance to the hollow promises of liberal individualism. It was a liberal and democratic form of Socialism, with strong affinities to anarchism, though Orwell was never an anarchist in his view of the state. He encountered this Socialism in Barcelona when he went to fight in the Spanish Civil War. But he quickly realized that, in the context of the 1930s, this was a dissident form of Socialism. Its dominant Communist variety was authoritarian and dangerously open to the totalitarian temptation. After 1936, Orwell spent his life writing in support of the former and in condemnation of the latter. He believed that liberal Socialism was its original form and that its authoritarian version, especially when totalitarian, was a later corruption. It is perhaps an accident that Orwell encountered in Spain a Socialism that meshed with his strong individualist beliefs, but it is no accident that this was the sort of Socialism that could inspire him, nor that he was eager to write about Oscar Wilde's utopian vision. From the start, Orwell's Socialism was a means for securing justice and freedom for all. It was an answer to the question posed by his fiction of the 1930s, the same questions that animated Wilde's essay: what sort of society would encourage human individuality to flourish? How could we have real freedom and not the sham freedom of liberal capitalism?

The first part of this book examines the development and nature of Orwell's Socialism. His views were neither systematically developed nor as original as he sometimes made them out to be. But they are central to any understanding of the mind that produced *Animal Farm* and *Nineteen Eighty-Four*. The case presented here is a simple one: Orwell was a *revolutionary* Socialist until the end of his life; he was also a liberal, democratic and humanistic Socialist. It is sometimes implied that he couldn't have been both of these things, that his Socialism somehow weakened or was compromised by what I will refer to as his liberalism, that it waned over time. This is not so. At one time he hoped that revolution was just around the corner, and this view he did abandon. Though a supporter of the 1945 Labour government, he did not mistake its actions for the implementation of Socialism. If anything, it underlined the need for hope to be postponed; it clearly wasn't going to be fulfilled any time soon. Nonetheless, the world

---

[134]Wilde, 'Soul of Man under Socialism', p. 141.

needed revolutionary transformation to abolish privilege and inequality; it also needed transformation so that free individuals could flourish.

Much of this will be familiar. Orwell's first biographer to have full access to his archive, Bernard Crick was a political scientist, and his work paid particular attention to Orwell's political thought. It has done much to rescue Orwell from the misunderstandings of his critics on the Left and the Right, establishing the commitment to democratic Socialism as the main drive behind Orwell's writing from 1937 until his death. Crick rightly emphasized that 'Orwell's socialism is libertarian'. This label was used by contemporaries. Arthur Koestler received a letter in 1946 from Gilbert Hall, editor of *Common Wealth Review*, expressing his wish 'to propagate the ideas of libertarian socialism', the views in other words of 'people like yourself, George Orwell, Herbert Read [distinguished art critic and anarchist] and so on'.[135] David Martin, writing to interest Koestler in supporting a new journal for which he already had Orwell's support, referred to the 'powerful but scattered forces' of 'libertarian socialism'. He, too, wanted to bring together Koestler, Read and Orwell, under this banner.[136] The term seems to have had currency in 1945–6, the period of Orwell's most intense activism for liberal freedoms, as a label for the meeting place of liberals, Socialists and anarchists.

For Crick, Orwell's was an English Socialism, in the tradition of 'Morris, Blatchford, Carpenter, Cole, Tawney, Laski, Bevan and Foot'; and it accepted that 'liberty and equality were not merely not antithetical, but that more liberties could actually be exercised in an egalitarian society: they were conditions of each other'. This Socialism also entailed 'undisciplined commitment to free speech and truth'.[137] This book will reinforce these central aspects of Crick's interpretation. It will also, though, question whether Orwell's commitment to (violent) revolution was a 'phase', as Crick has it,[138] and whether he moved towards something different, '*Tribune* Socialism' it has been called;[139] more broadly, it has been asked whether Orwell was a Socialist or a liberal and 'was he moving towards liberalism' or to the Right?[140]

---

[135]Gilbert Hall to Arthur Koestler, 11 March 1946, Edinburgh University Library, Koestler Papers, MS 2363/4.

[136]David Martin to Arthur Koestler, 28 September 1945, Edinburgh University Library, Koestler Papers, MS 2363/4.

[137]Bernard Crick, 'Orwell and English Socialism', in Peter Buitenhuis & Ira B. Nadel (eds), *George Orwell: A Reassessment* (Basingstoke: Macmillan, 1988), pp. 4, 15, 13. On Orwell's Englishness, see especially the important study by Robert Colls, *George Orwell: English Rebel* (Oxford: Oxford University Press, 2013).

[138]Crick, 'Orwell and English Socialism', p. 19.

[139]Crick, 'Orwell and English Socialism', p. 4.

[140]These questions were posed in the discussions of Crick's essay from which I have been quoting: 'Panel Discussion', in Buitenhuis & Nadel (eds), *Orwell: A Reassessment*, p. 178. Crick reaffirmed in this discussion his belief that Orwell thought liberty and equality both to be important (pp. 179–80).

There is thus an extensive debate about the character and direction of Orwell's later thought. Was the *Tribune* Socialist losing his revolutionary edge?[141] The debate is very much one of nuance. Orwell clearly aligned himself with the *Tribune* Labour left, but just what did this mean? The writers for *Tribune* were not a cohesive group. Did his (qualified) support for Attlee's Labour government suggest a move to the right? Some go further and doubt that Orwell was meaningfully Socialist at the end, or even that he ever was. It is certainly not obvious what Orwell's attachment to *Tribune* actually means for his identity as a Socialist.[142] I wonder whether Orwell did in any significant way move to the right at all. He postponed his hopes for revolutionary change, but he did not abandon them. The Labour government deserved support – it was the best that might be hoped for in the austere post-war conditions – but Orwell had no illusions that it was actually implementing Socialism. And even at his most revolutionary, Orwell never pinned his hopes *just* on the working class – indeed the revolution he preached was a patriotic one that transcended class divisions. The argument of the book that follows is, in essence, that the later Orwell – it seems an uncomfortable phrase to use of someone who died before there was a later – became engrossed by a number of liberal causes. But this is a sign of the maintenance of his original Socialist convictions not their weakening. To appreciate this fully, it is important to understand just what sort of Socialist he was. This book begins by doing that before moving to its primary focus, Orwell's activism is the cause of intellectual freedom.

There are risks in writing, as I do in this book, primarily about George Orwell's political ideas. Stephen Ingle, writing at the end of his own study of Orwell's social and political thought, delineates them well:

If I have been critical of some of the central ideas of Orwell's social and political thought, it was primarily because I did not really think it

---

[141]See Paul O'Flinn, 'Orwell and *Tribune*', *Literature and History*, 6 (1980), pp. 201–18, 173; Paul Anderson (ed.), *Orwell in Tribune: 'As I Please' and Other Writings 1943–7* (London: Politico's, 2006), Introduction; Paul Anderson, 'In Defence of Bernard Crick', and John Newsinger, 'Orwell's Socialism', both in Richard Lance Keeble (ed.), *George Orwell Now!* (New York: Peter Lang, 2015), chs 5 & 7; John Newsinger, 'Orwell, the Labour Party and the Atlee Government', *George Orwell Studies*, 2:1 (2017), pp. 78–87; Paul Anderson, 'So What Sort of Democratic Socialist Was He?', *George Orwell Studies*, 2:1 (2017), pp. 97–111. More generally Newsinger's two books are still the best introduction to Orwell's Socialist ideas, *Orwell's Politics* (Basingstoke: Palgrave, 1999) and *Hope Lies in the Proles: George Orwell and the Left* (London: Pluto Press, 2018), ch. 5 of which is most relevant to the debate discussed here.
[142]Cf. the reflections in Alex Woloch, *Or Orwell: Writing and Democratic Socialism* (Cambridge, MA: Harvard University Press, 2016), pp. 317–19, engaging Scott Lucas, *Orwell* (London: Haus, 2003) and Colls, *George Orwell: English Rebel*. On the latter and its excessive blunting of Orwell's radicalism, see also John Newsinger, 'Defusing George Orwell', *International Socialist*, 143 (2014), available online: http://isj.org.uk/defusing-george-orwell/ (accessed 5 June 2022).

best to understand it as political thought at all. If we take Orwell as a political thinker, then, immediately, basic shortcomings, inconsistencies and apparently irresolvable tensions appear, but if we shift our focus, a different picture emerges. In categorising Orwell as a moralist and a writer, I do not wish for a moment to suggest that he was not, therefore a socialist sympathiser or, more simply, a socialist. But what I want to stress is that he approached socialism, not as a spokesman for this or that ideological stratum or substratum, but as a moralist and a writer, and that is how he should be considered.[143]

Indeed, Orwell was only in the loosest sense a political thinker – still less was he a political theorist or political philosopher. He was, as Ingle has it, a writer and a moralist. His Socialism began and ended in the two values he stressed in *The Road to Wigan Pier*, justice and liberty.[144] That does not mean, though, that it cannot be fruitful to consider the implication of Orwell's ideas for political theory or philosophy;[145] his political thinking is interesting for what it is. But it does mean the best recent writing on Orwell recognizes that he was above all else a writer, and that his Socialism was in good part intimately connected to his identity as a writer,[146] or it focuses on his core moral values, recognizing that his deep attachment to these values (which could be in tension with one another) does not make for a consistent or systematic thinker.[147] The account that follows does, I hope, recognize that Orwell was not just a writer but one who cared and thought deeply about the craft of writing. Though I say a lot in the last part of the book about Orwell as an 'activist' in the narrow sense, he was as well always after 1936 an activist writer. Nor, I hope, does this account make Orwell sound too much like a careful political thinker: he was above all an impassioned moralist.

*****

Orwell's novels of the 1930s were an unresolved problem, but his non-fiction began to move towards a Socialism that would subsume – but not obliterate – his individualism. It was a Socialism that didn't just allow for

---

[143]Stephen Ingle, *The Social and Political Thought of George Orwell: A Reassessment* (London: Taylor & Francis, 2006), p. 178.

[144]Orwell, *Road to Wigan Pier*, p. 201.

[145]Two illuminating attempts are Craig L. Carr, *Orwell, Politics and Power* (London: Bloomsbury, 2010); and Ezio di Nucci & Stefan Storrie (eds), *1984 and Philosophy: Is Resistance Futile* (Chicago, IL: Open Court, 2018) – the latter is an especially stimulating book.

[146]Alex Woloch, *Or Orwell: Writing and Democratic Socialism*.

[147]David Dwan, *Liberty, Equality and Humbug: Orwell's Political Ideals* (Oxford: Oxford University Press, 2018).

individual freedom; it required it. It enabled Orwell to understand why intellectual freedom was essential and what was needed to maintain it. He never lost a rich sense of what a flourishing human life might be like. 'Man needs warmth, society, leisure, comfort and security: he also needs solitude, creative work and the sense of wonder.'[148] The second part of the book, building on the foundation established by the first, will reconstruct in detail Orwell's writing about freedom of thought and expression. It will also uncover his activism in this cause. By the end of the war, Orwell came to see the defence of freedom (and especially of intellectual freedom) as the most important task that needed doing to ensure the victory of a healthy rather than a diseased version of Socialism. (He assumed that some form of collectivism was inevitable.) Orwell put all of the energy that he could muster into this task, probably hastening his death as a result.

---

[148]Orwell, 'Pleasure Spots', January 1946, CW, XVIII, p. 32.

# Part One

## Orwell's Socialism

George Orwell was an unlikely Socialist. His birth, background and education seemingly provided little grounding for Socialism, even in a country that spawned a good many privileged supporters of the cause. But, more significantly, Orwell's fundamental belief in the importance of individual freedom, and his personal resistance to being part of any group, makes his sustained attachment to collectivist political and economic principles more puzzling than it is generally taken to be. It is hardly surprising that his critics on the Left have felt that something does not quite add up. That so many scholars have puzzled over 'the problem of Orwell's socialism' is, no doubt, something that would have entertained as well as irritated the man himself.[1]

'Despite his socialism, Orwell was instinctively an *individualist*.'[2] Stuart Hall's judgement may be better in reverse: despite his individualism, Orwell became a Socialist. The individualism, as we have seen, came first, and it never abated. The Socialism was adapted to it. Much of Orwell's political thinking involved wrestling with his early perception 'that the essential aims of Socialism are justice and liberty'.[3] *Social* justice and *individual* liberty: how could they go together?

---

[1]The phrase is from the seminal essay by Peter Sedgwick, 'George Orwell, International Socialist?', *International Socialism*, (First Series), No 37 (1969), pp. 28–34 (also available on the Marxists Internet Archive, https://www.marxists.org/archive/sedgwick/1969/xx/orwell.htm, accessed 31 March 2018); reprinted in Paul Flewers (ed.), *George Orwell: Enigmatic Socialist* (London: Socialist Platform, 2005), pp. 3–19. This remains an excellent and careful analysis of Orwell's development into a socialist. The far Left's suspicion of Orwell pre-dates but has been re-fuelled by efforts to claim him for the Right: for a survey, see C. J. Fusco, *Our Orwell, Right or Left: The Continued Importance of One Writer to the World of Western Politics* (Newcastle: Cambridge Scholars, 2008); for an example Scott Lucas, *Orwell* (London: Haus, 2014), and, more debatably, Raymond Williams, *Orwell* (London: Flamingo, new. ed. 1984).

[2]Stuart Hall, 'Conjuring Leviathan: Orwell on the State', in Christopher Norris (ed.), *Inside the Myth – Orwell: Views from the Left* (London: Lawrence & Wishart, 1984), pp. 217–41, at p. 218.

[3]George Orwell, *The Road to Wigan Pier* [CW, V] (London: Secker & Warburg, 1986), p. 199. The Penguin Classics ed. has the same pagination as CW.

# 1. Before Orwell; before Socialism:
# A Tory Anarchist?

Eric Blair adopted the pen name George Orwell for the publication of his first book, *Down and Out in Paris and London*, in 1933. Thereafter he answered to both names, but wrote only as Orwell. Eric Blair's early political commitments are hard to track, possibly because they were weak or ill-defined. 'I was not a rebel, except by force of circumstances. I accepted the codes that I found in being,' he recalled of his time at St Cyprian's, the preparatory school that he attended from 1911 to 1916, before progressing to Eton.[4] Cyril Connolly, his friend from St Cyprian's, remembered things differently: 'I was a stage rebel, Orwell a true one'; he was 'an intellectual and not a parrot'.[5] Of his time at Eton, Orwell would later say, 'I loosely described myself as a Socialist. But I had not much grasp of what Socialism meant, and no notion that the working class were human beings.'[6] Though it is a mistake to assume that Orwell can be identified with any of the central characters in his novels, nonetheless some of his memories of Eton probably informed this account of the school days of Gordon Comstock, the central character in *Keep the Aspidistra Flying*:

> And at that moment, in the years just after the War, England was so full of revolutionary opinion that even the public schools were infected by it. The young, even those who had been too young to fight, were in a bad temper with their elders, as well they might be; practically everyone with any brains at all was for the moment a revolutionary. Meanwhile the old – those over sixty say – were running in circles like hens, squawking about 'subversive ideas'. Gordon and his friends had quite an exciting time with their 'subversive ideas'. For a whole year they ran an unofficial monthly paper called the *Bolshevik*, duplicated with a jellygraph. It advocated Socialism, free love, the dismemberment of the British Empire, the abolition of the Army and Navy, and so on and so forth. It was great fun. Every intelligent boy of sixteen [Orwell's age in 1919] is a Socialist. At that age one does not see the hook sticking out of the rather stodgy bait.[7]

---

[4]Orwell, 'Such, Such Were the Joys', 1939–48. CW, XIX, p. 372.
[5]Cyril Connolly, *Enemies of Promise*, Part 3 (1938), in *The Selected Works of Cyril Connolly*, ed. Matthew Connolly (London: Picador, 2 vols, 2002), II, pp. 22–3.
[6]Orwell, *Road to Wigan Pier*, pp. 132–3.
[7]Orwell, *Keep the Aspidistra Flying* [CW, IV] (London: Secker & Warburg, 1987), pp. 45–6. The Penguin Classics ed. has the same pagination as CW.

Bernard Crick, however, is probably right to caution that these retrospective accounts from the mid-1930s might have 'drawn from experience, but experience reinterpreted for a purpose, not simply recalled'.[8]

Whatever his schoolboy radicalism might have been, it does not seem to have long survived Orwell's departure from Eton in 1921. From 1922 to 1927 he served in Burma with the Indian Imperial Police, rather than going to university. Why he did so remains unclear. Christopher Hollis, a contemporary at Eton, visited Blair in Burma, and detected in him 'no trace of liberal opinions'. He added: 'I should certainly have dismissed him as an example of that common type which has a phase of liberal opinion at school, but relapses easily after into conventional reaction.'[9] Returning to England in 1927, Blair resigned from the Imperial Police while on leave and was discharged in early 1928. The experience of Empire clearly disgusted him, though his return to England was actually prompted by ill-health, but his political views remained inchoate. It was in these years after Burma that he lived the 'down and out' life that was crafted into his first book, but his political views remain elusive. He had some connections at the very beginning of his writing career with Parisian Communist circles in the years 1928–9, through his aunt, Nellie Limouzin. His first professional journalism was published amidst this milieu.[10] Nellie was also a friend of the Westropes, Frank and Myfanwy, who owned the Hampstead bookshop, Booklover's Corner, where Orwell worked during 1934–6. She in particular was deeply committed to the Left and both were Marxists and ILP members.[11] Also part of this circle was Mabel Fierz, one of Orwell's lovers.[12] How much this tells us about Orwell's own views at the time is harder to say.[13] The surveillance files kept on Orwell by the SIS and by Special Branch are another potential source of information. They picked up an 'interest in the activities of the French Communist Party' during his Paris days (though could not determine whether he was an active supporter of the revolutionary movement), his

---

[8]Crick, *George Orwell: A Life* (Harmondsworth: Penguin, new edition, 1992), p. 128.

[9]Christopher Hollis, *A Study of George Orwell: The Man and His Works* (New York: Racehorse, 2017), pp. 27–8. It may be, as Gordon Bowker has suggested, that Hollis was misled by Orwell's public face, a face that disguised his growing disquiet at what he saw in Burma: Gordon Bowker, *George Orwell* (London: Little, Brown, 2003, Abacus pbk 2004), p. 86.

[10]Bowker, *George Orwell*, pp. 105–10; Darcy Moore, 'Orwell's Aunt Nellie', *George Orwell Studies*, 4:2 (2020), pp. 30–44; Ann Kronbergs, 'Orwell's Favourite Aunt', *Orwell Society Journal*, 16 (Spring 2020), pp. 8–11; and Masha Karp, 'Lanti and the Soviet Union', *Orwell Society Journal*, 16 (Spring 2020), pp. 12–16.

[11]Gordon Bowker, *George Orwell*, pp. 160–1.

[12]See D. J. Taylor, 'George and Mabel: An Unlikely Romance', available online https://www.sothebys.com/en/articles/george-and-mabel-an-unlikely-romance (accessed 5 June 2022).

[13]Crick, *George Orwell*, pp. 254–6.

connection with the Westropes (Frank was 'known to hold Socialist views')[14] and his attendance at (indeed 'addressing') Communist meetings in Wigan in 1936.[15] But neither his friendships nor his political curiosity tell us much about Orwell's own thinking.

In 1947, looking back on his life, he declared that 'as to politics, I was only intermittently interested in the subject until about 1935, though I think I can say I was always more or less "left"'.[16] Another account from about the same time implies a slightly different chronology. 'Up to 1930 I did not upon the whole look upon myself as a Socialist. In fact I had as yet no clearly defined political views.'[17] At the time, writing to his friend Eleanor Jaques, he was even blunter: 'I don't understand or take any interest in the political situation.'[18]

In spite of these comments, when Eric Blair entered the circle of the leftish magazine *The Adelphi* in 1930, he provided himself with a political label. As one contemporary put it, 'Orwell [then still just Eric Blair] described himself as a Tory anarchist, but admitted *The Adelphi*'s socialist case on moral grounds.'[19] Much has been made of this label, and it is a convenient starting point for a discussion of Orwell's path to Socialism, as others have found. It can, for example, be appropriated as a label for a phase in Orwell's thinking: 'He called himself "a Tory anarchist" until the mid-1930s. After that, experience made him a democratic socialist.'[20] Orwell's biographer, Bernard Crick, uses the term several times to refer to Orwell's inchoate pre-Socialist political views.[21] But this approach is too simple for some, who suggest instead that 'the qualities that he possessed that had made him refer to himself as a Tory anarchist remained throughout his life'.[22] 'Orwell liked to describe himself as a "Tory anarchist" ... A writer and not a party man, he stayed on the same side throughout his life'.[23]

---

[14]Memo of 11 March 1936 in Orwell's MI5 file, TNA, KV2/2699.

[15]Scattered documents in both TNA KV2/2699 and in Orwell's Special Branch file MEPO 38/69.

[16]Orwell to Richard Usborne, 26 August 1947, in Peter Davison (ed.), *George Orwell: A Life in Letters* (London: Penguin, 2011), p. xi.

[17]Orwell, 'Preface to the Ukrainian Edition of *Animal Farm*', March 1947, CW, XIX, p. 87.

[18]Orwell to Eleanor Jaques, 22 October 1931, UCL Orwell/G/14/2. Cf. D. J. Taylor, *On Nineteen Eighty-Four: A Biography* (New York: Abrams Press, 2019), p. 31. This is one of a number of newly discovered letters to Eleanor Jaques that have only just become accessible to researchers. See also D. J. Taylor, 'Don't Fear That I Will Leave Your Letter Lying about – George Orwell's Notes for His Lover', *The Times*, 10 July 2018.

[19]Rayner Heppenstall, *Four Absentees* (London: Barrie & Rockliff, 1960), p. 32.

[20]Paul Richards, 'George Orwell: From Tory Anarchist to Democratic Socialist', *Labour List*, https://labourlist.org/2010/11/george-orwell-from-tory-anarchist-to-democratic-socialist/ (accessed 1 April 2018).

[21]Crick, *George Orwell*, pp. 16, 21, 174, 205, 211, 233, 254, 256.

[22]Peter Wilkin, 'George Orwell: The English Dissident as Tory Anarchist', *Political Studies*, 61 (2003), pp. 197–214, at pp. 217–18.

[23]Stuart Hampshire, 'The Tory Anarchist', *New York Review of Books*, 30 January 1992.

Just how illuminating is this label? It has, for example, been said that he 'described himself as a Tory anarchist to numerous friends and acquaintances at least until he went to Spain in 1936'.[24] But did he? What is the evidence for such a claim? It is interesting that the statement by Heppenstall, quoted above, occurs in a paragraph about Jack Common and his view of Orwell. Common was, in 1929, when he met Orwell for the first time, working for *The Adelphi*, edited by John Middleton Murry, at least on paper, who was joined in the role by Sir Richard Rees in 1930. Rees in his later book about Orwell also notes in passing that 'up to about 1930 he had remained some sort of Bohemian tory-anarchist'.[25] When Rees repeated the comment in a 1972 interview for BBC Omnibus, he abridged it to 'he had a kind of Bohemian Anarchist attitude'.[26] This is vaguer than Heppenstall's account, and it may be that both men were drawing upon their experience (direct or indirect) of a conversation with Orwell to which Jack Common alludes in his account of his early meetings with Orwell.

Common's first encounter with Orwell (in 1929) left a mixed impression:

He was sitting in [the late wife of John Middleton Murry] Katherine Mansfield's arm-chair one dusky afternoon talking to Richard Rees and Max Plowman, the editors [of *The Adelphi*]. Like that, at that low level at which one took in first the scrub of hair and curiously-ravaged face, he looked the real thing, outcast, gifted pauper, kicker against authority, perhaps near-criminal. But he rose to acknowledge the introduction and shake hands. Manners showed through. A sheep in wolf's clothing, I thought, taking in his height and stance, accent and cool built-in superiority, the public school presence. What he said in subsequent conversation that day I do not remember – perhaps because of the let-down in how he said it.

In their next meeting, Orwell declared his wish to spend Christmas in gaol, 'one of the statements he loved to use for shock value and which made him appear like an *enfant terrible* in decay'. As the thirties progressed, political positioning became more important and more fraught.

It was typical of the way things were going that *The Adelphi*, formerly a monthly ivory tower sheltering or gathering together the devotees of truth-beauty, beauty-truth in writing, was now a political lighthouse in which doughty polemicists argued about which way to direct the beam. At

---

[24]Wilkin, 'George Orwell', p. 201.
[25]Richard Rees, *George Orwell: Fugitive from the Camp of Victory* (London: Secker & Warburg, 1961), p. 48.
[26]Richard Rees, in Audrey Coppard & Bernard Crick (eds), *Orwell Remembered* (London: Ariel Books/BBC, 1984), p. 124.

that same old blooming asbestos gas-fire where Eric Blair airily described himself over a cup of tea as a Tory Anarchist and nobody objected to such a harmless description, now Marxist and Fascist and acidulated Liberal fought wickedly to establish a derogatory meaning to each other's phrases and cigarettes were sucked to death in short, sharp puffs.

By the mid-1930s (Common's chronology is a bit vague), though Orwell 'made no violent change of political conviction, but somehow one gathered he now approved of socialism on moral grounds'.[27] That last phrase is closely echoed by Heppenstall, and it seems likely that the three accounts (Heppenstall, Rees, Common) are inter-dependent. So just how often did Orwell refer to himself as a Tory Anarchist? Once?

In 1935 Orwell shared a flat with Heppenstall and Michael Sayers (also a contributor to *The Adelphi*). Gordon Bowker interviewed Sayers for his biography of Orwell, and gives a vivid picture of their literary and political conversations. They provide an interesting picture of Orwell's politics in the mid-'30s:

> They talked about *The Communist Manifesto*, and agreed 'that it was one of the most powerful and beautifully written political documents imaginable ... an epic poem in the magnificence of its vocabulary and passion'. Orwell, however, still referred to himself as a Tory Anarchist. 'He was sympathetic to the idea of a change but didn't think it was possible to retain the values that made life worth living. He said the leadership of such movements could not be trusted and pointed to the outcome of the French Revolution.'[28]

It is not clear, however, whether Sayers himself was the source for the claim that Orwell still referred to himself as a Tory Anarchist, or whether Bowker is interpolating contextual information based on Common, Heppenstall and Rees.[29]

Other accounts are more enigmatic. Stephen Spender, who first met Orwell only late in 1937, by which time he was a Socialist, recalls:

> But we always come back to the position with Orwell that his integrity lay in the life he led. So it didn't matter very much that some of the things he said were wrong. One always respected he was living out this more or less working-class life. He was really a radical conservative, which

---

[27]Jack Common, in Coppard & Crick, *Orwell Remembered*, pp. 139–40, 142.

[28]Bowker, *George Orwell*, p. 174.

[29]However, Gordon Bowker has confirmed by email (via his agents) that 'this definitely came from Sayers ... It looks as if they all [Sayers, Rees, Heppenstall] pinned that label on him because that is what he called himself at the time' (Personal email, 9 April 2018).

has a very respectable English history, going back to the nineteenth century, to people like Cobbett. What he valued was the old concept of England based on the English countryside, in which to be conservative is to be against changes taking place, especially changes in the direction of producing inequality. He was opposed to the whole hard-faced industrial middle class which arose in the nineteenth century.[30]

These reflections were recorded in 1983, and are Spender's attempt to characterize Orwell's thought, not to capture what Orwell might have said of himself.

We should be careful not to read too much into a possibly isolated comment, uttered by an *'enfant terrible'*, conceivably for its 'shock value'. Orwell did, of course, use the phrase 'Tory anarchist' in print, not of himself but of one of the writers he most admired, Jonathan Swift:

We are right to think of Swift as a rebel and iconoclast, but except in certain secondary matters, such as his insistence that women should receive the same education as men, he cannot be labelled 'Left'. He is a Tory anarchist, despising authority while disbelieving in liberty, and preserving the aristocratic outlook while seeing clearly that the existing aristocracy is degenerate and contemptible.[31]

If this provides a definition of a 'Tory anarchist', it is not one that could ever have applied to Orwell. He may have despised authority all his life, but he never disbelieved in liberty. As he examined Swift's politics further, Orwell undermines even this definition of Tory anarchism. The label is self-contradictory, 'the anarchist outlook covering an authoritarian cast of mind'.[32] On closer examination, the Tory anarchist was *both* hostile to liberty (or individual freedom) *and* authoritarian.

Orwell, during his time at the BBC, had written and broadcast an imaginary conversation with Swift, in which he said to the eighteenth-century author, 'Since your day something has appeared called totalitarianism.' Totalitarianism was not altogether new, however, but had been made practicable by modern technologies. Orwell was even able to find a hint of it in *Gulliver's Travels*. The final part of that book mentioned in passing the 'ruling *Yahoo*' that most Yahoo herds possessed.[33] Orwell commented, 'each

[30]Stephen Spender in Stephen Wadhams (ed.), *The Orwell Tapes* [previously published by Penguin as *Remembering Orwell*] (Vancouver: Locarno Press, 2017), p. 136.

[31]George Orwell, 'Politics vs. Literature: An Examination of *Gulliver's Travels*', September–October 1946, in CW, XVIII, p. 425.

[32]Orwell, 'Politics vs. Literature', CW, XVIII, p. 426.

[33]The passage is in *The Essential Writings of Jonathan Swift*, ed. Claude Rawson & Ian Higgins (New York: Norton, 2010), p. 479.

tribe of Yahoos had a dictator, or Fuehrer and this Dictator liked to surround himself with yes-men'.[34] The implication is that modern totalitarianism was traditional tyranny amplified by technology; tyranny that could reach to 'total' control through modern methods of communication.

Orwell's later essay on Swift found a very different anticipation of totalitarianism in the country of the Houyhnhnms.

> Part IV of *Gulliver's Travels* is a picture of an anarchist Society, not governed by law in the ordinary sense, but by the dictates of 'Reason', which are voluntarily accepted by everyone ... This illustrates very well the totalitarian tendency which is implicit in the anarchist or pacifist vision of Society. In a Society in which there is no law, and in theory no compulsion, the only arbiter of behaviour is public opinion. But public opinion, because of the tremendous urge to conformity in gregarious animals, is less tolerant than any system of law. When human beings are governed by 'thou shalt not', the individual can practice a certain amount of eccentricity: when they are supposedly governed by 'love' or 'reason', he is under continuous pressure to make him behave and think in exactly the same way as everyone else ... [The Houyhnhnms] had reached, in fact, the highest stage of totalitarian organisation, the stage when conformity has become so general that there is no need for a police force.[35]

It was not amongst the brutish, human Yahoos, but amongst the rational, civilized and equine Houyhnhnms that totalitarianism was to be found. Orwell had identified the problem of what Sir Isaiah Berlin would come to call two concepts of liberty. An anarchist society like the country of the Houyhnhnms seems free, in the negative sense that one was free from direct coercion (no police force). But these societies cohered, in the absence of political authority, because everyone shared and found their freedom positively in adherence to values or principles like love or reason. People were 'free' when forced to conform to the needs of their 'higher' selves. This produced a drive to conformity that was hard to avoid, partly because it was invisible to its victims. It operated through cultural hegemony to achieve willing subjection. Herein lay the chief way in which totalitarian threats to intellectual freedom functioned.

Orwell thus gave two different accounts of the way in which *Gulliver's Travels* could be charged with anticipating the politics of totalitarianism, and in the later of them 'Tory anarchism' itself was indicted. Its

---

[34]Orwell, 'Imaginary Interview: George Orwell and Jonathan Swift', broadcast 6 November 1942, in CW, XIV, p. 158.
[35]Orwell, 'Politics vs Literature', CW, XVIII, pp. 424–5.

anti-authoritarianism, exemplified by the society of the Houyhnhms, led to totalitarianism. And, as well, it was opposed to individual liberty by definition.

There are figures besides Swift who have been associated with the 'Tory anarchist' tradition. Orwell showed little interest in any of them, with one (dubious) exception. The writer most often associated with Tory anarchism or radicalism is William Cobbett. Spender, as quoted above, makes this connection, as does Paul Potts: 'He was by temperament a Tory radical. He had more in common with William Cobbett than he did with Tom Paine.'[36] Yet, Orwell mentioned Cobbett only three times. The first mention, passing in the extreme, was in a 1936 review of an anthology of writing on rural culture;[37] the second in a 1944 review of an edition of extracts from nineteenth-century diaries. Orwell betrayed no particular interest or sense of affinity (less, perhaps, than he did with Tom Paine).[38] The third mention, which displays no greater knowledge of Cobbett, is nonetheless more interesting, and points us to a major topic in Orwell's writing. Reviewing H.J. Massingham's edited collection *The Natural Order: Essays on the Return to Husbandry*, Orwell announced that 'one does not have to be a mediævalist to feel that the modern world has something seriously wrong with it'.[39] The sight of any city 'would convince the most cheery optimist that scientific progress has not been an unmixed blessing'. Most would attribute our ills to 'an outworn economic system which makes it impossible to consume all the goods that are produced and leads inevitably to struggles for markets and hence to Imperialist wars'. But was it possible 'that machine civilisation is itself the enemy'? While many may see the machine as something that 'can set us free from brute labour', there was another view.

> Ever since the early days of the Industrial Revolution, however, there has been an opposite school of thought – it included such thinkers as Cobbett, Ruskin, Chesterton – which refused to admit that the machine could be the friend of humanity if its products were distributed more evenly. According to this school creative labour is psychologically necessary to the human being.

No one has ever advocated the complete scrapping of mechanical progress, but it is argued that a truly human life – and, consequently,

---

[36]Paul Potts in Coppard & Crick, *Orwell Remembered*, p. 254.
[37]George Orwell, 'Review of *The Open Air* by Adrian Bell', 2 December 1936, CW, X, p. 525.
[38]George Orwell, 'Review of *English Diaries of the Nineteenth Century*, edited by James Aitken', July 1944, CW, XVI, 309; on Paine see George Orwell, 'As I Please', 6, 7 January 1944, CW, XVI, p. 56; Orwell to K.S. Shelvankar, 6 August 1942, CW, XIII, p. 451.
[39]Orwell, 'Review of *The Natural Order: Essays on the Return to Husbandry*, edited by H.J. Massingham', 25 January 1945, CW, XVII, p. 27.

private happiness and international peace – is only possible on a basis of hand labour and wide distribution of property.[40]

Cobbett, Ruskin, Chesterton – this, at least, is a grouping that makes sense. All three shared with Orwell a sense of the damage that industrialization and technology might do to ways of living that promoted human flourishing. Mechanization created work that was 'soul-destroying'; even worse, 'those whose work is soul-destroying tend to seek mechanical mass-produced amusements (the film and the radio) in their spare time'. A culture was under threat. Yet Orwell could not really share the perspectives of Massingham's team of writers (nor of Cobbett, Ruskin and Chesterton). Most people preferred machine civilization to life in the rural village. Countries that did not industrialize would be militarily vulnerable. Like it or not, machine civilization 'cannot be got rid of'. There is no mistaking the note of regret in Orwell's conclusion, nor that in reaching it he described as 'probably a fallacy' one of the core beliefs of many (especially Marxist) Socialists: that mechanization would reduce the hours of work, leaving more time for creative leisure.[41]

Orwell's concerns about mechanization and its consequences were forcefully expressed in the later 1930s, especially in *The Road to Wigan Pier* and *Coming Up for Air*. They will get fuller attention later in this chapter.

Among other writers who have been associated with a Tory anarchist tradition are William Hazlitt, G.K. Chesterton and Evelyn Waugh – possibly Charles Dickens too. Or, at any rate, they have been associated with such a tradition by Orwell commentators.[42] Listing these names is itself enough to suggest that the 'Tory anarchist' tradition has been concocted, with varying assortments of people attached, to provide an invented context for views deemed to be essential to Orwell. Hazlitt, who would have been surprised to be described as any sort of Tory, is another writer of whom Orwell was aware, but in whom he had no real interest. His references to Hazlitt – passing in the extreme – were mostly products of his work for BBC radio.[43]

---

[40]CW, XVII, p. 27.
[41]CW, XVII, p. 28.
[42]Especially Wilkin, 'George Orwell: The English Dissident as Tory Anarchist'; and William E. Laskowski Jnr, 'George Orwell and the Tory-Radical Tradition', in Jonathan Rose (ed.), *The Revised Orwell* (East Lansing, MI: Michigan State University Press, 1992), pp. 149–90. Also Peter Wilkin, *The Strange Case of Tory Anarchism* (Faringdon: Libri, 2010), where the main connections are with Evelyn Waugh and forward to the likes of Peter Cook and Spike Milligan.
[43]Orwell to Edmund Blunden, 3 December 1942, CW, XIV, p. 215; Orwell, 'Memorandum to Miss Playle, *The Listener*', 21 December 1942, CW, XIV, p. 249; Orwell to Edmund Blunden, 23 December 1942, CW, XIV, p. 253. Also George Orwell, 'Review of *The Two Carlyles* by Osbert Burdett', March 1931, CW, X, p. 196; and a passing reference in George Orwell, 'Lear, Tolstoy and the Fool', March 1947, CW, XIX, p. 55.

Orwell's relationship to the other three writers is more substantial and more complex.

Dickens was the subject of one of Orwell's finest essays, published in his 1940 collection, *Inside the Whale*. Here, at the end of his formative political decade, Orwell strained hard to capture Dickens's political identity; but he showed neither an awareness of a Tory anarchist tradition, nor a wish to find Tory or anarchist elements in Dickens. He did the opposite:

> His radicalism is of the vaguest kind, and yet one always knows that it is there. That is the difference between being a moralist and a politician. He has no constructive suggestions, not even a clear grasp of the nature of the society he is attacking, only an emotional perception that something is wrong. All he can finally say is, 'Behave decently', which ... is not necessarily so shallow as it sounds. Most revolutionaries are potential Tories, because they imagine that everything can be put right by altering the *shape* of society; once that change is effected, as it sometimes is, they see no need for any other. Dickens has not this kind of mental coarseness. The vagueness of his discontent is the mark of its permanence. What he is out against is not this or that institution, but, as Chesterton put it, 'an expression on the human face'.[44]

Is this a self-portrait? Orwell, like Dickens, was a moral rather than a political critic of the social order, and his discontent, too, was permanent. Though in his own way a revolutionary, Orwell had a sense that revolution was never achieved, always still needed, unlikely to produce something that could thereafter be conserved. And he also was someone for whom the expression on the human face mattered most. Both men were advocates for the 'bourgeois' values of the working classes, or for what Orwell would call 'common decency'.[45]

From the Marxist or Fascist point of view, nearly all that Dickens stands for can be written off as 'bourgeois morality'. But in moral outlook, no one could be more 'bourgeois' that the English working classes ... But in

---

[44]George Orwell, 'Charles Dickens', March 1940, CW, XII, p. 54.

[45]See John Rodden, 'Decency and Democracy: George Orwell, "the Aspiring Plebeian"', *Prose Studies*, 12:2 (1989), pp. 174–192, which formed ch. 9 of Rodden, *The Politics of Literary Reputation: The Making and Claiming of 'St George' Orwell* (New York: Oxford UP, 1989); Kristian Williams, 'On Common Decency', in Williams (ed.), *Between the Bullet and the Lie: Essays on Orwell* (Chico, CA: AK Press, 2017). More broadly, with a focus on the fiction: Anthony Stewart, *George Orwell, Doubleness and Value of Decency* (London: Routledge, 2010).

his own age and ours he [Dickens] he has been popular chiefly because he was able to express in a comic, simplified and therefore memorable form the native decency of the common man.[46]

Both men built their politics on vague but powerful commitments to freedom and equality. Dickens appealed to 'a certain cultural unity' that crossed class divisions: 'All through the Christian ages, and especially since the French Revolution, the Western world has been haunted by the idea of freedom and equality; it is only an *idea*, but it has penetrated to all ranks of society.'[47] Both men combatted the orthodoxies of the age, waging battles on multiple fronts, and (at least in Orwell's case) displayed a disconcerting enthusiasm for attacking friend and enemy alike:

> ... a man who is always fighting against something, but who fights in the open and is not frightened, the face of a man who is *generously angry* – in other words, of a nineteenth-century liberal, a free intelligence, a type hated with equal hatred by all the smelly little orthodoxies which are now contending for our souls.[48]

Neither man was a Tory.

Chesterton and Waugh were writers with whom Orwell had much less sympathy, partly because of his sustained hostility to Roman Catholic ideas (which he nonetheless took very seriously).[49] Chesterton attracted his attention in several essays. Orwell was especially scathing about Chesterton's antisemitism,[50] but it was his 'medievalism' (which, as we have seen, created in Orwell's mind an affinity between Chesterton, Cobbett and Ruskin[51]) that is significant to Tory Anarchism. Orwell considered the idea in one of four essays for *The Manchester Guardian* in 1946 which together surveyed the main

---

[46]Orwell, 'Charles Dickens', CW, XII, p. 55.

[47]Orwell, 'Charles Dickens', CW, XII, p. 55.

[48]Orwell, 'Charles Dickens', CW, XII, p. 56. The label 'nineteenth-century liberal' was applied to Orwell himself in an early assessment of his politics by George Woodcock, 'George Orwell, 19th Century Liberal', *Politics*, December, 1946, in Jeffrey Meyers (ed.), *George Orwell: The Critical Heritage* (London: Routledge & Kegan Paul, 1975), pp. 235–46.

[49]For this context, see John Rodden, 'Orwell, the Catholics, and the Jews', in Rodden (ed.), *Scenes from an Afterlife: The Legacy of George Orwell* (Willmington, DE: ISI Books, 2003), ch. 14; and Michael G. Brennan, *George Orwell and Religion* (London: Bloomsbury, 2017). Orwell's relationship to Chesterton is exhaustively documented in Luke Seaber, *G.K. Chesterton's Literary Influence on George Orwell: A Surprising Irony* (Lewiston, NY: Edwin Mellen Press, 2012). Seaber argues that, though Orwell's references to Chesterton 'are almost universally negative', nonetheless his influence was pervasive and Orwell 'less than honest' in denying it (pp. 3, 7). This is an extraordinary argument – not in a good way.

[50]See George Orwell, 'Anti-Semitism in Britain', April 1945, CW, XVII, pp. 68–9.

[51]C.S. Lewis also shared this 'horror of modern machine civilisation': George Orwell, 'Review of *That Hideous Strength* by C.S. Lewis ...', August 1945, CW, XVII, p. 250.

political ideas of the time. The third of them was on 'The Christian Reformers', a group with several sub-groups. The most interesting of these (which included Chesterton, Belloc and T.S. Eliot) included 'those who admit the injustice of present-day society and are ready for drastic changes but reject Socialism and, by implication, industrialism'. Chesterton, with 'the mental background of a nineteenth-century radical', wished for a return to a simpler peasant society that possessed a wide distribution of property. This medievalism was, in Orwell's view, 'not serious politics', but 'merely a symptom of the malaise which any sensitive person feels before the spectacle of machine civilisation'.[52] The evils of the machine age were no justification for reactionary politics.

Chesterton died in 1936, but his fellow Catholic Evelyn Waugh was Orwell's contemporary. The two bumped into one another from time to time, in print and, at the end of Orwell's life, in person.[53] In Orwell's literary world, Waugh's was 'the only loudly discordant voice', bravely defending 'a reactionary political tendency' that was 'false and to some extent perverse'.[54] His standpoint was that of a 'Conservative', someone 'who disbelieves in progress and refuses to differentiate between one version of progress and another'.[55] This last comment was from Orwell's review of Waugh's short novel (or long short story) *Scott-King's Modern Europe*. Scott-King was a school master, who made an ill-fated trip to the country of 'Neutralia'. Orwell picks up the story following his return to England:

> Back at Granchester, amid the botched desks and the draughty corridors, the headmaster informs him sadly that the number of classical scholars is falling off and suggests that he shall combine his teaching of the classics with something a little more up-to-date:
> Parents are not interested in producing the 'complete man' any more. They want to qualify their boys for jobs in the modern world. You can hardly blame then, can you?
> 'Oh, yes,' said Scott-King, 'I can and I do.'

Later he adds: 'I think it would be very wicked indeed to do anything to fit a boy for the modern world.' And when the headmaster objects that this is a short-sighted view, Scott-King retorts, 'I think it is the most long-sighted view it is possible to take.'[56]

---

[52]George Orwell, '[The Intellectual Revolt] 3. The Christian Reformers', February 1946, CW, XVIII, p. 66.
[53]Waugh visited Orwell in hospital several times during his final illness: Crick, *George Orwell*, p. 556. For more on their relationship, see Richard Lance Keeble, 'In the Waugh-Zone' in Keeble (ed.), *Orwell's Moustache: Addressing More Orwellian Matters* (Bury St Edmunds: Abramis, 2021), ch. 4.
[54]George Orwell, 'Evelyn Waugh', April? 1949, in CW, XX, p. 75.
[55]Orwell, 'Review of *Scott-King's Modern Europe* by Evelyn Waugh', February 1949, CW, XX, p. 46.
[56]Orwell, 'Review of ... Waugh', CW, XX, p. 45.

Orwell's comments were sympathetic, up to a point.

> The modern world, we are meant to infer, is so unmistakably crazy, so certain to smash itself to pieces in the near future, that to attempt to understand or to come to terms with it is simply a purposeless self-corruption. In the chaos that is shortly coming, a few moral principles that one can cling to, and perhaps even a few half-remembered odes of Horace or choruses from Euripides, will be more useful than what is now called 'enlightenment'.
>
> There is something to be said for this point of view, and yet one must always regard with suspicion the claim that ignorance is, or can be, an advantage.

Whatever there was to be said for Waugh's view, the key problem was the one Orwell had identified, Waugh's refusal to distinguish between different forms of progress, combined with the unwillingness to recognize the impossibility of either preventing change or returning to the land of lost content. Waugh was seeking 'to use the feverish, cultureless modern world as a set off for his own conception of a good and stable way of life'.[57] One might agree with Waugh, 'that a classical education is the best prophylactic against insanity, and yet still feel that he could fight the modern world more effectively if he would turn aside to read a six-penny pamphlet on Marxism'.[58] Orwell shared the Tory-Conservative dislike of many of the changes that were transforming his world; he did not share their response to those changes. The correct response was Socialism, which – in Orwell's view – was the struggle to maintain freedom *and* equality in the face of the technological change that was producing mass collectivized societies.

Much of what has been mistaken in Orwell for a continuing adherence to a 'Tory radical' tradition comes from his exploration of questions that interested many on the Left. Was there a 'native' English radical tradition? Was Socialism anything more than an alien ideology, too doctrinaire and too rigid to appeal to the English people? In 1935, at the 7th International Congress of the Communist International (Comintern), its President, Georgi Dimitrov, encouraged Communists 'to link up the present struggle with the people's revolutionary traditions and past'.[59] This was a cultural dimension to the People's Front policy, in which Communists sought to make common cause with left and liberal groups in anti-Fascist solidarity. In England this stimulated a wealth of writing and scholarship, eventually to fertilize the

---

[57] Orwell, 'Evelyn Waugh', CW, XX, p. 76.
[58] Orwell, 'Review of ... Waugh', CW, XX, p. 46.
[59] Quoted in Philip Bounds, *British Communism and the Politics of Literature 1928–1939* (Pontypool: Merlin, 2012), p. 181.

better-known work of the Communist Party Historians Group after the Second World War (1946–56). Writing for a collection that Orwell read and referred to,[60] the Communist poet and critic, Edgell Rickword constructed a radical English pedigree for the supposedly alien ideas that he and his comrades shared:

> Such men as Everard and Winstanley, Lilburne and Chamberlen ... were striving for an ideal of social justice for which the material conditions were not yet ripe. The noble anger of Milton at tyranny and injustice, as of Swift in the next century; the struggle round *habeas corpus*, Wilkes and the writer of the Junius letters; the idealism of Shelley, the searing contempt of Byron and Cobbett, all these exertions of the finest minds in aid of an oppressed humanity could influence but could not determine the outcome of that historical conflict which complacent politicians would like to convince us had no further significance for us to-day. The attempt to stigmatise the class struggle as the fantastic invention of an alien and deadly philosophy is belied by every fact that official history keeps in the background.[61]

During the later 1930s there was a broad left-wing effort to uncover a tradition of native English radicalism, from which Orwell very likely learnt much. English Communists shared an interest in some of Orwell's own cultural heroes, including Dickens and Swift.[62]

Furthermore, Orwell's attachment to traditional Englishness was far from uncritical. As well as looking for the radical within it, he appreciated that it was a barrier to revolution.

> In England we could not have a civil war, not because tyranny and injustice do not exist, but because they are not obvious enough to stir the common people to action. Everything is toned down, padded, as it were, by ancient habits of compromise, by representative institutions, by liberal aristocrats and incorruptible officials, by a 'superstructure' that has existed so long that it is only partly a sham.[63]

Nonetheless, when he came to expound his own brand of revolutionary Socialism in *The Lion and the Unicorn* (1941) Orwell made it a principle

---

[60]George Orwell, 'Inside the Whale', March 1940, CW, XII, p. 108.
[61]Edgell Rickword, 'Culture, Progress and English Tradition', in Cecil Day Lewis (ed.), *The Mind in Chains: Socialism and the Cultural Revolution* (London: Frederick Muller, 1937), pp. 242–3.
[62]Philip Bounds, *Orwell and Marxism: The Political and Cultural Thinking of George Orwell* (London: I. B. Tauris, 2009, pbk ed. 2016), ch. 3.
[63]Orwell, 'Review of *The Forge* by Arturo Barea ...', September 1941, CW, XIII, p. 34.

of hope that a revolution in England might turn out better than elsewhere because it could draw upon deeply rooted traditions of civil liberty and free speech. 'No revolution in England as a chance of success unless it takes account of England's past.'[64] *The Lion and the Unicorn* (discussed in full later in this chapter) provides an amusing coda to the discussion of Orwell's Tory anarchism. His wife Eileen informed one of her friends late in 1940 that 'George has written a little book ... explaining how to be a Socialist though Tory'.[65] The book was, of course, *The Lion and the Unicorn*, the fullest development of his Socialist thinking. Perhaps her words reflect a familiar joke within the Orwell marriage.

The idea that Orwell was ever much of a *Tory* anarchist deserves scepticism; the idea that he remained one, at some level, deserves even more. But Orwell's *anarchism* is a different matter. Notwithstanding his frequent expressions of overt loathing for anarchists, Orwell was on good terms with many of them and his affinity for anarchist ideas – some of them, at least – is often remarked. George Woodcock, one of his anarchist friends, has summarized:

After he returned to England in 1927 and resigned from the Imperial police in Burma, he described himself rather vaguely as an Anarchist, and continued to do so for several years; even after he began to call himself a Socialist in 1936, he significantly fought beside the Anarchists in the internecine struggle between the Communists and their libertarian opponents during the Barcelona May Days of 1937. From that time until his death his relation with the Anarchists was noticeably ambivalent.[66]

A more recent commentator has noted that

While he resolutely denounced pacifists in public and criticized anarchism as a political philosophy, Orwell's own brand of socialism – never precisely defined – veered toward the antibureaucratic and libertarian, and he shared many of the anarchists' suspicions about the people directing the war on Britain's behalf, their motives, and his own assigned role in the war effort.[67]

---

[64]Orwell, 'Will Freedom Die with Capitalism?', April 1941, CW, XII, p. 463.

[65]Eileen Blair to Norah Myles, *c.*5 December 1640, in Peter Davison (ed.), *The Lost Orwell: Being a Supplement to the Complete Works of George Orwell* (London: Timewell Press, 2006), p. 80.

[66]George Woodcock, *The Crystal Spirit: A Study of George Orwell* (Montréal: Black Rose Books, 2005 [original edition 1966]), p. 19. There is a fascinating account of Woodcock's portraits of Orwell in Rodden, *Politics of Literary Reputation*, pp. 156–70.

[67]Eric Laursen, *The Duty to Stand Aside: Nineteen Eighty-Four and the Wartime Quarrel of George Orwell and Alex Comfort* (Chico, CA: AK Press, 2018), p. 17.

For all his hostility to anarchists, which mostly arose from his association of anarchists with pacifism during the war years, Orwell never lost his libertarian instincts. Taking issue in 1948 with Malcolm Muggeridge's account of Samuel Butler, he emphasized that 'the real division is not between conservatives and revolutionaries but between authoritarians and libertarians'.[68] From Woodcock, Comfort and Read onwards, anarchists have found a kindred spirit in Orwell, whose libertarian Socialism was rooted in an appreciation of human individualism. As one noted anarchist scholar has said, quoting another: 'as the major anarchist writer Colin Ward maintained approvingly, Orwell version of socialism is "pretty anarchical" and the equally hostile assessment of Isaac Deutscher ... was that Orwell was "at heart ... a simple minded anarchist"'. Orwell's major concern was that Socialism should not lead to 'the extinction of liberty'.[69]

# 2. The Birth of George Orwell's Socialism

Writing from Barcelona in June 1937, Orwell told Cyril Connolly 'I have seen such wonderful things & at last really believe in Socialism, which I never did before'.[70] Of course, at one level Orwell was already a Socialist before leaving for Spain in December 1936. In the second half of *The Road to Wigan Pier* (published while he was in Spain), Orwell recounted his political evolution during the Blair years, and declared his Socialism, though largely by the peculiar method of denigrating in the most colourful and sweeping fashion most other professed Socialists. Of *The Road to Wigan Pier*, Fredric Warburg was later to say that it was 'perhaps the most luke-warm advocacy of a creed ever penned';[71] 'it was obviously intended to be basically a book in defence of socialism, but it had a good slam at practically every type of socialist'.[72] Orwell himself put it like this:

---

[68]Orwell to Malcolm Muggeridge, 4 December 1948, in Davison (ed.), *The Lost Orwell*, p. 116. The letter was sent on the same day that Orwell dispatched the MS of *Nineteen Eighty-Four* to his agent and publisher.

[69]David Goodway, 'Orwell and Anarchism', *George Orwell Studies*, 1:1 (2916), pp. 50–1. The reference to Deutscher is, of course, to his famous essay, perhaps the key piece of hard-Left Orwell denunciation, '"1984" – The Mysticism of Cruelty', in Deutscher, *Marxism, Wars and Revolutions: Essays from Four Decades* (London: Verso, 1984), pp. 60–71, originally published 1955. See also David Goodway, *Anarchist Seeds beneath the Snow: Left Libertarian Thought and British Writers from William Morris to Colin Ward* (Oakland, CA: PM Press, 2012, orig. ed., 2006), ch. 6; and the fine tribute to Orwell by the Freedom Press anarchists (on whom see the discussion in the next part of this book), Vernon Richards (ed.), *George Orwell at Home (and among the Anarchists): Essays and Photographs* (London: Freedom Press, 1998).

[70]Orwell to Cyril Connolly, 8 June 1937, CW, XI, p. 28.

[71]Fredric Warburg, *An Occupation for Gentlemen* (London: Hutchinson, 1959), p. 229.

[72]Coppard & Crick, *Orwell Remembered*, p. 193.

In *Wigan Pier* I first tried to thrash out my ideas. I felt, as I still do, that there are huge deficiencies in the whole conception of Socialism, and I was still wondering whether there was any other way out. After a fairly good look at British industrialism at its worst, i.e. in the mining areas, I came to the conclusion that it is a duty to work for Socialism even if one is not emotionally drawn to it, because the continuance of present conditions is simply not tolerable, and no solution except some kind of collectivism is viable, because that is what the mass of the people want.[73]

This account perhaps has something of the tidiness of hindsight, but it captures both the sense that Socialism didn't come naturally or easily to Orwell, and that his initial acceptance of it came in spite of the limited affinity he felt with Socialism (and, more to the point, his limited liking for Socialists). Spain was to change this, at least to a degree: the wonderful things he saw there brought with them a real emotional commitment to the Socialist cause.

Orwell was clear that his journey to the north of England (and consequently the writing of *The Road to Wigan Pier*) was undertaken 'as part of my approach to Socialism'. The book's second half is, indeed, the story of this approach, his journey down 'the road from Mandalay to Wigan'.[74] Placing himself as 'lower-upper-middle class', but also as part of a post-War generation hostile to the 'old men' who were held responsible for all that had gone wrong with the world, Orwell recounted his development as 'both a snob and a revolutionary'.[75] It is not easy to trace the details of Orwell's political development from this account, nor to match it up with other evidence. About his early views, while at Eton he said, as we saw earlier, 'I loosely described myself as a Socialist. But I had not much grasp of what Socialism meant, and no notion that the working class were human beings.'[76] There is not much other evidence to suggest that Orwell was a Socialist this early. He then describes his time in the Indian Police, noting that by the end of his time in Burma 'I hated the imperialism I was serving with a bitterness which I probably cannot make clear'.[77] His experience of policing India, vividly captured in some of his early essays, led Orwell in a different direction. He 'worked out an anarchist theory that all government was evil, that the punishment always does more harm than the crime and that people can be trust to behave decently if only you will let them alone'.[78] This, perhaps, was the Orwell of Tory Anarchism.

---

[73]Orwell to Richard Usborne, 26 August 1947, in Davison (ed.), *Life in Letters*, p. xi.
[74]Orwell, *Road to Wigan Pier*, p. 113.
[75]Orwell, *Road to Wigan Pier*, pp. 129–30.
[76]Orwell, *Road to Wigan Pier*, pp. 132–3.
[77]Orwell, *Road to Wigan Pier*, p. 134.
[78]Orwell, *Road to Wigan Pier*, p. 137.

This anarchism he came to see as 'sentimental nonsense'.[79] But the mood that produced it was a critical turning point for Orwell. He could no longer stomach being one of the oppressors. 'I felt I had to escape not merely from imperialism but from every form of man's dominion over man. I wanted to submerge myself, to get right down among the oppressed, to be one of them and on their side against the tyrants.'[80] His immersion in the world of the oppressed was, of course, the subject of *Down and Out in Paris and London*; and his journey to the coal-mining north continued his exploration of poverty. Respectable poverty, like that of the miners, was harder for Orwell to get closer to than was the poverty of the down and out tramps, beggars and prostitutes. The latter were diverse in origin, almost classless; the former had very strong group identities that Orwell could not pretend to share. His Socialism was initially rooted in seeking to overcome the differences between himself and the 'respectable' poor.

This was the Orwell who went to fight and to write in Spain. His journey to Socialism had begun on the road to Wigan Pier, but he had not travelled far. As Simon Leys put it: 'After his journey to Wigan Pier, when he first joined the socialist cause, he was merely devoting himself to a dream. But ... since Spain, he knew: socialism was actually feasible; for a short, unforgettable time, it had been a living reality, in which he took a direct part and found his place.'[81] His views before Spain were formless and vague, moral but without much political tinge, and negative rather than positive. He knew the things he hated better than he knew what he wanted to replace them with.

In his review of Borkenau's *Spanish Cockpit* published in July 1937, after he had returned to England, Orwell summed up the key political dynamic that he had (in part) witnessed in Spain:

In August the Government was almost powerless, local soviets were functioning everywhere and the Anarchists were the main revolutionary force; as a result everything was in terrible chaos, the churches were still smouldering and suspected Fascists were being shot in large numbers, but there was everywhere a belief in revolution, a feeling that the bondage of centuries had been broken. By January power had passed, though not so completely as later, from the Anarchists to the Communists, and the Communists were using every possible method, fair and foul, to stamp out what was left of the revolution.[82]

---

[79]Orwell, *Road to Wigan Pier*, p. 137.
[80]Orwell, *Road to Wigan Pier*, p. 138.
[81]Simon Leys, 'Orwell: The Horror of Politics', in Leys (ed.), *The Angel and the Octopus: Collected Essays 1983–1998* (Sydney: Duffy & Snellgrove, 1999), p. 168.
[82]George Orwell, 'Review of *The Spanish Cockpit* by Franz Borkenau ...', July 1937, CW, XI, p. 51.

Orwell shared Borkenau's view that the clash between revolutionary and non-revolutionary principles was embodied in the clash between Anarchists (with whom the POUM were aligned) and the Communists.[83] The Socialism in which Orwell came to 'really believe' in Spain was thus 'revolutionary' Socialism, and Orwell's hostility to Soviet Communism grew from this experience of the ways in which it thwarted revolution.

Orwell arrived in Spain with assistance from Fenner Brockway (Chairman of the Independent Labour Party, the ILP), and the ILP connection led to him being associated with the ILP contingent in Spain, which formed part of the POUM 29th Division. The POUM (Partido Obrero de Unificácion Marxista) was anti-Stalinist, revolutionary and Communist, willing to work in broad revolutionary alliance with other Communists, Socialists and anarchists. This included the official Spanish Communist party, aligned with the Comintern. It was the crushing of the POUM and anarchists in the Barcelona 'May Days' that convinced him that 'the Communist Party is now (presumably for the sake of Russian foreign policy) an anti-revolutionary force'.[84]

There was, perhaps, nothing foreordained in Orwell's association with the POUM. He only sought Brockway's assistance in getting to Spain because his earlier request for help had been turned down by the General Secretary of the Communist Party of Great Britain, Harry Pollitt. Pollitt decided that Orwell was 'politically unreliable' and warned him about 'Anarchist terrorism'.[85] Though he would not make this commitment to Pollitt, Orwell for much of time in Spain was determined on joining the International Brigade, the main contingent of 'official' Communist volunteers. One of his contemporaries in Spain recalled that at first 'he was leaning slightly towards the communists'.[86] As late as 30 April, Orwell approached a British Communist official in Barcelona, Walter Tapsell, and declared that 'he has grown to dislike the POUM'.[87] Only after experiencing the May violence against the POUM did he change his mind and decide that he could never side with official Communist groups.[88] For Orwell, May 1937 destroyed forever the credibility of the Popular Front.

---

[83]Orwell, 'Review of *The Spanish Cockpit*', CW, XI, p. 52.

[84]Orwell, 'Review of *The Spanish Cockpit*', CW, XI, p. 51.

[85]George Orwell, 'Notes on the Spanish Militias', written early 1939?, CW, XI, p. 136.

[86]Wadhams (ed.), *Orwell Tapes*, p. 111.

[87]Richard Baxell, *Unlikely Warriors: The British in the Spanish Civil War and the Struggle against Fascism* (London: Aurum Press, 2014), p. 188.

[88]Orwell, *Homage to Catalonia* [CW, VI] (London: Secker & Warburg, 1986), p. 126 (Penguin ed. pp. 133–4). Bob Edwards particularly emphasized that Orwell was a very slow convert to the POUM view of what was happening in Spain: see his 'Introduction' to Orwell, *Homage to Catalonia* (London: Folio Society, 1970), p. 8.

After his interview with Orwell, Tapsell reported to Harry Pollitt that 'he has little political understanding and ... is not interested in party politics'.[89] He was not alone in reaching this conclusion. The political activists who were Orwell's comrades in the ILP brigade found him politically naïve when he joined them, his search for Socialism not yet quite completed.

Stafford Cottman, like the Communist Walter Tapsell, recalled that Orwell 'wasn't really a political animal, in the sense that he wasn't partisan to any particular group'.[90] 'Politically virginal' was Harry Milton's verdict. He was 'ideologically very confused' and 'only after he left Spain did he become politically aware'.[91] The Socialist commitments that Orwell forged in Spain and in the months following his return to England took on characteristics that were to endure for the rest of his life. Jon Kimche, a friend with whom Orwell had worked at Booklovers' Corner, disagreed with some of Orwell's assessment of Spanish politics, noting that Barcelona's early 'revolutionary excitement was lovely ... but it couldn't win the war'.[92] Orwell was not disposed to see things this way.[93]

> Orwell, you see, always *reacted* to situations, to people, to individuals. He had certain basic gut attitudes. Very decent but not attuned, I would say, to complicated political or military situations. He was a gut socialist. He was never very analytical, never theoretically searching out how to deal with a situation or what is the fundamental problem of a situation. That's why he wrote so very clearly and very simply. Because that's how he saw things.[94]

The central tension in Orwell's thinking was identified by Jennie Lee, who first met him in Barcelona: 'Part of his malaise was that he was not only a socialist but profoundly liberal. He hated regimentation wherever he found it, even in the socialist ranks.'[95] Orwell's politics were captured in the simple terms in which he held them in his later reflections on Spain. He wanted 'a

---

[89]Baxell, *Unlikely Warriors*, p. 188.
[90]Wadhams (ed.), *Orwell Tapes*, p. 109.
[91]Wadhams (ed.), *Orwell Tapes*, p. 109.
[92]Wadhams (ed.), *Orwell Tapes*, p. 123.
[93]After Franco's victory Orwell's perspectives broadened and he referred to the conflicts within the Left as 'unimportant ... secondary issues' (George Orwell, 'Looking Back on the Spanish War', 1942?, CW, XIII, p. 503). What defeated the Left were not its lethal internal conflicts but the lack of international support; 'the Trotskyist thesis that the war could have been won if the revolution had not been sabotaged was probably false' (ibid., pp. 507–8). See also Orwell, 'Caesarean Section in Spain', March 1939, CW, XI, pp. 332–5. For a fuller discussion see Paul Preston, 'Lights and Shadows in George Orwell's *Homage to Catalonia*', *Bulletin of Spanish Studies* (2017), DOI: 10.1080/14753820.2018.1388550.
[94]Wadhams, *Orwell Tapes*, pp. 123–4.
[95]Jennie Lee to Margaret Goalby, 23 June 1950, in CW, XI, p. 5.

world of free and equal human beings', a world in which all people could 'live the decent, full human life which is now technically achievable'. And he wanted this sooner rather than later. The main obstacle to the realization of this vision was also simple, 'the simple intention of those with money or privileges to cling to them'.[96]

Spain had an overwhelming impact on Orwell. His Socialism remained formless, in the sense that it was never forced into conformity with any party or ideological position. But the emotional and moral commitment intensified, and Orwell arrived at clarity about fundamental principles. Orwell's journey to Socialism was in all essentials complete. He said of his first three or four months in Spain that 'they taught me things I could not have learned in any other way'.[97] He realized that he was 'amidst the most revolutionary sentiment in the country'.

> I had dropped more or less by chance into the only community of any size in Western Europe where political consciousness and disbelief in capitalism were more normal than their opposites. Up here in Aragón one was among tens of thousands of people, mainly though not entirely, of working-class origin, all living at the same level and mingling on terms of equality. In theory it was perfect equality, and even in practice it was not far from it. There is a sense in which it would be true to say that one was experiencing a foretaste of Socialism, by which I mean that the prevailing mental atmosphere was one of Socialism. Many of the normal motives of civilized life – snobbishness, money-grubbing, fear of the boss, etc. – had simply ceased to exist. The ordinary class-division of society had disappeared to an extent that is almost unthinkable in the money-tainted air of England; there was no one there except the peasants and ourselves, and no one owned anyone else as his master. Of course such a state of affairs could not last. It was simply a temporary and local phase in an enormous game that is being played over the whole surface of the earth. But it lasted long enough to have its effect on anyone who experienced it. However much one cursed at the time, one realized afterwards that one had been in contact with something strange and valuable. One had been in a community where hope was more normal than cynicism or apathy, where the word 'comrade' stood for comradeship and not, as in most countries, for humbug. One had breathed the air of equality.[98]

This hope was an antidote to the view that Socialism was all about 'planned state-capitalism with the grab motive left intact'. For most, Socialism meant

---

[96]Orwell, 'Looking Back on the Spanish War', CW, XIII, p. 509.
[97]Orwell, *Homage to Catalonia*, p. 82 (Penguin ed. p. 86).
[98]Orwell, *Homage to Catalonia*, p. 83 (Penguin ed. pp. 87–8).

'a classless society'. In Spain, Orwell witnessed 'a crude forecast of what the opening stages of Socialism might be like'. This was an altogether different Socialism, and 'it deeply attracted me', Orwell reported, and 'the effect was to make my desire to see Socialism established much more actual than it was before'. It probably helped that this experience was with Spaniards, 'who, with their innate decency and their ever-present Anarchist tinge, would make even the opening stages of Socialism tolerable if they had the chance'.[99]

Orwell's first impressions of Barcelona were particularly vivid and concrete and give us the best sense of what he witnessed.

Practically every building of any size had been seized by the workers and was draped with red flags or with the red and black flag of the Anarchists; every wall was scrawled with the hammer and sickle and with the initials of the revolutionary parties; almost every church had been gutted and its images burnt. Churches here and there were being systematically demolished by gangs of workmen. Every shop and café had an inscription saying that it had been collectivized; even the bootblacks had been collectivized and their boxes painted red and black. Waiters and shop-walkers looked you in the face and treated you as equal. Servile and even ceremonial forms of speech had temporarily disappeared. Nobody said 'Señor' or 'Don' or even 'Usted'; everyone called everyone else 'Comrade' and 'Thou', and said 'Salud!' instead of 'Buenos días'. Almost my first experience was receiving a lecture from an hotel manager for trying to tip a lift-boy. There were no private cars, they had all been commandeered, and all the trams and taxis and much of the other transport were painted red and black. The revolutionary posters were everywhere, flaming from the walls in clean reds and blues that made the few remaining advertisements look like daubs of mud. Down the Ramblas, the wide central artery of the town where crowds of people streamed constantly to and fro, the loudspeakers were bellowing revolutionary songs all day and far into the night. And it was the aspect of the crowd that was the queerest thing of all. In outward appearance it was a town in which the wealthy classes had practically ceased to exist. Except for a small number of women and foreigners there were no 'well-dressed' people at all. Practically everyone wore rough working-class clothes, or blue overalls or some variant of the militia uniform. All this was queer and moving. There was much in it that I did not understand, in some ways I did not even like it, but I recognized it immediately as a state of affairs worth fighting for.[100]

---

[99]Orwell, *Homage to Catalonia*, p. 84 (Penguin ed. p. 88).
[100]Orwell, *Homage to Catalonia*, pp. 2–3 (Penguin ed. pp. 3–4).

Orwell had seen in Spain a glimpse of a hint of a hope, but it was enough to convince him that there was the possibility of a Socialism that was liberating and not authoritarian, combined freedom with equality, social solidarity with individualism. Crucially for Orwell, notwithstanding the brutality and the war, 'there was a spirit of tolerance, a freedom of speech and the press, which no one would have thought possible in time of war'.[101] There was 'a belief in the revolution of the future, a feeling of having suddenly emerged into an era of equality and freedom'.[102] It was a revolution, certainly, but primarily a 'revolution of ideas' that produced 'a feeling of liberation and hope', showed 'what human beings are like when they are trying to behave as human beings and not as cogs in the capitalist machine'. No one who witnessed those 'months when people still believed in revolution will ever forget that strange and moving experience'.[103]

# 3. The Development of Orwell's Socialism

The Socialist hopes that Orwell acquired in Spain never left him, and the sort of Socialism that attracted him in 1937 remained recognizably the same until his death in 1950. But his views certainly did not remain unchanging. To take an obvious example, in the years immediately after Spain Orwell believed that Socialists needed to oppose war-mongering and to oppose those clamouring for an anti-Fascist war against Hitler's Germany. He was never exactly a pacifist,[104] but it was only after the outbreak of war that he both abandoned his opposition to war with Germany and developed his intense hostility to pacifism. This in turn led him to repudiate sharply the anarchist tinges to his own Socialism. Yet there were other ways in which Orwell's obsessions – and they do at times come across as obsessions – remained consistent. His fears about the emergence of mass societies based on mechanization, and whether they could ever be hospitable places for intellectual freedom, took various forms, but were a continual feature of his thinking. The following sections examine the main features of Orwell's Socialism by looking at these obsessions, temporary and permanent. As will become apparent, even the temporary ones usually reveal a set of problems that Orwell wrestled with longer term. His views of war and pacifism, for example, were part of a longer and deeper interest in political violence and in

---

[101]George Orwell, 'Caesarean Section in Spain', March 1939, CW, XI, p. 333.
[102]Orwell, *Homage to Catalonia*, p. 4 (Penguin ed. p. 4).
[103]George Orwell, 'Review of *Red Spanish Notebook* by Mary Low ...', October 1937, CW, XI, p. 87.
[104]Cf. Crick, *George Orwell*, p. 365: Crick prefers the term 'anti-militarist'.

the relationship between ends and means. My organization of this material is, on the face of it, thematic, but I hope that readers will soon discern a chronological structure too.

## (a) Peace, Empire and Internationalism

From June 1937 to the declaration of war in September 1939, Orwell's writing and his Socialism were developed under the shadow of a threatened war to which he was vehemently opposed. John Sceats, who met Orwell probably in May or June 1938, gave this snapshot of him:

> Despite his recent association with POUM, he had already decided he was not a Marxist, and he was more than interested in the philosophy of Anarchism. As he saw things then, it was a matter of months before either Fascism or War landed him in the Concentration Camp (British); whatever the future held he could not believe it would allow him to go on writing. He was of course anti-Nazi, but could not … stomach the idea of an anti-German war: in fact, talking to Max Plowman (who called in the afternoon) he implied that he would join him in opposition to such a war with whatever underground measures might be appropriate.[105]

Writing from Morocco to Jack Common (who was house-sitting in Wallington for the Orwells), Orwell outlined his analysis of the political situation. His hope was that, if Chamberlain began preparing for war, this would force the Labour Party into a clear anti-war position. Its current

> policy of simultaneously shouting for a war policy and pretending to denounce conscription, rearmament etc. is utter nonsense and the general public aren't such bloody fools as not to see it. As to the results if war comes, although *some* kind of revolutionary situation will no doubt arise, I do not see how it can lead to anything except Fascism *unless* the Left has been anti-war from the outset. I have nothing but contempt for the fools who think that they can first drive the nation into a war for democracy and then when the people are a bit fed up suddenly turn around and say 'Now we'll have the revolution.' What sickens me about left-wing people, especially the intellectuals, is their utter ignorance of the way things actually happen.[106]

The final flourish was essence of Orwell.

---

[105]John Sceats quoted in CW, XI, p. 228.
[106]Orwell to Jack Common, 12 October 1938, CW, XI, pp. 222–3.

A year or so after returning from Spain, Orwell joined the Independent Labour Party. His membership card was dated 13 June 1938; he resigned from the ILP soon after the outbreak of war in September 1939, as 'they were talking nonsense and proposing a line of policy that could only make things easier for Hitler'.[107] The ILP, unlike Orwell, maintained its pacifist position into the war. Soon after he had joined the party, Orwell published a justification for doing so. As a writer, he said, his first instinct was to keep out of politics: what a writer 'wants is to be left alone so that he can go on writing in peace'. But this was hardly feasible at the present. He had both personal and public reasons for joining the ILP. The personal ones go to the heart of this book and will be explored more fully in the next chapter. As a writer Orwell needed freedom of expression, and a Socialist regime was likely to be the only one in which that would be possible. The public reasons for joining the ILP grew out of Orwell's experience. The ILP was the only party 'which aims at anything I should regard as Socialism'. It was the only party that matched Orwell's anti-Imperialism (acquired in Burma), his concern to tackle poverty and unemployment (acquired in Wigan), and his form of anti-Fascism, hostile to the Popular Front (acquired in Spain).[108]

These things were all connected, at least in Orwell's mind. Anti-Fascism, as most people understood it, was 'simply a thin disguise for jingo imperialism'.[109] Socialist anti-Fascism should not involve pursuit of a European war. Just as war was about to erupt, Orwell still maintained that 'a Left-wing party, which, within a capitalist society, becomes a war party, has already thrown up the sponge, because it is demanding a policy which can only be carried out by its opponents'.[110]

Why did he believe that real Socialists should believe these things? During May and June 1938 Orwell wrote a short pamphlet, 'Socialism and War' (5,000–6,000 words), that would have explained the connections. He variously described the pamphlet as 'more or less on the subject of pacifism' and 'my anti-war pamphlet'.[111] Unfortunately, Orwell's literary agent, Leonard Moore, was unable to find a publisher for the pamphlet.[112] The typescript has been lost, but its argument is probably preserved in a couple of things he did succeed in publishing in 1938 and 1939. In a letter

---

[107]Orwell to Stanley J. Kunitz & Howard Haycraft, 17 April 1940, CW, XII, p. 148.

[108]George Orwell, 'Why I Join the I.L.P.', June 1938, CW, XI, pp. 167–9.

[109]George Orwell, 'Review of *The Mysterious Mr. Bull* by Wyndham Lewis ...', June 1939, CW, XI, p. 354.

[110]George Orwell, 'Democracy in the British Army', September 1939, CW, XI, p. 406.

[111]Orwell to Leonard Moore, 28 June 1938, CW, XI, p. 169; Orwell to Jack Common, 12 October 1938, CW, XI, p. 223. For a full account of Orwell's views of pacifism, see Lawrence Rosenwald, 'Orwell, Pacifism, Pacifists', in Thomas Cushman & John Rodden (eds), *George Orwell into the Twenty-First Century* (Boulder, CO: Paradigm, 2004), pp. 111–25.

[112]Orwell to Leonard Moore, 28 November 1938, CW, XI, p. 241.

to the editor of the *New English Weekly*, written at the time when he was working on the pamphlet, Orwell defended pacifism. He believed that it would be possible to create an 'effective anti-war movement in England … [by] mobilising the dislike of war that undoubtedly exists in ordinary decent people'. It was imperative to create this movement because militarism was used as a weapon to prevent social reform:

> The truth is that any real advance, let alone any genuinely revolutionary change, can only begin when the mass of the people definitely refuse capitalist-imperialist war and thus make it clear to their rulers that a war-policy is not practicable. So long as they show themselves willing to fight 'in defence of democracy', or 'against Fascism', or for any other fly-blown slogan, the same trick will be played upon them again and again: 'You can't have a rise in wages *now*, because we have got to prepare for war. Guns before butter!'[113]

He later warned that, once war begins, 'left-wing parties will have the choice of offering unconditional loyalty or being smashed'. Most British people would oppose war, so the Left should oppose militarism, to avoid the 'fascising process that war-preparation implies'. War or the preparation for war 'can be used as an excuse for anything'.[114]

The link between anti-militarism and Socialism was clear: militarism was an excuse for doing nothing about inequality and social justice, and it impelled a country towards Fascism. The Popular Front would dupe people into a pursuit of an 'anti-Fascist' war that would perpetuate their own disadvantage and make their own societies resemble those of the Fascists they were opposing. There might be less 'colour prejudice' in French Morocco than in British India, he told Charles Doran, but 'economically it is just the usual swindle for which empires exist'.[115]

But what about imperialism and the 'capitalist-imperialist' war that Orwell feared and opposed? Orwell's anti-imperialism was not a product of his Socialism. It was rooted in his experience in Burma: 'I was in the Indian police five years and by the end of that time I hated the imperialism I was serving with a bitterness which I probably cannot make clear … [I]t is not possible to be a part of such a system without recognising it as an unjustifiable tyranny.'[116]

Orwell grafted his Socialism onto this anti-imperialism, and held consistently to the view that, as a Socialist and man of the Left, he was

---

[113]Orwell, 'To the Editor, *New English Weekly*', May 1938, CW, XI, p. 153.
[114]George Orwell, 'Political Reflections on the Crisis', December 1938, CW, XI, p. 245.
[115]Orwell to Charles Doran, 26 November 1938, CW, XI, p. 239.
[116]Orwell, *Road to Wigan Pier*, p. 134.

compelled to fight imperialism abroad as well as injustice and unfair privilege at home. They were part of the same struggle. In his 1939 essay 'Not Counting Niggers', Orwell accused the militarist Left of 'humbug', of 'shamming', because they would tolerate no drop in living standards and therefore had no willingness to address the injustices of imperialism that maintained those living standards. 'One threat to the Suez canal and "antifascism" and "defence of British interests" are discovered to be identical.'[117] He was reviewing a book by Clarence Streit called *Union Now*, which advocated a union of the United States, the UK and other democratic nations, and Orwell took violent exception to Streit's list of the 'democratic' countries, which included Britain and France, both with empires that were 'in essence nothing but mechanisms for exploiting cheap coloured labour'. These empires, far from being democracies, included 'six hundred thousand disenfranchised human beings', and Streit's proposal would simply 'put the huge strength of the U.S.A. ... behind the robbery of India and Africa'.

> The unspoken clause is always 'not counting niggers'. For how can we make a 'firm stand' against Hitler if we are simultaneously weakening ourselves at home? In other words, how can we 'fight Fascism' except by bolstering up a far vaster injustice?[118]

It is necessary to remember 'that the overwhelming bulk of the British proletariat does not live in Britain, but in Asia and Africa'. This is a striking and powerful statement, drawing no distinctions of ethnicity or nationality. Socialist justice needed to extend to all British proletarians wherever in the world they laboured, and whatever the colour of their skins. What would be the benefit of a war to bring down Hitler 'in order to stabilise something that is far bigger and in its different way just as bad?'[119] The way forward was, instead, to 'mobilise the decency of the English people', thus to produce 'a real mass party whose first pledges are to refuse war and to right imperial injustice'.[120]

In 1938–9 Orwell spent nearly seven months in Marrakech (where he wrote *Coming Up for Air*), and this experience probably strengthened his disgust with imperialism. In his essay 'Marrakech' he elaborated on the core thought in 'Not Counting Niggers', the moral depravity of empire,

---

[117]George Orwell, 'Review of *Union Now* by Clarence K. Streit' [published as 'Not Counting Niggers'], July 1939, CW, XI, p. 358. On the editorial decision to make less prominent the original title in the CW edition – not, it must be admitted, particular to this essay – see Anthony Stewart, 'Vulgar Nationalism and Insulting Nicknames: George Orwell's Progressive Reflection on Race', in Cushman & Rodden (eds), *George Orwell into the Twenty-First Century*, p. 150.
[118]Orwell, 'Review of *Union Now*', CW, XI, p. 360.
[119]Orwell, 'Review of *Union Now*', CW, XI, p. 361.
[120]Orwell, 'Review of *Union Now*', CW, XI, p. 361.

which rendered some people invisible and thus dehumanized them and their suffering. They ceased to be *individuals*:

> When you walk through a town like this – two hundred thousand inhabitants, of whom at least twenty thousand own literally nothing except the rags they stand up in – when you see how the people live, and still more how easily they die, it is always difficult to believe that you are walking among human beings. All colonial empires are in reality founded upon that fact. The people have brown faces – besides, there are so many of them! Are they really the same flesh as yourself? Do they even have names? Or are they merely a kind of undifferentiated brown stuff, about as individual as bees or coral insects? They rise out of the earth, they sweat and starve for a few years, and then they sink back into the nameless mounds of the graveyard and nobody notices that they are gone. And even the graves themselves soon fade back into the soil. Sometimes, out for a walk, as you break your way through the prickly pear, you notice that it is rather bumpy underfoot, and only a certain regularity in the bumps tells you that you are walking over skeletons.[121]

This anti-imperialism persisted as an essential feature of Orwell's brand of Socialism, rooted in the belief in the mutual affinity of Fascism and imperialism. During the war, he noted that 'the most intelligent imperialists have been in favour of compromising with the Fascists ... because they have seen that only thus could imperialism be salvaged'. Admittedly, Orwell thought, India might never be fully independent, because it would depend on other powers for its military defence. Some sort of international federation, along with the defeat of the Axis powers, would be in India's best interest. Even so:

> [T]he necessary first step, before we can make our talk about world federation sound even credible, is that Britain shall get off India's back. This is the only large scale decent action that is possible in the world at this moment. The immediate preliminaries would be: abolish the Viceroyalty and the India Office, release the Congress prisoners, and declare India formally independent. The rest is detail.[122]

In early 1945, for example, he attended a meeting of the League for European Freedom, which he saw as 'dominated by the anti-Russian wing of the Tory party'. He found it difficult to believe that such people were 'really interested

---

[121]George Orwell, 'Marrakech', CW, XI, p. 417.
[122]George Orwell, 'Gandhi in Mayfair: Review of *Beggar My Neighbour* by Lionel Fielden', September 1943, CW, XV, pp. 214, 213.

in political liberty as such'. They were more concerned that Britain did not seem likely at the Teheran Conference to receive its fair share of the world to dominate. 'I am all in favour of European freedom', Orwell declared, 'but I feel happier when it is coupled with freedom elsewhere – in India for example'.[123] Later in the year, the Duchess of Atholl invited Orwell to speak on behalf of the League. His resounding reply is well-known:

> I cannot associate myself with an essentially Conservative body which claims to defend democracy in Europe but has nothing to say about British imperialism. It seems to me that one can only denounce the crimes now being committed in Poland, Jugoslavia etc. if one is equally insistent on ending India's rule in India. I belong to the Left and must work inside it, much as I hate Russian totalitarianism and its poisonous influence in this country.[124]

In July 1945 a Labour government was elected. Orwell wrote a lukewarm early assessment of it, in which he affirmed the anti-imperialism of his prewar days. 'The first task of the Labor government is to make people realize that Britain is not self-contained, but is part of a world-wide network. Even the problem of introducing Socialism is secondary to that. For Britain cannot become a genuinely Socialist country while continuing to plunder Asia and Africa.'[125]

His anti-imperialism persisted, but Orwell's opposition to an anti-Fascist war barely lasted beyond 3 September 1939. As early as 9 September he wrote to the Ministry of Labour and National Service offering to help the war effort,[126] and soon after appears to have told Ethel Mannin (a Quaker and life-long pacifist) that he wished to join the army. She was stunned:

> Is it because you like fighting for its own sake? Or what? After all you wrote in *Coming Up For Air*. I don't understand it. It leaves me bitched buggered and bewildered ... I thought you went off the boil in 1916! I though you thought it all crazy, this smashing in of Nazi faces. For the luv of Mike write a few lines to enlighten our darkness.[127]

But Orwell was never again to bring light to this particular darkness. A year later he sought to explain himself, though in a tone that might suggest a certain discomfort. In a notable understatement he admitted that 'for several

[123]George Orwell, 'As I Please', 56, 26 January 1945, CW, XVII, pp. 29–30.
[124]Orwell to Katharine, Duchess of Atholl, 15 November 1945, CW, XVII, p. 385.
[125]George Orwell, 'The British General Election', November 1945, CW, XVII, p. 340.
[126]See editor's note, 'Application for War Service', CW, XI, p. 410.
[127]Ethel Mannin to Orwell, 30 October 1939, UCL Orwell Archive, Orwell/H/2/6/2; also Editor's note, 'Correspondence with Ethel Mannin', CW, XI, p. 413.

years the coming war was a nightmare to me, and at times I even made speeches and wrote pamphlets against it'. But he then recounts a sort of dream conversion experience that changed his view overnight.

> But the night before the Russo-German pact was announced I dreamed that the war had started. It was one of those dreams which, whatever Freudian inner meaning they may have, do sometimes reveal to you the real state of your feelings. It taught me two things, first, that I should be simply relieved when the long-dreaded war started, secondly, that I was patriotic at heart, would not sabotage or act against my own side, would support the war, would fight in it if possible.[128]

Dreams are a useful way of evading scrutiny – including self-scrutiny – and Orwell was candid that his response was 'emotional'. He did say that he thought he could give good reasons for his change of heart, but they did not go far. Indeed they were a simple statement of ideas on which he had hitherto poured scorn. 'There is no real alternative,' Orwell said, 'between resisting Hitler and surrendering to him'. Furthermore, 'from a Socialist point of view ... I can see no argument for surrender that does not make nonsense of the Republican resistance in Spain'.[129] His main point in this essay was to defend the compatibility of patriotism and revolutionary Socialism, a point to which we shall return.

After the war, Orwell would express a degree of sheepish regret for the crudity of his attacks on pacifism.

> Whenever A and B are in opposition to one another, anyone who criticises A is accused of aiding and abetting B. And it is often true, objectively and on a short term analysis, that he *is* making things easier for B. Therefore say the supporters of A, shut up and don't criticise: or at least criticise 'constructively', which in practice always means favourably. And from this it is only a short step to argue that the suppression and distortion of known facts is the highest duty of a journalist.[130]

Orwell's hostile comments on pacifism had often taken precisely this form, as he seemed to acknowledge:

> The whole argument that one mustn't speak plainly because it 'plays into the hands of' this or that sinister influence is dishonest, in the sense that people only use it when it suits them ... Beneath this argument there

---

[128]George Orwell, 'My Country Right or Left', Autumn 1939, CW, XII, p. 271.
[129]Orwell, 'My Country Right or Left', CW, XII, p. 271.
[130]George Orwell, 'Through a Glass, Rosily', November 1945, CW XVII, p. 396.

always lies the intention to do propaganda for some single sectional interest, and to browbeat critics into silence by telling them that they are 'objectively' reactionary. It is a tempting manœuvre, and I have used it myself more than once, but it is dishonest. I think one is less likely to use it if one remembers that the advantages of a lie are always short-lived.[131]

Orwell had long been aware of the dangers of the sort of argument he was here rejecting. Writing to Naomi Mitchison in 1938, he noted that there was a risk that in opposing Communists one might be accused of 'objectively if not intentionally, aiding the Fascists'. But he was not going to let this argument silence him (even if there was truth in it). 'This last argument,' he said, 'is, of course, dragged forth on every occasion. Nevertheless, I believe it is right to try & keep alive the older version of Socialism even when it doesn't seem strategically opportune.' The 'objectively' argument was 'the C.P. line of talk', and he rejected the Communist view that 'People's motives do not matter; the only thing that matters is the objective result of their actions'.[132] Even during the war Orwell was aware of the pressure to dishonesty, noting the use of the phrase 'playing into the hands of'. 'When you are told that by saying this, that or the other you are "playing into the hands of" some sinister enemy, you know that it is your duty to shut up immediately.' Among the examples he gave was the usefulness of Gandhi to the Japanese. But he concluded with Spain, and the pressure not to tell the truth about the clash between Communists and Anarchists for fear of what use the *Daily Mail* might make of it. He concluded that the result of this was 'that the left-wing cause as a whole was weakened'. The *Daily Mail* might have found less fuel for their anti-Left furnaces, 'but some all-important lessons were not learned, and we are suffering from the fact to this day'.[133] Furthermore, as he recognized elsewhere, it just wasn't true that subjective opinions didn't matter. He gave an example. 'A pacifist is working in some job which gives him access to important military information, and is approached by a German secret agent. In those circumstances his subjective feelings *do* make a difference. If he is subjectively pro-Nazi he will sell his country, and if he isn't, he won't.'[134]

The pacifists and anarchists who were the objects of Orwell's tongue-lashing during the war might, if they could read these comments, be forgiven a rueful smile. In a verse exchange with Alex Comfort (writing under the name Obadiah Hornbooke), Orwell admitted:

---

[131]Orwell, 'Through a Glass, Rosily', CW, XVII, p. 398. He was even clearer in 'As I Please', 51, 8 December 1944, CW, XVI, pp. 495–6.
[132]Orwell to Naomi Mitchison, 17 June 1938, CW, XI, pp. 163–4.
[133]George Orwell, 'As I Please', 28, 9 June 1944, CW, XVI, pp. 252–3.
[134]Orwell, 'As I Please', 51, 8 December 1944, CW, XVI, p. 495.

All propaganda's lying, yours or mine;
It's lying even when its facts are true;
That goes for Goebbels or the 'party line',
Or the Primrose League of P.P.U.
But there are truths that smaller lies can serve,
And dirtier lies that scruples can gild over;
To waste your brains on war may need more nerve
Than to dodge facts and live in mental clover;
It's mean enough when other men are dying,
But when you lie, it's much to know you're lying.[135]

Orwell was here defending his work for the BBC in particular, but the comments could apply just as well to some of his other activity, not least his attacks on pacifism and anarchism, which he tended to see as closely intertwined if not the same thing. It seems that in 1938, 1943, 1944 and 1945 Orwell knew well enough what intellectual dishonesty was, but his mode of attacking pacifism (characterized by just this sort of dishonesty) was, presumably, one of the smaller lies. In his March–April 1942 'London Letter' to *Partisan Review* (a journal based in New York), Orwell shamelessly used an argument he knew, by his own account, to be dishonest:

[N]ot many English pacifists have the intellectual courage to think their thoughts down to the roots, and since there is no real answer to the charge that pacifism is objectively pro-Fascist, nearly all pacifist literature is forensic – i.e. specialises in avoiding awkward questions.[136]

He went further, to assert that there was 'an increasing overlap between Fascism and pacifism', describing Julian Symons as writing 'in a vaguely Fascist strain', Hugh Ross Williamson as a long-term Fascist in the same 'section' as Lord Haw-Haw, and so on. Alex Comfort got off lightly: 'a "pure" pacifist of the other-cheek school'. And throughout pacifism was lumped together indiscriminately with many other forms of defeatism.[137] The editors of *Partisan Review* published three replies to Orwell in September 1942, along with his own belligerently unapologetic response. For the most part, Orwell was unimpressed by his adversaries and merely reiterated his views: 'Pacifism is objectively pro-Fascist. This is elementary common sense. If you hamper the war effort of one side you automatically help that of the other.'[138] Their denial that they 'are tending towards active

---

[135]George Orwell, 'As One Non-Combatant to Another (A Letter to "Obadiah Hornbooke")', June 1943, CW, XV, p. 144.

[136]George Orwell, 'London Letter, 1 January 1642', in CW, XIII, p. 110.

[137]Orwell, 'London Letter', CW, XIII, p. 111.

[138]George Orwell, with D.S. Savage, George Woodcock & Alex Comfort, 'Pacifism and the War: A Controversy', September–October 1942, CW, XIII, p. 396.

pro-Fascism' was just 'intellectual cowardice'. '[P]eace propaganda is just as dishonest and intellectually disgusting as war propaganda.'[139] The charge that seems to have stung was George Woodcock's claim that Orwell's own record, from Burma onwards, showed the same 'over-lapping of left-wing, pacifist and reactionary tendencies of which he accuses others'.[140] Orwell responded with a pained defence of his anti-imperialism, his support for the POUM (even though he didn't really agree with them), and his broadcasts to India, made in the belief that a Fascist victory would destroy India's hopes of independence.[141]

Though these exchanges are Orwell's best-known clashes with pacifists, the logic of his thinking was better laid out elsewhere. In his first 'London Letter' to *Partisan Review* he explored whether there was any space in England for a policy that combined anti-Fascism and Socialist revolution, and concluded that 'there does not effectively exist any policy between being patriotic in the "King and Country" style and being pro-Hitler'.[142] If there is a defence to be made of Orwell against the charge of bad faith and dishonesty in his vituperation of pacifists, it lies in his sense that the war years were unusual years in which some principles might need to be compromised. There was not the space to advance the right views, and there was an urgency about defeating Hitler that overrode many other scruples. We will, in the next chapter, explore this matter more fully in relation to Orwell's views on intellectual freedom.

Orwell came to believe by 1941 that pacifism was not just 'objectively' but actually close to Fascism. 'The most interesting development of the anti-war front has been the interpenetration of the pacifist movement by Fascist ideas, especially antisemitism.' Pacifism had suffered 'a moral collapse', and pacifists 'now spin a lie of talk indistinguishable from that of the Blackshirts ("Stop this Jewish war" etc.), and the actual membership of the P.P.U. [Peace Pledge Union] and the British Union [of Fascists] overlap to some extent'.[143] Pacifism was giving comfort to the enemy, actively as well as 'objectively'.

The problems with pacifism went deeper, however. They were not just circumstantial. In a review of Alex Comfort's pacifist novel, *No Such Liberty,* Orwell laid down the fundamental principles that made pacifism unacceptable. 'Civilization,' he said, 'rests ultimately on coercion'. Society might cohere thanks to the 'goodwill of common men', but that goodwill was 'powerless unless the policeman is there to back it up'. Therefore,

---

[139]Orwell et al., 'Pacifism and the War', CW, XIII, pp. 397–8.
[140]Orwell et al., 'Pacifism and the War', CW, XIII, p. 395.
[141]Orwell et al., 'Pacifism and the War', CW, XIII, pp. 398–9.
[142]Orwell, 'London Letter', 3 January 1941, CW, XII, p. 353.
[143]Orwell, 'London Letter', CW, XII, pp. 353–4.

any government which refused to use violence in its own defence would almost immediately cease to exist, because it could be overthrown by any body of men, or even any individual, that was less scrupulous. Objectively, whoever is not on the side of the policeman is on the side of the criminal, and vice versa. In so far as it hampers the British war effort, British pacifism is on the side of the Nazis, and German pacifism, if it exists, is on the side of Britain and the U.S.S.R.

Furthermore, pacifism was a particular threat to democracy, because in democratic societies pacifists had more freedom to act. 'Objectively, the pacifist is pro-Nazi.'[144]

Orwell here was linking his thought on pacifism to the wider question of political violence: 'Since coercion can never be altogether dispensed with, the only difference is between degrees of violence.' England has been a relatively peaceful and anti-militarist country, and this has led many into the delusion that violence is not necessary. 'To abjure violence it is necessary to have no experience of it.'[145] There was no 'short term' case for pacifism: if you don't resist the Nazis they will beat you, and they are likely to be rather less benign rulers than those who have hitherto governed England. These circumstances made the moral purity of pacifism untenable:

The notion that you can somehow defeat violence by submitting to it is simply a flight from fact. As I have said, it is only possible to people who have money and guns between them and reality. But why should they want to make this flight anyway? Because, rightly hating violence, they do not wish to recognize that it is integral to modern society and that their own fine feelings and noble attitudes are all the fruit of injustice backed up by force. They do not want to learn where their incomes come from. Underneath this lies the hard fact, so difficult for many people to face, that individual salvation is not possible, that the choice before human beings is not, as a rule, between good and evil but between two evils. You can let the Nazis rule the world; that is evil; or you can overthrow them by war, which is also evil. There is no other choice before you, and whichever you choose you will not come out with clean hands.[146]

The stakes were too high, the violence too real: a dishonest argument became the only viable argument.

Orwell's many insinuations of a *rapprochement* between pacifism and Fascism eventually built into a second core argument against pacifism

---

[144]George Orwell, 'No, Not One', October 1941, CW, XIII, p. 40.

[145]Orwell, 'No, Not One', CW, XIII, pp. 40–1.

[146]Orwell, 'No, Not One', CW, XIII, p. 43.

and anarchism. Pacifism not only 'acts objectively in favour of violence', it also 'tends to turn into power worship'.[147] By the time of his essay on Jonathan Swift (quoted previously in this chapter), Orwell had come to believe that pacifism and anarchism (united, so far as he was concerned, in their non-violence and alleged non-coerciveness[148]) were dangerous because they relied on the 'soft' coercive power of compulsory conformity and induced agreement. They were therefore a threat to intellectual freedom and inherently or incipiently Fascist. Orwell developed the ideas further in his account of Tolstoy. Tolstoy, Orwell wrote, 'abjured violence in all its forms … but it is not so easy to believe that he abjured the principle of coercion'. He drew attention to the sort of coercion that a father exercises not by smacking a child but by exerting psychological pressure to conform to some norm – 'Now, darling, *is* it kind to mummy to do that?' Both are 'tyrannous'.

> The distinction that really matters is not between violence and non-violence, but between having and not having the appetite for power. There are people who are convinced of the wickedness both of armies and of police forces, but who are nevertheless much more intolerant and inquisitorial in outlook than the normal person who believes that it is necessary to use violence in certain circumstances. They will not say to somebody else, 'Do this, that and the other or you will go to prison', but they will, if they can, get inside his brain and dictate his thoughts for him in the minutest particulars. Creeds like pacifism and anarchism, which seem on the surface to imply a complete renunciation of power, rather encourage this habit of mind. For if you have embraced a creed which appears to be free from the ordinary dirtiness of politics … surely that proves you are in the right? And the more you are in the right, the more natural that everyone else should be bullied into thinking likewise.[149]

As with so much of his attack on other writers and thinkers of the Left, it was the odour mixed of self-assumed sanctity, self-righteousness and bad faith that Orwell could not stomach. He could, however, recognize that not all pacifists carried this odour – one in particular seemed to earn Orwell's grudging respect, Mahatma Gandhi. Orwell was always ambivalent about

---

[147]Orwell to John Middleton Murry, 11 August 1944, CW, XVI, p. 333.
[148]In a response to this essay, George Woodcock rightly took Orwell to task for his assumption (or pretence) that anarchism and pacifism were the same: 'Orwell confuses the issue by identifying anarchist with pacifist. Many anarchists believe in violence; on the other hand, many pacifists admit the need for law and coercion on a lower level than that of war.' Woodcock, 'Anarchism & Public Opinion', *Freedom (Anarchist Fortnightly)*, 28 June 1947, p. 2.
[149]George Orwell, 'Lear, Tolstoy and the Fool', March 1947, CW, XIX, pp. 65–6.

Gandhi's political thought, admiring his 'personal integrity', but doubtful that his non-violent methods would prove adequate to getting the British to leave India. He was scornful of the very idea of 'moral force' and tended to see Gandhi as playing into British hands: it was only violence the British feared. On the other hand, in his diary, after admitting that 'his pacifism may be genuine', Orwell compared Gandhi to Rasputin; and later he listed him alongside Hitler, Mussolini and Franco as one of the 'superhuman fuehrers'.[150] Orwell's final thoughts on Gandhi were written after Indian independence and Gandhi's assassination. He remained ambivalent, and was especially hostile to Gandhi's anti-humanist religious politics. Gandhi, Orwell thought, also failed to understand totalitarianism, and that the moral force on which he relied could not be effective in countries where there was not a reasonable level of freedom of expression. That said, though, Gandhi was successful in his major aim (a peaceful end to British rule, albeit not peaceful for long).

Orwell came to appreciate the strengths of non-violent *resistance* (and the fact that it was not a form of inaction). Even though he thought that in international politics 'pacifism either stops being pacifist or it becomes appeasement', he doubted whether 'civilization can stand another war'. 'It is at least thinkable,' he mused, 'that the way out lies through non-violence'.[151] But, above all, he recognized in Gandhi an honest pacifist.

Even after he had completely abjured violence he was honest enough to see that in war it is usually necessary to take sides. He did not ... take the sterile and dishonest line of pretending that in every war both sides are exactly the same and it makes no difference who wins. Nor did he, like most western pacifists, specialize in avoiding awkward questions. In relation to the late war, one question that every pacifist had a clear obligation to answer was: 'What about the Jews? Are you prepared to see them exterminated? If not, how do you propose to save them without resorting to war?' I must say that I have never heard, from any western pacifist, an honest answer to this question ... Gandhi's view was that the German Jews ought to commit collective suicide, which 'would have aroused the world and the people of Germany to Hitler's violence'. After the war he justified himself: the Jews had been killed anyway, and might as well have died significantly ... Gandhi was merely being honest.[152]

---

[150]Orwell to Rev. Iorwerth Jones, 8 April 1941, CW, XII, pp. 466–7; Orwell et al., 'Pacifism and War', CW, XII, p. 397; Orwell, 'War-Time Diary', 3 April 1942, CW, XIII, p. 259 [Orwell, *Diaries* (London: Penguin, 2010), p. 328]; Orwell to Noel Willmett, 18 May 1944, CW, XVI, p. 190.
[151]George Orwell, 'Reflections on Gandhi', January 1949, CW, XX, pp. 9–10.
[152]Orwell, 'Reflections on Gandhi', CW, XX, p. 9.

## (b) Revolution and Political Violence

Orwell's Socialism from its inception in Spain was, as we have seen, revolutionary Socialism. He saw in the Communists the opponents of revolution, actively suppressing those who had created a revolutionary moment in Barcelona. Orwell repudiated this position, even though he probably suspected at the time and certainly suspected later that the Communist position was a more likely route to beating Franco, and entrusted his hopes to a Socialist(-anarchist) vision for the revolutionary reconstruction of society. We have also seen that Orwell was not squeamish about violence used for political ends. Even during his anti-militarist phase, his objection was not to violence in principle but to a particular war that was looming. Violent revolution was, in some circumstances, to be welcomed; it was indeed often the only way to achieve one's goals. The ends might not justify any means – but they justified a good many.

We have already heard Orwell, in his attacks on pacifism, declare that without the policeman society could not cohere for long. 'What holds society together is not the policeman but the goodwill of common men, and yet that goodwill is powerless unless the policeman is there to back it up.'[153] The statement is often taken to contradict something that Orwell had written in *Homage to Catalonia*: 'I have no particular love for the idealized "worker" as he appears in the bourgeois Communist's mind, but when I see an actual flesh-and-blood worker in conflict with his natural enemy, the policeman, I do not have to ask myself which side I am on.'[154] But there is no need to think that Orwell was contradicting himself. In one case he was describing a workers' revolution; in the other, a society that needed to hang together to defeat Hitler. The policeman was a necessary adjunct of order, but order sometimes needed to be maintained and sometimes overthrown. The important point is that Orwell was always alive to the violence, real or implicit, that might be needed to achieve political goals. In any particular case, circumstances dictated the ways in which violence might be used and the extent to which it might be required.

But there were limits as well. Orwell twice cited a remark of Nietzsche's, first in his 1938 review of Koestler's *Spanish Testament*: 'this book lays bare the central evil of modern war – the fact that, as Nietzsche puts it, "he who fights the dragons becomes a dragon himself"'.[155] Nietzsche's aphorism

---

[153]Orwell, 'No, Not One', CW, XIII, p. 40.
[154]Orwell, *Homage to Catalonia*, p. 104 (Penguin ed. p. 109).
[155]Orwell, 'Review of *The Tree of Gernika* by G.L. Steer; *Spanish Testament* by Arthur Koestler', February 1938, CW, XI, p. 113; Nietzsche, *Beyond Good and Evil*, par. 146: 'Whoever fights monsters should see to it that in the process he does not become a monster. And when you look long into an abyss, the abyss also looks into you', Walter Kaufmann (ed.), *Basic Writings of Nietzsche* (New York: Modern Library, 1992), p. 279.

captured a fear that haunted Orwell throughout the war – that, in fighting it, even those on the right side would lose their humanity – but the fear is relevant to his thoughts on political violence more broadly. In 1938, he thought the problem identified by Nietzsche was insoluble. There was no doubt that some of what happened in Spain was bestial.

> And the horror we feel of these things has led to this conclusion: if someone drops a bomb on your mother, go and drop two bombs on his mother. The only apparent alternatives are to smash dwelling houses to powder, blow out human entrails and burn holes in children with lumps of thermite, or to be enslaved by people who are more ready to do these things than you are yourself; as yet no one has suggested a practicable way out.[156]

I don't think Orwell ever found a way out of this dilemma. The important thing was to recognize its existence, and therefore to recognize the necessity of making invidious choices.

Orwell's second deployment of Nietzsche was in a discussion of 'an exceptionally disgusting photograph' published in the *Star*. The picture was of two female collaborators, publicly shamed by having had their hair shaved. Orwell could understand the hostility to collaborators shown by the French, but deplored the pleasure that might be taken in their humiliation by others. He recalled the similar treatment previously meted out to Jews by the Nazis, also 'exhibited in the British press'. Another example also came to mind:

> Recently another newspaper published photographs of the dangling corpses of Germans hanged by the Russians in Kharkov, and carefully informed its readers that these executions had been filmed and that the public would shortly be able to witness them at the news theatres. (Were children admitted, I wonder?)

He quoted a different version of Nietzsche, 'he who fights too long against dragons becomes a dragon himself: and if thou gaze too long into the abyss, the abyss will gaze into thee'. The 'too long' is an interpolation, not present in Nietzsche's German, but Orwell glossed it 'as meaning "after the dragon is beaten"'.[157] We might need to do things in wartime that compromised our humanity, but there was no justification for them when the war was won.[158]

---

[156]Orwell, 'Review of … *Spanish Testament*', CW, XI, p. 113.
[157]Orwell, 'As I Please', 41, 8 September 1944, CW, XVI, p. 387.
[158]These paragraphs are indebted to the fine analysis in Kristian Williams, '"Between the Bullet and the Lie": Ethics in Warfare', in Williams, *Between the Bullet and the Lie*, ch. 4.

In wartime (and presumably in violent revolutions) there was sometimes no choice. 'You may not understand this,' Orwell wrote to John Middleton Murry, 'but I don't think it matters killing people so long as you don't hate them'. He continued: 'I also think that there are times when you can only show your feeling of brotherhood for somebody else by killing him, or trying to. I believe most ordinary people feel this and would make a peace in that sense if they had any say in the matter. There has been very little popular resistance to this war, and also very little hatred. It is a job that has to be done.'[159] Recognizing that all sides lied in their propaganda, Orwell nonetheless believed there was something qualitatively different this time: 'Nazism is a quite exceptionally evil thing, and it has been responsible for outrages quite unparalleled in recent times. It is definitely worse than British Imperialism, which has plenty of crimes of its own to answer for.'[160] This evil had to be beaten, even at the risk of making oneself into a dragon.

Replying to someone who objected to the 'barbarous methods' being used by the Allies in the war (but who also recognized that 'the Hun had got to be beaten'), Orwell wrote:

> Now, it seems to me that you do less harm by dropping bombs on people than by calling them 'Huns'. Obviously one does not want to inflict death and wounds if it can be avoided, but I cannot feel that mere killing is all-important. We shall all be dead in less than a hundred years, and most of us by the sordid horror known as 'natural death'. The truly evil thing is to act in such a way that peaceful life becomes impossible. War damages the fabric of civilisation not by the destruction it causes (the net effect of a war may be to increase the productive capacity of the world as a whole), nor even by the slaughter of human beings, but by stimulating hatred and dishonesty. By shooting at your enemy you are not in the deepest sense wronging him. But by hating him, by inventing lies about him and bringing children up to believe them, by clamouring for unjust peace terms which make further wars inevitable, you are striking not at one perishable generation, but at humanity itself.

Hatred, jeering, failing to respect the humanity of your enemies – these were the sorts of thing 'that damages the very roots of human solidarity in a way that no mere act of violence could do'.[161]

These attitudes to violence serve as a backdrop to Orwell's thinking about revolution and revolutionary means. As we have seen, in Spain he came to see what revolution could make possible, and defended those

---

[159]Orwell to John Middleton Murry, 11 August 1944, CW, XVI, p. 333.
[160]Orwell, 'As I Please', 37, 11 August 1944, CW, XVI, p. 330.
[161]Orwell, 'As I Please', 36, 4 August 1944, CW, XVI, pp. 317–8.

who struggled to achieve this vision in the face of Stalinist attempts to stamp out the revolutionary impulse. Even during the later 1930s, when he opposed militarism, he did so because he thought a war would be fatal to the aspirations for Socialism and revolutionary change. But he was still prepared to use illegal, if not revolutionary, means to achieve his goals. Writing to his anarchist friend, Herbert Read, he lamented that 'actual pacifists ... had a sort of lingering moral objection to illegality and underground work'. He proposed to Read that those opposed to war should set about to construct an underground organization and 'to start organising for illegal anti-war activities'.[162]

It was in the early years of the war, however, once his anti-militarism had been repudiated, that Orwell's revolutionary aspirations reached their apogee. During 1940 and 1941 Orwell believed that conditions were perfect for revolution in England. Without one the war might be lost, and would, in any case, hardly be worth fighting.

Orwell's most revolutionary piece of writing dates from this period – *The Lion and the Unicorn: Socialism and the English Genius*, published early in 1941. The book was animated by Orwell's passionate conviction that 'we cannot win the war without introducing Socialism, nor establish Socialism without winning the war'.[163] Furthermore, wartime patriotism created an opportunity for Socialists: 'an intelligent socialist movement will *use* [the people's] ... patriotism, instead of merely insulting it'. Patriotism could be the means to create a genuine mass movement in favour of Socialism 'because patriotism is finally stronger than class hatred'.[164] As Orwell said in his contribution to Victor Gollancz's *The Betrayal of the Left*, 'the feeling of all true patriots and all true Socialists is at bottom reducible to the "Trotskyist" slogan: "The war and the revolution are inseparable".'[165] Patriotism provided the opportunity to forge a new type of revolution. Socialists had hitherto talked of proletarian revolution, but this divided the working class from the middle class, and the latter included all those technocrats and professionals needed to run a modern economy and society. Patriotism could bring them together, and a revolution that was 'more or less a voluntary act of the people – the only kind of revolution that is conceivable under modern Western conditions' could ensue. The key thing on which to focus was persuading the middle class that Socialism was necessary to defeat Hitler. Patriots and revolutionaries must be brought together in a coalition that spanned classes. 'Do you want to defeat Hitler? Then you must be ready

---

[162]Orwell to Herbert Read, 4 January 1939, CW, XI, p. 313.
[163]George Orwell, *The Lion and the Unicorn: Socialism and the English Genius* (1941), in Orwell, CW, XII, p. 421.
[164]Orwell, *Lion and Unicorn*, CW, XII, pp. 421–2.
[165]George Orwell, 'Our Opportunity', January 1941, reprinted as 'Patriots and Revolutionaries', March 1941, CW, XII, pp. 345–6.

to sacrifice your social prestige. Do you want to establish Socialism? Then you must be ready to defend your country.'[166]

In *The Lion and the Unicorn* Orwell expressed an almost Burkean view of the English nation and its perdurance – a country possessed of a continuity that could be interrupted by nothing short of foreign occupation.

> The gentleness, the hypocrisy, the thoughtlessness, the reverence for law and the hatred of uniforms will remain along with the suet puddings and the misty skies. It needs some very great disaster, such as prolonged subjugation by a foreign enemy, to destroy a national culture. The Stock Exchange will be pulled down, the horse plough will give way to the tractor, the country houses will be turned into children's holiday camps, the Eton and Harrow match will be forgotten, but England will still be England, an everlasting animal stretching into the future and the past, like all living things, having the power to change out of recognition and yet remain the same.[167]

Divided by class though it might be, England nonetheless possessed 'emotional unity, the tendency of nearly all its inhabitants to feel alike and act together in moments of supreme crisis'.[168] Since Dunkirk this emotional unity had created the possibility of Socialist revolution – in 'that spectacular disaster the working class, the middle class and even a section of the business community could see the utter rottenness of private capitalism'.[169] Now, 'it is only by revolution that the native genius of the English people can be set free'. There is the real chance that for the first time the 'initiative will ... come from below' and a Socialist movement 'that actually has the mass of the people behind it' can be created.[170] It was possible for the first time to be 'both revolutionary and realistic'.[171] The revolution may happen 'with or without bloodshed' – circumstances would decide – but it would be decidedly like the revolution in Barcelona, rooted in a destruction of the culture of social privilege and inequality.

> In the short run, equality of sacrifice, 'war communism', is even more important than radical economic changes. It is very necessary that industry should be nationalized, but it is more urgently necessary that such monstrosities as butlers and 'private incomes' should disappear forthwith. Almost certainly the main reason the Spanish Republic could

---

[166]Orwell, 'Our Opportunity', CW, XII, p. 347.
[167]Orwell, *Lion and Unicorn*, CW, XII, p. 409.
[168]Orwell, *Lion and Unicorn*, CW, XII, p. 400.
[169]Orwell, *Lion and Unicorn*, CW, XII, p. 412.
[170]Orwell, *Lion and Unicorn*, CW, XII, p. 418.
[171]Orwell, *Lion and Unicorn*, CW, XII, p. 421.

keep up the fight for two and half years against impossible odds was that there were no gross contrasts of wealth. The people suffered horribly, but they suffered alike.[172]

Orwell presented a vision of what Socialism should look like. The means of production would be in common ownership, though people would still have 'private possessions'. This would 'solve the problems of production and consumption', enabling the planned mobilization of England's productive capacity that was needed to win the war. But more was needed. 'One must also add the following: approximate equality of incomes (it need be no more than approximate), political democracy, and abolition of all hereditary privilege, especially in education.' This was needed to prevent the formation of a 'self-elected political party', and the return of 'oligarchy and privilege'.[173]

Orwell's vision was distilled into a political programme with six immediate objectives:

I.     Nationalization of land, mines, railways, banks and major industries.

II.    Limitation of incomes, on such a scale that the highest tax-free income in Britain does not exceed the lowest by more than ten to one.

III.   Reform of the education system along democratic lines.

IV.    Immediate Dominion status for India, with power to secede when the war is over.

V.     Formation of an Imperial General Council, in which the coloured peoples are to be represented.

VI.    Declaration of formal alliance with China, Abyssinia and all other victims of the Fascist powers.[174]

It was important that this Socialism could emerge in the 'English-speaking world', for this gave it the chance of becoming 'a society of free and equal human beings'.[175] English patriotism was not conservative. Quite the opposite, 'since it is devotion to something that is always changing and yet is felt to by mystically the same'. 'No real revolutionary has ever been an internationalist',[176] presumably because revolution has to be rooted in patriotism. English Socialism would be a humane Socialism, for 'by revolution we become more ourselves, not less'. Given the peculiarities of the

---

[172]Orwell, *Lion and Unicorn*, CW, XII, p. 415.
[173]Orwell, *Lion and Unicorn*, CW, XII, p. 410.
[174]Orwell, *Lion and Unicorn*, CW, XII, p. 422.
[175]Orwell, *Lion and Unicorn*, CW, XII, p. 430.
[176]Orwell, *Lion and Unicorn*, CW, XII, p. 428.

English, that would produce an odd revolution, but one that was without the dogmatism and totalitarian tendencies of other revolutions.

> It will not be doctrinaire, not even logical. It will abolish the House of Lords, but quite probably will not abolish the Monarchy. It will leave anachronism and loose ends everywhere, the judge in his ridiculous horsehair wig and the lion and the unicorn on the soldier's cap-buttons. It will not set up any explicit class dictatorship ... But it will never lose touch with the tradition of compromise and a belief in law which is above the State. It will shoot traitors, but it will give them a solemn trial beforehand, and occasionally it will acquit them. It will crush any open revolt promptly and cruelly, but it will interfere very little with the spoken and written word. Political parties with different names will still exist, revolutionary sects will still be publishing their newspaper and making as little impression as ever. It will disestablish the Church, but will not persecute religion. It will retain a vague reverence for the Christian moral code, and from time to time will refer to England as 'a Christian country' ... It will show a power of assimilating the past which will shock foreign observers and sometimes make then doubt whether any revolution has happened.

This was a new revolution – patriotic not class-based – and the English would muddle their way through it as they muddled their way through much else. But no one should be in any doubt that this odd revolution 'will have done the essential thing. It will have nationalized industry, scaled down incomes, set up a classless educational system.'[177]

During the war years, Orwell's confidence in the likelihood of this revolution fluctuated, but, by war's end, it had considerably reduced. His first 'London Letter' to *Partisan Review*, dated 3 January 1941 (just before the publication of *The Lion and the Unicorn*), argued that 'in the summer [of 1940] what amounted to a revolutionary situation [had] existed in England'. Though the reactionaries had recovered a little, the opportunity of a patriotic-Socialist union of middle and working classes still remained.[178] Over a year later, the readers of *Partisan Review* were informed that 'we are back to the "revolutionary situation" which existed but was not utilized after Dunkirk'. He declared, with perhaps an excess of optimism, that 'one can after all discern the outlines of a revolutionary world war' and was particularly encouraged by the weakening of imperialist attitudes.[179] Orwell looked to Stafford Cripps as a potential leader for the Left. He recorded

---

[177]Orwell, *Lion and Unicorn*, CW, XII, p. 427.
[178]Orwell, 'London Letter', 3 January 1941, CW, XII, pp. 352–3.
[179]George Orwell, 'London Letter', 8 May 1942, CW, XIII, pp. 307–8.

meeting Cripps (for the second time) on 7 June 1942. Cripps had said that many thought the war would be over by October, to which Orwell replied, 'I should look on that as a disaster pure and simple (because if the war were won as easily as that there would have been no real upheaval here and the American millionaires would still be in situ).' Cripps 'appeared not to understand'.[180] Orwell's disillusionment was palpable: it was perhaps no surprise that Cripps did not subsequently rise to Orwell's hopes. It is striking, nonetheless, that Orwell could hope for the war to be prolonged to ensure that revolution would be achieved. By early 1943, however, the opportunity had been lost, 'it is hard to see how any revolutionary situation can recur till the Western end of the war is finished'.[181] Dunkirk and the fall of Singapore had provided the opportunities – both were squandered.

Orwell's assessments of the Labour Government, elected in July 1945, make it clear that he never again thought that England had an opportunity for revolution. Soon after the election he told *Partisan Review* readers that 'one cannot take this slide to the Left as meaning that Britain is on the verge of revolution. In spite of the discontent smouldering in the armed forces, the mood of the country seems to me less revolutionary, less Utopian, even less hopeful than it was in 1940 or 1942.'[182] Though Orwell was always a (critical) supporter of the Labour government in most matters, he was under no illusions that it would introduce the degree of change that he wished for. The need was 'to persuade ... that Socialism is a *better* way of life but not necessarily, in its first stages, a more comfortable one'.[183] No one was even trying to make this case. 'Heaven knows,' he concluded, 'whether the government has any serious intention of introducing socialism, but if it has, I don't see what there is to stop it'.[184] It is an odd assessment: the mood was not a revolutionary one, but there were few barriers to revolutionary change if the government wished to set about it. A little under a year later, Orwell noted that 'what I have not heard any ordinary person say is that the government has not made any perceptible step towards the introduction of Socialism'. But the absence of such criticism was not because people were less interested in Socialism and more interested in the coal supply, housing, food shortages, high prices and so on. In fact:

Even allowing for the fact that everything takes time, it is astonishing how little change seems to have happened as yet in the structure of society. In a purely economic sense, I suppose, the drift is towards Socialism,

---

[180]Orwell, 'War-Time Diary', 7 June 1942, CW, XIII, pp. 351–2; Orwell, *Diaries*, Penguin ed. pp. 343–4.
[181]George Orwell, 'A Letter from England' [London Letter], 3 January 1943, CW, XIV, p. 292.
[182]George Orwell, 'London Letter', 15–16 August 1945, CW, XVII, p. 246.
[183]Orwell, 'London Letter', 1945, CW, XVII, p. 248.
[184]Orwell, 'London Letter', 1945, CW, CVII, p. 249.

or at least towards state ownership. Transport for example is being nationalised ... But in the social set-up there is no symptom by which one could infer that we are not living under a Conservative government. No move has been made against the House of Lords, for example, there has been no talk of disestablishing the Church, there has been very little replacement of Tory ambassadors, service chiefs or other high officials, and if any effort is really being made to democratise education, it has borne no fruit as yet.[185]

In his final verdict on Labour, Orwell again emphasized that most of those who voted the government into power were not really interested in the introduction of Socialism as such. They wanted particular improvements in their lives, more comfortable lives, and Orwell was consistently of the view that the introduction of Socialism might well mean the opposite in the short term. Labour, he thought, should have been more truthful that 'there were very hard times ahead, all the harder because the first steps towards socialism now had to be taken'. In a passage that he could have written in the later 1930s, Orwell noted the 'unsolved contradiction that dwells at the heart of the Socialist movement. Socialism, a creed which grew up in the industrialized Western countries, means better material conditions for the white proletariat; it also means liberation for the exploited colored peoples. But the two aims, at least temporarily, are incompatible.'[186] Progress towards Socialism was slow, and it was not clear that the British people would be prepared to put up with the privations that might be required along the way. In the meantime the Labour government deserved support: it was the best available option.

This last essay has led many to see Orwell as shifting to the Right in his final years, especially the statement 'that certain jobs which are vitally necessary are never done except under some kind of compulsion. As soon as you have full employment, therefore, you have to make use of forced labor for the dirtier kinds of work (You can call it by some more soothing name, of course).'[187] This may be one uncomfortable truth too far for some. But it strikes me that this is – something very familiar to those on the Left – a sort of *consolation* for the experience of defeat. We couldn't have done better, given the circumstances, is what Orwell wanted to believe. But it does not mean that he had changed his mind about the desirability of revolutionary change or about the legitimacy of violent revolution. As Simon Leys put

---

[185]George Orwell, 'London Letter', Summer 1946, CW, XVIII, p. 286.

[186]George Orwell, 'The Labour Government after Three Years', October 1948, CW XIX, pp. 439–40.

[187]Orwell, 'The Labour Government after Three Years', CW, XIX, pp. 438–9. Cf. John Newsinger, *Hope Lies in the Proles: George Orwell and the Left* (London: Verso, 2018), p. 110; Newsinger, 'Orwell, the Labour Party and the Attlee Government', *Orwell Studies*, 2:1 (2017), pp. 85–6.

it, 'Orwell effectively ceased to believe in the imminent *possibility* of such revolutionary up-heavals; still, there is nothing in his writings that would allow us to conclude that he actually ceased to consider these *desirable*.'[188] Indeed, it is noticeable that his assessments of the Labour government, chastened though they were, measured its performance by the degree to which it had achieved revolutionary change. Furthermore, when he looked at the world more broadly, as he did in the essay he contributed to *Partisan Review*'s discussion of the future prospects for Socialism, Orwell could maintain a level of hope. He argued in that essay that the best hope for the future lay in a 'socialist United States of Europe'. Though the 'actual outlook ... is very dark', there were some grounds for optimism. The reality might be that what Orwell envisaged was 'a very unlikely event', but it was not altogether impossible, and certainly 'I ... can't at present see any other hopeful objective'. '[U]nexpected things might happen.'[189] This reflects the shifts in Orwell's vision of revolution that occurred in the mid-1940s, along with his growing sense that a brighter future might take longer to achieve than he had dared to expect in 1940 and 1941.

In the years 1943 to 1946 Orwell thought much harder about the politics and ethics of revolution than he had done before. Much of this was in dialogue with the writings of Arthur Koestler, and some of it was expressed in *Animal Farm*, Orwell's fable of how the Russian Revolution had been betrayed. *Animal Farm* was based closely on the events of 1917 and after, but 'they are dealt with schematically and their chronological order is changed'. Its underlying purpose was 'the destruction of the Soviet myth', namely 'the belief that Russia is a Socialist country'. This was a 'corruption of the original idea of Socialism' and smashing it was 'essential if we wanted a revival of the Socialist movement'.[190] So *Animal Farm* was an attempt to revitalize Socialism by distancing it from its debased Russian counterfeit. In that sense, it was a tract to counter Orwell's fears, evident by 1944, for the possibility of real revolutionary change. The Russian Revolution had produced totalitarianism, not any form of Socialism worth having.

*Animal Farm* ends enigmatically. The animals' new masters, the pigs, become indistinguishable from their previous human masters. 'The creatures outside looked from pig to man, and from man to pig, and from pig to man again: but already it was impossible to say which was which?'[191] Are we to conclude from this that revolutions can only succeed in replacing one set of oppressors with another? I don't think so. When Orwell reworked *Animal*

---

[188]Leys, 'Orwell: The Horror of Politics', in Leys, *The Angel and the Octopus*, p. 172.

[189]George Orwell, 'Toward European Unity', July–August 1947, CW, XIX, pp. 163–7.

[190]George Orwell, 'Preface to the Ukrainian Edition of *Animal Farm*', March 1947, CW, XIX, pp. 89, 87; also included in Orwell, *Animal Farm* (1945) [CW, VIII] (London: Secker & Warburg, 1986), pp. 112–13.

[191]Orwell, *Animal Farm*, p. 95 (Penguin ed. p. 102).

*Farm* into a radio script, he made a minor adjustment to the text at the point in the story where Napoleon, following Snowball's expulsion and the ending of the Sunday meetings, is seeking to quell resistance. He says, 'And one last word. Remember always that when there has been one Rebellion, there can never be another. That is the just rule of Rebellions.'[192] This seems to echo a well-known piece of dialogue in Zamyatin's *We*:

> He: 'This is mad. This doesn't hold water. You don't realize that what you are preparing is a revolution?'
> She: 'Yes it is a revolution. Why doesn't it hold water?'
> He: 'Because there can be no revolution. Because *our* revolution was the last and there can be no more. Everybody knows that ...'
> She: 'There is no such thing as the last revolution, the number of revolutions is infinite.'[193]

I quote this from Gleb Struve's *25 Years of Soviet Russian Literature*. Orwell will have read this passage just as he was completing the original manuscript of *Animal Farm* in February 1944. Struve had sent him a signed advance copy, and Orwell replied that the book 'has already roused my interest in Zamyatin's "We", which I had not heard of before'. Orwell concluded the letter with a reference to his work on *Animal Farm*: 'I am writing a little squib which might amuse you when it comes out, but it is so not O.K. politically that I don't feel certain in advance that anyone will publish it.'[194] Orwell eventually managed to find and read a copy of the French translation of *We*, and reviewed it for *Tribune* in January 1946. The only extensive quotation from Zamyatin's book that Orwell provided was this same passage;[195] he produced the radio script of *Animal Farm* late in 1946.

Orwell took the view that *We* was written too early (1923) to be a satire on Soviet Russia (though Gleb Struve wrote to *Tribune* to dispute this[196]), and that its real aim was a rationalized and mechanized world – 'the implied aims of industrial civilization' – or, as he put it later, 'it debunks the super-rational, hedonistic type of Utopia'.[197] It is a society that has sought happiness by abandoning freedom, though Orwell was unconvinced by the premise: 'though everyone is happy in a vacuous way, life has become so pointless that it is difficult to believe that such a society could endure'. Zamyatin probably agreed. He himself used the lines about

---

[192]Orwell, *Animal Farm*, p. 161.
[193]Gleb Struve, *25 Years of Soviet Russian Literature* (London: George Routledge, 1944), p. 136.
[194]Orwell to Gleb Struve, 17 February 1944, CW, XVI, p. 99.
[195]Orwell, 'Freedom and Happiness', January 1946, CW, XVIII, pp. 13–16.
[196]Struve in CW, XVIII, p. 16.
[197]Orwell to Fredric Warburg, 30 March 1949, CW, XX, p. 72.

there being only one revolution as the epigraph for an essay that comes closest to being his intellectual credo.

Revolution is everywhere, in everything. It is infinite. There is no final number, no final revolution. The social revolution is only one of an infinite number of numbers: the law of revolution is not a social law, but an immeasurably greater one. It is a cosmic, universal law – like the laws of the conservation of energy and of the dissipation of energy (entropy).[198]

Zamyatin, perhaps more strongly than Orwell himself, believed utopia to be a bad thing. Revolution, change, disorder, heresy – these were the forces of vitality in the world, and they all required freedom, especially freedom of thought. Orwell sensed a kindred spirit, another worshipper of perverse humanity, and his own hostility to hedonism (discussed later in this chapter) was rooted in a fear that it sapped the revolutionary spirit. Revolutions were betrayed as they ossified, as the spirit evaporated.

Orwell's allusion to Zamyatin in the radio script is a clarification of his intention in *Animal Farm*. The fable is certainly a fable of revolution betrayed, the Russian Revolution in particular; it may even be a fable of the inevitable failure of revolution. But this does not make the book an anti-revolutionary parable. Rather, it is an argument for what we might call the *open-endedness* of revolution. We can see that by looking at the way in which Orwell, soon after finishing *Animal Farm*, turned to gather his thoughts on Arthur Koestler. He began work on an essay about Koestler (finishing it on 11 September 1944). The essay was mostly about the three novels that formed Koestler's 'ends and means' trilogy, which together explored 'the central question of revolutionary ethics and of political ethics in general: the question whether, or to what extent, the end justifies the means'.[199] Orwell shared Koestler's interest in this question, but he resisted Koestler's answers. Writing of the first of Koestler's trilogy, *The Gladiators* (1939), an account of Spartacus's slave revolt and the attempt to institute a utopian 'Sun City', Orwell summarized the lesson of the book: 'Revolutions always go wrong.' But, he added, Koestler 'falters' in understanding '*why* they go wrong'.[200]

What, then, was Koestler's understanding? The answer is not simple. The Koestler of *The Gladiators* is, in some ways, more interesting than the Koestler

[198]Zamyatin, 'On Literature, Revolution, Entropy, and Other Matters', in *A Soviet Heretic: Essays by Yevgeny Zamyatin*, ed. & trans. Mirra Ginsburg (Chicago, IL: University of Chicago Press, 1970), pp. 107–8.

[199]Arthur Koestler, 'Postscript to the Danube Edition', *The Gladiators* (London: Vintage, 1999), p. 316. This was Koestler's first novel, published in 1939. The Danube edition was first published in 1965.

[200]Orwell, 'Arthur Koestler', 11 September 1944, CW, XVI, p. 394.

of the later novels in his trilogy, because in 1939 he had not altogether lost the revolutionary enthusiasm of his Communist years. He resigned from the party in two letters of 22 and 29 April 1938. In the first he repudiated any 'hostile intent' towards the party, and declared 'that I continue ... to regard the existence of the Soviet Union as a decisively positive factor in the political balance of our time, and that nothing is further from my mind than to abandon this conviction'. His second letter was much longer. It gave his reasons for leaving the party, which amounted to his deep concern over its 'progressive moral degeneration'. What concerned Koestler most was 'the absence of a system of revolutionary ethics'. Communists rejected the moral code of liberalism, but had nothing to put in its place except the view 'that the end justifies the means'. Anyone who opposed the purposes of the party, deemed by definition to be objectively correct, had to be destroyed by means fair or foul. Usually, indeed, by means murderous. This was made worse by the fact that Marxist theory had become rigid, unable to explain why or even admit that the masses so often supported parties that were (in Communist eyes) hostile to their own interests. 'We grew blinders. We trained ourselves to see things in a perspective that did not correspond to reality. We did our thinking within a closed logical system that has as little to do with the real world as the equally strict and twisted logic of schizophrenics.' Even here, though, Koestler did not repudiate the Russian Revolution, 'the foundation of the future'. 'But,' he added, 'whoever represents it as a finished prototype of the future ... is offering us a caricature of the future'. Free and open discussion was needed, not blind loyalty.[201]

The Gladiators was finished in July 1938 and Koestler immediately began work in its more famous successor, Darkness at Noon, to be published in 1940.[202] The Gladiators was a book very much underpinned by the same views that had been expounded in the two resignation letters. Koestler's account of Spartacus recognized not only the attractiveness of revolution and utopia, but also that without them injustice and inequality will remain, and humanity will be denied freedom. This takes on a tragic dimension: if revolutions must fail, then the wrongs they seek to address must persist. Koestler summarized his analysis of the ethics of revolution:

But why, then, did the revolution go to pieces? The reasons were, of course, of great complexity, yet one factor stood out clearly: Spartacus was a victim of the 'law of detours', which compels the leader on the road

[201]All quotations are from the translations in Michael Scammell, 'Arthur Koestler Resigns', New Republic, 4 May 1998, pp. 27–33. Also Michael Scammell, Koestler: The Indispensable Intellectual (London: Faber & Faber, 2010), pp. 161–3.
[202]John V. Fleming, The Anti-Communist Manifestos: Four Books That Shaped the Cold War (New York; Norton, 2009), pp. 52–4; Scammell, Koestler, pp. 164–7, 173–5; David Cesarani, Arthur Koestler: The Homeless Mind (London: William Heinemann, 1998), p. 151.

to Utopia to be 'ruthless for the sake of pity'. Yet he shrinks from taking
the last step – the purge by crucifixion of the dissident Celts and the
establishment of a ruthless tyranny; and through this refusal he dooms
his revolution to defeat.[203]

The law of detours was the principle that the greatest of God's curses on
man was 'that he must tread the evil road for the sake of the good and right,
that he must make detours and walk crookedly so that he may reach the
straight goal'.[204] Of course, evil ways carry the danger that the detour is
actually a road into the wilderness.

> In the beginning, the head will always order the fist to strike from lofty
> reasons; later on the fist strikes of its own accord and the head supplies
> the lofty reasons afterwards; and the person does not even notice the
> difference. Many a man has started out as a friend of the people and
> ended up as a tyrant; but history gives not a single example of a man
> starting out as a tyrant and ending up as a friend of the people. Therefore
> I tell you again: there is nothing so dangerous as a dictator who means
> well.[205]

For a while it seemed that Spartacus courted the fate of becoming a tyrant;
but what undid him in the end, and destroyed the Sun City, was his failure to
be sufficiently ruthless and to follow the detour all the way to its terminus.
The message seemed to be that, if you follow the principle that the end
justifies the means, the revolution will be irrevocably corrupted, but if you
don't, then the revolution will fail through ill-discipline. Spartacus died in
the final battle; his surviving supporters were brutally crucified. If this is
how revolutions end, it does not take away the need for them or the nobility
of their purposes. 'The century of abortive revolutions was completed, the
Party of Justice has lost out, its strength was spent and exhausted. Now
nothing could impede the greed for power, nothing barred the way to
despotism, no barrier to protect the people was left.'[206]

Orwell found fault with the character of Spartacus, who came across
as peculiarly passive, neither the 'visionary' nor simply 'power-hungry'.
He ought to have failed 'because of the impossibility of combining power
with righteousness'. The story therefore failed because 'the central problem
of revolution has been avoided, or at least has not been solved'.[207] By
this, he seems to mean that the book is both appreciative of the power

---

[203]Koestler, *Gladiators*, p. 317.
[204]Koestler, *Gladiators*, p. 130.
[205]Koestler, *Gladiators*, p. 204.
[206]Koestler, *Gladiators*, p. 310.
[207]Orwell, 'Arthur Koestler', CW, XVI, p. 395.

of revolutionary visions and the need for them, aware of the misery that follows their failure, yet unable to articulate a revolutionary path that does not detour into corruption or rush headlong to failure. He was not much more impressed by the later works in Koestler's trilogy either. *Darkness at Noon* tells the story of Rubashov, someone who 'follows the "law of detours" to the end';[208] but when the revolution turns on him, as the Russian Revolution had on the old Bolsheviks in Stalin's show trials of the later 1930s, he was without any ethical compass that could guide him to resisting his own condemnation and execution. The ends still justified the means, only now he was the murdered not the murderer. Orwell was resistant to the implications – Koestler 'comes near to claiming that revolutions are of their nature bad'. It is not a conclusion that is endorsed. Nor does he endorse these further implications of Koestler's novel: 'It is not merely that "power corrupts": so also do the ways of attaining power. Therefore, all efforts to regenerate society *by violent means* lead to the cellars of the Ogpu. Lenin leads to Stalin, and would have come to resemble Stalin if he happened to survive.'[209] Though there is much on these words that Orwell would have agreed with, there is no mistaking his discomfort with the thought that all violent revolutions are doomed to fail, even though he had not long before written a fable of just such a failure.

The third novel in the trilogy seemed even more troubling. By the time he wrote *Arrival and Departure* (1943), Koestler had begun to psychologize the motives of revolutionaries. Orwell bristled. A 'morbid guilt complex' may have driven the central character, Peter Slavek, to act in various ways. But so what? 'Marx's ultimate motives may well have been envy and spite, but this does not prove that his conclusions were false.' Koestler should have known that 'certain things have to be done, whether our reasons for doing them are "good" or "bad".' Koestler was heading into a 'blind alley' because of his inability to solve the central ethical problem of revolutions.[210] The solution, for Orwell, seemed to lie in shades of grey.

The problem, as Koestler saw, is that 'one must have a picture of the future'. There were two options. One was 'the earthly Paradise', and this is what Spartacus set out to achieve. This is also the vision that 'has haunted the imagination of Socialists, Anarchists and religious heretic for hundreds of years'. The other option is the religious one, to see 'this life as preparation for the next'. This last view was no longer credible, in Orwell's view (or Koestler's). The problem for Koestler is that he seems to have lost faith in the former too. '[H]is intelligence tells him that the Earthly Paradise is receding into the far distance and that what is actually ahead of is bloodshed, tyranny

---

[208]Koestler, *Gladiators*, p. 317.

[209]Orwell, 'Arthur Koestler', CW, XVI, p. 397.

[210]Orwell, 'Arthur Koestler', CW, XVI, p. 398.

and privation.' Orwell did not fully share the pessimism: 'It is quite possible that man's major problems will *never* be solved. But it is also unthinkable!' In the face of a very gloomy immediate future for humanity, Orwell's solution was to say that 'the real problem is how to restore the religious attitude while accepting death as final. Men can only be happy when they do not assume that the object of life is happiness.' In particular, they must abandon the belief that material prosperity – hedonism – was the essential foundation for human happiness and the good society.[211] The full meaning of these themes will be considered in the next section of this chapter, but what do they mean for the subject of revolution?

The bulk of the final paragraph of his Koestler essay needs to be quoted, because Orwell's conclusion is, by his standards, cryptic.

> The Russian Revolution, the central event in Koestler's life, started out with high hopes. We forget these things now, but a quarter of a century ago it was confidently expected that the Russian Revolution would lead to Utopia. Obviously this has not happened. Koestler is too acute not to see this, and too sensitive not to remember the original objective ... Therefore he draws the conclusion: This is what revolutions lead to. There is nothing for it but to be a 'short-term pessimist', i.e. to keep out of politics, make a sort of oasis within which you and your friends can remain sane, and hope that somehow things will be better in a hundred years. At the basis of this lies his hedonism, which leads him to think of the Earthly Paradise as desirable. Perhaps, however, whether desirable or not, it isn't possible. Perhaps some degree of suffering is ineradicable from human life, perhaps the choice before Man is always a choice of evils, perhaps even the aim of Socialism is not to make the world perfect but to make it better. All revolutions are failure, but they are not all the same failure. It is his unwillingness to admit this that has led Koestler's mind temporarily into a blind alley.[212]

The fact that revolutions (like the Russian) all fail does not mean that they all achieve nothing. Judged by the standard of whether they have created the perfect society, then of course they have failed. But is this standard the right one? Is not the most that we can hope for the revolution that makes things better, that fails better? Koestler was notorious for seeing only in black-or-white; if Orwell does not exactly see the world in technicolour, he can at least perceive shades of grey.

Koestler's consideration of revolutionary ethics continued in his essay collection *The Yogi and the Commissar* (published in 1945). Orwell

---

[211]Orwell, 'Arthur Koestler', CW, XVI, p. 399.
[212]Orwell, 'Arthur Koestler', CW, XVI, p. 400.

reviewed the book in an important essay, 'Catastrophic Gradualism'. The title referred to a theory used 'whenever it is necessary to justify some action which conflicts with the sense of decency of the average human being'. It has two parts: (1) nothing can be achieved without 'bloodshed, lies, tyranny and injustice'; (2) nothing can be achieved very fast, change may be imperceptibly slow. Thus, Stalin can be defended: the methods may be monstrous (but that is inevitable); the achievements may seem elusive (but that too is inevitable); this is the only way progress can happen. 'The formula usually employed is "You can't make an omelette without breaking eggs". And if one replies, "Yes, but where is the omelette?", the answer is likely to be: "Oh well, you can't expect everything to happen all in a moment".'[213] The ill consequences of revolutions shouldn't be used against them. Orwell thought the theory absurd. 'Crime follows crime, one ruling class replaces another, the Tower of Babel rises and falls, but one mustn't resist the process – indeed, one must be ready to applaud any piece of scoundrelism that comes off – because in some mystical way, in the sight of God, or perhaps in the sight of Marx, this is Progress.'[214]

Was this, then, the end of the road for revolution in Orwell's mind? Actually he remained resistant to the conclusion that revolutions achieved nothing. A few years later in his famous manifesto of anti-Communism, Koestler wrote:

> It is ... true that in the face of revolting injustice the only honourable attitude is to revolt, and to leave introspection for better times. But if we survey history and compare the lofty aims, in the name of which revolutions were started, and the sort end to which they came, we see again and again how a polluted civilization pollutes its own revolutionary offspring.[215]

Orwell had some sympathy for the position. Revolutions were necessary, could be noble in aspiration, but they fell short. Koestler said the same in *The Yogi and the Commissar*. These were ideal types: the commissar was the revolutionary; the yogi was the saint, whose goal was to reform himself, in particular to renounce the lust for power. Orwell, at least in 1944, thought that a synthesis of both was necessary, and however unlikely in the short term, not impossible. (The terms of this discussion are reminiscent of Orwell's earlier discussion of Charles Dickens and his politics.) It is true that 'throughout history, one revolution after another – although usually producing a temporary relief, such as a sick man gets by turning over in

---

[213]Orwell, 'Catastrophic Gradualism', November 1945, CW, XVII, p. 342.

[214]Orwell, 'Catastrophic Gradualism', CW, XVII, p. 343.

[215]Arthur Koestler in Richard Crossman (ed.), *The God That Failed* (New York: Bantam, 1949, reprinted 1972), p. 17.

bed – has simply led to a change of masters, because no serious effort has
been made to eliminate the power instinct'. This will not happen – nor will
a genuine Socialist revolution that improves the human lot – 'without a
change in the individual heart. To that extent, though no further, the Yogi is
right as against the Commissar.'[216]

Orwell took stock of his political thinking in a series of short essays for
the *Manchester Evening News* in January and February 1946. They surveyed
the various shades of opinion amongst those who revolted against the values
of machine civilization, and especially the view that all other things should
be traded for economic security.[217] The second essay 'What Is Socialism?' is
particularly interesting as a statement of his beliefs by this time. Socialism
before the 1930s was, in Orwell's view, always 'in some sense Utopian': it
was always imagined, not something that had been tried out, and 'it was
bound up with the idea of liberty and equality'. It had a visionary quality:
'Only let economic injustice be brought to an end and all other forms of
tyranny would vanish also. The age of human brotherhood would begin,
and war, crime, disease, poverty, and overwork would be things of the past.'
Orwell held fast to this original Socialist vision, indeed he was seeking to
restore it to vitality. '[T]he Utopians, at present a scattered minority, are
the true upholders of the Socialist tradition'. However, in the 1930s, things
darkened. Soviet Russia provided an example of Socialism in practice, but
'the Russian Communists were forced to abandon, at any rate temporarily,
some of the dreams with which they had started out'. The things abandoned
included 'economic equality', 'freedom of speech' and 'internationalism' – all
of course integral components of what Orwell thought Socialism was about.
Even worse Nazism – National Socialism – embodied Socialist features 'in
one of the most cruel and cynical regimes the world has ever seen'. Where
did that leave Socialism and revolution? Orwell summarized – seemingly in
agreement – Koestler's argument:

[R]evolutions have to happen, there can be no moral progress without
drastic economic changes, and yet the revolutionary wastes his labour
if he loses touch with ordinary human decency. Somehow the dilemma
of ends and means must be resolved. We must be able to act, even to use
violence, and yet not be corrupted by action. In specific political terms,
this means rejection of Russian Communism on the one hand and of
Fabian gradualism on the other.

Socialists have to believe 'the "earthly paradise"' to be possible – 'Socialism
is in the last analysis an optimistic creed and not east to square with the

---

[216]Orwell, 'Catastrophic Gradualism', CW, XVII, pp. 343–4.
[217]Orwell, '1. The Intellectual Revolt', 24 January 1946, CW, XVIII, p. 57.

doctrine of original sin'. Absolutely crucial for Orwell – and this is what he added to Koestler's analysis of revolution – is the claim that 'a Socialist is not obliged to believe that human society can actually be made perfect, but almost any Socialist does believe that it could be a great deal better than it is at present'. People who no longer suffer injustice and inhumanity will be better people and able to build a better world. 'The basis of Socialism is humanism.'[218]

Orwell did not always use terms consistently. In this 1946 article he sounds like a Utopian, but his political thought was, as we will see later, generally anti-Utopian (even here) in that it was rooted in a rejection of the idea that a perfect human society could be achieved. All revolutions which aimed at this perfection would fail, but some failed better than others. At least in principle, a revolution that improved things was feasible. And even the hope invested in Utopianism was important in motivating people to keep on searching for a better future. We shall explore many of these themes further in the next section, but first need to refocus our attention on the subject of revolution.

We have moved a long way from *Animal Farm*, and can now return to the book. It tells, of course, a story of a revolution that was corrupted, very closely based on the Russian Revolution and its degeneration into Stalinist tyranny. It was, as we have seen, an attempt to destroy the 'Soviet myth' and revive Socialism.[219] Old Major, a pig, denounces the oppression of the animals of Manor Farm by human beings, and prophesies revolution: 'I do not know when that rebellion will come, it might be in a week or in a hundred years, but I know, as surely as I see this straw beneath my feet, that sooner or later justice will be done.' Major issues a warning, though: 'remember that in fighting against Man, we must not come to resemble him … no animal must ever tyrannise over his own blood'.[220] He tells the other animals of a dream 'of the golden future time', when the animals are and free from oppression.[221] Major is a sort of Marx figure; he dies before the revolution, which is nonetheless based on his ideas reduced to 'a complete system of thought'. It is led by three other pigs (Napoleon, Snowball and Squealer) – the Old Bolsheviks of Manor Farm, which is renamed Animal Farm following the revolution. Snowball represents Trotsky, and he is expelled from the farm by Napoleon and his trained dogs, his role in the original revolution gradually erased by lies and distortions of history, which the other animals drink up, drip by drip.

Initially the revolution is liberation. It is easily achieved, the animals are happy and for a time better off. Furthermore, it was not a conspiratorial

---

[218]Orwell, '2. What Is Socialism?', 31 January 1946, CW, XVIII, pp. 60–2.
[219]Orwell, 'Preface to the Ukrainian Edition …', *Animal Farm*, p. 113.
[220]Orwell, *Animal Farm*, pp. 5–6 (Penguin ed. p. 6).
[221]Orwell, *Animal Farm*, pp. 6–8 (Penguin ed. pp. 7–9).

revolution, but one supported by all. This is the Barcelona moment for the inhabitants of Animal Farm.[222] But Napoleon and the other pigs, supported by their trained canine killers, gradually turn the revolution to their advantage not that of the animals at large. Orwell's intentions are best gauged by looking at the Russian parallels. Napoleon is an amalgam of Lenin and Stalin,[223] and thus signals Orwell's acceptance of the view (one of the most debated matters among the Left of the later 1930s and 1940s) that the Russian Revolution was doomed from the start – it was the wrong kind of Revolution. As he put it elsewhere, even if power had remained with Lenin or Trotsky,

> there is no strong reason for thinking that the main lines of development would have been very different. Well before 1923 the seeds of a totalitarian society were quite plainly there. Lenin is, indeed, one of those politicians who win an undeserved reputation by dying prematurely. Had he lived, it is probably that he would either have been thrown out, like Trotsky, or would have kept himself in power by methods as barbarous, or nearly as barbarous, as those of Stalin.[224]

Later still, Orwell recounted the betrayal of Marxism in Russia at some length. Marx's vision, like Major's, was a noble one of 'a free and just society based on the principle of "to each according to his needs"'. But Marx's Russian followers abandoned much of his teaching, and so the Russian Revolution became no more than 'the seizure of power by a small body of classless professional revolutionaries, who claimed to represent the common people but were not chosen by them nor genuinely answerable to them'. The result was 'terrorism'. Things got worse, and, though Orwell does say this time that things 'developed in a direction of which Lenin would probably not have approved if he had lived longer', there is no doubt that tyranny and dictatorship were designed into the revolution from the start.[225]

A key turning point in *Animal Farm* comes when the pigs decide to keep the milk and apples produced on the farm for themselves rather than sharing them amongst all the animals. It is the point at which the road towards corruption of the revolution and betrayal of Major's principles is taken. Orwell highlighted its significance by adding some extra lines to the

---

[222]See also Morris Dickstein, '*Animal Farm*: History as Fable', in John Rodden (ed.), *The Cambridge Companion to George Orwell* (Cambridge: Cambridge University Press, 2007), ch. 11, pp. 138–9.

[223]The importance of this conflation is stressed in John Molyneux, 'Animal Farm Revisited', *International Socialism*, 2 (1989), reprinted in Flewers (ed.), *George Orwell: Enigmatic Socialist*, pp. 23–35.

[224]Orwell, 'Second Thoughts on James Burnham', May 1946, CW, XVIII, p. 274.

[225]Orwell, 'Marx and Russia', 15 February 1948, CW, XIX, pp. 268–9.

radio script: 'Do you think that is quite fair? – What, keep all the apples for themselves? – Aren't we to have any? – I thought they were going to be shared out equally.'[226] Even Snowball [Trotsky] was in agreement with the decision, once again emphasizing that things might have been little different if he rather than Napoleon [Stalin] had been in control.

The revolution was initially made by the animals, but they were led by their intellectual elite, the pigs, who soon grasped the initiative. Very quickly the revolution was being controlled not *by* the animals but *for* them. This is the core problem. The only way of averting the betrayal of the revolution would have been for the animals to seize democratic control. They were given little chance. Napoleon abolished the original Sunday meetings, which had exercised a degree of democracy, and ruthlessly suppressed opposition. It is not the case that there were no attempts to resist. Nine hens were killed when they objected to Napoleon's decision that their eggs would be confiscated. Four pigs, allegedly the agents of Snowball, had their throats ripped out by Napoleon's dogs, as part of series of purges associated with Snowball's exclusion.[227] Clover, a gentle mare and friend of the Stakhanovite carthorse, Boxer, reflected on the situation:

> If she could have spoken her thoughts, it would have been to say that this was not what they had aimed at when they had set themselves years ago to work for the overthrow of the human race. These scenes of terror and slaughter were not what they had looked forward to on that night when old Major first stirred them to rebellion. If she herself had had any picture of the future, it had been of a society of animals set free from hunger and the whip, all equal, each working according to his capacity, the strong protecting the weak ... Instead – she did not know why – they had come to a time when no one dared speak his mind, when fierce, growling dogs roamed everywhere, and when you had to watch your comrades torn to pieces after confessing to shocking crimes. There was no thought of rebellion or disobedience in her mind. She knew that even as things were they were far better off than they had been in the days of Jones [the original owner of Manor Farm], and that before all else it was needful to prevent the return of the human beings. Whatever happened she would remain faithful ... But still, it was not for this that she and all the other animals had hoped and toiled.[228]

The revolution was kept in being by a mixture of fear, coercion and genuine belief that things were not as bad as they had been even if not as good as

[226]Orwell, *Animal Farm*, pp. 16, 22–3, 153–4 (Penguin ed. pp. 17–8, 25–6; the radio script is not in the Penguin ed.).

[227]Orwell, *Animal Farm*, pp. 36, 51, 56 (Penguin ed. pp. 39–40, 56, 62).

[228]Orwell, *Animal Farm*, pp. 58–9 (Penguin ed. pp. 63–4).

hoped. Returning to the past was a greater fear than the horrors of the present. Major had awoken the animals to their inherent strength: Napoleon had put them back to sleep. Immediately after Clover's reflections, the animals sang in mournful tones the utopian song of the revolution (Beasts of England). Napoleon, though, decreed that its dreams were now achieved and that it would be replaced by an anodyne song celebrating the achievement of their goals. The bleating of the sheep stifled any possible protest.[229] Things got worse, but the animals continued to believe the lies told to them, in defiance even of their own experience.

The book ends with Napoleon, in discussion with neighbouring farmers, renouncing the revolution, indicating that he would abolish the word 'comrade' and return Animal Farm to its original name of Manor Farm.[230] The pigs squabbled with the farmers anyway, and the book, as we have already seen, closed with these lines:

> Twelve voices were shouting in anger, and they were all alike. No question, now, what had happened to the faces of the pigs. The creature outside looked from pig to man, and from man to pig, and from pig to man again: but already it was impossible to say which was which.[231]

The bluntness of this has probably done more than anything else to establish the view that revolutions just replace one set of masters with another, very likely worse. But this does not cohere with other things Orwell said about revolution at this time and later. Furthermore, as seen, the book does suggest moments at which rebellion or resistance began, only to be crushed ruthlessly. Even more, in words that echo some of Orwell's other writing, towards the end, when only the donkey Benjamin could remember the past – from which memory he concluded, 'hunger, hardship and disappointment [were] … the unalterable law of life' – 'the animals never gave up hope'. The animal republic, Major's utopia, 'was still believed in. Some day it was coming: it might not be soon, it might not be within the lifetime of any animal now living, but still it was coming …'.[232] This persistence of hope, this belief that a better revolution might one day possible, was important to Orwell. Even a failed revolution might perpetuate its own dreams. Only months after finishing *Animal Farm*, Orwell told a correspondent that 'I would support the USSR against Germany because I think the USSR cannot altogether escape its past and retains enough of the original ideas of the Revolution to make it a more hopeful phenomenon than Nazi Germany'.[233]

---

[229]Orwell, *Animal Farm*, pp. 59–60 (Penguin ed. pp. 64–5).
[230]Orwell, *Animal Farm*, pp. 93–4 (Penguin ed. pp. 100–2).
[231]Orwell, *Animal Farm*, p. 95 (Penguin ed. p. 102).
[232]Orwell, *Animal Farm*, pp. 87–8 (Penguin ed. pp. 94–5).
[233]Orwell to Noel Willmett, 18 May 1944, CW, XVI, p. 191.

It should be possible to see why Orwell's own accounts of what that book was intended to say can be taken at face value. In December 1946, responding to some queries from Dwight Macdonald about the meaning of *Animal Farm*, Orwell wrote:

> Of course I intended it primarily as a satire on the Russian revolution. But I did mean it to have a wider application in so much that I meant that *that kind* of revolution (violent conspiratorial revolution, led by unconsciously power-hungry people) can only lead to a change of masters. I meant the moral to be that revolutions only effect a radical improvement when the masses are alert and know how to chuck out their leaders as soon as the latter have done their job. The turning point of the story was supposed to be when the pigs kept the milk and apples for themselves (Kronstadt). If the other animals had had the sense to put their foot down then, it would have been all right. If people think I am defending the *status quo*, that is, I think, because they have grown pessimistic and assume that there is no alternative except dictatorship or *laissez-faire* capitalism. In the case of Trotskyists, there is the added complication that they feel responsible for events in the USSR up to about 1926 and have to assume that a sudden degeneration took place about that date. Whereas I think the whole process was foreseeable – and was foreseen by a few people, eg. Bertrand Russell – from the very nature of the Bolshevik party. What I was trying to say was, 'You can't have a revolution unless you make it for yourself; there is no such thing as a benevolent dictat[or]ship.'[234]

Orwell's commitment remained after the war, as it had been in 1937, to *revolutionary* Socialism, even though he was much more aware by this time of the potential of revolutions to fail. In *Nineteen Eighty-Four*, he put into O'Brien's mouth the statement:

> We know that no one ever seizes power with the intention of relinquishing it. Power is not a means; it is an end. One does not establish a dictatorship in order to safeguard a revolution; one makes the revolution in order to safeguard the dictatorship. The object of persecution is persecution. The object of torture is torture. The object of power is power.[235]

But this is not Orwell speaking. Revolutions don't have to end in dictatorship, or have no other purpose but the lust for power. This is why he resisted

---

[234]Orwell to Dwight Macdonald, 5 December 1946, CW, XVIII, p. 507. As early as 1920, Russell, though sympathetic to the aims of Socialism, found 'it impossible to believe that later developments [in Soviet Russia] will realize more fully the Communist ideal' there – Bertrand Russell, *The Practice and Theory of Bolshevism* (Nottingham: Spokesman, 1995; reprint of 2nd ed. 1949; orig, ed. 1920), p. 119.
[235]Orwell, *Nineteen Eighty-Four* [CW, IX] (London: Secker & Warburg, 1987), p. 276 (Penguin ed. p. 302).

the crude psychologizing that Koestler could indulge in. Things could be otherwise; and even an imperfect humanity, whatever dark motives drove individuals, could – or so one had to hope – be the agent of social justice and liberty. In short, Orwell's final verdict on revolution was not O'Brien's. It was this: 'The most encouraging fact about revolutionary activity is that, although it always fails, it always continues.'[236]

## (c) Nostalgia, Progress and Utopia

Returning from Spain, Orwell could relish again the things that made England special to him – and at the same time express his concern about the complacency of a nation that was an island in more senses than one:

> Down here it was still the England I had known in my childhood: the railway-cuttings smothered in wild flowers, the deep meadows where the great shining horses browse and meditate, the slow-moving streams bordered by willows, the green bosoms of the elms, the larkspurs in the cottage gardens; and then the huge peaceful wilderness of outer London, the barges on the miry river, the familiar streets, the posters telling of cricket matches and Royal weddings, the men in bowler hats, the pigeons in Trafalgar Square, the red buses, the blue policemen – all sleeping the deep, deep sleep of England, from which I sometimes fear that we shall never wake till we are jerked out of it by the roar of bombs.[237]

There is an unmistakable note of nostalgia in this – though Orwell's tone of voice is harder to judge – as it is elsewhere in his writing. *Coming Up for Air* (1939) was suffused with a melancholy sense of the passing of a wholesome and stable world. George Bowling's effort to remember and then revisit the tranquillity and security of his childhood in Little Binfield is, however, the basis for a more sophisticated exploration of nostalgia – its attractions and its problems – than has often been allowed.[238] Consider, for example, this passage:

> [I]n a manner of speaking I *am* sentimental about my childhood – not my own particular childhood, but the civilisation which I grew up in

---

[236]Orwell, 'Introduction to *British Pamphleteers*, Volume I, edited by George Orwell and Reginald Reynolds', written Spring 1947?, published November 1948, CW, XIX, p. 109.

[237]Orwell, *Homage to Catalonia*, p. 187 (Penguin ed. p. 196).

[238]I am indebted here to a number of critics. Loraine Saunders, *The Unsung Artistry of George Orwell: The Novels from* Burmese Days *to* Nineteen Eighty-Four (Aldershot: Ashgate, 2008) is particularly good at defending the novels of the 1930s from the simplistic readings and cursory dismissal they often receive. On *Coming Up for Air*, I have found helpful Joseph Brooker,

and which is now, I suppose, just about at its last kick. And fishing is somehow typical of that civilisation. As soon as you think of fishing you think of things that don't belong to the modern world. The very idea of sitting all day under a willow tree beside a quiet pool – and being able to find a quiet pool to sit beside – belongs to the time before the war, before the radio, before aeroplanes, before Hitler. There's a kind of peacefulness even in the names of English coarse fish. Roach, rudd, dace, bleak, barbell, bream, gudgeon, pike, chub, cap, tench. They're solid kind of names. The people who made them up hadn't heard of machine guns, they didn't live in terror of the sack or spend their time eating aspirins, going to the pictures, and wondering how to keep out of the concentration camps.[239]

Yes there is nostalgia here, the memory of a quieter world. But here and throughout the book there is an awareness of the limitations of nostalgia, an acknowledgement of 'sentimentality'. There is acknowledgement in the book, too, that the past was not all fishing and Sunday church ('the drunks are puking in the yard'). He remembers the stench and the flies – but then reflects 'which would you sooner listen to, a bluebottle or a bombing plane?'[240] Nor is the book sentimental about boyhood, showing the attractions of violence and cruelty even in Lower Binfield when 'Vicky's at Windsor' still.[241] Life was harder then, 'people ... worked harder, lived less comfortably, and died more painfully'.[242] Throughout, simple nostalgia is punctuated. The pool in which the young Bowling spotted an enormous carp remained unfished even in childhood and youth. 'I never went back. One never goes back.'[243] The nostalgia becomes weaponized: it becomes a critique of the age of the machine and of totalitarianism, but not a realistic way forward. There was something wrong with the modern world. At the heart of the critique was the sense that the fundamental values of a decent society – love of nature, a sense of good and evil, security – were being lost. Nowadays, in 'this life we lead – I don't mean human life in general, I mean

---

'Forbidden to Dream Again: Orwell and Nostalgia', *English*, 55 (2006), pp. 281–97; Patricia Rae, '"There'll be no more fishing this side of the grave": Radical Nostalgia in George Orwell's *Coming Up for Air*', in Tammy Clewell (ed.), *Modernism and Nostalgia: Bodies, Locations, Aesthetics* (Basingstoke: Palgrave Macmillan, 2013), pp. 149–65; Christine Berberish, 'A Revolutionary in Love with the 1900s: Orwell in Defence of "Old England"', in Alberto Lázaro (ed.), *The Road from George Orwell: His Achievement and Legacy* (Bern: Peter Lang, 2001), pp. 33–52; and Laura Coffey, *The Recovery of History through Memory and Nostalgia in the Mid Twentieth-Century Novel* (PhD Thesis, Birkbeck College, University of London, 2005).
[239]Orwell, *Coming Up for Air* [CW, VII] (London: Secker & Warburg, 1986), p. 76. The Penguin Classic ed. has the same pagination as CW.
[240]Orwell, *Coming Up for Air*, pp. 31, 56.
[241]Orwell, *Coming Up for Air*, pp. 66–70, 31.
[242]Orwell, *Coming Up for Air*, p. 109.
[243]Orwell, *Coming Up for Air*, p. 81.

life in this particular age and this particular country – we don't do the things we want to … There's time for everything except the things worth doing.'[244] People before had less concern for the future:

> [I]t's precisely in a settled period, a period when civilisation seems to stand on its four legs like an elephant, that such things as a future life don't matter. It's easy enough to die if the things you care about are going to survive. You've had your life, you're getting tired, it's time to go underground – that's how people used to see it. Individually they were finished, but their way of life would continue. Their good and evil would remain good and evil.[245]

Before setting off on his return to Lower Binfield, Bowling visits his friend Porteous, a retired school master living in an introverted world of books and literature from the past. Porteous can see nothing of the changes around him, he thinks England is the world and the world will never change. 'But what about,' thinks Bowling, 'the new kind of men from eastern Europe, the streamlined men who think in slogans and talk in bullets?'[246] When Bowling does return to Lower Binfield in search of 'peace and quiet', he discovers that the place is transformed. The only thing unchanged is the church; everywhere else it was hard to see much of the past remaining in the present.[247] Symbolic of this was meeting his former love, Elsie. She didn't recognize Bowling, while he found her a 'great round-shouldered hag', 'shapeless', 'a kind of soft lumpy cylinder, like a bag of meal'.[248] There comes a moment when Bowling fears that Hitler's war has begun, though it turns out that a bomb had been accidentally dropped on the town by a bomber from the local airfield. And the fishing pond with the enormous carp …?

One never goes back. Bowling had returned to Lower Binfield to find an answer to the question 'can we go back to the life we used to live or is it gone for ever?' The answer was clear: 'The old life's finished, and to go about looking for it is just a waste of time. There's no way back to Lower Binfield.'[249] What was worse,

> *It's all going to happen.* All the things you've got at the back of your mind, the things you're terrified of, the things that you tell yourself are just a nightmare or only happen in foreign countries. The bombs, the food-queues, the rubber truncheons, the barbed wire, the coloured

---

[244]Orwell, *Coming Up for Air*, p. 82.
[245]Orwell, *Coming Up for Air*, p. 111.
[246]Orwell, *Coming Up for Air*, pp. 168–9.
[247]Orwell, *Coming Up for Air*, p. 201.
[248]Orwell, *Coming Up for Air*, pp. 217–18.
[249]Orwell, *Coming Up for Air*, p. 237.

shirts,[250] the slogans, the enormous faces, the machine guns squirting out of bedroom windows. It's all going to happen, I know it – at any rate, I knew it then.[251]

Those last words should remind us that Orwell is not Bowling. There is no going back, but is there a going forward? Is totalitarian horror inevitable? *Coming Up for Air* is a critique of the politics of nostalgia, though the nostalgia does nonetheless convey the message that what is happening to Europe in the 1930s is destroying the foundations of a decent and human society. As Bowling tries to tell Porteous, the changes they were witnessing were different in kind, and threatened not just a quiet corner of merry England. They threatened the fundamental values of Western civilization itself, values that Socialism both shared and could improve. Nonetheless, Orwell left open the question of whether a better future than the one Bowling feared was possible.

These nostalgic tones have, of course, helped to fuel the idea that Orwell was always a conservative of sorts, or even an enemy of progress. Even some who knew him well accepted such a view of him. His publisher, Fredric Warburg, commented:

> I don't think he was ever a socialist. After all, socialism is supposed to be a creed in favour of progress and efficiency. And one of the things that Orwell has a most eloquent passage about in *The Road to Wigan Pier*, is what a menace to everything progress is ... He didn't like progress; he preferred the old ways, the traditional ways, which is surely not the road of socialism.[252]

Just as surely, though, this is going too far. Orwell, unlike George Bowling, accepted both the inevitability of change and the possibility of progress (most of the time). 'Whatever else history may do, it never travels backwards.'[253] He retained always a belief in the possibility of a better future, though his assessment of its imminence or likelihood varied.

Fundamental to Orwell's thinking about these matters was the distinction between material progress, on the one hand, and moral or intellectual progress on the other. In a review of two of H.G. Wells's film scenarios, Orwell diagnosed the key flaw in Wells's imagination of future worlds as being:

> ... his confusion of mechanical progress with justice, liberty and common decency. The kind of mind that accepts the machine and despises the past

---

[250]Presumably black or brown, rather than, say, pink.
[251]Orwell, *Coming Up for Air*, p. 238.
[252]Coppard & Crick, *Orwell Remembered*, pp. 193–4.
[253]George Orwell, 'Culture and Democracy', 22 November 1941, CW, XIII, p. 75.

is supposed to be, automatically, the kind of mind that longs for a world of free and equal human beings.[254]

This assumption, Orwell notes, is 'quite false'. The confusion was between technological advance and moral or social progress. The terminology is unstable, however, and 'progress' might be used for either concept, though when Orwell sounded most pessimistic about 'progress', it was moral progress that he meant. In his 'Imaginary Interview' with Jonathan Swift, 'Orwell' asked 'Swift' to 'admit that we have made a certain amount of progress'; Swift replied:

> Progress in quantity yes. The buildings are taller and the vehicles move faster, Human beings are more numerous and commit greater follies. A battle kills a million where it used to kill a thousand. And in the matter of great men, as you still call them, I admit that your age outdoes mine Whereas previously some petty tyrant was considered to have reached the highest point of human fame if he laid waste a single province and pillaged half a dozen towns, your great men nowadays can devastate whole *continents* and condemn entire races of men to *slavery*.[255]

Though Orwell would never deny the reality of material and technological improvement, he could sound decidedly pessimistic about the prospect of real moral progress, or even about the chances that what he called 'decency' might survive. In a review of a book attacking public schools, he could write this:

> Again, when he [T.C. Worsley] says that the public schools breed an undemocratic mentality, he appears to mean that they do not turn out boys who can accommodate themselves to a world of equal suffrage, free speech, intellectual tolerance and international co-operation. This would be a valid criticism if any such world lay ahead of us. But unfortunately that version of democracy is even more a lost cause than feudalism. What is ahead of us is not an age of reason but an age of bombing planes.[256]

In his essay on Henry Miller and the writers of the 1930s, written just at the outbreak of the Second World War, Orwell gave his verdict on the

[254]George Orwell, 'Review of *A Hero of Our Own Times* by Mikhail Yurevich Lermontoff; *Priest Island* by L.E. Grant Wilson; *Film Stories* by H.G. Wells', June 1940, CW, XII, p. 191.
[255]George Orwell, 'Imaginary Interview: George Orwell and Jonathan Swift', November 1942, CW, XIV, pp. 157–8.
[256]George Orwell, 'Review of *Barbarians and Philistines: Democracy and the Public Schools* by T.C. Worsley', September 1940, CW, XII, p. 261.

illusions of that sorry decade: 'Progress and reaction have both turned out to be swindles.' He seemed to hold out little hope as the decade descended into war:

> What is quite obviously happening, war or no war, is the break up of laissez-faire capitalism and of the liberal-Christian culture. Until recently the full implications of this were not foreseen, because it was generally imagined that Socialism could preserve and even enlarge the atmosphere of liberalism. It is now beginning to be realised how false this idea was. Almost certainly we are moving into an age of totalitarian dictatorships – and age in which freedom of thought will be at first a deadly sin and later on a meaningless abstraction. The autonomous individual is going to be stamped out of existence.[257]

Without moral progress, scientific and material progress can actually make things worse. 'So long as the world tendency is towards nationalism and totalitarianism, scientific progress simply helps it along.'[258]

On balance, though, Orwell's optimism outweighed his pessimism (in spite of appearances to the contrary). Thinking of Victorian slums and Victorian writers, he noted that the former had been improved and that no contemporary writer could share the inhuman social attitudes of the latter. So, he said: 'Progress does happen, hard though it may be to believe it, in this age of concentration camps and big beautiful bombs.'[259] Importantly, this was moral progress, an improvement in social attitudes to the working class. Orwell was particularly alert to the lazy anti-progressive ideas of reactionary thinkers. His contempt for Chesterton's bald assertion that 'there are no new ideas' led Orwell to what may be his most eloquent account of human moral and intellectual progress. Chesterton's idea – shared by many – 'is rooted in the fear of progress'. It implies that 'what will never come – since it has never come before – is that hated, dreaded thing, a world of free and equal human beings'.

> In fact, there *are* new ideas. The idea that an advanced civilisation need not rest on slavery is a relatively new idea, for instance: it is a good deal younger than the Christian religion. But even if Chesterton's dictum were true, it could only be true in the sense that a statue is contained in every block of stone. Ideas may not change, but emphasis shifts constantly. It could be claimed, for example, that the most important part of Marx's theory is contained in the saying: 'Where your treasure is, there will

---

[257]George Orwell, 'Inside the Whale', March 1940, CW, XII, pp. 110–11.
[258]George Orwell, 'As I Please', 24, 12 May 1944, CW, XVI, p. 184.
[259]George Orwell, 'As I Please', 1, 3 December 1943, CW, XVI, p. 14.

your heart be also'. But before Marx developed it, what force had that saying had? Who had paid any attention to it? Who had inferred from it – what it certainly implies – that laws, religions and moral codes are all a superstructure built over existing property relations? It was Christ, according to the gospel, who uttered the text, but it was Marx who brought it to life. And ever since he did so the motives of politicians, priests, judges, moralists and millionaires have been under the deepest suspicion – which, of course, is why they hate him so much.[260]

Even after the war, as his hopes for a real Socialist revolution faded and he found in the Labour government about as much as might be expected in an age of lowered expectations, Orwell was still clear that 'there is such a thing as intellectual progress, so that the ideas of one age are sometimes demonstrably less silly than those of the last'.[261] The remarks were, though, balanced by what may be Orwell's final explicit reflections on the subject of nostalgia. 'There is now a widespread idea that nostalgic feelings about the past are inherently vicious. One ought, apparently, to live in a continuous present, a minute-to-minute cancellation of memory, and if one thinks of the past at all it should merely be in order to thank God that we are so much better than we used to be.'[262] Put like this, the folly of believing that holding on to the good things of the past is somehow incompatible with fighting for progress is all too plain. You can believe in the need to retain both liberal freedoms and the space to take delight in the natural world and also believe that 'there can be no more question of restoring the Edwardian age than of reviving Albigensianism'.[263] At much the same time, Orwell admitted that 'the shadow of the atomic bomb' made it difficult 'to talk confidently about progress'; but *if* the world were not destroyed by atomic weapons, then 'there are many reasons ... for thinking that the present age is a good deal better than the last one'.[264] This was all from the man supposedly overwhelmed by morbid pessimism at the time he was writing *Nineteen Eighty-Four*.

While he valued progress, and thought it real enough, if slow to come about, Orwell nonetheless, as we have seen, loathed something that he usually called mechanization. This loathing often comes across as a species of nostalgia, but there was more to it than a regret for the passing of the remembered, though possibly imaginary, world of his youth. He wanted to protect Socialism against hedonism, and the material improvements brought

---

[260]George Orwell, 'As I Please', 13, 25 February 1944, CW, XVI, pp. 104–5.
[261]George Orwell, 'Review of *Great Morning* by Osbert Sitwell', July–September 1948, CW, XIX, pp. 396–7.
[262]Orwell, 'Review of *Great Morning*', CW, XIX, p. 397.
[263]Orwell, 'Review of *Great Morning*', CW, XIX, p. 396.
[264]George Orwell, 'George Gissing', May–June 1948?, CW, XIX, p. 347.

by mechanization could easily lead to the worship of plenty and comfort as the highest goods.

> Man needs warmth, society, leisure, comfort and security: he also needs solitude, creative work and the sense of wonder. If he recognised this he could use the products of science and industrialism eclectically, applying always the same test: does this make me more human or less human? He would then learn that the highest happiness does not lie in relaxing, resting, playing poker, drinking and making love simultaneously. And the instinctive horror which all sensitive people feel at the mechanisation of life would be seen not to be a mere sentimental archaism, but to be fully justified, For man only stays human by preserving larges patches of simplicity in his life, while the tendency of many modern inventions – in particular the film, the radio and the aeroplane – is to weaken his consciousness, dull his curiosity, and, in general, drive him nearer to the animals.[265]

The attitude was not nostalgic ('sentimental archaism'), but rooted in an anti-hedonistic analysis of human need. Certainly, this meant that there were a lot of things that human beings should hold on to and ensure were not expunged from the world, as George Bowling appreciated in his own fashion. At bottom, these were the simple pleasures and the common decencies. Orwell produced a series of essays for the *Evening Standard* celebrating the pleasures of an open coal fire; the ideal English pub (The Moon under Water: 'uncompromisingly Victorian'); the perfect cup of tea (if there is one piece of Orwellian advice that is worth taking, it is that 'one should pour tea into the cup first'); and good English cooking ('kippers, Yorkshire pudding, Devonshire cream, muffins and crumpets', various sauces, Oxford marmalade, Stilton and Wensleydale cheese, Cox's Orange Pippins, and so on).[266] Orwell's taste is not everyone's: his point that the French don't have a word for suet might for some of us constitute a clinching argument against Brexit.

But it was delight in the natural world that showed Orwell at this best, and which is so powerfully present in his work, from the landscapes of Burma in his first novel to the trip into the countryside taken by Winston Smith and Julia in his last.[267] He recalls from his miserable days at St Cyprians the small consolations, 'the pleasure of keeping caterpillars – the silky green

---

[265]George Orwell, 'Pleasure Spots', January 1946, CW, XVIII, p. 32.

[266]George Orwell, 'The Case for the Open Fire', December 1945, CW, XVII, pp. 419–20; 'The Moon under Water', February 1946, CW, XVIII, pp. 98–100; 'A Nice Cup of Tea', January 1946, CW, XVIII, pp. 33–35; 'In Defence of English Cooking', December 1945, CW, XVII, pp. 446–8.

[267]See now Rebecca Solnit, *Orwell's Roses* (London: Granta, 2021).

and purple puss-moth, the ghostly green poplar-hawk, the privet hawk', and 'the excitement of dredging the dew-ponds on the Downs for enormous newts with orange-coloured bellies'.[268] An *Evening Standard* essay even managed to find something like perfection in the English climate, listing the natural delights of each month ('November – Raging gales. The smell of rubbish fires').[269] But nothing else in his writing matches Orwell's glorious celebration of Spring. He stressed the wonders of the under-appreciated toad, which 'has about the most beautiful eye of any living creature', and tells of their emergence in the Spring into 'intense sexiness' and reproduction. But this appreciation of the natural world was not just a nostalgia for boyhood pleasures. Even in the grime of the city, nature could be enjoyed:

> The point is that the pleasures of Spring are available to everybody, and cost nothing. Even in the most sordid street the coming of Spring will register itself by some sign or other, if it is only a brighter blue between the chimney pots or the vivid green of an elder sprouting on a blitzed site. Indeed it is remarkable how Nature goes on existing unofficially, as it were, in the very heart of London. I have seen a kestrel flying over the Deptford gasworks, and I have heard a first-rate performance by a blackbird in the Euston Road. There must be some hundreds of thousands, if not millions, of birds living inside the four-mile radius, and it is a rather pleasing thought that none of them pays a halfpenny of rent.[270]

Orwell worried, though, that his delight in nature might seem like sentimental escapism:

> [I]s it politically reprehensible, while we are all groaning ... under the shackles of the capitalist system, to point out that life is frequently more worth living because of a blackbird's song, a yellow elm tree in October, or some other natural phenomenon which does not cost money and does not have what the editors of Left-wing newspapers call a class angle?[271]

The attitude might be thought 'sentimental' on two grounds, and Orwell thought there were two things behind this. One was the concern that the enjoyment of nature could encourage quietism, making people satisfied with a life that they should be fighting to improve; the other, the fear that the attitude was rooted in a reactionary and anti-progressive rejection of

---

[268]George Orwell, 'Such, Such Were the Joys', 1939–48?, CW, XIX, p. 367.
[269]George Orwell, '"Bad" Climates are Best', February 1946, CW, XVIII, pp. 90–2.
[270]George Orwell, 'Some Thoughts on the Common Toad', April 1946, CW, XVIII, pp. 238–9.
[271]Orwell, 'Some Thoughts on the Common Toad', CW, XVIII, p. 239.

machines and technology. Orwell rejected these attitudes. The question, as always, was what sort of life Socialism could make possible:

> Certainly we ought to be discontented, we ought not simply to find out ways of making the best of a bad job, and yet if we kill all pleasure in the actual process of life, what sort of future are we preparing for ourselves? If a man cannot enjoy the return of Spring, why should he be happy in a labour-saving Utopia? What will he do with the leisure that the machine will give him? I have always suspected that if our economic and political problems are ever really solved, life will become simpler instead of more complex, and that the sort of pleasure one gets from finding the first primrose will loom larger that the sort of pleasure one gets from eating an ice to the tune of a Wurlitzer. I think that by retaining one's childhood love of such things as trees, fishes, butterflies and ... toads, one makes a peaceful and decent future a little more probable, and that by preaching the doctrine that nothing is to be admired except steel and concrete, one merely makes it a little surer that human beings will have no outlet for their surplus energy except in hatred and leader worship.[272]

It's a lot to hope for from the common toad, but not the least of the pleasures that Orwell took from the enjoyment of Spring and the beauty of the toad's eye was the thought that 'they can't stop you enjoying it'. He ended the essay with this thought: 'The atom bombs are piling up in the factories, the police are prowling through the cities, the lies are streaming from the loudspeakers, but the earth is still going around the sun, and neither the dictators nor the bureaucrats, deeply as they disapprove of the process, are able to prevent it.'[273] There are some fundamental things – of nature and of culture too – that must belong to a decent future as much as they may have also belonged to the past.

The decencies of public life were just as important as the quiet enjoyment of small, quotidian pleasures. One loss that Orwell lamented – the loss of religious faith – underlay much of his concern about the threats to political decency.

> Material progress, which is necessary if the average human being is to be anything better than a drudge, has only been achieved at a fearful price. Somehow the religious attitude to life must be restored, and yet the only body of doctrine available to the Western world is one which the great mass of people are obviously less and less willing to accept.[274]

---

[272]Orwell, 'Some Thoughts on the Common Toad', CW, XVIII, p. 240.
[273]Orwell, 'Some Thoughts on the Common Toad', CW, XVIII, p. 240.
[274]George Orwell, 'Review of *Christianity and Democracy* by Jacques Maritain', June 1945, CW, XVII, p. 176.

This concern about the loss of faith was not an isolated one. In 1942 Orwell had declared that 'the major problem of our time is the decay of the belief in personal immortality'.[275] Reviewing C.S. Lewis, he lamented that 'the drift away from the churches, and the decay of the religious attitude to life, continue. One has only to look out of the nearest window to see that this is a disaster, but it is inevitable so long as the real reasons for it are not faced.'[276] This seems an odd thing for a lifelong atheist and opponent of organized religion (especially Catholicism) to say. The nearest that Orwell came to explaining what he meant was in an essay from March–April 1940, 'Notes on the Way'. He recounted a story:

> I thought of a rather cruel trick I once played on a wasp. He was sucking jam on my plate, and I cut him in half. He paid no attention, merely went on with his meal, while a tiny stream of jam trickled out of his severed œsophagus. Only when he tried to fly away did he grasp the dreadful thing that had happened to him. It is the same with modern man. The thing that has been cut away is his soul, and there was a period – twenty years, perhaps – during which he did not notice it.

This was not another exercise in nostalgia, nor a belief that the faith of the past could be recovered: 'it was absolutely necessary that the soul should be cut away'. (Elsewhere, Orwell was clear that the 'silly-clever' attempts to resuscitate Christian belief of people like C.S. Lewis were usually politically reactionary, 'an outflanking movement in the big counter-attack against the Left.'[277]) Conventional religion was a lie, 'a semi-conscious device for keeping the rich rich and the poor poor'. This lie that pervaded all of capitalist society had to be expunged: 'it was absolutely necessary to rip [it] out'. For the best part of two centuries, writers and thinkers had set about the task; most writers became 'destroyers, wreckers, saboteurs'. But they were sawing away at the branch on which they sat, and when that branch crashed to the ground everyone discovered that they had fallen, not into a 'bed of roses', but into a 'cesspool full of barbed wire'.[278] This led Orwell to one of his bleakest assessments of the world around him:

> It is as though in the space of ten years we had slid back into the Stone Age. Human types supposedly extinct for centuries, the dancing dervish, the robber chieftain, the Grand Inquisitor, have suddenly reappeared, not as inmates of lunatic asylums, but as the masters of the world. Mechanization

---

[275]George Orwell, 'Looking Back on the Spanish War', probably written 1942, CW, XIII, p. 510.
[276]George Orwell, 'Unpublished Review of *Beyond Personality* by C.S. Lewis', October 1944?, CW, XVI, p. 438.
[277]George Orwell, 'As I Please', 46, 27 October 1944, CW, XVI, pp. 440–1.
[278]George Orwell, 'Notes on the Way', March–April 1940, CW, XII, p. 124.

and a collective economy seemingly aren't enough. By themselves they lead merely to the nightmare we are now enduring; endless war and endless underfeeding for the sake of war, slave populations toiling behind barbed wire, women dragged shrieking to the block, cork-lined cellars where the executioner blows your brains out from behind. So it appears that amputation of the soul *isn't* just a simple surgical job, like having your appendix out. The wound has a tendency to go septic.[279]

If you believe that, without God and his sanctions, there is no possibility of moral order and therefore of building a good society, then there is little hope. It was the loss of 'belief in individual immortality' that mattered most, and mattered more than the loss of belief in God. 'There is little doubt that the modern cult of power-worship is bound up with the modern man's feelings that life here and now is the only life there is. If death ends everything, it becomes much harder to believe that you can be in the right even if you are defeated.'[280]

The challenge, though, was to fill the gap left by the death of faith and of the soul. There was no going back: 'I do not want the belief in life after death to return, and in any case it is not likely to return.'[281] 'The Kingdom of Heaven, old style, has definitely failed.' But Marxist Communism has also failed, 'whatever it may achieve materially'. The alternative? The only choice left is 'the much-derided "Kingdom of Earth", the concept of a society in which men know that they are mortal and are nevertheless willing to act as brothers'. We will not escape a miserable fate 'unless we can reinstate the belief in human brotherhood, without the need for a "next world" to give it meaning'.[282] Man will not 'salvage civilisation unless he can evolve a system of good and evil which is independent of heaven and hell'.[283]

This also came down to a rejection of hedonism, or the belief that material pleasure alone sufficed for human happiness. Hedonism was associated with capitalism. Discussing his view that capitalist societies had a lower birth rate than non-capitalist ones, Orwell claimed that it was 'due to something that goes with capitalist democracy, and that is the principle of hedonism'. Capitalist societies inculcated a 'consumer mentality'. 'The chief feature of life in capitalist society during the past twenty years has been an endless struggle to sell goods which there is never enough money to buy; and this has involved teaching ordinary people that things like cars, refrigerators, movies, cigarettes, fur coats and silk stockings are more important than

[279]Orwell, 'Notes on the Way', CW, XII, pp. 124–5.
[280]George Orwell, 'As I Please', 14, 3 March 1944, CW, XVI, p. 112.
[281]Orwell, 'As I Please', 14, CW, XVI, p. 113.
[282]Orwell, 'Notes on the Way', CW, XII, pp. 125–6.
[283]Orwell, 'As I Please', 14, CW, XVI, p. 113.

children.'[284] As so often Christianity and capitalism went hand-in-glove, and Orwell was to argue also that traditional Christianity had, in fact, reinforced hedonism, albeit through a logic of deferred gratification:

> But a normal human being does not want the Kingdom of Heaven: he wants life on earth to continue. This is not solely because he is 'weak', 'sinful', and anxious for a 'good time'. Most people get a fair amount of fun out of their lives, but on balance life is suffering, and only the very young or the very foolish imagine otherwise. Ultimately it is the Christian attitude which is self-interested and hedonistic, since the aim is always to get away from the painful struggle of earthly life and find eternal peace in some kind of Heaven or Nirvana. The humanist attitude is that the struggle must continue and that death is the price of life. 'Men must endure. Their going hence, even as their coming hither: Ripeness is all' – which is an un-Christian sentiment. Often there is a seeming truce between the humanist and the religious believer, but in fact their attitudes cannot be reconciled: one must choose between this world and the next. And the enormous majority of human beings, if they understood the issue, would choose this world.[285]

The cure for humanity's disease lay in this world, it lay with the humanist not the religious believer; but it also lay in a 'religious' rejection of hedonism. Orwell found this part of his message proclaimed by the unlikely pairing of Karl Marx and Adolf Hitler. Commenting on Marx's famous reference to religion as the 'opium of the people', Orwell noted that 'Marx did not say ... that religion is merely a dope handed out from above; he said that it is something people create for themselves, to supply a need that he recognized to be a real one'. Marx's words in full – 'religion is the sigh of the soul in a soulless world. Religion is the opium of the people' – imply his recognition 'that man does *not* live by bread alone, that hatred is *not* enough, that a world worth living in cannot be founded on "realism" and machine guns'.[286] Hitler also had 'grasped the falsity of the hedonistic attitude to life', and propounded views 'psychologically far sounder than any hedonistic conception of life'. He said to his people, '"I offer you struggle, danger and death," and as a result a whole nation flings itself at his feet'.[287] Communism and Fascism were therefore both attempts – albeit monstrous ones – that went beyond hedonism and materialism. The task for democratic Socialists was to do the same, but with the values of decency replacing those of the monstrosities that threatened the world with slavery and tyranny.

---

[284]Orwell, 'Culture and Democracy', CW, XIII, p. 69.
[285]Orwell, 'Lear, Tolstoy and the Fool', CW, XIX, p. 64.
[286]Orwell, 'Notes on the Way', CW, XII, p. 126.
[287]George Orwell, 'Review of *Mein Kampf* by Adolf Hitler', March 1940, CW, XII, p. 118.

There was, however, a major obstacle in the way. Socialists were themselves in the grip of hedonistic attitudes. Orwell praised Jack London for

> his perception that hedonistic societies cannot endure, a perception which isn't common among what are called progressive thinkers. Outside Soviet Russia, left-wing thought has generally been hedonistic, and the weaknesses of the Socialist Movement spring partly from this.[288]

This view had been part of Orwell's Socialism from its initial conception in *The Road to Wigan Pier*. There he discussed the 'spiritual' objections to Socialism in the unsatisfactory form in which it was espoused by most of its adherents. 'I have very seldom met a convinced Socialist who could grasp that thinking people may be repelled by the *objective* towards which Socialism appears to be moving.' The 'spiritual recoil from Socialism' was rooted in the feeling that there are 'certain things (patriotism, religion, etc.) which lay deeper than the economic motive'.[289] Socialism had become hitched to a worship of machine production and industrial society, promising a 'vision of the future as a sort of glittering Wells-world [from which ... ] sensitive minds recoil'. Only now, Orwell thought, are we actually beginning to '*feel* the tendency of the machine to make a fully human life impossible'.[290] Socialists had not thought enough about these problems, and as a result had not thought enough about what would happen after Socialism was established:

> Most Socialists are content to point out that once Socialism has been established we shall be happier in a material sense, and to assume that all problems lapse when one's belly is full. But the truth is the opposite: when one's belly is empty, the only problem is an empty belly. It is when we have got away from drudgery and exploitation that we shall really start wondering about man's destiny and the reason for his existence.[291]

Socialism could remove us from the realm of necessity, but there was no guarantee that it would take us to the realm of freedom.

In fact, Orwell came to believe that the key challenge the world faced was not how to achieve Socialism. That was inevitable, at least in the sense of the emergence of a collectivist society with a planned economy. What lay in doubt was the particular form that this Socialism might take. In early 1940 he declared that 'the world-struggle is no longer between Socialism and capitalism. In so far as Socialism means no more than centralized

---

[288]George Orwell, 'Jack London, "Landmarks in American Literature", 5', March 1943, CW, XV, p. 6.
[289]Orwell, *Road to Wigan Pier*, pp. 173–4.
[290]Orwell, *Road to Wigan Pier*, pp. 175–8.
[291]Orwell, 'As I Please', 14, CW, XVI, p. 113.

ownership and planned production, all the industrialized countries will be "Socialist" before long'. So what was the world-struggle about? 'The real issue is between democratic Socialism and some form of rationalized caste-society.' Socialism in and by itself was not enough to guarantee a humane and flourishing society. 'Socialism in the narrow economic sense has nothing to do with liberty, equality or common decency.'[292] There's the rub. Socialism had to preserve some core values of liberal societies, however imperfectly they had been exemplified under capitalism, which for Orwell were, precisely, liberty, equality and decency. But Socialism could rely neither on the ideologies of capitalism nor on traditional Christian faith, both of which had buttressed these values:[293] it needed a form of moral progress (or even moral revolution) that would establish a secular brotherhood of man.

There was hope – though, possibly, it was hope without optimism. For a start, Orwell could see around him some signs that people were, in practice, already acting on values that were neither hedonistic nor totalitarian, and he built some aspects of the Socialism of *The Lion and The Unicorn* on this. 'Intelligent hedonism is a poor guide in a world where millions of people are willing to shed their own or anyone else's blood in the name of half-a-dozen kinds of folly.'[294] But it wasn't all folly. In particular, patriotism was a positive value that led many people to act against their own narrow material interests.

The special atmosphere of the English-speaking countries in the last twenty years has allowed the intelligentsia to rid themselves of patriotism, and from this they have proceeded to argue that patriotism doesn't exist. Meanwhile, the whole of contemporary history contradicts them. Most men will, in fact, die 'for their country' rather more readily than they will go on strike for higher wages. Isn't it just possible, therefore that there is something wrong with the 'commonsense', hedonistic view of life?[295]

The war boosted Orwell's hopes for Socialism because he could see that war was waged with a commitment to values that were not hedonistic, and that could be harnessed to the Socialist cause, giving it the spiritual dimension it needed. Patriotism was paramount here, and (as we have seen) patriotism was not the same as nationalism.

---

[292]Orwell, 'Notes on the Way', CW, XII, p. 123.

[293]It was the particular purpose of Christianity to preserve the illusion of equality in the face of the economic inequalities of capitalism – 'Notes on the Way'.

[294]George Orwell, 'Review of *The Adventures of the Young Soldier in Search of the Better World* by C.E.M. Joad', October 1943, CW, XV, p. 292.

[295]George Orwell, 'Review of *Journey through the War Mind* by C.E.M. Joad ...', June 1940, CW, XII, p. 178.

By 'patriotism' I mean devotion to a particular place and a particular way of life, which one believes to be the best in the world but has no wish to force on other people. Patriotism is of its nature defensive, both militarily and culturally. Nationalism, on the other hand, is inseparable from the desire for power. The abiding purpose of every nationalist is to secure more power and more prestige, *not* for himself but for the nation or other unit in which he has chosen to sink his own individuality.[296]

The dissolution of individuality into nationalism was for Orwell, no doubt, a critical point against it: his patriotism was in part the love of a culture in which individuality was protected and encouraged. The nationalist placed 'a single nation ... beyond good and evil and recogniz[ed] no other duty than that of advancing its interests'.[297] Patriotism gave people an awareness 'of some organism greater than themselves, stretching into the future and the past, within which they feel themselves to be immortal'. People are willing to die for 'fragmentary communities – nation, race, creed, class'. Perhaps not all of these emotions and values are beneficent ones, but there remained the hope that men might transcend their fragmented world. 'A very slight increase of consciousness, and their sense of loyalty could be transferred to humanity itself, which is not an abstraction.'[298] The 'very slight' is indicative of just how strong Orwell's hopes in the early years of the war were.

Orwell's hopes diminished over time, hand-in-hand with his declining belief in the imminence of revolution, but they never altogether vanished. Crucially, though his hopes waxed and waned, they were at all times built on a hostility to Utopian politics. In 'Notes on the Way' he had summarized a view which he attributed to Malcolm Muggeridge and others: 'We are living in a nightmare precisely *because* we have tried to set up an earthly paradise. We have believed in "progress", trusted to human leadership, rendered unto Caesar the things that are God's ...'[299] This was not Orwell's view, but he came close to sharing some of these implicitly anti-Utopian arguments. In an important discussion of what he called 'neo-pessimism' – a view he identified with T.E. Hulme and later writers influenced by him, Wyndham Lewis, T.S. Eliot, Aldous Huxley, Malcolm Muggeridge, Evelyn Waugh, Graham Greene – Orwell argued that those who shared this view had in common 'their refusal to believe that human society can be fundamentally improved. Man is non-perfectible, merely political changes can effect nothing, progress is an illusion.' They were political reactionaries, but it was important to take

---

[296]George Orwell, 'Notes on Nationalism', October 1945, CW, XVII, p. 142.
[297]Orwell, 'Notes on Nationalism', CW, CVII, p. 141.
[298]Orwell, 'Notes on the Way', CW, XII, pp. 125–6.
[299]Orwell, 'Notes on the Way', CW, XII, p. 125.

them seriously because 'up to a point they are right'. It is true that 'plans for human betterment do normally come unstuck'.

The real answer is to dissociate Socialism from Utopianism. Nearly all neo-pessimist apologetics consists in putting up a man of straw and knocking him down again. The man of straw is called Human Perfectibility. Socialists are accused of believing that society can be – and, indeed, after the establishment of Socialism, will be – completely perfect; also that progress is *inevitable*. Debunking such beliefs is money for jam of course.

The answer, which ought to be uttered more loudly than it usually is, is that Socialism is not perfectionist, perhaps not even hedonistic. Socialists don't claim to be able to make the world perfect: they claim to be able to make it better. And any thinking Socialist will concede to the Catholic that when economic injustice has been righted, the fundamental problem of man's place in the universe will still remain. But what the Socialist does claim is that that problem cannot be dealt with while the average human being's preoccupations are necessarily economic. It is all summed up in Marx's saying that after Socialism has arrived, human history can begin.[300]

Socialism was not utopian and did not promise a perfect society. It was a foundation: equality was necessary before a society of free and flourishing humanity could be constructed. But it was in itself no guarantee of such a society. The Christmas Eve issue of *Tribune* that included this column also contained another article by Orwell (writing pseudonymously as John Freeman) in which he reflected further on utopianism and Socialism.[301] The burden of Orwell's Christmas message was that Utopias were, on the whole, unappealing and unpleasant places. 'All efforts to describe *permanent* happiness ... have been failures.' As for Utopias, even 'the "favourable" ones are invariable appetising, and usually lacking in vitality as well'. The sort of future envisaged by H.G. Wells particularly bothered Orwell (as he said on many other occasions too):

It is a world whose keynotes are enlightened hedonism and scientific curiosity. All the evils and miseries that we now suffer from have vanished. Ignorance, war, poverty, dirt, disease, frustration, hunger, fear, overwork, superstition – all vanished. So expressed, it is impossible to deny that that is the kind of world we all hope for. We all want to abolish the things that

---

[300]George Orwell, 'As I Please', 4, 24 December 1943, CW, XVI, pp. 34–5.
[301]The reasons for attributing the essay to Orwell are given by Peter Davison in CW, XVI, pp. 37–8.

Wells wants to abolish. But is there anyone who actually wants to live in a Wellsian Utopia? On the contrary, *not* to live in a world like that, *not* to wake up in a hygienic garden suburb infested by naked schoolmarms [!?], has actually become a conscious political motive.[302]

Huxley's *Brave New World* expressed the fear of 'the rationalised hedonistic society' with which Wells threatened his readers. Other Utopias fared no better in Orwell's hand. Morris's *News from Nowhere* was a 'goody-goody version', leaving its reader with a feeling of 'watery melancholy'. Lord Samuel's *An Unknown Country* was 'even more dismal', while the society of Swift's Houyhnhnms provided 'a tepid existence, hardly worth leading'. Portrayals of the perfect society that consigned it to a future life were no better: 'Heaven is as great a flop as Utopia.'[303] Other visions of perfect happiness that were not utopian or heavenly were 'merely sensual'.[304] All of these visions have in common the fact that they worked by contrast: they imagine a world in which the main problems of the present are ended. 'Nearly all creators of Utopias have resembled the man who has toothache, and therefore think that happiness consists in not having toothache.'[305]

Orwell's Socialism, in contrast, was rooted in a rejection of the utopian impulse and a disgust with all Utopias and the happy lives that were led by their citizens. They were not the sort of place for a perverse humanity.

I suggest that the real objective of Socialism is not happiness. Happiness hitherto has been a by-product, and for all we know it may always remain so. The real objective of Socialism is human brotherhood ... Men use up their lives in heart-breaking political struggles, or get themselves killed in civil wars, or tortured in the secret prisons of the Gestapo, not in order to establish some central-heated, air-conditioned, strip-lighted Paradise, but because they want a world in which human beings love one another instead of swindling and murdering one another. And they want that world as a first step. Where they go from there is not so certain, and the attempt to foresee it in detail merely confuses this issue.

Socialists should predict 'only in broad terms'. They want a world of peace, but no one can say in detail what such a world would be like. 'The wiser course would be to say that there are certain lines along which humanity must move, the grand strategy is mapped out, but detailed prophecy is not our business.' The predictors of happiness reveal only their own emptiness.[306]

---

[302]George Orwell, 'Can Socialists Be Happy?', December 1944, CW, XVI, pp. 39–40.
[303]Orwell, 'Can Socialists Be Happy?', CW, XVI, p. 40.
[304]Orwell, 'Can Socialists Be Happy?', CW, XVI, p. 41.
[305]Orwell, 'Can Socialists Be Happy?', CW, XVI, p. 43.
[306]Orwell, 'Can Socialists Be Happy?', CW, XVI, pp. 42–3.

Socialists had to be 'both revolutionary and realistic', had to avoid both 'humbug and Utopianism'.[307]

Orwell's post-war attitudes were best summed up in a comment made in one of his 'As I Please' columns from 1946:

When one considers how things have gone since 1930 or thereabouts, it is not easy to believe in the survival of civilisation. I do not argue from this that the only thing to do is to abjure practical politics, retire to some remote place and concentrate either on individual salvation or on building up self-supporting communities against the day when the atom bombs have done their work. I think one must continue the political struggle, just as a doctor must try to save the life of a patient who is probably going to die.

These remarks prefaced thoughts that were, for Orwell, unusually open-ended, expressions of puzzlement not certainty. The world in which he lived seemed to make no sense for Orwell. 'Political behaviour is largely non-rational'; 'the world is suffering from some kind of incurable mental disease'. Hedonism again came into play, as he noted the common assumption 'that what human beings want is to be comfortable'. The puzzle for Orwell was that, if this was what human beings wanted, there was no reason why they couldn't have it. Nature was, more or less, conquered; the wealth being generated was enough that it could be diffused to ensure that all had sufficient; superstition was largely expunged, making a rational view of the world possible. Progress was real, but its promise went unfulfilled. People, in spite of all that they had, fought with renewed viciousness for resources that were no longer scarce, tyrannized over people who, if things were better ordered, would have less and less reason for discontent; and free thought was suppressed notwithstanding the triumph of reason. All senseless and unnecessary.

It was not just shallow hedonism that was given the lie by all of this: there seemed to be no economic explanation of any sort for why things were as they were. 'The desire for pure power seems to be much more dominant than the desire for wealth.' The key question for understanding the world – to which Orwell had no answer – was a psychological one: 'what is the special quality in modern life that makes a major human motive out of the impulse to bully others?'[308]

Socialism had to make its way in a world that read like an amalgam of Hobbes and Dostoevsky. It was dominated by the desire for power and domination, by self-interest, by the fragility of order and decency; it was a world in which human suffering was immense, though unnecessary, and in

---

[307]Orwell, *Lion and Unicorn*, CW, XII, p. 421.
[308]George Orwell, 'As I Please', 63, 29 November 1946, CW, XVIII, pp. 503–4.

which there were many who took pleasure in the suffering of others. But there were countervailing forces, and for Socialism to bring about decency, equality and freedom it had to be more than an economic system that levelled inequalities of wealth: it had to have a spiritual dimension. Socialism like revolution was caught in a dilemma: a better world would be built by better people. But where, in this world, could the better people be found? Orwell was a chastened and a disenchanted Socialist. The perfection of Utopia was not to be found or established, on earth or in heaven. But the struggle must go on, against whatever odds, to make our world a bit better, a bit less bad, and something closer to a place of human flourishing for the many and not just the few. Progress happened and could continue to happen, but nothing was inevitable. We needed to work with the forces that were transforming the earth, willy nilly, and nudge them towards a democratic Socialist future. Otherwise we would end up in Oceania – a world of constant surveillance, no freedom or individuality, no concept of truth, tyranny loved by those whom it oppressed. Socialism, perhaps, but not in any sense worth having. For a while it had seemed that the world was heading towards 'a completely materialistic vulgar civilisation based on hedonism'; in reality the risk to be averted was not this but 'the centralised slave state, ruled over by a small clique'.[309]

The last word should be given to Orwell himself, a passage (the first sentence of which has been quoted once already) about the need to follow a vision that will never be realized:

> The most encouraging fact about revolutionary activity is that, although it always fails, it always continues. The vision of a world of free and equal human beings, living together in a state of brotherhood – in one age it is called the Kingdom of Heaven, in another the classless society – never materialises, but the belief in it never seems to die out.[310]

---

[309]Orwell to S. Moos, 16 November 1943, CW, XV, p. 308.
[310]George Orwell, 'Introduction to *British Pamphleteers*, Volume I, edited by George Orwell and Reginald Reynolds', written Spring 1947?, published November 1948, CW, XIX, p. 109.

# Part Two

## Orwell and Freedom of Thought

*You are perhaps right in thinking I am over-pessimistic. It is
quite possible that freedom of thought etc. may survive in an
economically totalitarian society. We can't tell until a collectivised
economy has been tried out in a western country. What worries
me at present is the uncertainty as to whether the ordinary people
in countries like England grasp the difference between democracy
and despotism well enough to want to defend their liberties.
One can't tell until they seem themselves menaced in some quite
unmistakeable manner. The intellectuals who are at present
pointing out that democracy and fascism are the same thing etc.
depress me horribly. However, perhaps when the pinch comes
the common people will turn out to be more intelligent than the
clever ones. I certainly hope so.*

ORWELL TO VICTOR GOLLANCZ, 8 JANUARY 1940 [CW, XII, P. 5]

Twice in his lifetime Orwell received a boost in the unlikely pages of *Vogue*
magazine. Identified by Auden and Isherwood as one of the 'Young British
Writers in the Way Up' in 1939,[1] Orwell was only a few years later caught
in a spotlight shone by the magazine's features editor, Allene Talme. Now,
benefitting from 'a new fame' since the publication of *Animal Farm*, Orwell

---

[1]W.H. Auden & Christopher Isherwood, 'Young British Writers on the Way Up', *Vogue*,
15 August 1939. This was the last collaboration between Auden and Isherwood. Both *Vogue*
features on Orwell are online in the *Vogue* archive, though behind a paywall: https://archive.
vogue.com/.

was given something like a celebrity profile, complete with picture.[2] The profile ended with a sentence in which it is hard not to hear Orwell's own voice: 'Fairly much a leftist, George Orwell is a defender of freedom, even though most of the time he violently disagrees with the people beside whom he is fighting.'[3] Orwell, of course, was fairly much a leftist from at least 1936 through to his death in January 1950. Socialism, he was convinced, was coming – sooner or later. Nonetheless, the years 1945–6 were watershed years. By this time, later was looking increasingly more probable. The question that really concerned Orwell was whether the arrival of Socialism would prove compatible with the survival of freedom. It was freedom, especially the freedom to write and say what you thought, that mattered most to Orwell, in part because this sort of freedom was fundamental for someone who lived by writing and cared to write with integrity. Concern for the future of this freedom was not new for Orwell, but it was in these years after the war that defending freedom became the dominant feature of his writing and thinking. The war had been won, but there was every chance that the peace might be lost. Socialism had to be defended against the Soviet myth; it had to be preserved in its original liberal and humanist form, now threatened by the belief that freedom lay in loyal and unquestioning service to the Communist cause. These pivotal years for Orwell were darkened by the fear that human liberty would be expunged, a fear that drove him into writing *Nineteen Eighty-Four* in frantic isolation on the island of Jura. Through his writing, of course, but also through his actions, Orwell worked to avert the terrifying future that he portrayed in his last book. It was written in defiance of ill-health, in a desperate effort to frighten the world into freedom. Orwell died before he could know whether he had succeeded.

Famously, *Nineteen Eighty-Four* declared that, if there was any hope, it lay in the Proles. It was the same hope he had expressed to Victor Gollancz in 1940. The intellectuals couldn't be trusted to defend freedom, but maybe the common people could. 'I certainly hope so.'[4] Neither hope carries much conviction. But together they point to the continuities in Orwell's thinking. His determination to defend freedom (above all, intellectual freedom) grew naturally from his previous ideas, as did his doubt that intellectuals as a group were as determined as he was in their loyalty to this cause. Here we will trace the interplay between Orwell's individualist commitment to intellectual freedom and his Socialism from his early writings, through the pivotal years that followed *Animal Farm*, to his death.

---

[2]The picture was one of those taken by Vernon Richards in Orwell's Canonbury Square flat, early 1946. (Vernon Richards (ed.), *George Orwell at Home (and among the Anarchists)* (London: Freedom Press, 1998), p. 54.) The interview on which the *Vogue* profile was based took place in the same flat: George Bowker, *George Orwell* (London: Abacus, 2004), p. 358.
[3]Allene Talmey, 'Vogue Spotlight', 15 September 1946, in CW, XVIII, p. 396.
[4]Orwell to Victor Gollancz, 8 January 1940, CW, XII, p. 5.

# 1. From Eric Blair to George Orwell: Englishness and Freedom

Eric Blair's first published article as a professional writer was for the French journal *Monde*, and appeared on 6 October 1928. 'La Censure en Angleterre' ['Censorship in England'] was the work of an author who was not yet George Orwell, and (of course) entirely unknown to readers. Just over two months later Blair could take pride in his first professional publication in English, an article for *G.K.'s Weekly* that appeared on 29 December 1928. It, too, was about freedom of expression.

The essay on censorship explored the illogicality of a system that suppressed contemporary literature and plays, largely for their sexual content, but left unmolested the bawdy literature of the past. Blair was fascinated by the prudery that had overcome English literature in the nineteenth century and the impact of this prudery, but looked forward to the end of the hypocrisy entailed by a censorship that left public morality in the hands of the outraged few. 'If a government dared to abolish all moral literary censorship we should find that we have been ill-used for decades by a smallish minority.'[5] In the persona that Eric Blair would create, George Orwell was to become a writer free from both prudery and licentiousness.

'A Farthing Newspaper', the essay for *G.K.'s Weekly*, similarly sounded a theme that would later be central to the concerns of George Orwell: freedom of the press. The farthing newspaper in question was in fact a ten-centime newspaper, the Parisian *Ami du People*. It was being sold extremely cheaply, 'rather less than a farthing' in Blair's estimate. (In comparison, the cover price of *The Times* on the day his essay was published was 4d.). Blair seems to have been a little unsure whether he approved or not. An ostensible goal of the paper was 'to combat the powerful newspapers which are strangling free speech in France'. The *Ami du Peuple* would become not just the friend of the people but their voice too. This 'stand for democracy' might have been more palatable were it not the case that the paper's proprietor was 'M. Coty, a great industrial capitalist'. The price was, of course, intended to increase circulation, seemingly with considerable success. Blair encouraged England's newspaper barons to follow suit. Then, 'at any rate the poor devils of the public will at last feel that they are getting the correct value for their money'. This conclusion, though, came only after the rather weightier point that 'every paper of this kind, whatever its intentions, is the enemy of free speech'. Why? Because they increased their circulation at the cost of driving other publications out of business. The very real freedom of the press enjoyed by the French rested on the range and diversity of its newspapers. It rested on a

---

[5]Orwell, 'Censorship in England', 6 October 1928, CW, X, pp. 117–19; French original 'La Censure en Angleterre', CW, X, pp. 148–50.

cacophony of voices, 'nationalist, socialist, and communist, clerical and anti-clerical, militarist and anti-militarist, pro-semitic and anti-semitic'.[6] George Orwell, following the Eric Blair of 1928, would also be alert to the risks that capitalism posed to freedom of thought. He may be remembered today chiefly as the enemy of totalitarianism, but he was no friend of capitalism either.

Notwithstanding this start, intellectual freedom was not an obvious theme in Orwell's early writing. But it is there nonetheless. From the beginning, he had a keen eye for the conditions that enabled people to think freely. Bozo, the London pavement artist, whom we encounter with Eric Blair in his first outing as George Orwell, in *Down and Out in Paris and London* (1933) noted that you 'can have cartoons about any of the parties, but you mustn't put anything in favour of Socialism, because the police won't stand it'.[7] Bozo spoke of the value of education – if you have that, he said, 'it don't matter to you if you're on the road for the rest of your life'. Orwell, or at any rate the narrator of the book, demurred. A man was nothing without money. Bozo was not persuaded.

'No, not necessarily. If you set yourself to it, you can live the same life, rich or poor. You can still keep on with your books and ideas. You just got to say to yourself, "I'm a free man in *here*"' – he tapped his forehead – 'and you're all right.'[8]

This was a view that Orwell later rejected. Roaming freely inside your own head was a freedom of no use to the writer. Nor, as Flory discovered in Burma, was this freedom much use to those living in 'the atmosphere of imperialism' (or of any other despotism).

It is a stifling, stultifying world in which to live. It is a world in which every word and every thought is censored. In England it is hard even to imagine such an atmosphere. Everyone is free in England; we sell our souls in public and buy them back in private, among our friends. But even friendship can hardly exist when every white man is a cog in the wheels of despotism. Free speech is unthinkable. All other kinds of freedom are permitted. You are free to be a drunkard, an idler, a coward, a backbiter, a fornicator; but you are not free to think for yourself. Your opinion on every subject of any conceivable importance is dictated for you by the pukka sahibs' code.[9]

---

[6]Orwell, 'A Farthing Newspaper', 29 December 1928, CW, X, pp. 119–21.

[7]George Orwell, *Down and Out in Paris and London* [CW, I] (London: Secker & Warburg, 1986), p. 164 (Penguin ed. p. 174).

[8]Orwell, *Down and Out*, p. 167 (Penguin ed. p. 176).

[9]Orwell, *Burmese Days* [CW, II] (London, 1986), pp. 68–9. The Penguin Classics ed. has the same pagination.

Friendship was impossible; but, worse than that, 'the secrecy of your revolt poisons you like a secret disease'. You become 'a creature of the despotism'. Flory could 'secretly, in books and secret thoughts', ponder the evils of the imperialism from which he profited, 'but it is a corrupting thing to live one's real life in secret'.[10] Flory's quest was for someone – a wife – who could understand him, with whom he could share the burdens of his secret thoughts.[11] The quotations come from a chapter that begins with Flory's cowardice and ends with his ineffectiveness: he was never going to have the pluck needed to defy the social conventions that compelled him to think freely only in secret. But his example made it clear that a freedom confined to the inside of one's own skull was no freedom at all.

Orwell's other early novels, as we have seen, are all about people who feel that the communities in which they live are in some respect frustrating their individuality, though *A Clergyman's Daughter* stands a bit removed from this theme, as it is as much about living with and without religious faith. But these novels do not address directly questions of intellectual freedom. The one that comes closest to doing so is probably *Keep the Aspidistra Flying*. Gordon Comstock's repudiation of the money God, his doomed quest, simultaneously hectic and feckless, to find a way of living that would be free from the compromises needed to live under capitalism, is ostensibly about the pursuit of a life of artistic integrity. But it is not easy to take this pursuit at face value. His decision to settle for a life with wife, baby, capitalism and aspidistra brings the novel to a clumsy end. What was Orwell's verdict on the matter? Comstock was such a poor vessel for artistic idealism and his final capitulation to the money God so perfunctory that it is difficult to be sure, but it may well be that he shared at this time – the book was finished in January 1936, just before Orwell's trip to Wigan – Comstock's repudiation of the alternatives to capitalism. Socialism, suicide and Catholicism, he wanted none of them. Did that mean that the best chance for artistic freedom and integrity still lay with capitalism? Perhaps, but part of Comstock's capitulation was abandoning his hope of being a successful poet.

In *The Road to Wigan Pier* Orwell associated Socialism with the inevitable triumph of collectivism – 'an *ordered* world, an *efficient* world' – but he had misgivings. It may be, he suspected, that a classless society 'means a bleak world in which all our ideals, our codes, our tastes – our "ideology" in fact – will have no meaning'.[12] While his book was still in press, Orwell headed for Spain, where he experienced the real Socialism of Barcelona. This inspired a hope in Socialism that never left him. But Spain also increased his fear that a different sort of collectivism might triumph in the name

---

[10]Orwell, *Burmese Days*, pp. 69–70.
[11]Orwell, *Burmese Days*, p. 73.
[12]Orwell, *The Road to Wigan Pier* [CW, V] (London, 1986), pp. 175–6, 156. The Penguin Classics ed. has the same pagination.

of Socialism. Witness to the attempts by orthodox Stalinists to crush the genuinely revolutionary elements among the anarchist and Socialist groups, Orwell awakened to the peculiar dangers of totalitarianism. At first, once he had returned to England, the threat still seemed distant:

> It is not easy to convey the nightmare atmosphere of that time [the Barcelona May Days] – the peculiar uneasiness produced by rumours that were always changing, by censored newspapers and the constant presence of armed men. It is not easy to convey it because, at the moment, the thing essential to such an atmosphere does not exist in England. In England political intolerance is not yet taken for granted. There is political persecution in a petty way; if I were a coalminer I would not dare to be known to the boss as a Communist; but the 'good party man', the gangster-gramophone of continental politics, is still a rarity, and the notion of 'liquidating' or 'eliminating' everyone who happens to disagree with you does not yet seem natural. It seemed only too natural in Barcelona.[13]

Orwell quickly realized, though, that the dangers that threatened Europe would not leave England's slumber undisturbed. On 13 June 1938, he joined the Independent Labour Party. He did so in order to defend free speech. His self-justification anticipated things that he would say in 1945 and 1946, when he was again involved in political groups that aimed to defend intellectual freedom. As a writer, his first instinct was to avoid politics and 'to be left alone so that he can go on writing books in peace'. But this was not possible when Fascism threatened. Sides had to be taken. 'To begin with,' Orwell said, 'the era of free speech is closing down'. It had always been 'something of a fake' in England anyway, 'because in the last resort money controls opinion'. But – the crucial point – while a legal right to free speech still existed, then 'there are always loopholes for an unorthodox writer'. Like Orwell, you could with a little ingenuity even contrive to make the Capitalists pay for your writings against Capitalism.

> But I do not delude myself that this state of affairs is going to last forever. We have seen what has happened to the freedom of the Press in Italy and Germany, and it will happen here sooner or later. The time is coming – not next year, perhaps not for ten or twenty years, but it is coming – when every writer will have the choice of being silenced altogether or of producing the dope that a privileged minority demands.

These threats had to be resisted, and Orwell saw in the ILP the only party that 'aims at anything I should regard as Socialism'. It opposed both capitalism

---

[13]Orwell, *Homage to Catalonia* [CW, VI] (London, 1986), p. 151 (Penguin ed. pp. 158–9).

and imperialism. What was it that Orwell regarded as true Socialism? His answer to this was to develop over time, but one thing was clear in 1938: 'the only regime which in the long run, will dare to permit freedom of speech is a Socialist regime'.[14] As we have seen, Orwell's earliest and deepest commitments were to a liberal individualism that gave an anarchist and libertarian tinge to his Socialism. And Socialism itself was a vehicle for fulfilling the promise of liberal individualism – it would bring freedom and justice *for all*. In 1938, and later, it was the liberalism in his Socialism (what he would later call 'democratic Socialism') that could move Orwell to political activism.

In joining the ILP, Orwell rejected the politics of the Popular Front, which involved working with capitalists and Communists. This was no more than 'an unholy alliance between the robbers and the robbed' that would entrench capitalism more firmly.[15] He did not believe that the Popular Front, which brought illiberal Communists and illiberal Capitalists together, could possibly defend the sort of Socialism that he valued. Much has been written on the subject of Orwell's 'pessimism', especially the supposed pessimism of his final years and of *Nineteen Eighty-Four*. Isaac Deutscher denounced that book as 'a document of dark disillusionment … with every form and shade of socialism', the work of a man overcome by 'a quasi-mystical pessimism'.[16] Many others have followed, and the view of Orwell as someone who ended his days intellectually bankrupt and bereft of hope has been particularly attractive to his critics on the Left.[17] But the trajectory is all wrong. Orwell's despair, such as it was, was deepest at the end of the 1930s. The war rescued him from this. First, as we saw in the previous chapter, it seemed to create the conditions for a Socialist revolution in England. This opportunity was lost. Orwell never abandoned his revolutionary Socialist hopes, but, like many before and after, he postponed their realization indefinitely. Instead, he settled for the distinctively second-best option presented by a Labour government that was not what it could have been but was better than anything else on offer. At the same time, though, Orwell became animated by a new cause: keeping alive and in good health the ideal of a liberal (libertarian some may say), democratic and humanistic Socialism. This was, in Orwell's view, the original form of Socialism. This task inspired him as a writer to combat the Soviet *mythos*, most effectively in *Animal Farm*; it also inspired

---

[14]Orwell, 'Why I Join the I.L.P.', 24 June 1938, CW, XI, pp. 167–8.

[15]Orwell, 'Review of *Workers' Front* by Fenner Brockway', 17 February 1938, CW, XI, p. 124.

[16]Isaac Deutscher, '"1984" – The Mysticism of Cruelty', in Deutscher (ed.), *Heretics and Renegades and Other Essays* (London: Hamish Hamilton, 1955), pp. 45–6.

[17]Alex Zwerdling, *Orwell and the Left* (New Haven: Yale University Press, 1974), esp. ch. 4. For an assessment of Orwell's pessimism see Erika Gottlieb, *The Orwell Conundrum: A Cry of Despair or Faith in the Spirit of Man?* (Ottawa: Carleton University Press, 1992).

him as both a writer and activist to the defence of freedom, especially of intellectual freedom. Activism was not Orwell's usual mode. He was driven to it by the Spanish Civil War and the threat of Fascism; he was driven to it again after 1945 by the threat to freedom. As it turned out, this later threat was something he had been made aware of by his Spanish experience. The Soviet Union was the biggest threat to the success and to the ideals of Socialism. The activism after 1945 was undermined by his ill health and by the priority he accorded to being a writer. *Nineteen Eighty-Four* instead absorbed most of his dying energy. We will return to that book, which Orwell's critics are not wrong in finding problematic; but first we need to establish Orwell's identity as a writer and activist for freedom.

By the end of the 1930s, Orwell was as close as he got to despair. This despair was rooted in the realization 'that this is not a writer's world'.[18] He told Eleanor Jaques early in 1938 that 'there is a very definite possibility that the next big slump will result in some kind of Fascism. If so, good-bye to all literary gents. I am told that in Germany now you can't even publish an anonymous pamphlet with safety because the Government keeps a large tribe of literary experts at work determining the authorship of anonymous pamphlets by comparison of literary style. Whichever way you look it seems to be a most horrible nightmare.'[19] As a writer of fiction, Orwell was aware that he had not yet left his journeyman years. Now he must have wondered whether he ever could become the master that he aspired to be. He had since 1937 declared firmly his Socialism, still believing perhaps 'that Socialism could preserve and even enlarge the atmosphere of liberalism'. But he had come to see that this was not possible. It was totalitarianism that was taking over the world. Totalitarianism might be, in some cases, a sort Socialism, but it wasn't liberal. 'The autonomous individual is going to be stamped out of existence.' The creative writer 'can take no part in the process *as a writer*. For *as a writer* he is a liberal, and what is happening is the destruction of liberalism.' In 'the remaining years of free speech' the only creative writing that could survive would have to take a 'passive attitude'. It would be apolitical, recognizing that 'progress and reaction have both turned out to be swindles'. His model for this sort of writing was Henry Miller, a writer 'completely negative, unconstructive, amoral ... a passive accepter of evil'. Even this would not, presumably, last long, for freedom of thought would soon be a 'deadly sin' and then 'a meaningless abstraction'.[20] A merely passive acceptance of evil might not be enough to permit even bare survival. As his fears accumulated through the later 1930s, Orwell came to focus his writing and thinking on one

---

[18] Orwell, 'Inside the Whale', 11 March 1940, CW, XII, p. 111.
[19] Orwell to Eleanor Jaques, 25 January 1938, UCL Orwell Archive, Orwell/G/4/20.
[20] Orwell, 'Inside the Whale', CW, XII, pp. 110–12.

principal task: 'to oppose a humaner, freer form of collectivism to the purge-and-censorship variety'.[21]

The onset of war changed Orwell's perspective on the world more or less overnight, but he did not immediately abandon his pessimism. He came to value England's embedded habits of freedom, though it was far from clear whether they could be preserved. In England:

> The liberty of the individual is still believed in, almost as in the nineteenth century. But this has nothing to do with economic liberty, the right to exploit others for profit. It is the liberty to have a home of your own, to do what you like in your spare time, to choose your own amusements instead of having them chosen from above. The most hateful of all names in an English ear is Nosey Parker. It is obvious, of course, that even this purely private liberty is a lost cause. Like all other modern peoples the English are in process of being numbered, labelled, conscripted, 'co-ordinated'. But the pull of their impulses is in the other direction, and the kind of regimentation that can be imposed on them will be modified in consequence. No party rallies, no Youth Movements, no coloured shirts, no Jew-baiting or 'spontaneous' demonstrations. No Gestapo either, in all probability.[22]

A lost cause – but one worth fighting for.

The statement just quoted was written during the summer and autumn of 1940.[23] The connection he made between Englishness and freedom stuck with Orwell through his later writings on intellectual freedom.[24] But the pessimism faded. It didn't become optimism, but the cause came to seem not so definitively lost. In his later writings on intellectual freedom, Orwell would argue that England, with its long liberal tradition from Milton's *Areopagitica* (1644) onwards, was especially suited to being the place where Socialism learnt (or remembered) how to retain its liberal dimension. As he said, in a letter that sketched out some of the ideas that would coalesce into *Nineteen Eighty-Four*, 'I believe very deeply, as I explained in my book "The Lion and the Unicorn", in the English *people* and in their capacity to centralise their economy without destroying freedom in doing so'.[25] He elaborated the case in his short book *The English People*, which recast the ideas of *The Lion and*

---

[21]Orwell, 'Review of *The Totalitarian Enemy* by F. Borkenau', 4 May 1940, CW, XII, p. 159.

[22]George Orwell, *The Lion and the Unicorn: Socialism and the English Genius*, 19 February 1941, CW, XII, p. 394.

[23]Orwell, *The Lion and the Unicorn*, CW, II, p. 391.

[24]Robert Colls, *George Orwell: English Rebel* (Oxford: Oxford University Press, 2013), pp. 107–8 (and passim); David Dwan, *Liberty, Equality and Humbug: Orwell's Political Ideals* (Oxford: Oxford University Press, 2018), pp. 63–4.

[25]Orwell to Noel Willmett, 18 May 1944, CW, XVI, p. 191.

*the Unicorn* (with its call for violent revolution) in a less incendiary mode. It was finished by May 1944 but not published until 1947. Orwell later dismissed the book as 'silly', 'a piece of propaganda', 'a little propaganda book', and in notes that he made not long before his death it joined *The Lion and the Unicorn* as one of his books that ought not to be reprinted.[26] But there is more to the book than Orwell's own dismissal of it may suggest.[27] It pulled into focus his conviction that the English were at heart a freedom-loving people. The stubbornness of their attachment to freedom impressed him most: 'the feeling that your spare time is your own and that a man must not be persecuted for his opinions ... is deeply ingrained, and the centralising processes inevitable in wartime ... have not destroyed it'. The attitude derived in part from 'respect for integrity of conscience' but perhaps more from 'the prevailing lack of intellectuality'. The 'ordinary Englishman ... almost never grasps the full logical implications of the creed he professes: almost always he utters heresies without noticing it. Orthodoxies, whether of the Right or the Left, flourish chiefly among the literary intelligentsia, the people who ought in theory to be the guardians of freedom of thought.'[28]

This was perhaps not the strongest of foundations and it should surprise no one that the freedom resting upon it was far from perfect. For a start, freedom of the press required a more conscious and deliberate defence. The English might boast of press freedom, but it was 'theoretical rather than actual'. It was undermined by 'the centralised ownership of the press [which] means in practice that unpopular opinions can only be printed in books or in newspapers with small circulation'. But more than that, the people didn't really care about this aspect of freedom, and did not in great number protest at its infringements. Only a 'small minority' probably opposed the wartime suppression of the *Daily Worker*. Free speech, though, was a different matter. It was a reality. 'Extremely few English people are afraid to utter their political opinions in public, and there are not even very many who want to silence the opinions of others.' Totalitarianism, the control of thoughts as well as words, was in Orwell's view, 'hardly imaginable' among such a people.[29]

*The English People* ended with some thoughts on the future. The English had relied on stupidity for the protection of free speech: 'the people are not intellectual enough to be heresy-hunters'. But this would not be enough in the future. The general contempt for things intellectual and cultural would become 'serious liabilities'. For one thing, the contempt for ideas

[26]Orwell to Julian Symons, 9 October 1947, CW, XIX, p. 212; Orwell to Leonard Moore, 23 June 1945, CW, XVII, p. 189; Orwell, 'Notes for My Literary Executor', 31 March 194, CW, XVII, p. 114; 'Orwell's Notes on His Books and Essays', 1949, CW, XX, p. 226.

[27]Some others saw this too: see Peter Davison (ed.), *Orwell's England* (London: Penguin, 2001), pp. 290–1, 333, supplementing the editorial material in CW, XVI, pp. 199, 228.

[28]Orwell, *The English People*, 1947, written May 1944, CW, XVI, p. 208.

[29]Orwell, *The English People*, CW, XVI, p. 208.

drove English intellectuals into dangerous positions. It was bad enough that already they 'are markedly hostile to their own country'. Partly this was because capitalism gave them 'security without much responsibility'. (The irresponsibility of intellectuals was a major threat, in Orwell's view, to intellectual freedom.) But there was no doubt that 'the philistinism of the English public alienates the intelligentsia still further', with the result that they were 'hardly able to make contact with the masses and grow less and less interested in English problems'.

Orwell instead placed his hopes elsewhere.[30] The people – ordinary people, that is, not intellectuals – needed to be better educated and intellectually livelier; they needed to 'pay more attention to the world' and to love their country more intelligently. If they could do this, then no people were better placed to 'give the example that millions of human beings are waiting for'. In a world that had had its fill of chaos and dictatorship, the English were just what might be needed. 'Of all peoples the English are likeliest to find a way of avoiding both.' They were ready to accept the changes needed, especially to the economy, but had no wish to conquer others and 'no desire ... for violent revolution'. This is perhaps where the false note of propaganda intrudes, eliding both the realities of Empire and the desirability of revolution, both subjects on which Orwell had more complex views. Nonetheless, he did genuinely believe that England was better placed than elsewhere to preserve liberty and embrace Socialism. A revolution of sorts would be needed, though, because this embrace could happen only 'if the ordinary English in the street can somehow get their hands on power'. If England is to remain a great nation, 'it is the common people who must make it so'.[31] This faith in the people rather than in intellectuals is one of Orwell's signature tunes, but it was always problematic – a few lines of melody rather than a complete song. A hope in pursuit of a plan. In *The English People* this is particularly plain, with wishful thinking the dominant note in these final pages.

# 2. Libel, Obscenity and Politics: Orwell's Early Experience of Censorship

Freedom of expression may not have been a central theme in Orwell's early fiction, but it was nonetheless an inescapable concern for Orwell the professional writer. The difficulty that Orwell had in finding a publisher for *Animal Farm* in 1944 and 1945 – it was rejected by three publishers all seemingly concerned not to offend England's Russian allies – intensified his

---

[30]Orwell, *The English People*, CW, XVI, pp. 225–7.
[31]Orwell, *The English People*, CW, XVI, pp. 227–8.

fears for free speech in an age of ideological polarization and intellectual bad faith. The dishonesty of publishers who found ingenious reasons for refusing to publish a book that they disliked largely because of its criticism of England's ally, the Soviet Union, for whose Communism they may also have had some covert sympathy, infuriated Orwell. We will explore later his writing on these themes in the mid-1940s. But long before he became concerned with the political suppression of intellectual freedom, Orwell confronted other sorts of censorship.

His books of the 1930s were censored on their journey to publication for two major reasons. One of the causes of censorship was publishers' very considerable fear of action for libel or defamation, which led to some extraordinary alterations to Orwell's texts before their publication. For the most part, he accepted the constraint and worked with publishers and lawyers to do what was needed to get his work into print. English libel law (then and now) joined the same category as death and taxes: not something to be welcomed but not likely to go away either.

Orwell also accommodated himself, grudgingly, to the other major constraint on his freedom of expression: the risk of prosecution for obscenity (and blasphemy). Scholars have devoted less attention to Orwell's views about censorship and obscenity than they have to his views of the totalitarian threat to intellectual freedom. In spite of the accommodation, Orwell was clearly of the view that censorship on grounds of obscenity was self-evidently absurd, and showed an interest in matters of obscenity throughout his professional career. Arguably, his approach to obscenity provided a template for his consideration of intellectual freedom more generally.

The effort of getting his first book, *Down and Out in Paris and London*, into print was an education in the limits to free expression.[32] Orwell had a shorter version of the book (in diary form, and perhaps confined just to the Paris material[33]) rejected by Jonathan Cape, and then an expanded version was rejected both by Cape and by T.S. Eliot for Faber. (Eliot would later render the same service to *Animal Farm*.) Orwell's manuscript was then sent to his literary agent Leonard Moore by his friend Mabel Fierz. Orwell himself seems to have rather lost heart in the book and doubted whether it merited publication, but he left open the hope that Moore might be able to place the manuscript for him.[34] Moore sent it to Victor Gollancz, whose

[32]Peter Davison, *George Orwell: A Literary Life* (Basingstoke: Macmillan, 1996) gives a good account of Orwell's pursuit of the writing profession, including the difficulties of getting his early books into print – see especially pp. 56–8.
[33]Peter Stansky & William Abrahams, *The Unknown Orwell* (New York: Knopf, 1972; reprinted Stanford, CA: Stanford University Press, 1994), pp. 271–2.
[34]Orwell to Leonard Moore, 6 January 1932, CW, X, p. 241; Orwell to T.S. Eliot, 17 February 1932, CW, X, p. 242; Orwell to Leonard Moore, 26 April, 1932, CW, X, pp. 242–3; Gillian Fenwick, *George Orwell: A Bibliography* (Winchester: St Paul's Bibliographies, 1988), pp. 1–4 gives a neat summary of the book's composition history.

reader (Gerald Gould) provided an enthusiastic report, urging publication but warning about the risks of prosecution for libel and defamation, or for obscenity and blasphemy. The lawyers were summoned, and naturally even more dire warning followed.[35] Orwell went to see Gollancz and then summarized in a letter to Moore the changes he was required to make: 'Names are to be changed, swearwords etc. cut out, & there is one passage which is to be either changed or cut out – a pity, as it is about the only good bit of writing in the book, but he says the circulating libraries would not stand for it.' On the face of it, Orwell got on with making the changes required uncomplainingly.[36] But he was only prepared to go so far. He took only a week or so to make the necessary changes and reported to Moore that 'I have made the alterations of names etc. that he asked for, & I think there is now nothing that can cause offence. The passage between pp. 6 & 13 that was objected to cannot be altered very radically. I have crossed out or altered the phrases that seemed to show too definitely what was happening & perhaps like this it might pass inspection. If not, I think the only thing to do is to remove Chap. II in toto, as Chap. III follows fairly consecutively from Chap. I.'[37] Chapter II did indeed pass inspection. Toned down though it may have been, the chapter is a jarringly jaunty account of sexual violence and rape, possibly more offensive now than when first published, albeit on different grounds.[38]

Editing *Down and Out in Paris and London* for his edition of Orwell's *Complete Works*, Peter Davison has been able to restore some of Orwell's original, making use of the evidence of his dealings with Gollancz, of a proof copy of the first edition, and of the French translation of 1935, with which Orwell was directly involved. Thus, the English version published in 1935 substituted a dash ('—') for most swear words, which Davison has often been able to restore (mainly from the proof) to a slightly more forthcoming state: 'f—' for fuck(ing), even 'c—' for cunt on occasion.[39] Occasionally, using the French version, he has gone even further as in this discussion of swearing itself:

The whole business of swearing, especially English swearing, is mysterious. Of its very nature swearing is as irrational as magic – indeed, it is a species of magic. But there is also a paradox about it, namely this: Our intention in swearing is to shock and wound, which we do by mentioning

---

[35]Bernard Crick, *George Orwell: A Life* (London: Penguin, rev. ed., 1992), pp. 223–4.

[36]Orwell to Leonard Moore, 1 July 1932, CW, X, p. 252.

[37]Orwell to Leonard Moore, 6 July 1932, CW, X, p. 253.

[38]George Orwell, *Down and Out in Paris and London* [CW, I] (London: Secker & Warburg, 1986), pp. 6–11 (Penguin ed. pp. 6–12).

[39]E.g. Orwell, *Down and Out in Paris and London*, pp. 143, 138 (Penguin ed. pp. 150–1, 145). For a full discussion and summary see the editor's 'Textual Note', pp. 217–30 (not in Penguin).

something to do with the sexual functions. But the strange thing is that when a word is well established as a swear word, it seems to lose its original meaning; that is, it loses the thing that made it into a swear word. A word becomes an oath because it means a certain thing, and, because it has become an oath, it ceases to mean that thing. For example, 'fuck'. The Londoners do not now use, or very seldom use, this word in its original meaning; it is on their lips from morning till night, but it is a mere expletive and means nothing. Similarly with 'bugger', which is rapidly losing its original sense. One can think of similar instances in French – for example, *'foutre'* [fuck] which is now a quite meaningless expletive. The word *'bougre'* [bugger], also, is still used occasionally in Paris, but the people who use it, or most of them, have no idea what it once meant. The rule seems to be that words accepted as swear words have some magical character, which sets them apart and makes them useless for ordinary conversation.[40]

The tone – matter-of-fact, unshocked, comfortable and familiar with the demotic – typifies Orwell's discussions of obscenity, especially of obscene language. The passage continues with a discussion of words used to insult, and here a satirical edge at the absurdity and irrationality of what is considered taboo, and what not, edges in.

Why is 'bastard' the worst insult in English, when 'taken for what it means, [it] is hardly an insult at all'? Why is 'cow' an insult to women when 'cows are among the most likeable of animals'? Why can you print *je m'en fous* [I don't give a fuck, approximately speaking] in England when the phrase has to end with 'f—' in France? Why is 'barnshoot' a word of gentle 'badinage in English', while its Hindi original *bahinchut* [sister-fucker, or, more literally, sister's-cunt] is a 'vile and unforgiveable insult in India'?

Orwell concluded that Londoners were more careful not to swear in front of women than Parisians. Indeed, in Paris 'the women [themselves] swear freely'.[41]

Orwell no doubt learnt from the experience of working with Gollancz on *Down and Out in Paris and London*, and certainly seems quickly to have acquired a keener sense of what could and what couldn't be printed. That did not, however, spare him from wrangling over the text of his next few books.

---

[40]Orwell, *Down and Out in Paris and London*, pp. 178–9 (Penguin ed. pp. 189–90). All of the words in this part of the discussion (including 'bastard') were printed in the English edition of 1933. See also George Orwell, *Down and Out in Paris and London*, ed. John Brannigan (Oxford: Oxford University Press, World's Classics edition, 2021), pp. 139–41 and the explanatory notes. This edition prints the 1933 first edition text.

[41]Orwell, *Down and Out in Paris and London*, pp. 179–80 (Penguin ed. pp. 190–1).

His second book (and first novel) *Burmese Days* was first published in the United States in October 1934, but an English edition did not appear until June 1935. Leonard Moore had greater difficulty placing the book with an English publisher. This may have been in part for political reasons. Orwell was later to recall that *Animal Farm* 'had to be peddled from publisher to publisher over a year or so, just as had happened earlier with my novel *Burmese Days*, which attacked another vested interest, British Imperialism'.[42] There is no contemporary evidence to support this claim, though Orwell did tell Henry Miller that the book had to be published first in the United States 'because my publisher was afraid the India Office might take steps to have it suppressed'.[43] Nonetheless, both Gollancz and Heinemann rejected the book primarily for fear of libel or defamation. The American publishers, Harpers', had similar concerns but opted to take the risk. Jonathan Cape also rejected the book before Gollancz decided in February 1935 to reconsider, perhaps emboldened by the American publication.[44] This did not mean, however, that Gollancz would be happy to publish the text that had appeared in America. As Orwell told Leonard Moore, 'he thinks that if time were taken the libellous points might be cleared up'.[45] Time was taken. Orwell met Gollancz and his lawyers and reported to Moore that they were quite willing to publish 'subject to a few trifling alterations which will not take more than a week'.[46] A raft of changes was made to the text. Orwell considered the English first edition to have been 'a garbled version'.[47] The Penguin edition of 1944 and the Uniform Edition of 1949 both derived from the American first edition, though Orwell added some further revisions of his own. The changes that were made for the Gollancz edition of 1935 were extensive, but virtually all of them were designed to make it impossible to identify places and people in the book with real locations or individuals. For example, the fictional setting of the novel, Kyauktada, had been based on the real town of Katha, and Orwell revised the text to obscure this. Names of people were changed – the chief Burman villain, U Po Kyin, was renamed U Po Sing (as Orwell said, this was 'not a possible Burmese name'); Dr Veraswami, friend of the main character Flory, was renamed Murkhaswami, again a name

---

[42] Orwell, Annotations to Randall Swingler, 'The Right to Free Expression', *Polemic*, September–October 1946, CW, XVIII, p. 442.

[43] Orwell to Henry Miller, 26/7 August 1936, CW, X, p. 496.

[44] Peter Stansky & William Abrahams, *Orwell: The Transformation* (New York: Knopf, 1979; reprinted Stanford, CA: Stanford University Press, 1994), pp. 50–8; Crick, *George Orwell*, pp. 245–7. For comments on the account provided by Stansky and Abrahams, see the editor's comments on Orwell, Telegram to Victor Gollancz, 19 February 1935, CW, X, pp. 375–6.

[45] Orwell to Leonard Moore, 2 February 1935, CW, X, p. 372.

[46] Orwell to Leonard Moore, 22 February 1935, CW X, p. 378; George Orwell, *Burmese Days* [CW, II] (London: Secker & Warburg, 1986), 'Appendix' and 'Textual Note', pp. 303–22 (not in Penguin ed., which for the main text has the same pagination).

[47] 'Orwell's Notes on His Books and Essays', CW, XX, p. 224.

'which could not actually belong to any real individual'. Orwell checked the names of British officials against the Burma Civil List for 1929, to make sure that no one of the same name was in Burma, and changed the name Lackersteen to Latimer on the grounds that he did 'once hear of somebody called Lackersteen'.[48] Some of this was summarized in a new author's note, which declared: 'All the characters in this book are entirely fictitious ... I have thought it better to sacrifice a little probability than to risk even seeming to caricature individuals – than which nothing could be further from my intention.'[49]

Fear of libel and defamation continued to haunt the publication of Orwell's next two novels, A Clergyman's Daughter (published in England before Burmese Days) and Keep the Aspidistra Flying, both published by Gollancz. By the time the second of these books was published, Orwell was clearly becoming weary of the excessive caution of his publishers and their lawyers. When Keep the Aspidistra Flying was undergoing its final changes in proof, Orwell was in the North, on the journey that led to the writing of The Road to Wigan Pier. From Wigan, he sent an exasperated telegram to Gollancz: 'ABSOLUTELY IMPOSSIBLE MAKE CHANGES SUGGESTED WOULD MEAN COMPLETE REWRITING.'[50] He made many of the changes anyway, explaining his exasperation to his literary agent: 'I have made the alterations Gollancz asked for ... It seems to me to have utterly ruined the book, but if they think it worth publishing in that state, well and good. Why I was annoyed was because they had not demanded these alterations earlier.' Being asked to make extensive changes to the proof while 'equalizing the letters' was unreasonable.[51]

A considerable number of changes were made to both of these novels, many concerned to reduce the risk of libel or defamation. Names were queried and checked; locations were blurred; even details that risked inadvertently making a character resemble a real person were removed.[52] The most notable example of this last tactic was the suppression in A Clergyman's Daughter of some of the detail about Mr Blifil-Gordon, Conservative party candidate and factory owner, originally portrayed as a Jewish convert to Roman Catholicism. Orwell admitted that 'I do know one M.P. who answers to this

[48]The changes are summarized in Orwell to Victor Gollancz Ltd, 28 February 1935, CW, X, pp. 379–81; and detailed in the 'Textual Note' to Orwell, Burmese Days, pp. 313–22.
[49]Orwell, Burmese Days, pp. 313–14.
[50]Orwell to Victor Gollancz Ltd, 19 February 1936, CW, X, p. 280.
[51]Orwell to Leonard Moore, 24 February 1936, CW, X, pp. 434–5.
[52]Full details are provided by Peter Davison in George Orwell, A Clergyman's Daughter [CW, III] (London: Secker & Warburg, 1986), pp. 299–307; and George Orwell, Keep the Aspidistra Flying [CW, IV] (London: Secker & Warburg, 1986), pp. 279–87. Subsequent to the publication of these editions, Davison gained access to the proof copies of both novels and these revealed further changes: see Peter Davison (ed.), George Orwell: A Life in Letters (London: Penguin, 2011), pp. 491–2.

description. So I will make the necessary alterations here.'[53] Similarly he had to provide extensive reassurance to the publishers that the character of the bookshop owner, Mr McKechnie, in *Keep the Aspidistra Flying* was not a portrait of his former employer at Booklover's Corner, Francis Westrope.[54] Some of the changes made seemed excessively cautious. Dorothy in *A Clergyman's Daughter* visits Lambeth Public Library in Orwell's original text, but he was persuaded to change this to 'the nearest public library'.[55] No doubt Gollancz could rest more easily once the threat of being sued by the militant librarians of Lambeth was averted. Almost all of the extensive changes made to the text of *Keep the Aspidistra Flying* related to the risk of libel. The book's satirical onslaught on the world of advertising carried some risk of inadvertent libel or defamation, so the examples given of product names and advertising copy were scrutinized closely.

But with these two books concerns about potential obscenity and other issues also returned. Gollancz's initial response to the typescript of *A Clergyman's Daughter* led Orwell to confide to Leonard Moore that 'I knew there would be trouble over that novel'. Some of the trouble related to 'points about libel, swearwords etc.' but these were 'a very small matter & could be put right by a few strokes of the pen'.[56] Early in the book, Orwell removed a suggestion that Mr Warburton had 'tried to rape' Dorothy, with the statement that he had 'begun making love to her, violently, outrageously, even brutally'.[57] It is an unfortunate sanitization of the book, though no reader today could miss the fact that Warburton subjected Dorothy to repeated sexual assault amounting to attempted rape. More direct acknowledgement of the fact might have done more to enable contemporary readers to understand Dorothy's revulsion at any thought of sexual activity.[58] The swearwords were potentially significant for the book's hop-picking scenes and especially for the section in which Orwell portrays, purely in dialogue, the experience of the book's central character, Dorothy, in living rough on the streets of central London.[59] He told Brenda Salkeld that the book 'is tripe, except for chap 3, part 1, which I am pleased with'.[60] 'Tripe' may be going too far, even for what is often considered to be Orwell's worst book, but he was surely right to take pride in his attempt to

---

[53]Orwell to Victor Gollancz Ltd, 1 February 1935, CW, X, p. 371.
[54]Orwell to Norman Collins, 18 February 1936, CW, X, p. 429.
[55]Orwell to Victor Gollancz Ltd, 10 January 1935, CW, X, p. 368.
[56]Orwell to Leonard Moore, 14 November 1934, CW, X, p. 358.
[57]Orwell, *A Clergyman's Daughter*, pp. 41, 299; Orwell to Victor Gollancz Ltd, 17 December 1934, CW, X, p. 361.
[58]Orwell, *A Clergyman's Daughter*, pp. 81–2, 100, 283. She does seem to tolerate some 'furtive fondling' among the London homeless, though largely because she 'is too far gone to care' (100).
[59]Orwell, *A Clergyman's Daughter*, pp. 151–84 (ch. 3, section i).
[60]Orwell to Brenda Salkeld, 7 March 1935, CW, X, p. 382.

capture the speech of London's down and out in this scene. Of course, the censorship of its language meant that this scene was unusually full of dashes, and Orwell must surely have regretted this, even if he had resigned himself to the inevitable from the start. With *Keep the Aspidistra* he was forced to fight back an attempt by the publishers to tone down the language even further. As he told them, 'The word "sod". I really cannot cut this out. I have used it in all my books before. A book like, for instance, Robert Graves's "Goodbye to All That", which was a best-seller, used "sod" freely.' Orwell won this battle and 'sod' withstood the attempt to replace it with 'swine'.[61]

A *Clergyman's Daughter* faced more substantial criticism for the Gollancz readers. Towards the end of the book, just before she returns home, Dorothy works in Mrs Creevy's school for girls. Orwell paints a devastating picture of the appalling standards, the cynicism, and the swindle constituted by such schools. Even the printed version is blunt and Orwell's strength of feeling leads him to editorialize on the matter, though the story itself is damning enough without this.[62] This printed version, though, had been extensively modified. Indeed the changes were on such a scale that they seem to have permanently darkened Orwell's view of a book, which, though it is psychologically unconvincing and involves awkward transitions between its scenes, in defiance of the reader's credulity and adding further to the sense of a book that does not hang together, is nonetheless magnificent in parts. Orwell did not give in on all points. His initial defensiveness – 'I am willing to admit that the part about the school, which is what seems to have aroused people's incredulity, is overdrawn, but not nearly so much as people think' – gave way to a mix of truculence and a willingness to do as much as necessary to get the book into print.[63] He considered cutting the material altogether (often his preferred response to censorship) but realized that this would 'make the ending of the book too abrupt'. Instead, he would spend a month rewriting the chapter.[64] It is clear that he extensively toned down some passages, but also that he stood his ground in places too. He sought to give 'a less exaggerated impression of the low standard prevailing', and even tried 'to make the standard at the school higher than I made it before' – anyone who has read the chapter will be wondering how it could ever have been much lower. But he would not alter the account he gave of the textbooks used in the school 'as it is substantially true' and 'I have seen schoolbooks similar to the ones I have described, though ... I have parodied them'; nor would he alter the passages dealing with Dorothy's clash with the parents, 'as, making allowance for a slight touch of burlesque, this

[61]Orwell to Norman Collins, 18 February 1936, CW, X, p. 429; Orwell, *Keep the Aspidistra Flying*, p. 282.
[62]Orwell, *A Clergyman's Daughter*, pp. 239–41.
[63]Orwell to Leonard Moore, 14 November 1934, CW, X, p. 358.
[64]Orwell to Leonard Moore, 20 November 1934, CW, X, p. 359.

is the kind of thing that does happen in these schools'. He defended his editorializing remarks that schools of this type were subject to no inspection of their educational quality. Orwell's references to parody and burlesque are significant, for they signal, I think, his awareness of the literal-mindedness of his censors and their failure to appreciate the quality of the *satire* with which he endeavoured to get across his point that these schools 'are apt to be more or less of a swindle, existing only to make money and not giving much more than a pretence of education'. None of his changes, fortunately, prevented Orwell from delivering his message.[65]

Orwell did what was necessary to get his work into print, but it is clear enough that he thought the censorship of obscenity was largely absurd. His reflections on the matter of swear words, begun in *Down and Out in Paris and London*, were later resumed in a way that made his attitude clear. The discussion is worth quoting in full:

Early this year I met an American publisher who told me that his firm had just had a nine-months lawsuit from which it had emerged partially victorious, though out of pocket. It concerned the printing of a four-letter word which most of us use every day, generally in the present participle [i.e. 'fucking'].

The United States is usually a few years ahead of Britain in these matters. You could print 'b—' ['bugger'] in full in American books at a time when it had to appear in English ones as B dash. Recently it has become possible in England to print the word in full in a book, but in periodicals it still has to be B dash. Only five of six years ago it was printed in a well-known monthly magazine, but the last-minute panic was so great that a weary staff had to black the word out by hand.

As to the other word, the four-letter one, it is still unprintable in periodicals in this country, but in books it can be represented by its first letter and a dash. In the United States this point was reached at least a dozen years ago. Last year the publishing firm in question tried the experiment of printing the word in full. The book was suppressed, and after nine months of litigation the suppression was upheld. But in the process an important step forward was made. It was ruled that you may now print the first and last letters of the word with two asterisks in between, clearly indicating that it had four letters. This makes it reasonably sure that within a few years the word will be printable in full.

So does progress continue – and it is genuine progress, in my opinion, for if only our half-dozen 'bad' words could be got off the lavatory wall

---

[65]Orwell to Victor Gollancz Ltd, 17 December 1934, CW, X, pp. 361–2; Orwell to Victor Gollancz Ltd, 1 February 1935, CW, X, pp. 370–1.

and on to the printed page, they would soon lose their magical quality, and the habit of swearing, degrading to our thoughts and weakening to our language, might become less common.[66]

The last paragraph is particularly telling. Orwell was not fond of obscenity as such. The degradation and weakening of language was, by 1946, one of his central preoccupations, and it seems that habits of swearing contributed to the problem. But the remedy was to allow the language of the street – and of the lavatory wall – to be printed openly so that it could be demystified. In this matter, as in so many, Orwell's instincts were to oppose censorship. It was absurd to keep out of print words that people used every day; it inhibited the ability of writers to capture demotic speech authentically; and hiding it from view only made mindless swearing seem a more daring thing to do.

As a writer, Orwell – apart from the use of four-letter words – was not inclined to obscenity. His approach to sex in his fiction, from *Burmese Days* to *Nineteen Eighty-Four*, was more coy than explicit. But he certainly read extensively writers who took a different approach, notably James Joyce (especially *Ulysses*), D.H. Lawrence and Henry Miller. And he wrote about all of them, his discussions of Miller being especially relevant to the topic of obscenity. Orwell read all three writers during the 1930s. In his first writings he had commented on the 'illogical censorship' arising from prudery that had led to the suppression of Joyce's *Ulysses*, though it seems he only read the book later.[67] His correspondence, especially with Brenda Salkeld, was eloquent about his encounter with *Ulysses*, though he also reported to her his reading of Lawrence's *Sons and Lovers*. He recalled reading it before in 1924, 'the unexpurgated version that time'.[68] It was Joyce that captured his imagination. He had to borrow a copy of *Ulysses* from a friend in order to be able to read it in 1933,[69] only getting his own copy (from Paris presumably) a year or so later:

> I managed to get my copy of 'Ulysses' through safely this time. I rather wish I had never read it. It gives me an inferiority complex. When I read a book like that and then come back to my own work, I feel like a eunuch who has taken a course in voice production and can pass himself off

[66]Orwell, 'As I Please', 64, 6 December 1946, CW, XVIII, pp. 511–12.

[67]Orwell, 'Censorship in England', December 1928, CW, X, pp. 117–18.

[68]Orwell to Brenda Salkeld, 7 May 1935, CW, X, p. 386. Lawrence was one of the authors about whom Orwell wrote the most, but not generally with respect to his obscenity. See Richard Lance Keeble, 'Love of Lawrence', in Keeble, *Orwell's Moustache: Addressing More Orwellian Matters* (Bury St Edmunds: Abramis, 2021), ch. 5.

[69]Orwell to Eleanor Jaques, 30 November 1932, CW, X, p. 276.

fairly well as a bass or baritone, but if you listen closely you can hear the good old squeak just the same as ever.[70]

Orwell's initial response to *Ulysses* did not dwell on the book's obscenity, though he did emphasize the feature of the book that was most linked to it: 'instead of taking as his material the conventional and highly simplified version of life presented in most novels, Joyce attempts to present life more or less as it is lived'.[71] But his encounter with the more vivid obscenity, the 'callous coarseness', of Henry Miller put things in perspective. As with Joyce, the obscenity was not without purpose, being used to 'describe sexual life from the point of view of the man in the street'. Referring to one of his favourite authors, he noted that:

A book like *Tropic of Cancer*, which deals with sex by brutally insisting on the facts, swings the pendulum too far, no doubt, but it does swing it in the right direction. Man is not a Yahoo. But he is rather like a Yahoo and needs to be reminded of it from time to time.

Yet, though he remained always an admirer of Miller's early work, especially *Tropic of Cancer*, Orwell had no doubt of Joyce's superiority. *Tropic of Cancer* was likely to be coupled in critical discussion with *Ulysses*, thanks to their common obscenity but 'quite wrongly'. '*Ulysses* is not only a vastly better book, but also quite different in intention. Joyce is primarily an artist; Mr. Miller is a discerning though hardboiled person giving his opinions about life.'[72] This verdict should only be tempered a little by Orwell's later admission that he had underpraised Miller because 'I did not wish to seem or to be impressed by mere obscenity'.[73] The remark captures his ambivalence well. He appreciated the realistic purposes of the obscenity that was intended to put the 'thinking man' back into contact with the 'man-in-the-street'. But a certain distaste remains evident. As he told a correspondent, there was no doubt about 'the disgusting subject matter of much of Miller's writing, and the narrowing down of vision that this implies'. But nonetheless, 'he was being true to experience'. Miller lived among derelict people and 'wrote truthfully about them'. *Tropic of Cancer* was 'a disgusting book, but it is not pornographic'. Pornography was written 'to arouse sexual desire' but the use of obscenity in the description of sexual activity does not necessarily

[70]Orwell to Brenda Salkeld, Early September? 1934, CW, p. 348.
[71]Orwell to Brenda Salkeld, 10 December 1933, CW, X, p. 326; also Orwell to Brenda Salkeld, 10 March 1933, CW, X. p. 307.
[72]Orwell, 'Review of *Tropic of Cancer* by Henry Miller; *The World at the Door* by Robert Francis', November 1935, CW, X, pp. 404–5.
[73]Orwell, 'Review of *Black Spring* by Henry Miller [etc.]', September 1936, CW, X, p. 499.

do this, 'very often quite the contrary'.[74] Orwell captured well the use (valid in both cases) that Joyce and Miller made of obscenity:

> *Tropic of Cancer* ... is by no means a book of pornography, but the dirty words are integral to it and no expurgated edition would be possible, because it is a straightforward attempt to describe life as it is seen and lived by the average sensual man. I emphasise 'straightforward', because Miller is in a sense not attempting very much. If one wants to describe life as it really is, there are two main difficulties to be got over. The first is that our language is so crude compared with our mental processes that communication between human beings is chancy at best. The second is that so much in our lives is normally considered unprintable that the most ordinary words and actions, once they get onto paper, are given a false emphasis. Joyce in *Ulysses* was dealing with both these problems, but primarily with the first; Miller is only dealing with the second, and dealing with it by pretending that it does not exist.[75]

It is important to remember that the books that Orwell was reading and discussing were suppressed in England. His most immediate brush with the laws relating to obscenity came in 1939. He had accumulated a number of Henry Miller's books while working on 'Inside the Whale'. This had not gone unnoticed, with consequences that Orwell noted in his diary: 'All my books from the Obelisk Press this morning seized by the police, with warning from Public Prosecutor that I am liable to be prosecuted if importing such things again. They had opened my letter addressed to Obelisk Press evidently at Hitchin. Do not know yet whether because of the address or because my own mail is now scrutinised.'[76] He explained further to Victor Gollancz:

> I cannot *at this moment* lend you 'Tropic of Cancer', because my copy has been seized. While I was writing my last book two detectives suddenly arrived at my house with orders from the public prosecutor to seize all books which I had 'received through the post'. A letter of mine addressed to the Obelisk Press had been seized and opened in the post. The police

---

[74]Orwell to Miss Shaw, 5 September 1946, CW, XVIII, p. 388.
[75]Orwell, 'The End of Henry Miller', December 1942, CW, XIV, p. 217. See also Orwell, 'Inside the Whale', March 1940, CW, XII, esp. pp. 89–90.
[76]Orwell, 'Diary of Events Leading Up to War', 12 August 1939, CW, XI, p. 393; Orwell, *Diaries*, ed. Peter Davison (London: Penguin, 2010), p. 191. One of things Orwell traced in this diary was the gradual imposition of wartime regulations on speech and other activities, including the passage of the Emergency Powers Act. He noted a couple of days after being raided by the police: 'It appears that the opening of letters to persons connected with leftwing parties is now so normal as to excite no remark', CW, XI, p. 394; *Diaries*, p. 193. Obelisk Press was a Paris-based publisher that specialized in printing English-language books that could not legally be printed in the United States or the UK.

were only carrying out orders and were very nice about it, and even the public prosecutor wrote and said that he understood that as a writer I might have a need for books which it was illegal to possess. On these grounds he sent me back certain books, e.g. 'Lady Chatterley's Lover', but it appears that Miller's books have not been in print long enough to have become respectable. However, I know that Cyril Connolly has a copy of 'Tropic of Cancer'. He is down with flu at present, but when I can get in touch with him again I will borrow the book and pass it on to you.[77]

There is no doubt a very English decency in this episode that Orwell would have appreciated.

Obscenity was, of course, not just a matter of literary art. In other domains, it could achieve something more noble in Orwell's eyes. It could be our rebellion against the heroic. His famous essay on the comic postcard, an object available everywhere but associated specially with the seaside resort, acknowledged that their 'outstanding characteristic' was obscenity.[78] Half or more of them involved sex jokes, and amongst printed or written material they were alone in their degree of frankness, though the music hall equalled them. A small number were so obscene that 'Newsagents are occasionally prosecuted for selling them',[79] though most were protected by the plausible deniability provided by their reliance on the *double entendre*. Orwell's interpretation of the smutty postcard was oddly ambivalent. On the one hand, they were 'not intended as pornography but, a subtler thing, as a skit on pornography'. Indeed, their 'brand of humour only has meaning in relation to a fairly strict moral code'.[80] The postcards' central subject was marriage, lampooned as invariably a victory for wives over husbands in their inevitable struggle for power. But the smutty postcard was a form of transgression that reinforced a social order. The implication was 'that marriage is something profoundly exciting and important, the biggest event in the average human being's life'. Postcards 'imply a stable society in which marriage is indissoluble and family loyalty taken for granted'.[81] This was an order to which we were sentenced for life. But as the essay progressed, Orwell moved beyond this sort of stock argument to something more celebratory.

The dirty postcard represented the 'Sancho Panza' view of life. Mostly in art and literature, it is the heroic, the saintly or the visionary that is celebrated (even in delusionary form, like Don Quixote). But none of us wants to live by these qualities all of the time: 'part of you is a little fat man

---

[77]Orwell to Victor Gollancz, 8 January 1940, CW, XII, p. 5. The second paragraph of this letter is the source of the epigraph to Part II of this book.
[78]George Orwell, 'The Art of Donald McGill', September 1941, CW, XIII, p. 25.
[79]Orwell, 'Art of Donald McGill', CW, XIII, p. 28.
[80]Orwell, 'Art of Donald McGill', CW, XIII, p. 27.
[81]Orwell, 'Art of Donald McGill', CW, XIII, p. 27.

whose sees very clearly the advantages of staying alive with a whole skin'. This part of us is less interested in tilting at windmills and more interested in 'soft beds, no work, pots of beer and women with "voluptuous" figures'.[82] And the seaside postcard is Sancho Panza's small act of rebellion against the canons of politeness:

> Whatever is funny is subversive, every joke is ultimately a custard pie, and the reason why so large a proportion of jokes centre round obscenity is simply that all societies, as the price of survival, have to insist on a fairly high standard of sexual morality. A dirty joke is not, of course, a serious attack upon morality, but it is a sort of mental rebellion, a momentary wish that things were otherwise.[83]

Though 'high sentiment always wins in the end' – 'when it comes to the pinch, human beings are heroic' – nonetheless that other side of us, the unheroic and hen-pecked, needs on occasional outing, usually to the seaside.[84] 'On the whole, human beings want to be good, but not too good, and not quite all the time.'[85]

Certainly, this can be seen as a 'defence', even a 'celebration', of obscenity.[86] But there is a little more to it than this. It was less obscenity as such and more obscenity as an aspect of vulgar humour that Orwell was celebrating.[87] 'Every joke is a tiny revolution,' he later said.[88] Jokes punctured orthodoxy; they punctured the dignity of those who served the establishment. But they did not *need* to be obscene to do this. What Orwell saw as a modern preference for 'clean fun' and the avoidance of vulgar obscenity was actually the symptom of a wider problem: 'a general unwillingness to touch upon any serious or controversial subject'.

> Obscenity is, after all, a kind of subversiveness. Chaucer's 'Miller's Tale' is a rebellion in the moral sphere, as *Gulliver's Travels* is a rebellion in the political sphere. The truth is that you cannot be memorably funny

---

[82]Orwell, 'Art of Donald McGill', CW, XIII, pp. 28–9.

[83]Orwell, 'Art of Donald McGill', CW, XIII, p. 29.

[84]Orwell, 'Art of Donald McGill', CW, XIII, p. 29.

[85]Orwell, 'Art of Donald McGill', CW, XIII, p. 30.

[86]The terms are from the valuable essay by David Pascoe, 'Orwell's Dirty Postcards', in Mina Gorji (ed.), *Rude Britannia* (London: Routledge, 2007), ch. 5, p. 76; also Richard Lance Keeble, '"The Art of Donald McGill": Orwell and the Pleasures of Sex', in Richard Lance Keeble (ed.), *George, Orwell, the Secret State and the Making of* Nineteen Eighty-Four (Bury St Edmunds: Abramis, 2020), ch. 7.

[87]On Orwell's much-neglected humour, see especially Richard Lance Keeble, '"There Is Always Room for One More Custard Pie": Orwell's Humour', in Keeble (ed.), *George, Orwell, the Secret State and the Making of* Nineteen Eighty-Four, ch. 8.

[88]Orwell, 'Funny, but Not Vulgar', 1 December 1944. CW, XVI, p. 483.

without *at some point* raising topics which the rich, the powerful and the complacent would prefer to see left alone.

Yes, 'you *cannot* be funny without being vulgar', but vulgarity doesn't have to be about sex. It is vulgar to talk about 'death, childbirth and poverty' too. There are serious matters but 'to be funny ... you have got to be serious'. Serious in the way that Boccaccio was in ridiculing the ideas of Hell and Purgatory, or that Swift was in stripping humanity of its dignity or that Falstaff was in his praise of cowardice and rejection of honour. Obscenity was just one of the ways in which humour provided 'a temporary rebellion against virtue'.[89]

Obscenity could, then, serve at least two purposes for Orwell. It could aid the realistic portrayal of the way in which people lived and spoke; it could facilitate the mild rebelliousness of humour. These were good reasons to oppose its censorship. But Orwell's 'celebration' of obscenity was not unlimited. His essay on 'the ethics of the detective story' contrasted the ethos of E.W. Hornung's late-Victorian stories about the gentleman crook, Raffles, with that of the crime novels of James Hadley Chase, in particular *No Orchids for Miss Blandish* (1939).[90] Whereas the cricket-playing Raffles observed a gentleman's code and his crimes involved 'very few corpses, hardly any blood, no sex crimes, no sadism, no perversions of any kind', Chase portrayed a 'sordid and brutal' world. Blood flowed freely, but this was also a world of sexual violence, rape and cruelty. The book 'assumes great sexual sophistication in its readers', but has little place for 'normal sexuality'.[91] Though the book was eventually withdrawn, it seems to have caused little outrage amongst readers, so far as Orwell could see. But it outraged Orwell, not so much for its obscenity and sexual perversion but for its unjudgemental acceptance of a world driven only by 'the pursuit of power'. It was not its display of sexual *libido* that disgusted Orwell; it was the *libido dominandi*, the lust for power that undelay violence, whether sexual or not, that he found appalling. *No Orchids for Miss Blandish* was a marker of the 'power-worship' that had come to dominate the modern world. Though in no way political, the book was 'pure Fascism'. It was a symptom of the same reality whose other symptoms included bombing

---

[89]Orwell, 'Funny, but Not Vulgar', CW, XVI, pp. 484–6.

[90]'Ethics of the Detective Story: From Raffles to Miss Blandish' was the title under which the essay appeared in its first American edition (in Dwight Macdonald's journal *politics*, November 1944). This was also the first to be uncensored. The publication in *Horizon* 10: 58 (October 1944), which appeared simply as 'Raffles and Miss Blandish' had toned down two of Orwell's swipes at Stalinist apologist intellectuals – see Orwell to Dwight Macdonald, 15 September 1944, CW, XVI, p. 405; Fenwick, *George Orwell: A Bibliography*, pp. 210–11.

[91]Orwell, 'Raffles and Miss Blandish', August 1944, CW, XVI, pp. 347–52.

civilians, torturing, 'flogging with rubber truncheons', and the systematic falsification of evidence. In this sort of world,

> A tyrant is all the more admired if he happens to be a bloodstained crook as well, and 'the end justifies the means' often becomes, in effect, 'the means justifies itself provided it is dirty enough'. This idea colours the outlook of all sympathisers with totalitarianism, and accounts, for instance, for the positive delight with which many English intellectuals greeted the Nazi-Soviet pact. It was a step only doubtfully useful to the USSR, but it was entirely unmoral, and for that reason to be admired; the explanations of it, which were numerous and self-contradictory, could come afterwards.[92]

Not all obscenity was healthy. What mattered is what the obscenity was linked to. Its use in humour that punctured the dignity of the rich and powerful was something to be thankful for. Obscenity in the service of portraying the gritty realities of ordinary lives was just truth-telling. So, in a sense was the obscenity that featured in Chase's novels, featuring a brutal realism that was a symbol of a world losing its decency. That loss clearly came from a moral decay that was as much a cause of totalitarian attitudes as a consequence of them. Should Chase's books really be taken to heart by English readers, this 'would be good grounds for dismay'. We would know that 'emancipation is complete: Freud and Machiavelli have reached the outer suburbs'.[93] None of this means that Orwell was in favour of censorship.

A little before writing this, Orwell had given his attention to the work of Salvador Dali. Here his disgust at the obscenity was even stronger. Ironically, Orwell's essay, written for publication in 1944, was itself withdrawn on grounds of obscenity, its publisher (Hutchinson) having it cut out of the annual *Saturday Book* for which it was intended. It was first published in book form in Orwell's *Critical Essays* of 1946.[94] It is a pity, perhaps, that Orwell read Dali entirely at face value, though he is far from alone in doing so. Had he seen the book as a deliberate attempt to outrage and to shock, he might have found in Dali a kindred spirit, someone of 'astonishing imagination and wit ... [with] fierce contempt as a free-thinking artist for any efforts to enforce conformity to consensus values'.[95] But Orwell's essay was grimly determined to believe everything that Dali said of himself, and

---

[92]Orwell, 'Raffles and Miss Blandish', CW, XVI, pp. 351–5.

[93]Orwell, 'Raffles and Miss Blandish', CW, XVI, p. 356.

[94]Fenwick, *George Orwell: A Bibliography*, pp. 166–7; Orwell, 'As I Please', 58, 9 February 1945, CW, XVII, pp. 43–4, where he comments on the fact that none of the reviewers of the *Saturday Book* that still listed him as a contributor noticed the absence of his essay.

[95]Charles Stuckey, 'Dali Defiled', *Art in America*, 87:7 (July 1999), p. 29.

frank in its account of Dali's autobiography, noting for example that 'well into adult life he keeps up the practice of masturbation, and likes to do this, apparently, in front of the looking-glass'. He diagnosed in Dali a fascination with 'sexual perversion and necrophilia' that was, again, imbued with social and political significance. Dali's was a 'perversion of instinct that has been made possible by the machine age', and is instructive for that reason.[96] It was the necrophilia that weighed most heavily for Orwell. 'It is a book that stinks.' But Orwell took in the case of Dali an attitude very similar to that he was later to take with Ezra Pound. There was artistic talent of a high order, perhaps more so with Dali than Pound. 'He has fifty times more talent than most of the people who would denounce his morals and jeer at his painting.' But this did not excuse him from moral blame. His defenders may claim that an 'artist is to be exempt from the moral laws that are binding on ordinary people'. Not so. 'If Shakespeare returned to the earth to-morrow, and if it were found that his favourite recreation was raping little girls in railway carriages, we should not tell him to go ahead with it on the ground that he might write another *King Lear*.' Dali might have committed no crime, and thus be unpunishable, but he still did real harm in 'encouraging necrophiliac reveries'. In short, he 'is a good draughtsman and a disgusting human being'. Neither invalidates the other, a view typical of Orwell's attitude to such matters.[97] So too was this:

> Not, of course, that Dali's autobiography, or his pictures, ought to be suppressed. Short of the dirty postcards that used to be sold in Mediterranean seaport towns, it is a doubtful policy to suppress anything, and Dali's fantasies probably cast useful light on the decay of capitalist civilization. But what he clearly needs is diagnosis.[98]

Orwell consistently defended a minimalist view of what limits should be placed on free expression, and he consistently defended the right to be heard even of those who disgusted or appalled, whether morally or politically. Dali, like *No Orchids for Miss Blandish*, was valuable evidence of the deep spiritual malaise that had engulfed the world. 'He is a symptom of the world's illness.' We needed to see this evidence. Dali was by instinct, Orwell told us, a talented artist in a style that was essentially Edwardian, but he was not content to be conventional. He wanted to be a Napoleonic genius, and so fled 'into wickedness'. The lessons here were not political. We need the psychologist or the sociologist to help us understand the case of Salvador Dali.[99]

---

[96]Orwell, 'Benefit of Clergy: Notes on Salvador Dali', June 1944, published 1946, CW, XVI, pp. 233–5.
[97]Orwell, 'Benefit of Clergy', CW, XVI, pp. 236–7.
[98]Orwell, 'Benefit of Clergy', CW, XVI, p. 238.
[99]Orwell, 'Benefit of Clergy', CW, XVI, pp. 238–40.

Orwell's final novel of the 1930s, *Coming Up for Air*, faced none of the censorship that his earlier books had done.[100] There was less artistic need here for obscenity or the language of the street, though the book is not without its modest share of 'f—'s and 'b—'s.[101] But, before leaving Orwell's experience of being censored, we should consider his two political books, *The Road to Wigan Pier* and *Homage to Catalonia*. Neither was mauled in the way that his early fiction or *Down and Out in Paris and London* had been,[102] but their publication history does foreshadow some of the challenges that Orwell faced in the 1940s. *The Road to Wigan Pier* had an easy ride through the publication process, partly because Orwell and his wife, Eileen, were both in Spain and could not read the proofs. Gollancz had commissioned the book and Orwell began the journey to the North West that is recorded in the *Road to Wigan Pier* in January 1936, seemingly with some money from Victor Gollancz to cover his research costs (maybe £50). Gollancz had commissioned the book. In late December, just as Orwell was leaving for Spain, Gollancz also decided on a Left Book Club edition, with much larger sales at a much lower cover price.[103] Gollancz made this decision after he had seen the manuscript, and in spite of being altogether appalled at the second part of the book, Orwell's attack on the fashionable middle-class Communists and Socialists of his day. Even Orwell himself, when he sent the typescript to Leonard Moore on 15 December, doubted that a Left Book Club edition would be possible, partly on the grounds that the book was 'on the surface, not very left-wing'.[104] It seems that Gollancz tried to persuade him to allow only the first part, the account of the miners of Wigan, to be published for the Left Book Club. This was refused. Gollancz published anyway, and *The Road to Wigan Pier* was the Left Book Club choice for March 1937, as well as being published in a trade edition. The Left Book Club version appeared with a Foreword by Gollancz, who had not sought Orwell's permission to include it.[105]

The Foreword is an extraordinary document. Read in retrospect, at least, it resonates with the bad faith of the fellow-traveller that Orwell was to

---

[100]See George Orwell, *Coming Up for Air* [CW, VII] (London: Secker & Warburg, 1986), pp. 249–55 (Peter Davison's 'Textual Note' – not in Penguin ed.).

[101]E.g. Orwell, *Coming Up for Air*, pp. 85, 159. The Penguin Classics ed. has the same pagination.

[102]Though a reference to 'rooks copulating' in the manuscript was changed to 'courting' for the proof, and then to 'treading' for the printed version: George Orwell, *The Road to Wigan Pier*, p. 228 (not in Penguin ed.).

[103]Orwell, '*The Road to Wigan Pier* Diary', CW, X, p. 417; Peter Davison's notes on Orwell to Victor Gollancz, 19 December 1936, CW, X, pp. 529–32. The amount of the advance is unclear, and I have followed Davison's judgement, but cf. Crick, *George Orwell*, pp. 278–9; Fenwick, *George Orwell: A Bibliography*, pp. 50–1.

[104]Orwell to Leonard Moore, 15 December 1936, CW, X, p. 528.

[105]Crick, *George Orwell*, pp. 309–10.

denounce in the 1940s. But the context here was different. The Foreword began with a rather pained attempt to make the point that the Left Book Club had no policy and its selectors enforced no party-line, except perhaps 'the fight against war and Fascism' for which the People's Front stood. This is ominous. It's the sort of thing that generally introduces an attempt to censor or suppress. To be fair, Gollancz says some good things about the book, 'so full of a burning indignation against poverty and oppression'. He captures well the point of the second part, which is to explain why 'so many of the best people detest Socialism'. This can be overcome 'by making the elemental appeal of "liberty" and "justice"' in ways that will cross class lines. Appealing though that might be, Gollancz nonetheless found more than a hundred passages in the book with which he might disagree (it's not a long book), and invited readers who might be provoked by what Orwell said to remember that he wrote as a member of the middle class. Gollancz argued that the very fact that Orwell could say some of the things he did was actually evidence for Gollancz's own case against him. Only a Socialist corrupted by his own middle-class attitudes could say what Orwell did. He was thus caught by his own denunciation of middle-class Socialism. Orwell exhibited the shame of the middle classes, for which the only remedy was a classless society. His attack on Socialists as being 'stupid, offensive and insincere' did not, Gollancz reassured readers in advance of their encounter with the book, match what he could see himself. Orwell's charge that Socialists were all cranks was just a product of his middle-class conventionality.

> His conscience, his sense of decency, his understanding of realities tell him to declare himself a Socialist: but fighting against this compulsion there is in him all the time a compulsion far less conscious but almost – though fortunately not quite – as strong: the compulsion to conform to the mental habits of his class.

He displayed himself as the 'frightful snob' who hated snobbery, the intellectual who hated intellectuals. Patronizing though this put down was, there is, of course some truth in it. Orwell was an intellectual deeply suspicious of intellectuals.[106]

Orwell's second wife was later to tell Bernard Crick that Orwell was 'very angry' about Gollancz's unauthorized Foreword, even though he was polite about it at the time. Indeed, his response to Gollancz was astonishingly mild-mannered. He only got to see the book during a period of leave in Barcelona, and soon after wrote to thank Gollancz for his introduction to the book. 'I like the introduction very much, though of course I could have

---

[106]Gollancz in Orwell, *Road to Wigan Pier*, pp. 216–21 (not in Penguin ed.).

answered some of the criticisms you made. It was the kind of discussion of what one is really talking about that one always wants & never seems to get from the professional reviewers.'[107]

In spite of the Foreword, it is to Gollancz's credit that he published *The Road to Wigan Pier*, presumably against advice that he would have received from Harry Pollitt, General Secretary of the Communist Party of Great Britain.[108] He was careful in the latter part of his Foreword to make sure that he defended the Soviet Union against Orwell's charge that it glorified a dehumanizing industrial civilization.[109] The decision to publish must have been a recognition of the high quality of Orwell's reportage in the first part of the book. The whole episode was a foretaste of Orwell's later experience with *Animal Farm*.

So too was the story of the publication of *Homage to Catalonia*. Almost immediately after returning from Spain, Orwell began work on this book. His writings on Spain, because of their powerful indictment of the Soviet Union's role in betraying the revolution, were politically suspect for Communists and those who, perhaps in the spirit of the Popular Front, sympathized with them. *The New Statesman* refused to publish two pieces on Spain because they contradicted its political policy.[110] It was clear to Orwell from the start that there was little chance that Gollancz, toeing a similar line to *The New Statesman*, would publish his book on Spain. Indeed, they more or less turned it down in July 1937 before any of it was written, Gollancz telling Orwell that though he wasn't a Communist he would publish nothing that would harm the united front against Fascism. At much the same time Orwell was contacted by Fredric Warburg, soliciting a book on Spain.[111] Secker and Warburg would indeed publish *Homage to Catalonia*, just as later they would be the publisher to accept *Animal Farm*. Orwell signed a contract for the book with Secker and Warburg on 1 September 1937.[112] The publishing

---

[107]Orwell to Victory Gollancz, 9 May 1937, CW, XI, pp. 22–3.

[108]Crick, *George Orwell*, p. 314.

[109]Gollancz in Orwell, *Road to Wigan Pier* pp. 221–3 (not in Penguin ed.).

[110]The pieces were Orwell, 'Review of *The Spanish Cockpit* by Franz Borkenau; *Volunteer in Spain* by John Sommerfield', July 1937, CW, XI, pp. 51–3, published instead in *Time and Tide*; and Orwell, 'Eye-Witness in Barcelona', August 1937, CW, pp. 54–9, published instead in *Controversy: The Socialist Forum*. For details see Orwell to Rayner Heppenstall, 31 July 1937, CW, XI, p. 53; Orwell to Geoffrey Gorer, 16 August 1937, CW, XI, pp. 68–9; and Orwell to Raymond Mortimer, 9 February 1938 (with additional material appended), CW, XI, pp. 116–20. Orwell had an enduring contempt for the pusillanimity of Kingsley Martin, editor of the *The New Statesman*.

[111]Orwell to Leonard Moore, 8 July 1937, CW, XI, pp. 37–9; Orwell to Rayner Heppenstall, 31 July 1937, CW, XI, p. 53. Though Warburg himself suggests that Orwell had come to see him as early as December 1936 to talk about a book on Spain: Fredric Warburg, *An Occupation for Gentlemen* (London: Hutchinson, 1959), pp. 231–2.

[112]Fenwick, *George Orwell: A Bibliography*, p. 64.

house had a reputation for publishing works of the non-Communist Left, as Orwell noted in a letter to *Time and Tide*. That letter sounded a note that presaged concerns of the future, sounding a warning about 'pro-Communist censorship'. 'Ten years ago it was almost impossible to get anything printed in favour of Communism; today it is almost impossible to get anything printed in favour of Anarchism or "Trotskyism".'[113]

Let us return, though, to Orwell at the beginning of the Second World War. The early years of the war – especially the defeats of Dunkirk in 1940 and Singapore in 1942 – sparked in Orwell a faith that Socialism would soon transform Britain and wipe away the arbitrary social privileges that disfigured its society and denied freedom and equality to the many. Initially, Orwell was frustrated that his personal war effort was confined to the Home Guard, which he joined in June 1940, even though he put great effort into making the Home Guard a potential guerrilla army to resist a German occupation of Britain. But on 18 August 1941 Orwell found another way to serve the anti-Fascist cause. He joined the staff of the British Broadcasting Corporation (BBC) and began a two-year stint working on wartime propaganda. The experience both challenged and helped to reshape his sense of intellectual responsibility.

# 3. 'All Propaganda Is Lies': Orwell, BBC Propaganda and Intellectual Responsibility

Fierce guardian of intellectual integrity (his own and others'), scornful of the dishonesty of propaganda, a paragon of truthfulness – George Orwell, though he was all of these things, spent more than two years producing and broadcasting wartime propaganda for the BBC's service to India.[114] Unable to serve the war effort in other ways (apart from his service in the Home Guard), Orwell accepted the chance to contribute to the anti-Nazi effort through propaganda work. 'Two wasted years', he was later to call them, and the only surprising thing about those years may seem to be that Orwell stuck with the BBC job for as long as he did. Orwell's reasons for leaving the BBC – on

---

[113]Orwell, 'To the Editor, *Time and Tide*', 4 February 1938, CW, XI, pp. 113–15. Warburg himself refers to his 'policy of anti-fascist publishing which paid no heed to communist susceptibilities': Warburg, *Occupation for Gentlemen*, p. 221.

[114]There has been a flurry of recent interest in Orwell's BBC years. See for example Peter Davison, 'Orwell at the BBC: Two Wasted Years?' (2011), available online: https://orwellsociety.com/orwell-at-the-bbc-two-wasted-years-by-prof-peter-davison/ (accessed 7 June 2022); Desmond Avery, *George Orwell at the BBC in 1942* (Wellingore: Garth Press, 2017); and Ron Bateman, *The Radio Front: The BBC and the Propaganda War 1939–45* (Cheltenham: The History Press, 2022), esp. ch. 12 on the Eastern Service.

23 November 1943 – were not primarily about the nature of the propaganda work or the censorship under which he laboured. His work was wasted partly because it was a distraction from what he considered more important work (he began writing *Animal Farm* almost immediately on leaving the BBC) and partly because he came to doubt altogether the effectiveness of the India broadcasts. He was, as he said in his resignation letter, 'wasting my own time and the public money on doing work that produces no result'. Returning 'to my normal work of writing and journalism I could be more useful than I am at present'.[115] Orwell had good cause to suspect the pointlessness of his BBC work. Laurence Brander, the BBC Eastern Services Intelligence Officer (and later author of the first book about Orwell), produced early in 1943 a damning report on the Eastern broadcasts: they reached a tiny audience.[116] Orwell had discussed the findings with Brander when he first returned from investigating the situation in India and noted in his diary: 'His conclusions so depressing that I can hardly bring myself to write them down.'[117] During Orwell's last months at the BBC, Brander reported as well on the audience response to individual broadcasters. Only 16 per cent of them enjoyed listening to Orwell (the same as Kingsley Martin, whom he loathed). This compares to 68 per cent for J.B. Priestley, 52 per cent for E.M. Forster and 56 per cent for C.E.M. Joad; most popular with listeners was Henry Wickham Steed (76 per cent), a former editor of *The Times*.[118]

The wasted years comment was made to the editor of *Partisan Review*, Philip Rahv, and immediately followed with the comment that, though he had immediately after leaving the BBC become literary editor of *Tribune*, he nonetheless had more time for his own creative work.[119] Alongside these things, there can be no doubt that Orwell was not really at home in a bureaucratic organization like the BBC. Indeed, it is hard to imagine him much at home in any organization: unlike Kafka, Orwell would not have made a good employee of an insurance company any more than of the BBC. One of his superiors, Norman Collins (the Empire Talks Manager), noted in December 1942 'that Blair is working rather too independently of the existing organisation'.[120] Before long the Assistant Controller of Overseas Broadcasts, R.A. Rendall, was also raising concerns 'that Blair is setting up an independent business as an Eastern Talks Director'.[121] Fortunately, Orwell had a defender. The Eastern Services Director, L.F. Rushbrook Williams, understood and appreciated the unusual qualities that Orwell

[115]Orwell to L.F. Rushbrook Williams, 24 September 1943, CW, XV, p. 251.
[116]CW, XV, pp. 343–56. The report was dated 11 January 1943.
[117]Orwell, *Diaries*, 5 October 1942, p. 366; CW, XIV, p. 76.
[118]CW, XV, pp. 247–8.
[119]Orwell to Philip Rahv, 9 December 1943, CW, XVI, p. 22.
[120]Norman Collins to L.F. Rushbrook Williams, 8 December 1942, CW, XIV, p. 226.
[121]Rendall's annotation to a memo sent on Orwell's behalf, 3 February 1943, CW, XIV, p. 335.

brought to the BBC. His marvellous annual assessment of his independent-minded employee is worth quoting at length:

> He has great facility in writing, and a literary flair which makes his work distinguished.
> Conscientiously as he endeavours to achieve objectivity, he finds it difficult to realise the shock which certain sentiments, to him plain matters of fact, may cause to the conservatively-minded. For which reason, his scripts require close scrutiny: and he is himself a poor judge of 'political expediency'.
> He supports uncomplainingly a considerable burden of poor health. This never affects his work, but occasionally strains his nerves.
> I have the highest opinion of his moral, as well as of his intellectual capacity. He is transparently honest, incapable of subterfuge, and, in early days, would have been either canonised – or burnt at the stake! Either way he would have sustained with stoical courage.
> An unusual colleague: but a mind, and a spirit, of real and distinguished worth.[122]

Orwell told Rahv that he would send him a copy of *Talking to India*, a selection of the talks broadcast to India, edited by Orwell.[123] The book included five of his own Weekly News Reviews under the title 'Five Specimens of Propaganda'. It also included an example from the other side, the text of a broadcast by Subhas Chandra Bose from Berlin in May 1942. Bose was an Indian nationalist who saw an opportunity to use the Axis powers to rid India of British imperialism. Orwell commented: 'There is a difference between honest and dishonest propaganda, and Bose's speech, with its enormous suppressions, obviously comes under the latter heading. We are not afraid to let these samples of our own and Axis broadcasts stand side by side.'[124] To Rahv he described the book as having 'some interest as a specimen of British propaganda (rather a favourable specimen, however, as we in the Indian Section were regarded as very unimportant and therefore left a fairly free hand)'.[125] He took a different line with Mark Benney, telling him that 'there was no "propaganda" in his slot – it was all modern poetry and belles-lettres'.[126] This, though, was only

---

[122]Quoted from Abha Sharma Rodrigues, 'George Orwell, the B.B.C. and India: A Critical Study', Unpublished PhD Thesis, University of Edinburgh, 1994, pp. 79–80. This thesis is the fullest account of Orwell's BBC years and their impact on his other work. Rushbrook Williams's appraisal of Orwell is dated 7 August 1943.

[123]On *Talking to India*, published 18 November 1943, see CW, XV, pp. 320–4.

[124]Orwell, '*Talking to India*: Introduction', CW, XV, p. 323.

[125]Orwell to Rahv, 9 December 1943, CW, XVI, p. 22.

[126]Quoted from Rodrigues, 'George Orwell, the B.B.C. and India', p. 75.

true if you ignore the many news reviews and commentaries that Orwell wrote, and some of which he read himself.[127]

The letter to Rahv suggests that Orwell saw his BBC work as honest propaganda. His resignation letter to Rushbrook Williams reinforced the view: 'I am not leaving because of any disagreement with BBC policy and still less on account of any kind of grievance. On the contrary I feel that throughout my association with the BBC I have been treated with the greatest generosity and allowed very great latitude. On no occasion have I been compelled to say on the air anything that I would not have said as a private individual.'[128] For Orwell, intellectual freedom was the freedom to be honest, and those intellectuals who abandoned their responsibility to the truth (or to truthfulness) were squandering the riches that freedom offered. The neat distinction between honest and dishonest propaganda suggested that it was possible to be a propagandist in wartime while retaining intellectual integrity.

Alas, if only this were so. Orwell had remarked in a blistering review of a book by one of his BBC bosses, Lionel Fielden, that 'Western civilization has given the intellectual security without responsibility'. That the propagandist mode came naturally to intellectuals was a measure of this irresponsibility. Orwell began the review – and remember this is the man whose loathing of advertising had been fully displayed in *Keep the Aspidistra Flying* – thus: 'If you compare commercial advertising with political propaganda, one thing that strikes you is its relative intellectual honesty. The advertiser at least knows what he is aiming at – that is, money – whereas the propagandist, when he is not a lifeless hack, is often a neurotic working off some private grudge and actually desirous of the exact opposite of the thing he advocates.'[129] Perhaps this is only meant to apply to the dishonest propaganda, but I think not. When Orwell resumed his war-time diary he had been working for the BBC for about six months, having started work on 18 August 1941. The first entry in the diary reflected on these six months, concluding: 'All propaganda is lies, even when one is telling the truth. I don't think this matters so long as one knows what one is doing, and why.'[130] Whether this lying mattered or not, it took its toll on Orwell. In the first indication of his intention to resign, he told Rayner Heppenstall, who must have accused him of cynicism:

---

[127]The exact number that he wrote is hard to determine, but Davison comes up with a total between 219 and 221, with just over half of these written to be translated into other languages: CW, XIII, p. 83.

[128]Orwell to Rushbrook Williams, 24 September 1943, CW, XV, p. 251.

[129]Orwell, 'Gandhi in Mayfair. Review of *Beggar My Neighbour* by Lionel Fielden', September 1943, pp. 215, 209.

[130]Orwell, *Diaries*, 14 March 1942, p. 322; CW, XII, p. 229.

Re. cynicism, you'd be cynical yourself if you were in this job. However I am definitely leaving it probably in about 3 months. Then by some time in 1944 I might be near human again & able to write something serious. At present I'm just an orange that's been trodden on by a very dirty boot.[131]

It is, in fact, hard to take at face value Orwell's claim that lying didn't matter if you were aware of what you were doing. It was important to him that – in private and in public – he maintained his intellectual integrity. Throughout his time at the BBC he continued to publish outside work, mainly essays and reviews, and was markedly reluctant to do as expected and seek the permission of his BBC superiors to undertake this publishing ('I can't be bothered with it any more,' he told them at one point).[132] When George Woodcock accused him of returning 'to his old imperialist allegiances and works at the B.B.C., conducting British propaganda to fox the Indian masses', Orwell asked him if he knew 'what kind of stuff I put out in these Indian broadcasts'. He listed some of the people who had broadcast for him (Herbert Read, an anarchist like Woodcock, Eliot, Forster, Spender and others), stressing in effect the literary, scientific and educational character of his work. He added: 'Most of our broadcasters are Indian leftwing intellectuals, from Liberals to Trotskyists, some of them bitterly anti-British. They don't do it to "fox the Indian masses" but because they know what a Fascist victory would mean to the chances of India's independence.'[133] But this still left a gap between the private acknowledgement of lying and the pained public defence of his integrity.

The conflict between the propagandist and the writer of integrity came to a head when Laurence Brander suggested that, as Orwell (working under the name Eric Blair) wrote the weekly news review for broadcast to India, then the BBC should capitalize on the propaganda value of his reputation as a writer by asking him to read the reviews under his pen name.[134] Rushbrook Williams and the Assistant Controller of Overseas Broadcasts, R.A. Rendall, agreed on the 'propaganda advantages of Orwell's name', notwithstanding the 'characteristically honest and straightforward note' (these are not terms of praise in bureaucratic jargon) that Orwell had written on the subject. He had agreed to take on the reading of the broadcasts, but wrestled with the need to maintain the integrity of his writing persona. These were the terms that he laid down and that were, in effect, accepted by the BBC:

---

[131]Orwell to Rayner Heppenstall, 24 August 1943, CW, XV, p. 206.
[132]Bowker, *George Orwell*, pp. 285, 297, 299–300.
[133]'Pacifism and the War: A Controversy', CW, XIII, pp. 395, 398–9.
[134]Laurence Brander to L.F. Rushbrook Williams, 8 October 1942, CW, XIV, p. 89.

If I broadcast as George Orwell I am as it were selling my literary reputation, which so far as India is concerned probably arises chiefly from books of anti-imperialist tendency, some of which have been banned in India. If I gave broadcasts which appeared to endorse unreservedly the policy of the British government I should quite soon be written off as 'one more renegade' and should probably miss my potential public, at any rate among the student population. I am not thinking about my personal reputation, but clearly we should defeat our own object in these broadcasts if I could not preserve my position as an independent and more or less 'agin the government' commentator. I would therefore like to be sure in advance that I can have reasonable freedom of speech. I think this weekly commentary is only likely to be of value if I can make it from an anti-fascist rather than imperialist standpoint and avoid mention of subjects on which I could not conscientiously agree with current Government policy.

Orwell did not see that this should cause any difficulty. His main areas of disagreement with the government were over Indian policy, and the broadcasts mostly avoided Indian politics. Furthermore, they 'have always followed what is by implication a "left" line, and in fact have contained very little that I would not sign with my own name'. But there was no guarantee that this would always be so, and there could be circumstances in which 'I should have to say that I could not in honesty do the commentary for that week'.[135]

These words were not empty, and Orwell seems to have been sincere in saying that he was never made to say anything against his will. This does not mean that he didn't lie. Admitting that 'one rapidly becomes propaganda-minded', he gave an example: 'I am regularly alleging in my newsletters that the Japanese are plotting to attack Russia. I don't believe this to be so.'[136] This was the sort of lie he was willing to tell. Candidly, he declared that occasionally 'a well-timed lie ... may produce a great effect,' but he continued, 'in general propaganda cannot fight against the facts, though it can colour and distort them'.[137] Relatively honest propaganda was likely to be the best. When speaking as himself Orwell could be much more careful about proving his honesty. Asked to give a talk on social changes in towns, he agreed but made it clear 'I am not going to say anything I regard as untruthful'.[138] He was prepared, too, to make use of what freedom he could

[135]Orwell to Eastern Services Director [Rushbrook Williams], 15 October 1942, CW, XIV, pp. 100–1; my earlier quotations are from the supplementary material for this item, CW, XIV, pp. 101–2.
[136]Orwell, Diaries, 14 March 1942, p. 322; CW, XIII, p. 229.
[137]Orwell, 'Review of Voices in the Darkness by Tangye Lean', 30 April 1943, CW, XV, p. 86.
[138]Orwell to A.L.C. Bullock, European Services Talks Director, 25 January 1943, CW, XIV, p. 328.

find to advance views he thought important, as with his coverage of Sir Stafford Cripps' visit to India.[139] BBC staff were provided with careful notes on how to cover the Cripps mission, originating with the Ministry of Information. Orwell was inclined to go about this in his own way. 'I propose in my newsletters, having been instructed to give Cripps a buildup, to build him up as a political extremist. This draws the warning, "Don't go too far in that direction", which raises the presumption that the higher-ups haven't much hope of full independence being granted to India.'[140] And in his newsletter Orwell did, indeed, manage to colour the facts in his own way. While the briefing he received stressed that Cripps was not a member of any political party, Orwell presented him 'as the ablest man in the British Socialist movement ... respected for his absolute integrity [who] has given away most of his earnings at the Bar to the cause of Socialism and to the support of his weekly Socialist paper, "The Tribune"'. Orwell recounted Cripps' efforts before the war to prod the Labour Party into 'a more radical Socialist policy, and a firmer front against the Fascist aggression'.[141]

The fact that Orwell was prepared to include in *Talking to India* under his own name and as examples of 'good' propaganda, material from his newsletters is itself telling. He is hardly likely to have done this if he felt that this writing was compromised by either dishonesty or censorship. Particularly interesting in what was included are two discussions of propaganda itself. The first was a revealing exposure of the deceitfulness of German propaganda in general.[142] Even more interesting was an analysis of German propaganda to India, in which Orwell's candour comes through clearly:

For Germany to call Britain Imperialistic is at best the pot calling the kettle black. Nevertheless, the Axis propagandists are not so silly as this may seem to imply. They go upon two principles, both of them sound in the short run, though probably not in the long run. The first principle is that if you promise people what they want, they will always believe you. The second is that every few people either know or are interested in knowing what is being done or said in other parts of the world than their own.[143]

It is not then surprising that Orwell was, on the whole, a defender of the BBC, certainly in public. In the privacy of his diary he could be more dismissive. There he railed against 'the huge bureaucratic machine in which

---

[139] What follows is indebted to the account in Rodrigues, 'George Orwell, the B.B.C. and India', pp. 91–6.
[140] Orwell, *Diaries*, 14 March 1942, p. 321; CW, XIII, p. 229.
[141] Orwell, 'Weekly News Review, 14', 14 March 1942, CW, XIII, pp. 224–5.
[142] Orwell, 'Weekly News Review, [2?]', 29 November 1941, CW, XIII, pp. 92–4.
[143] Orwell, 'Weekly News Review, 32', 25 July 1942, CW, XIII, p. 429.

we are all caught up'; nor was he blind to 'the moral squalor and the ultimate futility of what we are doing', not to mention 'the impossibility of getting anything done', the 'ill-defined' policy and 'the fear and hatred of intelligence' which could result in good work being blocked.[144] His work for the BBC was, of course, subject to censorship, both within the BBC and from the Ministry of Information. Everything he wrote was vetted on both security grounds and for its conformity with government policy. Orwell did not in principle challenge the need for this in wartime – indeed for the most part he operated happily enough under a regime of censorship. Beating the Fascists was more important.[145] Even so, writing to a friend he declared the BBC to be 'a mixture of whoreshop and lunatic asylum',[146] suggesting perhaps a place for the unfortunate and the afflicted more than one for the wicked. Nonetheless, Orwell considered the BBC better than the newspapers as a source of news. '"I heard it on the wireless" is now almost equivalent to "I know it must be true",' for many people. Were they right? 'So far as my own experience goes,' Orwell declared, 'the B.B.C. is much more truthful, in a negative way, than the majority of newspapers, and has a much more responsible and dignified attitude towards news. It tells less direct lies, makes more effort to avoid mistakes, and ... keeps the news in better proportion'. It wasn't perfect, and 'though it doesn't tell deliberate lies, it simply avoids every awkward question'.[147] Challenged on this by a reader, Orwell qualified his praise a little further. He wasn't claiming that the BBC was seen as 'interesting, or grown-up, or democratic, or progressive', only that it was 'a relatively sound source of news'. And this view he stuck by. The BBC, he said, has 'a responsible attitude towards news and does not disseminate lies simply because they are "newsy"'. When untruths are broadcast, it is usually from error, and it 'sins much more by simply avoiding anything controversial than by direct propaganda'. The BBC was respected across the globe more than any other news organization, and even if it 'passes on the British official lies, it does make some effort to sift the others'.[148] There is, perhaps, special pleading and a guilty conscience lurking in this. Once you concede the passing on of our own lies, the questioning of others' seems hardly a defence.

---

[144]Orwell, *Diaries*, 23 July 1942 & 21 June 1942, pp. 354, 348–9; CW, XIII, pp. 425–6, 366–7.

[145]Most attention to this has been given by W.J. West, though his accounts are undermined by error and exaggeration. They nonetheless draw a picture of how censorship worked, and of Orwell's attitude to it. See W.J. West, *The Larger Evils: Nineteen Eighty-Four – The Truth behind the Satire* (Edinburgh: Canongate Press, 1992), chs 6–8 & 10; and the more detailed and documented accounts in West (ed.), *Orwell: The War Broadcasts* (London: Duckworth / BBC, 1985), Introduction & Appendix A; and West (ed.), *Orwell: The War Commentaries* (London: Duckworth / BBC, 1985), Introduction. For a more balanced view, see D.J. Taylor, *Orwell: The Life* (New York: Henry Holt, 2003), pp. 312–13.

[146]Orwell to Alex Comfort, 11 July 1943, CW, XV, p. 166.

[147]Orwell, 'As I Please', 19, 7 April 1944, CW, XVI, p. 147.

[148]Orwell, 'As I Please', 21, 21 April 1944, CW, XVI, pp. 164–5.

And the distinction between careful silences and 'direct' propaganda, had he heard it said by others, would have given Orwell some good critical sport.

At best, Orwell's effort to remain self-reflectively aware of what he was doing might hope to inoculate him against the worst corruptions of being a propagandist, but he clearly did not think this was a general solution. The propaganda mind was, above all else, destructive of intellectual honesty. Analysing the impact of the 'propaganda tricks' found in the political pamphlets that he collected assiduously, Orwell declared that they showed nothing more than 'the extraordinary viciousness and dishonesty of political controversy in our time'. Pamphlets of all political persuasions shared the same 'mental atmosphere': 'Nobody is searching for the truth, everybody is putting forward a "case" with complete disregard for fairness or accuracy, and the most plainly obvious facts can be ignored by those who don't want to see them.'[149] The words echo the passionate outburst Orwell committed to his diary while working at the BBC:

> We are all drowning in filth. When I talk to anyone or read the writings of anyone who has any axe to grind, I feel that intellectual honesty and balanced judgement have simply disappeared from the face of the earth. Everyone's thought is forensic, everyone is simply putting a 'case' with deliberate suppression of his opponent's point of view, and, what is more, with complete insensitiveness to any sufferings except those of himself and his friends ... One notices this in the case of people one disagrees with, such as Fascists or pacifists but in fact everyone is the same, at least everyone who has definite opinions. Everyone is dishonest, and everyone is utterly heartless towards people who are outside the immediate range of his own interests. What is most striking of all is the way sympathy can be turned on and off like a tap according to political expedience ... I am not thinking of lying for political ends, but of actual changes in subjective feeling.[150]

What might these 'changes in subjective feeling' be?

It was during his time at the BBC that Orwell wrote one of his most important political essays, 'Looking Back on the Spanish War'. It gives us some insight into these 'changes in subjective feeling'; at any rate, it gives us insight into the insidious effects of propaganda in the totalitarian age. Orwell recalled that he had once said to Arthur Koestler 'History stopped in 1936'. Koestler understood him immediately – 'we were both thinking of totalitarianism in general, but more particularly of the Spanish Civil War'. There Orwell saw something new. He saw reportage that wasn't just

---

[149]Orwell, 'As I Please', 51, 8 December 1944, CW, XVI, p. 495.
[150]Orwell, *Diaries*, 27 April 1942, pp. 335–6; CW, XIII, pp. 288–9.

lying; he saw an effort to conjure into existence a fake reality. '[I]n Spain, for the first time, I saw newspaper reports which did not bear any relation to the facts, not even the relationship which is implied in an ordinary lie.' There were plenty of those lies, battles reported where not had occurred and the like, 'history being written not in terms of what happened but of what ought to have happened according to various "party lines"'. But things went beyond this, especially in Fascist propaganda. For example, against overwhelming evidence, they continued to propagate the myth that there was a Russian army fighting in Spain. This is the sort of thing Orwell found 'frightening': 'it often gives me the feeling that the very concept of objective truth is fading out of the world'. If the wrong side were to win, then these lies might well become history, taught and believed across the generations.

> I know it is the fashion to say that most of recorded history is lies anyway. I am willing to believe that history is for the most part inaccurate and biased, but what is peculiar to our own age is the abandonment of the idea that history *could* be truthfully written. In the past people deliberately lied, or they unconsciously coloured what they wrote, or they struggled after the truth, well knowing that they must make many mistakes; but in each case they believed that 'the facts' existed and were more or less discoverable. And in practice there was always a considerable body of fact which would have been agreed to by almost everyone ... It is just this common basis of agreement, with its implication that human beings are all one species of animal, that totalitarianism destroys. Nazi theory indeed specifically denies that such a thing as 'the truth' exists. There is, for instance, no such things as 'science'. There is only 'German science', 'Jewish science' etc. The implied objective of this line of thought is a nightmare world in which the Leader, or some ruling clique, controls not only the future but *the past*. If the Leader says of such and such an event, 'It never happened' – well, it never happened. If he says that two and two are five – well, two and two are five. This prospect frightens me much more than bombs – and after our experiences of the last few years that is not a frivolous statement.[151]

Looking into the abyss, Orwell was determined to resist becoming the monster he saw there. His anguished self-examination and sometimes tortuous public pronouncements of the BBC years were testimony to a struggle to maintain decency. Lying was one thing; it didn't matter – *provided* that the very idea of truth was not lost in the process. The liar who knows he is lying also knows what the truth is, but totalitarianism rests upon fantasies for which truth and falsehood are irrelevances. It is not

---

[151]Orwell, 'Looking Back on the Spanish War', 1942?, CW, XIII, pp. 503–4.

surprising that Orwell has come to have such relevance to our own world of 'post-truth' and 'fake news'.[152]

Faced with the possibility of such a world, Orwell did not abandon hope. His work at the BBC, combatting totalitarian propaganda, was part of the struggle, as was ensuring that the propaganda was both effective and responsible. Orwell thought that there were two things that might withstand the waves of totalitarianism. One was the hope 'that however much you deny the truth, the truth goes on existing, as it were, behind your back, and you consequently can't violate it in ways that impair military efficiency'. We could put this more broadly as a sort of pragmatism: the truth is what enables us successfully to act in and on the world. Those who denied the truth long enough would lose out to those who did not. The second source of hope was 'that so long as some parts of the earth remain unconquered, the liberal tradition can be kept alive'.[153] Both of these hopes would be dashed by a Fascist victory; both demanded honesty, integrity and the maintenance of liberal values, above all of free speech.

The writer played a particular role in this which Orwell had analysed in a series of radio talks commissioned and delivered even before he joined the BBC as an employee. The last talk, especially, explored the plight of the writer in 'an age of partisanship' – 'an age in which the autonomous individual is ceasing to exist'. But literature as we know it is based on individualism. 'The whole of modern European literature ... is built on the concept of intellectual honesty, or, if you like to put it that way, on Shakespeare's maxim, "To thine own self be true". The first thing that we ask of a writer is that he shan't tell lies, that he shall say what he really thinks, what he really feels. The worst thing we can say about a work of art is that it is insincere.' More succinctly, 'Modern literature is essentially an individual thing. It is either the truthful expression of what one man thinks and feels, or it is nothing.' Totalitarianism was destroying the conditions that made this possible. Centralized economies, some of them Socialist, were replacing 'free capitalism'. People had been blind to the risks in this, believing too readily that Socialism and 'intellectual liberty' would be compatible. 'Art could flourish just as it had done in the liberal-capitalist age, only a little more so, because the artist would not any longer be under economic compulsions.' Totalitarianism had shown that this easy assumption couldn't be relied on.

Totalitarianism has abolished freedom of thought to an extent unheard of in any previous age. And it is important to realise that its control

---

[152]For example Michiko Kakutani, *The Death of Truth* (London: William Collins, 2018), pp. 12, 165–8. Orwell's 'Looking Back on the Spanish War' is a key starting point for Mathew D'Ancona, *Post Truth: The New War on Truth and How to Fight Back* (London: Ebury Press, 2017), pp. 3–5.
[153]Orwell, 'Looking Back on the Spanish War', CW, XIII, p. 505.

of thought is not only negative, but positive. It not only forbids you to express – even to *think* – certain thoughts but it dictates what you *shall* think, it creates an ideology for you, it tries to govern your emotional life as well as setting up a code of conduct. And as far as possible it isolates you from the outside world, it shuts you up in an artificial universe in which you have no standards of comparison. The totalitarian state tries, at any rate, to control the thoughts and emotions of its subjects at least as completely as it controls their actions.

The worst thing about totalitarianism for the writer was the instability of what it asked you to believe. Its truths changed with political need. 'It declares itself infallible, and at the same time it attacks the very concept of objective truth.' The only reality was the reality of obedience to the state and whatever it required you to accept.[154]

Bleak though things were, Orwell did not believe that because 'liberal capitalism' was doomed then 'freedom of thought is also inevitably doomed'. Hope lay in the right people winning the war. 'I believe the hope of literature's survival lies in those countries in which liberalism has struck its deepest roots, the non-military countries, Western Europe and the Americas, India and China ... [T]hose countries will know how to evolve a form of Socialism which is not totalitarian, in which freedom of thought can survive the disappearance of economic individualism.'[155]

It was soon after writing this that Orwell had joined the BBC to ensure the defeat of Fascism, the most immediate totalitarian threat. He left it in 1943 to continue the broader anti-totalitarian struggle as a writer. The day after he left radio he took up the post of literary editor for *Tribune*, and almost as quickly began writing *Animal Farm*. At this point in the war, our allies were as much a danger as our enemies, and in leaving the BBC Orwell could open his own second front.

# 4. Writing for Freedom: *Tribune*, *Animal Farm* and Free Speech

In the years 1944–6, Orwell was, as much as he was doing anything else, writing for freedom of expression, exploring its requirements and the responsibilities it imposed on the writer and intellectual. He wrote *Animal Farm* between November 1943 and February 1944 as an analysis of how revolutions could betray their original intention to liberate people, but then

---

[154]Orwell, 'Literature and Totalitarianism', 21 May 1941, CW, XII, pp. 502–4.
[155]Orwell, 'Literature and Totalitarianism', CW, XII, p. 505.

struggled to get his fable into print.[156] It did not appear until August 1945. His frustration at this delay provoked Orwell to think deeply about the things necessary to maintain freedom of thought and expression. For fifteen months or so of this time he was also the literary editor of *Tribune*. That experience, and his BBC propaganda work, also contributed to this reflection, which culminated in a series of substantial essays that were among his finest work. Before that, he was able to use *Tribune* as a forum for putting into practice and promoting his views of intellectual freedom as an example to others on the Left. The years 1945 and 1946 also saw Orwell involved in practical initiatives to support freedom of thought, though illness sapped the energy he could put into this work, and he was forced in the end to focus most of what remained of it on completing *Nineteen Eighty-Four*.

In November 1943 Orwell became literary editor for *Tribune*. The newspaper represented, as he later noted, 'the left wing of the Labour Party'.[157] More expansively, he declared in one of his columns for the paper in 1947, that 'it is the only existing weekly paper that makes a genuine effort to be both progressive and humane – that is, to combine a radical Socialist policy with a respect for freedom of speech and a civilised attitude towards literature and the arts'.[158] Just over a year after he took on this role, Orwell explained his literary policy to the paper's readers. He defended himself, first, against the charge that *Tribune* was 'lowbrow' and dominated by 'cliques' of limited talent, pointing out the large number and wide range of its contributors, but also proudly taking a stand against the esoteric. 'Nor will we print anything that is verbally unintelligible. I have had several angry letters because of this, but I refuse to be responsible for printing anything that I do not understand. If I can't understand it, the chances are that many of our readers will not be able to either.'[159]

This approach helped Orwell to respond to a second, and more important, line of criticism: the view that coverage of literature and the arts 'can be of no interest to the working man and of no direct use to the Socialist movement'. Orwell quoted a letter from a reader, Mrs O. Grant, who put her point even more memorably in a later letter that was part of the correspondence excited by Orwell's policy statement. Mrs Grant declared her 'desire to leave the world a little better than I found it', and she looked to *Tribune* to supply her with the ammunition needed for this task. This did not require a supply

---

[156]For an account of *Animal Farm* in the context of Orwell's ideas about revolution, see Part I, Section 3.ii above.

[157]George Orwell, *Animal Farm: A Fairy Story* [CW, VIII] (London: Secker & Warburg, 1946), p. 114 (Penguin ed. p. 119); Orwell, Preface to the Ukrainian Edition of *Animal Farm*', March 1947, CW, XIX, p. 89.

[158]Orwell, 'As I Pleased', 73, 31 January 1947, CW, XIX, p. 38. See also Orwell, 'Britain's Left-Wing Press', June 1948, CW, XIX, pp. 296–7.

[159]Orwell, 'Books and the People: A New Year Message', 5 January 1945, CW, XVII, p. 9.

of articles on general cultural matters. Her aim would be achieved 'not by setting the example of a cultured and broadminded old lady, but (forgive me, Mr. Orwell, I must have a one-track-mind) by kicking Tories. When one reaches 60 the path is not only straight and narrow – it is also short.'[160]

Though he would fail to persuade Mrs Grant, Orwell's policy statement was an emphatic defence of seeking diversity of opinion and allowing freedom of expression.

> Even the most unpolitical book, even an outright reactionary book, can be of value to the Socialist movement if it provides reliable information or forces people to think ... Obviously, we cannot print contributions that grossly violate *Tribune*'s policy. Even in the name of free speech a Socialist paper cannot, for instance, throw open its columns to anti-semitic propaganda. But it is only in this negative sense that any pressure is put on contributors to the literary end of the paper. Looking though the list of our contributors, I find among them Catholics, Communists, Trotskyists, Anarchists, Pacifists, Left-Wing Conservatives, and Labour Party supporters of all colours ... [N]one of them has ever been asked to modify what he had written on the ground that it was 'not policy'.[161]

This was particularly important with book reviewing, and *Tribune*'s reviewers were free to say what they thought of a book. 'And if, as a result, unorthodox opinions are expressed from time to time – even, on occasion, opinions that contradict some editorial statement at the other end of the paper – we believe that our readers are tough enough to stand a certain amount of diversity. We hold that the most perverse human being is more interesting than the most orthodox gramophone record.'[162]

In saying this Orwell was repeating points he had made to the readers of *Tribune* in July 1944. Taken to task for publishing *The Little Apocalypse of Obadiah Hornbooke*, Alex Comfort's pacifist poem, Orwell acknowledged that every paper published only the material that was compatible with its particular line, and none would publish attacks on its own core principles. But beyond that, at least in its literary pages, it was 'literary merit' that mattered. Intellectual freedom was not just something to be claimed, as a defence of one's own work, but something to be exercised and practised in relation to other people's work. It was a responsibility. It was especially a responsibility in war time:

---

[160]Orwell, 'Books and the People', CW, XVII, pp. 9–11.
[161]Orwell, 'Books and the People', CW, XVII, p. 10.
[162]Orwell, 'Books and the People', CW, XVII, pp. 10–11. This, of course, is the source for the title of the present book.

Besides, if this war is about anything it at all, it is a war in favour of freedom of thought. I should be the last to claim that we are morally superior to our enemies, and there is quite a strong case for saying that British imperialism is actually worse than Nazism. But there does remain the difference, not to be explained away, that in Britain you are relatively free to say and print what you like. Even in the blackest patches of the British Empire, in India, say, there is very much more freedom of expression than in a totalitarian country. I want that to remain true, and by sometimes giving a hearing to unpopular opinions, I think we help it to do so.[163]

Orwell's editorial policy was built from materials that he thought essential to a culture of free expression: tolerance of and latitude for unorthodox views and outspoken people, the willingness to be provoked into thought by enemies as well as friends – and tough readers. Orwell concluded his policy statement with a declaration of faith: 'we believe that anyone who upholds the freedom of the intellect, in this age of lies and regimentation, is not serving the cause of Socialism so badly either.'[164] Maybe this is not the most resounding credo, but it lay at the heart of Orwell's Socialism from 1937 until his death.

Provoked by the difficulty that he had in getting *Animal Farm* published and his sense that there were sinister forces behind this difficulty, Orwell produced a series of major essays in 1945 and 1946 that together formed his most considered and mature analysis of intellectual freedom and its responsibilities. The most important of these pieces were 'The Freedom of the Press' (written as a preface to *Animal Farm*, probably during the first half of 1945, but not published until 1972),[165] 'The Freedom of the Park' (*Tribune*, 7 December 1945), 'The Prevention of Literature' (*Polemic*, January 1946), 'Politics and the English Language' (*Horizon*, April 1946), 'Why I Write' (*Gangrel*, Summer 1946), and his annotations to Swingler's 'Right to Free Expression' (*Polemic*, September/October 1946). He was to return to the same themes one last time in 'Writers and Leviathan' (*Politics and Letters*, Summer 1948). Together, these essays explored closely interlinked topics: the importance of freedom of expression, the things that threatened it, the dangers of self-censorship, the responsibility of writers to the idea of telling the truth, and the misuse of language as a betrayal of this responsibility. By the time he wrote these essays, Orwell had come to the view that the war was not going to be the one that would establish Socialism, as he had hoped

---

[163]Orwell, 'As I Please', 35, 28 July 1944, CW, XVI, p. 306.
[164]Orwell, 'Books and the People', CW, XVII, p. 11.
[165]*Times Literary Supplement*, no 3680, 15 September 1972, pp. 1037–9. The date of composition is discussed in Bernard Crick's accompanying piece, 'How the Essay Came to Be Written', ibid., pp. 1039–40.

in *The Lion and the Unicorn*. Instead, 'if this war is about anything at all, it is a war in favour of freedom of thought'.[166]

By 1940 Orwell had concluded despairingly that the world was not a congenial place for the creative writer. He wrangled with this realization for the rest of his life. In 1940, there seemed no way out; later he at least fought his way to a draw against the monster he feared. As early as 1941, enthused by war fever, he was arguing that there was a threat hanging over literature, but the necessary 'freedom of thought was not *inevitably* doomed to die with liberal capitalism'. He thought that countries with well entrenched liberal traditions might evolve a form of liberal Socialism.[167] That hope too faded, though without altogether disappearing. Orwell invariably approached the subject of free speech and freedom of the press from the perspective of a professional writer. Being a writer was integral to his identity, and he took the responsibilities of the role as seriously as he took its privileges and needs.

Orwell's best-known account of the sort of writer that he wanted to be was the essay 'Why I Write'. From 'a very early age', he tells us, 'I knew that when I grew up I should be a writer.' By the he early 1930s, 'I wanted to write enormous naturalistic novels with unhappy endings, full of detailed descriptions and arresting similes, and also full of purple passages in which words were used partly for the sake of their sound.' The result was *Burmese Days*. There were 'four great motives' for writing – 'sheer egoism', 'aesthetic enthusiasm', 'historical impulse' and 'political purpose'. Orwell considered that he was naturally someone for whom the first three of these motives were most important, that 'in a peaceful age I might have written ornate or merely descriptive books, and might have remained almost unaware of my political loyalties'. He was denied this luxury. He was 'forced into becoming a sort of pamphleteer'. Burma, Wigan, Spain, Hitler – they all contributed to making him a political writer. The result:

> Every line of serious work that I have written since 1936 has been written, directly or indirectly, *against* totalitarianism and *for* democratic Socialism, as I understand it. It seems to me nonsense, in a period like our own, to think that one can avoid writing of such subjects.

Yet, as a writer, his key ambition had been 'to make political writing into an art'. He wrote to expose lies and to get a hearing for the truth, but he was not prepared 'to abandon the world-view that I acquired in childhood'. He cared about prose style, loved 'the surface of the earth', and took 'pleasure in solid object and scraps of useless information'. All of this infused his writing. But politics was paramount. It led him, as in *Homage to Catalonia*,

---

[166]Orwell, 'As I Please', 35, 28 July 1944, CW, XVI, p. 306.
[167]Orwell, 'Literature and Totalitarianism', 21 May 1941, CW, XII, pp. 502, 505.

to prioritize clarity of message over perfection of form, and compelled him to write more directly – 'one constantly struggles to efface one's own personality' (really?). 'Good prose is like a window pane.' Where the writing 'lacked a *political* purpose ... I wrote lifeless books'.[168]

It was in this mood, so much more optimistic than that of 1939–40, that Orwell commented on Zhdanov's tightening of Russian literary censorship in 1946. He declared, no doubt with a touch of irony, that he felt sorrier, for the persecutors than the persecuted. They censored and suppressed, issued instructions and diktats, and 'yet for some reason a vigorous and original literature, unmistakably superior to that of capitalist countries, fails to emerge'.

> The thing that politicians are seemingly unable to understand is that you cannot produce a vigorous literature by terrorising everyone into conformity. A writer's inventive faculties will not work unless he is allowed to say approximately what he feels. You can destroy spontaneity and produce a literature which is orthodox but feeble, or you can let people say what they choose and take the risk that some of them will utter heresies. There is no way out of that dilemma so long as books have to be written by individuals.[169]

Here was faith that not even totalitarianism could subdue the irrepressible spirit of the writer.

'Why I Write' was an attractive and relatively sunny credo. It's free of the bitter sense of watching his vocation crushed under the jackboot that Orwell had expressed on earlier occasions. He had found himself compelled by the state of his world to become a political writer, but at least he could make an art of it. When he returned to the subject of the writer in one of his final essays, Orwell's mood was again a little less sunny. 'Writers and Leviathan' was not a return to the despair of 1939 and 1940, but it was less easy in acknowledging the political motive for writing than 'Why I Write'. The threat to the writer was now more insidious, less the triumph of oppressive totalitarian dictatorships, more the totalitarianism that lurked within.[170] 'Group loyalties are necessary, and yet they are poisonous to literature, so long as literature is the product of individuals.' The writer of integrity could not be the mouthpiece of a political group. A 'sharper distinction' was needed 'between our political and our literary loyalties'. Then it would be clear that 'when a writer engages in politics he should do so as a citizen, as a

---

[168]Orwell, 'Why I Write', Summer 1946, CW, XVIII, pp. 316–21.
[169]Orwell, 'As I Please', 68, 3 January 1947, CW, XIX, p. 7.
[170]Not, of course, in itself a new theme for Orwell. In 1941 he talked of the 'necessity of resisting totalitarianism, whether it is imposed on us from without or from within': Orwell, 'Literature and Totalitarianism', CW, XII, p. 505.

human being, but not *as a writer* ... his writing is a thing apart'. The writer has to be loyal to the truth as he sees it: 'he should never turn back from a train of thought because it may lead to a heresy, and he should not mind very much if his unorthodoxy is smelt out, as it probably will be'. The writer 'lives and writes in constant dread ... of public opinion within his own group'. 'To yield ... to a group ideology, is to destroy yourself as a writer.' Consequently, you must 'keep part of yourself inviolate'. Here is a different credo from that of 1946: 'But his writings ... will always be the product of the saner self that stands aside, records the things that are done and admits their necessity, but refuses to be deceived by their true nature.'[171] This is more like the Orwell of the BBC propaganda machine: you might have to engage in the dirty work but, if you were to retain any integrity as a writer, you needed an honest acknowledgement of the dirt in which you wallowed.

What remained consistent in Orwell's understanding of the writer was that his honesty and commitment to truth depended on the individual. Literature could only be the work of the 'autonomous individual', working in solitude. 'Serious prose ... has to be composed in solitude.'[172] But there were qualifications to be made. Indeed, Orwell could assert, in what looks like the starkest self-contradiction, that it is 'the greatest mistake ... to imagine that the human being is an autonomous individual'.[173] In writing this, though, Orwell was exploding the 'fallacy ... that under a dictatorial government you can be free *inside*'. While the leader is worshipped in the streets and the crudest propaganda blares, 'up in the attics the secret enemies of the regime can record their thoughts in perfect freedom'. *Nineteen Eighty-Four* was, you could say, written to destroy just this delusion. Modern dictatorships left fewer 'loopholes' than older ones; they also systematically sapped 'the *desire* for intellectual liberty'. More importantly,

> The secret freedom which you can supposedly enjoy under a despotic Government is nonsense, because your thoughts are never entirely your own. Philosophers, writers, artists, even scientists, not only need encouragement and an audience, they need constant stimulation from other people, It is almost impossible to think without talking ... Take away freedom of speech, and the creative faculties dry up.[174]

Literature depended on the free individual, but individuals needed social connection of a particular sort. The society that makes individual thought and creativity possible is one that guarantees freedom of speech. Unfettered

[171]Orwell, 'Writers and Leviathan', Summer 1948, CW, XIX, pp. 288–93.
[172]Orwell, 'Prevention of Literature', CW, XVII, p. 377.
[173]Orwell, 'As I Please', 22, 28 April 1944, CW XVI, p. 172.
[174]Orwell, 'As I Please', 22, CW, XVI, pp. 172–3.

communication, allowing an intellectual feely to transmit and to receive ideas, was the essential feature of a liberal society.

Totalitarianism was not the only threat to intellectual freedom. In Orwell's view, 'intellectual liberty is under attack from two dimensions'. While one set of enemies attracted the bulk of his attention, 'the apologists of totalitarianism', there was another, 'monopoly and bureaucracy'.[175] This latter threat was important: 'in England the immediate enemies of truthfulness, and hence of freedom of thought, are the Press lords, the film magnates, and the bureaucrats'. The barriers writers faced included:

> the concentration of the Press in the hands of a few rich men, the grip of monopoly on radio and the films, the unwillingness of the public to spend money on books ... the encroachment of official bodies like the M.O.I. [Ministry of Information] and the British Council ... which waste his time and dictate his opinions, and the continuous war atmosphere ...[176]

Socialism was, of course, a cure for the disease, for the inequality that could make freedoms useless even when they existed in theory. 'One can accept,' Orwell wrote, 'and most enlightened people would accept, the Communist thesis that pure freedom will only exist in a classless society, and that one is most nearly free when one is working to bring about such a society'.[177] But in this thought lurked danger. For Orwell, 'the basis of Socialism is humanism', to sustain which 'freedom of speech and of the Press are of urgent importance';[178] but it did not follow that all of those who flocked under the banner of Socialism were the friends of freedom. Admittedly, it was as much a mistake even to believe that the Communists were really trying to create a classless society. In fact, as Orwell often said, the Soviet Union was the enemy of Socialism as much as it was the enemy of freedom; indeed it was the enemy of Socialism *because* it was the enemy of freedom. The risk was that those intellectuals who had been duped into believing that Russia, whatever its flaws, symbolized the possibility of a classless society would also believe that the hopes for true freedom lay in the same direction. Thus, the cause of freedom would – had – come to mean, not protecting and expanding valuable bourgeois commitments to free speech and freedom of the press, compromised as they were by the inequality of capitalist society, but using all necessary intellectual weapons to support the Soviet cause. These weapons could include suppressing contrary views. The pursuit of true and perfect freedom might, on this basis, require the suppression of those limited

---

[175]Orwell, 'The Prevention of Literature', January 1946, CW, XVII, p. 371.

[176]Orwell, 'Prevention of Literature', CW, XVII, pp. 374, 371.

[177]Orwell, 'Prevention of Literature', CW, XVII, p. 372.

[178]Orwell, 'The Intellectual Revolt: 2. What Is Socialism?', 31 January 1946, CW, XVIII, pp. 61–2.

but still necessary freedoms that allowed criticism of Communism.[179] In this undergrowth of bad faith was concealed Orwell's greatest fear: the triumph of a Socialism with 'no room in it for a humanistic culture'.[180]

It was important therefore to resist arguments for what we call today moral equivalence. Orwell had been making this point for some time. In November 1941, exploring the contrast between democracy and totalitarianism, he acknowledged that, in one sense, the Western democracies were not truly democratic because 'power is not in fact in the hands of the common people'. But they were, nonetheless, possessed of a democratic culture: 'it is necessary to say that democracy in the other senses – of freedom of speech, respect for the individual and all the rest of it – does have a reality, an importance, which cannot be made away with by mere juggling of words.' Of course there was truth in the claim that 'all the compulsions which are put upon the individual crudely and openly in a totalitarian state are put upon him in a slightly more subtle way by the money-squeeze in a so-called democratic society'. Of course, many intellectuals claimed that intellectual freedom 'isn't technically restricted in England, but in practice the whole of the Press that matters is in the hands of a small clique of millionaires who can prevent you from saying what you think'. But this last conclusion readily became 'nonsense'. Yes, 'the essential unfreedom of democratic society' was a reality; but compared to totalitarian societies, 'there does remain the residual difference that in a country like this we are not afraid to stand up and say what we think'. Even under war time conditions, we can criticize our leaders. Capitalist freedom was deeply flawed. Perhaps it differed in degree only from the unfreedom of totalitarianism – but differences of degree are still real differences. 'In England, absurdities just as great as any in the totalitarian states are being offered to you all the time, but you are not under any obligation to accept them.'[181]

The threat to intellectual freedom posed by the 'apologists of totalitarianism' was Orwell's main subject. Danger loomed wherever 'totalitarian habits of thought prevailed'.[182] Those habits of mind were most obviously manifest in direct attempts to censor or suppress the truth. In Orwell's view, 'organized lying' was 'integral to totalitarianism'.[183] By 1942, reflecting during his time at the BBC on what he had witnessed in Spain and later, Orwell had captured precisely the essence of totalitarianism. Lies have always been told, but the liar honours the truth in the breach if not the observance. This was different. The novelty of the modern world lay in

---

[179]Orwell, 'Prevention of Literature', CW, XVII, p. 372.

[180]Orwell, 'Literature and the Left', CW, XV, p. 126.

[181]Orwell, 'Culture and Democracy', 21 November 1941, CW, XIII, p. 68.

[182]Orwell, 'Annotations to Randall Swingler, "The Right to Free Expression"', September/October 1946, CW, XVIII, p. 439.

[183]Orwell, 'Prevention of Literature', CW, XVII, p. 373.

'the abandonment of the idea that history *could* be truthfully written'. This removed any 'common basis of agreement'. Whereas British and German histories of the First World War shared many facts and sought to demonstrate their validity with reference to those facts, this was no longer how things worked. Beneath the totalitarian mentality was an anti-humanism, the rejection of the belief 'that human beings are all one species of animal'. For the Nazi, there was no longer one science to the work of which all humanity might contribute; there were instead German science and Jewish science. Already in 1942 Orwell had conjured the world that would later become familiar to readers of *Nineteen Eighty-Four*:

> a nightmare world in which the Leader, or some ruling clique controls not only the future but *the past*. If the leader says of such an event, 'It never happened' – well, it never happened. If he says that two and two are five – well, two and two are five.[184]

The passage might have been lifted from Winston Smith's job description.

A few years on from the BBC, Orwell deftly summarized his position: 'From the totalitarian point of view history is something to be created rather than learned. A totalitarian state is in effect a theocracy, and its ruling caste, in order to keep its position, has to be thought of as infallible.' The result is not just 'outright falsification' but 'a disbelief in the very existence of objective truth'. Totalitarians exploited the fallacy of unattainable perfection: because *absolute* truth was unattainable, then anything goes.[185] Totalitarians pursued policies that would preserve their own power, 'no matter how contradictory'. Orwell had in mind particularly the dramatic change of Russian policy effected by the Nazi-Soviet pact of September 1939. This was something new. Previous cultures had promoted and enforced orthodoxy – medieval Catholicism, for example – but they still maintained a stable framework of ideas.[186] (Later, Orwell was quicker to condemn medieval orthodoxy. It resulted in a period of 'almost no imaginative prose literature and very little in the way of historical writing'.) Even so, totalitarianism was much worse, promising not an 'age of faith' but an 'age of schizophrenia'.[187] Totalitarian cultures were hyper-destructive of truth because they required belief in an ever-shifting orthodoxy. This shattered any expectation that truth was permanent and stable. 'The peculiarity of the totalitarian state is that though it controls thought, it doesn't fix it. It sets up unquestionable dogmas, and it alters them from day to day … It declares itself infallible,

---

[184]Orwell, 'Looking Back on the Spanish War', 1942, CW, XIII, pp. 503–4.
[185]Orwell, 'Prevention of Literature', CW, XVII, p. 374.
[186]Orwell, 'Culture and Democracy', 22 November 1941, CW, XIII, pp. 76–7.
[187]Orwell, 'Prevention of Literature', CW, XVII, p. 376.

and at the same time it attacks the very idea of objective truth.'[188] In those who follow, this corrodes both integrity and honesty. The writer is told to trust to 'the evidence of his own senses' when his thoughts are in line with orthodoxy, 'but as soon as he reveals something that the authorities dislike, he is reminded that all truth is relative'.[189]

Stalinists and Nazis in power were obvious threats to freedom; a more immediate and insidious threat came from the supporters of Stalinism among Western intellectuals. In November 1945 *Tribune* carried a story about the brutality of the Russian troops occupying Austria, including their responsibility for the appalling mass rape of Austrian women.[190] Some readers of the paper clearly thought that, even if true, this information was harmful to the cause of Socialism and shouldn't have been printed. Orwell, in response, conceded that the truth might sometimes bring comfort to one's enemies. It was true that left-wing criticism of British institutions and British imperialism during the war might well have been 'a gift for Goebbels'. Did that mean that such views should have been suppressed? No, it did not. Orwell could appreciate – indeed he had himself on occasion succumbed to – 'the fearful temptation to distort or suppress the facts, simply because any honest statement will contain revelations which can be made use of by unscrupulous opponents'.[191] But this was a 'dishonest' argument – and a counter-productive one. Hiding the truth from people is apt to encourage their disillusionment when they discover what you have been doing. They react with 'sudden revulsion'. That's why trying to obscure the truth about the Soviet Union had 'retarded the cause of Socialism'. Any benefit from lying was strictly 'short-lived'. But more importantly, the argument could be used to shield Communists and Nazis alike. Behind it 'always lies the intention to do propaganda for some single sectional interest'. Orwell's faith lay with free speech, liberalism and the values of enlightenment. The task was to destroy illusions, 'but the dropping of illusions means the publication of facts, and facts are apt to be unpleasant'. No truthfulness; no progress. 'And yet genuine progress can only happen through increasing enlightenment, which means the continuous destruction of myths.'[192]

In Western societies, the integrity of the writer was 'thwarted by the general drift of society rather than by active persecution'. Previously 'the idea of rebellion and the idea of intellectual integrity were mixed up', but now 'the rebels against the existing order ... are also rebelling against the

---

[188]Orwell, 'Literature and Totalitarianism', CW, XII, p. 504.
[189]Orwell, 'Annotations to Swingler', CW, XVIII, p. 439.
[190]The controversy is documented in CW, XVII, pp. 393–5.
[191]Orwell, 'Through a Glass, Rosily', 23 November 1945, CW, XVII, pp. 396–7. There is a fuller discussion of this argument in Part I of the present book.
[192]Orwell, 'Through a Glass, Rosily', CW, XVII, pp. 397–8.

idea of individual integrity'.[193] This was true not just of Communists, but more dangerously of those Socialists who remained trapped in the delusion that Communism still represented something progressive. Its blemishes were best left unmentioned, and the Socialist writer must stifle his or her instinct for truth-telling. Citing Milton, Orwell argued 'that intellectual freedom is a deep-rooted tradition without which our characteristic western culture could only doubtfully exist', but it was a tradition from which 'many of our intellectuals are visibly turning away'. Our 'liberals ... fear liberty'; our 'intellectuals ... want to do dirt on the intellect'.[194]

The writer working under conditions of intellectual bad faith was in an impossible situation:

> Not only will ideas refuse to come to him, but the very words he uses will seem to stiffen under his touch. Political writing in our time consists almost entirely of pre-fabricated phrases bolted together like the pieces of a child's Meccano set. It is the unavoidable result of self-censorship. To write plain, vigorous language one has to think fearlessly, and if one thinks fearlessly one cannot be politically orthodox.[195]

Western intellectuals censored themselves and encouraged others to self-censor. This was an impossible situation. A writer could not maintain integrity unless possessing 'the freedom to report what one has seen, heard, and felt, and not to be obliged to fabricate imaginary facts and feelings'.[196] The political writer must not be 'forced to write lies or suppress what seems to him important news'; the imaginative writer 'is unfree when he has to falsify his subjective feelings'. If these conditions are not met then writing of integrity and quality will disappear.[197] Any writer who submits even to the informal pressure of intellectual opinion 'destroys himself as a writer'.[198]

'The very words he uses will seem to stiffen under his touch': one of Orwell's deepest fears was that the degradation of the English language was also degrading the country's political culture. Clear language was necessary for clear thinking, and 'to think clearly is a necessary first step towards political regeneration'.[199] There was a 'special connection between politics and the debasement of language'.[200] It was therefore necessary to combat

---

[193]Orwell, 'Prevention of Literature', CW, XVII, p. 371.
[194]Orwell, 'Freedom of the Press', CW, XVII, pp. 259–60.
[195]Orwell, 'Prevention of Literature', CW, XVII, p. 376.
[196]Orwell, 'Prevention of Literature', CW XVII, p. 372.
[197]Orwell, 'Prevention of Literature', CW XVII, p. 375.
[198]Orwell, 'Prevention of Literature', CW XVII, p. 380.
[199]Orwell, 'Politics and the English Language', April 1946, written December 1945, CW, xvii, p. 421.
[200]Orwell, 'Politics and the English Language', CW, XVII, p. 427.

the decay of language to achieve a political world in which free intellectuals debated honestly. As things stood, though, stale, imprecise and vague language infested political writing and 'prose consists less and less of *words* chosen for the sake of their meaning, and more and more of *phrases* tacked together like the sections of a prefabricated henhouse'.[201] Orwell particularly reprehended the loss of concreteness and the dissolution of hard political realities into a soupy mush of abstractions. The willingness of writers to avoid the task of thinking by 'letting the ready-made phrases come crowding in' was not just laziness. It also performed 'the important service of partially concealing your meaning even from yourself', a most valuable service at a time when 'political speech and writing are largely the defence of the indefensible'.[202] In these circumstances it was necessary to avoid concrete and precise language. No political party could admit the unpalatable consequences of its own doctrines, so 'political language has to consist largely of euphemism'. The driving force was not saying what you meant; it was 'insincerity'.[203]

The situation was not irretrievable. Orwell encouraged writers to change their own habits and to jeer at the 'verbal refuse of others'. This was another dimension of the responsibility of the intellectual. Avoiding exhausted metaphors and similes, using short words in preference to long ones, using fewer words not more, writing in the active mood not the passive, avoiding foreign phrases and jargon, and breaking any of these rules to avoid saying 'anything outright barbarous' – these were political acts too.[204] They were necessary to the regeneration of political decency. It should be no surprise that, wherever good political writing could still be found, it was likely 'that the writer is some kind of rebel, expressing his private opinions and not a "party line". Orthodoxy, of whatever colour, seems to demand a lifeless, imitative style.'[205]

Freedom of speech and of the press were essential: the rebels could not challenge the orthodox unless they could speak without constraint. Free expression was a matter not just of legal rights and the freedom from official censorship. If the pressure to self-censor was to be lifted, then the informal pressure to conform had also to be lifted. Even during the war, formal censorship in England was 'pretty mild'. The bigger problem was 'intellectual cowardice'. Those who challenged prevailing orthodoxies were 'silenced with surprising effectiveness', their views 'almost never given a fair hearing, either in the popular press or in the highbrow periodicals'.[206] 'The enemy', he wrote, 'is the gramophone mind, whether or not one agrees with

---

[201]Orwell, 'Politics and the English Language', CW, XVII, pp. 422–3.
[202]Orwell, 'Politics and the English Language', CW, XVII, pp. 427–8.
[203]Orwell, 'Politics and the English Language', CW, XVII, p. 428.
[204]Orwell, 'Politics and the English Language', CW, XVII, p. 430.
[205]Orwell, 'Politics and the English Language', CW, XVII, p. 427.
[206]Orwell, 'Freedom of the Press', CW, XVII, pp. 354–5.

the record that is being played at the moment'. Free minds would flourish if the commissars of print and the commissars of publishing were exposed. Free speech needed constant defence. In the literary world, people were beginning 'to despise it, in theory and practice'. But they must be convinced otherwise. This was in essence what Orwell was seeking to do throughout his 1945–6 essays on intellectual freedom. The only way of combatting the tyranny of opinion was to change opinions. If opinion did not change, then the risks were plain: 'if you encourage totalitarian methods, the time may come when they will be used against you instead of for you.'[207]

Orwell was defending a tradition of ideas that he could trace from Milton to Voltaire to Luxemburg. Socialism was for him an extension of liberalism not its nemesis, and so he defended a position very similar to that of John Stuart Mill. Freedom of expression was critical for the pursuit of truth, and it was to be limited only when it risked doing what Mill called 'harm':

> Now, when one demands liberty of speech and of the press, one is not demanding absolute liberty. There always must be, or at any rather there always will be, some degree of censorship, so long as organised societies endure. But freedom, as Rosa Luxembourg said, is 'freedom for the other fellow'. The same principle is contained in the famous words of Voltaire: 'I detest what you say; I will defend to the death your right to say it'. If the intellectual liberty which without doubt has been one of the distinguishing masks of contemporary civilisation means anything it means that everyone shall have the right to say and to print what he believes to be the truth, provided only that it does not harm the rest of the community in some quite unmistakeable way.[208]

In defending free speech, Orwell was defending not just a liberal idea of freedom as a negative entitlement to say what you wished. He was also defending, as part of the intellectual's responsibility, what the Greeks called *parrhēsia*, or frank speech – the duty to speak truth to power, as our contemporary cliché puts it. The writer had a responsibility to speak truth as she or he saw it. Orwell's attempts to persuade other intellectuals were as much pleas for plain-spokenness as they were defences of freedom. This was, of course, precisely the freedom of speech that he himself practised. Orwell could be an intellectual thug. He almost never admitted error when challenged (though he might admit it on his own terms); he was a master of the counter-punch; he argued *ad hominem* and with sometimes outrageous

---

[207]Orwell, 'Freedom of the Press', CW, XVII, p. 258.
[208]Orwell, 'Freedom of the Press', CW, XVII, pp. 257–8. The famous words of Voltaire are no longer thought to have been uttered by the great Enlightenment *philosophe*. They were invented as a summary of his attitude by Evelyn Beatrice Hall (writing as S. G. Tallentyre) in her *The Friends of Voltaire* of 1906.

brutality, though also impersonally. Though he confronted many of his worst prejudices (like anti-Semitism), others were given licence to roam about his prose unmolested. Many of those people whom he pummelled later became friends (Stephen Spender, George Woodcock, Alex Comfort), recognizing a fierce truthfulness and honesty that were inseparable from Orwell the man. They came to respect and to like him both for this and in spite of it. It says much for the qualities of his friends that this was so – none more so, perhaps, than Richard Rees whose affection survived unscathed the portrait of him as the ineffectual, rich Socialist, Ravelston, in *Keep the Aspidistra Flying*. All of this should go without saying, as it often does for Orwell; but as we seem to live in an age where free speech is once again at risk of being taken for the freedom to espouse consensus views, and disruption of orthodoxy transformed into a sort of harm (giving offence) that should be suppressed, it is worth remembering that for Orwell freedom was not something that produced happy social harmony. More likely it would produce savage argument, intellectual combat and cacophonous discord. These, of course, were conditions in which he delighted.

Orwell, indeed, acknowledged that, though he deplored the pressure to conformity, he was also largely immune to it. Certainly, the inspiration for the great essays of 1945–6 lay in the long battle that Orwell fought to get *Animal Farm* into print. This informal censorship was real enough. Victor Gollancz, Jonathan Cape and Faber & Faber (in the person of T.S. Eliot) all refused to publish the book because it was offensive to Britain's Russian allies. Cape's refusal, against the advice of their own readers, was prompted by guidance from an official at the Ministry of Information.[209] Orwell never knew that the official was probably Peter Smollett, whom he would include in his list of Soviet sympathizers compiled for the Information Research Department in 1949. Smollett was later exposed as a Soviet spy.[210] Yet Orwell readily acknowledged that it was 'quite true that I have had great freedom to say what I wished, but I have only had it because I have not only ignored the pressures that are put on a writer by editors and publishers, but also public opinion inside the literary intelligentsia'. He had found it difficult 'to get anything of anti-Russian tendency into print', just as he had earlier struggled to find a publisher for the anti-imperialist *Burmese Days*.[211] This comment was Orwell's response to the Communist poet Randall Swingler's

---

[209]Crick, *George Orwell*, pp. 452–62.

[210]For Smollett, see Peter Davison (ed.), *The Lost Orwell* (London: Timewell Press, 2006), p. 210; and Bowker, *George Orwell* p. 312. Though all recent scholars assume that Smollett was the person who advised Jonathan Cape ('almost certainly' one account has it – Dorian Lynskey, *The Ministry of Truth: A Biography of George Orwell's 1984* (London: Picador, 2019, p. 204), I'm not aware of the evidence for the supposition. Orwell briefly recounted his struggle to get *Animal Farm* published in 'Freedom of the Press', CW, XVII, pp. 253–4.

[211]Orwell, 'Annotations to Swingler', CW, XVIII, p. 442.

*Polemic* critique of 'The Prevention of Literature'. These remarks remain among the least known of Orwell's writings, so it is worth quoting at length his account of why he was defending free speech, less on his own account and more for the benefit of others:

> Because I committed the crime known in France as *lese-Staline* I have been obliged at times to change my publisher, to stop writing for papers which represented part of my livelihood, to have my books boycotted in other papers, and to be pursued by insulting letters, articles similar to the one which Mr. Swingler has just written, and even threats of libel actions. It would be silly to complain of all this, since I have survived it, but I know that other thinner-skinned people often succumb to similar treatment, and that the average writer, especially the average young writer, is terrified of offending against the orthodoxy of the moment. For some years past, orthodoxy – at least the dominant brand of it – has consisted in not criticising Stalin, and the resulting corruption has been such that the bulk of the English literary intelligentsia has looked on at torture, massacre and aggression without expressing disapproval, and perhaps in the long run without feeling it. This may change, and in my opinion probably will change. In five years it may be as dangerous to praise Stalin as it was to attack him two years ago. But I should not regard this as an advance. Nothing is gained by teaching a parrot a new word. What is needed is the right to print what one believes to be true, without having to feel bullying or blackmail from *any* side.[212]

'Nothing is gained by teaching a parrot a new word' might join those phrases that encapsulate Orwell's commitment to a liberal and individualistic theory of intellectual freedom. '[A] bought mind is a spoiled mind' – 'the imagination will not breed in captivity'.[213] 'If liberty means anything at all, it means the right to tell people what they do not want to hear.'[214] 'We hold that the most perverse human being is more interesting than the most orthodox gramophone record.'[215]

How far would Orwell take his commitment to free speech? Would he, like so many, turn out to defend the freedom of his friends while seeking to restrict that of his enemies? Controversy over two writers accused of supporting Fascism – P.G. Wodehouse and Ezra Pound – gave Orwell opportunities to apply his principles. Wodehouse was living in France when the war began, and ended up being interred when France fell to the Germans.

---

[212]Orwell, 'Annotations to Swingler', CW, XVIII, pp. 442–3.
[213]Orwell, 'Prevention of Literature', CW XVII, p. 380.
[214]Orwell, 'Freedom of the Press', CW, XVII, p. 260.
[215]Orwell, 'Books and the People', CW, XVII, p. 11.

He was later sent to Berlin and there, in June and July 1941, recorded five broadcasts. Whatever Wodehouse's intentions, his broadcasts were used for propaganda purposes by the Germans. There was nothing pro-Nazi in the content of the broadcasts, which Wodehouse seems to have seen as a way of keeping in touch with his public.[216] Orwell examined the evidence for and against the view that Wodehouse's broadcasts were intended to be hostile to the English war effort, an extension of a body of writing by 'a penetrating satirist of English society'. Orwell would have none of this. Wodehouse's work was marked by a 'mild facetiousness covering an unthinking acceptance' of the English social order – or at least of the social order as it was in Edwardian times, for Wodehouse was decades out of date in his understanding of England. The broadcasts were the work of a political simpleton, no more than 'a few rather silly but harmless remarks by an elderly novelist'. One can understand that in 1941, when the war was not going well, feelings would run hot; but this was no longer so.

> In the desperate circumstances of the time, it was excusable to be angry at what Wodehouse did, but to go on denouncing him three or four years later – and more, to let an impression remain that he acted with conscious treachery – is inexcusable. Few things in this war have been more morally disgusting than the present hunt after traitors and Quislings. At best it is largely the punishment of the guilty by the guilty.

The problem with retribution after the fact was that the 'petty rats' are the ones caught and the 'big rats' slink off unscathed.[217] These remarks are typical of Orwell's post-war attitude: whatever the demands of war might have justified, it was time to return to decency (and along with it, the uncompromising defence of intellectual freedom). Wodehouse himself acknowledged the handsomeness of Orwell's attitude, writing in May 1946 that the 'criticism he did of my stuff was masterly. I was tremendously impressed by his fairmindedness in writing such an article at a time when it was taking a very unpopular view.'[218]

We might wonder, though, what Orwell would have said if he had believed that Wodehouse really was a Nazi sympathizer. The controversy that followed the award of the Bollingen Prize to Ezra Pound in 1949 may suggest some answers to the question. The Bollingen Foundation made

---

[216]P.G. Wodehouse, *A Life in Letters*, ed. Sophie Ratcliffe (London: Hutchinson, 2011), pp. 302–16.

[217]Orwell, 'In Defence of P.G. Wodehouse', 20 February 1945, published July 1945, CW, XVII, pp. 57, 60, 61.

[218]Wodehouse, *Life in Letters*, p. 388. Wodehouse was, however, less impressed by Orwell's account of 'my out-of-touchness with English life' (ibid., p. 444). See also the editorial note in CW, XVII, p. 63.

its inaugural award of an annual poetry prize to the best book of poetry published in 1948. The judges chose to honour Ezra Pound for *The Pisan Cantos*.[219] Pound was at the time in an asylum, certified insane, which fate had saved him from a treason trial. Like Wodehouse, he had made wartime broadcasts; unlike Wodehouse, he knew what he was doing in supporting the Axis powers.

William Barrett, associate editor of *Partisan Review*, voiced his disquiet at the Bollingen award in the magazine. Avoiding outright rejection of the judges' verdict, he ended with a question: 'How far is it possible, in a lyric poem, for technical embellishments to transform vicious and ugly matter into beautiful poetry?'[220] *Partisan Review* invited several writers to comment on the matter, and published seven responses (three of them from members of the panel that awarded the prize) and a further comment from Barrett. Of the three judges W.H. Auden and Karl Shapiro gave careful defences of the award to Pound; Allen Tate raged at the insult he had received from Barrett and demanded satisfaction.[221] Among all the comments, Orwell's stood out for its clear statement of principle: 'I think the Bollingen Foundation were quite right to award Pound the prize, if they believed his poems to be the best of the year, but I think also that one ought to keep Pound's career in memory and not feel that his ideas are made respectable by the mere fact of winning a literary prize.' He had said before that left-wing critics alienated many intelligent people by 'making ostensibly literary judgements for political ends'.[222] It was typical of Orwell to try to separate the writer from the political ideologue and to believe that the former should be judged for his writing and only for this. It was the only way in which intellectual freedom could be maintained in an ideological age. But he left no doubt about how appalling Pound's politics were. The excuses for Pound (e.g. that he was really just a pacifist or insane) were 'plain falsehood'. 'Pound was an ardent follower of Mussolini as far back as the nineteen-twenties, and never concealed it.' He was anti-Semitic to the core, and 'his broadcasts were disgusting': he 'approved the massacre of the East European Jews and "warned" the American Jews that their turn was coming presently'. But 'none of this is a reason against giving Pound the Bollingen Prize'. In a different time – for example, while the Jews were still being murdered in Europe – it might have been 'undesirable' (a weak word indeed). But now, one could separate 'aesthetic integrity and common decency'. But, even if Pound were a good writer (Orwell doubted it himself), we must be in no doubt that 'the opinions he has tried to disseminate by

---

[219]On the controversy, see Robert A. Corrigan, 'Ezra Pound and the Bollingen Prize Controversy', *Midcontinent American Studies Journal*, 8 (1967), pp. 43–57.
[220]William Barrett, 'A Prize for Ezra Pound', *Partisan Review*, 16:4 (April 1949), pp. 344–47.
[221]W.H. Auden et al., 'The Question of the Pound Award', *Partisan Review*, 16:5 (May 1949), pp. 512–22.
[222]Orwell, 'Literature and the Left', 3 June 1943, CW, XV, p. 126.

means of his works are evil ones'. It was a pity that the Bollingen judges had not said so 'more firmly'. [223]

This was Orwell's view in microcosm: even evil views should receive a hearing; even evil views could be well enough expressed to deserve a literary award – but evil they remained and no one should be deterred from unmasking or denouncing the evil. The broad embrace of Orwell's defence of intellectual freedom evident in his defence of Pound was just as apparent in his activism for the cause, the story of which has not been fully told or appreciated.

# 5. Activist for Intellectual Freedom: (I) The Freedom Defence Committee

Orwell was not a joiner. Apart from his brief membership of the Independent Labour Party (1938–9), he was never a member of any political party. When *Nineteen Eighty-Four* began to be interpreted by some readers as an attack on the post-1945 Labour government, Orwell was certainly quick to disavow the view. 'My recent novel is *not* intended as an attack on socialism or on the British Labor party (of which I am a supporter).'[224] But he was never a member of the Labour Party (and indeed his support for it was not exactly whole-hearted). It is therefore a sign of the importance that he attached to intellectual freedom that he was prepared to serve as Vice-Chair of one organization established for its defence, and to be a partner with Arthur Koestler in the attempt to set up a second such organization. (Koestler also relayed to Orwell the message that he would be welcomed as a member of the executive committee, or even as president, of the PEN Club, a writer's organization established in 1921 to support freedom of expression. Koestler's message was part of an effort to ensure that PEN took up 'an active fighting attitude against totalitarianism', but nothing came of this so far as Orwell was concerned,[225] though he did join PEN at about this time. His last two membership cards for 1949 and 1950 survive in his archive.[226])

---

[223]Orwell, 'A Prize for Ezra Pound', May 1949, CW, XX, p. 101. Orwell's friend Dwight Macdonald took a very similar line, arguing that maintaining 'clear distinctions ... between the various spheres, so that the value of an artist's work or a scientist's researches is not confused with the value of their politics' was the very essence of anti-totalitarianism (Macdonald, 'Homage to Twelve Judges: An Editorial', *Politics*, 6:1 (Winter, 1949), pp. 1–2).

[224]'Orwell's Statement on *Nineteen Eighty-Four*', CW, XX, p. 135. The 'statement' was published in multiple versions: the one quoted here was printed in *The New York Times Book Review*, 31 July 1949.

[225]Arthur Koestler to Orwell, *c*.6 March 1646, CW, XVIII, p. 138.

[226]UCL Orwell Archive, Orwell/J/31, digitized at https://ucl.primo.exlibrisgroup.com/view/delivery/44UCL_INST/12358707040004761 (accessed 17 July 2022).

The establishment of the Freedom Defence Committee was prompted by the persecution of British anarchist writers, in particular the editors of *War Commentary* (predecessor of *Freedom*), though other anarchists were arrested too.[227] *War Commentary* had published anti-militaristic stories throughout the war, seemingly with impunity. It was viewed as wrong but harmless by the authorities, who thought that its persecution would be counter-productive. But late in 1944 the government became concerned enough to attempt to prosecute anarchists, not because of their ineffectual opposition to the war, but because, as that war drew to a close, *War Commentary* began to point out that demobilization might create the potential for the same sort of revolutionary agitation that had been seen after the First World War. The offices of the paper were raided in December 1944.[228] The issue of *War Commentary* for 24 February 1945 included a 'stop press' announcement that four comrades had been arrested on 22 February. They were Marie-Louise Berneri and Vernon Richards, who were married to one another, and John Hewitson; a fourth editor, Philip Sansom, who was to be tried alongside them, was already in Brixton Prison in February. *War Commentary* announced the decision to 'form immediately a defence committee'. This was established in a meeting on 3 March with the objective, not only of defending the four and establishing a fund for their support, but 'to protest against any attacks on the freedom of speech and publication'.[229] This Freedom Press Defence Committee, with Herbert Read as its chair and two vice-chairs (Fenner Brockway and Patrick Figgis, with Richard Acland added later), was reconstituted with a broader remit in the summer of 1945 as the Freedom Defence Committee. A small pamphlet, 'The Aims and Constitution of the Freedom Defence Committee', was produced, declaring that the Committee 'was founded to uphold the essential liberty of individuals and organisations, and to defend those who are persecuted for exercising their rights to freedom of speech, writing and action'. It would help people 'irrespective of their political views'.[230] Read remained the chair, and now

---

[227]Rob Ray, *A Beautiful Idea: History of the Freedom Press Anarchists* (London: Freedom Press, 2018), pp. 73–85; Albert Meltzer, *The Anarchists in London 1935–1955* (Sanday: Cienfuegos Press, 1976), pp. 26–9.

[228]The fullest account of the subject (and an excellent one) is Carissa Honeywell, 'Anarchism and the British Warfare State: The Prosecution of the *War Commentary* Anarchists, 1945', *International Review of Social History*, 60 (2015), pp. 257–84. I am indebted to Honeywell's interpretation. Also: 'Anarchists in Court, England, April 1945', http://www.iisg.nl/collections/war-commentary/war-commentary.php (accessed 8 January 2020).

[229]*War Commentary*, 10 March 1945 (facsimile available at https://freedomnews.org.uk/archive/).

[230]The only copy of the 4 pp. pamphlet I have seen is in Arthur Koestler's papers: Edinburgh University Library, Koestler Papers, MS 2414/4. There is a different 2 pp. brochure available online: https://www.katesharpleylibrary.net/95x7mh (accessed 17 July 2022).

with Orwell as the sole vice-chair.[231] George Woodcock, who took over as secretary from Ethel Mannin, appears to have been the real organizer. The organization's constitution declared that it was 'founded to uphold the essential liberty of individuals and organisations, and to defend those who are penalised for exercising their rights to freedom of speech, writing and action'. The Committee would aid anyone whose liberties had been breached 'irrespective of their political views, the nature of the attack on their freedom being the sole criterion on which it will be determined whether or not action should be taken'.[232] Orwell wrote to Herbert Read on 18 August, suggesting that they might meet 'as I would like to talk to you about this Freedom Defence Committee. George Woodcock asked me to be vice-chairman, which I agreed to, but I haven't been very active, because I am really not much good at that kind of thing, and it's all still a bit vague in my mind'.[233] Orwell's talents were not organizational, and Herbert Read was later to say that 'when I took it on I had George Orwell as a vice-chairman, but he has been almost continuously ill, and no help at all'.[234]

That, however, is not the whole story. Woodcock described Orwell as 'a closely involved Vice-Chairman',[235] and he was active in pursuing or supporting individual cases. Woodcock, noting the things Orwell shared with anarchists, commented:

> He shared their sense of freedom as an absolute good, and showed this in the days when he and I worked together on the Freedom Defence Committee in the middle 1940s and he insisted that we must fight for fair treatment by the police and the courts, not only for those whose views we shared, but also for those whose views we detested, such as Communists and Fascists.[236]

Certainly, once the war was over, Orwell returned to a more expansive view of intellectual freedom. He gave a balanced view of the Committee (and

---

[231]The intention to continue the Freedom Press Defence Committee on a broader front was announced at the end of Herbert Read's pamphlet *Freedom: Is It a Crime? The Strange Case of the Three Anarchists Jailed at the Old Bailey, April 1945. Two Speeches by Herbert Read* (London, 1945), pp. 13–14, which was published in June.

[232]Freedom Defence Committee Constitution, UCL Orwell Archive, Orwell/I/5b (papers of Herbert Read).

[233]Orwell to Herbert Read, 18 August 1945, CW, XVII, pp. 263–4.

[234]Herbert Read to Victor Gollancz, 24 December 1948, UCL Orwell/I/5b (fol. 17).

[235]George Woodcock, *Anarchism: A History of Libertarian Ideas and Movements* (Toronto: Toronto University Press, 2009; original edition 1962, revised 1986), p. 385.

[236]George Woodcock, *Orwell's Message: 1984 and the Present* (Madeira Park, BC: Harbour, 1984), p. 127.

some more information about its background) in a 1947 letter to Arthur Koestler, advising his friend to support the organization:

> It is a very small organisation which does the best it can with inadequate funds ... I think up to date they have done a certain amount of good. They have certainly taken up quite a few cases and bombarded secretaries of state etc. with letters, which is usually about all one can do. The point is that the N.C.C.L. [National Council for Civil Liberties, established in 1934] became a Stalinist organisation, and since then there has been no organisation aiming chiefly at the defence of civil liberties. Even a tiny nucleus like this is better than nothing, and if it became better known it could get more money, and so become larger. I think sooner or later there may be a row about the larger aims of the Committee, because at present the moving spirits in it are anarchists and there is a tendency to use it for anarchist propaganda. However, that might correct itself if the organisation became larger, because most of the new supporters would presumably be people of ordinary liberal views.[237]

Whatever reservations he may have had, Orwell was happy to make common cause with anarchists and to defend their own freedom of expression, beginning with the case of the four anarchist editors of *War Commentary* themselves.

The four were charged with disaffecting members of the armed forces under Defence Regulation 39A. Their trial at the Old Bailey began on 23 April 1945. Three of them were convicted and sentenced to nine months' imprisonment on 26 April. (Marie-Louise Berneri was acquitted on a technicality: as a married woman she could not be guilty of conspiracy with her husband, Vernon Richards.[238]) The sentence reflected the fact that the case was a Pyrrhic victory for the government: the three could have received fifteen years' imprisonment. In sentencing them, the judge, Norman Birkett, noted that, though 'the views expressed might seem strange to many people[,] he was quite ready to believe that they were actuated by high motives'.[239] The National Council for Civil Liberties sent an observer to the trial. He reported: 'I understand that the jury came to their decision "with reluctance and great hesitation".'[240]

---

[237]Orwell to Arthur Koestler, 21 March 1947, CW, XIX, p. 84.
[238]Details of the trial can be found in the coverage in *War Commentary*, issues of 24 March 1945, 7 April 1945, 21 April 1945 and 5 May 1945. See also Crick, pp. 496–7; George Woodcock, *The Crystal Spirit: A Study of George Orwell* (Montréal: Black Rose Books, 2005), pp. 11–13.
[239]'Anarchists in Court, England, April 1945', http://www.iisg.nl/collections/war-commentary/war-commentary.php (accessed 8 January 2020); Ray, *Beautiful Idea*, p. 84.
[240]Hull History Centre, DCL/2/4, letter of J. Border to Miss Elizabeth Allen, 27 April 1945.

The position of the National Council for Civil Liberties is worth some comment. By 1945 they were widely seen as a Communist front (as Orwell pointed out to Koestler). This does not seem to be an altogether fair judgement,[241] though certainly some of the leading figures in the NCCL had Communist sympathies, notably its long-serving council member D.N. Pritt who, though never a party member, was an enthusiastic and incorrigible fellow-traveller with Stalinism.[242] Orwell described Pritt, by this time an MP, as an 'alleged "underground" Communist who has been perhaps the most effective pro-Soviet publicist in this country'.[243] Ronald Kidd, the NCCL's founding chairman, was suspected of being a Communist too, but the allegation seems to have been false.[244] The supporters of the NCCL were always ideologically diverse. Its reputation for being interested only in supporting the free speech of Communists may have been exacerbated by its decision, early in 1943, to mount a campaign to combat anti-semitism and Fascism. The latter was seen as the biggest threat to free speech. Consequently, Fascists themselves were not to be tolerated, so when Sir Oswald Mosley was released from internment in November 1943, on health grounds, the NCCL campaigned for his return to detention. The *Catholic Herald* commented: 'What more typical in this topsy-turvy phase of civilisation than that a National Council of Civil Liberties should be well to fore when it is a question of keeping in gaol for a long-term sentence a British citizen against whom no crime has ever been proved in a court of law?'[245] Orwell, in contrast, welcomed Mosley's release as consistent with the principles of *habeas corpus*.[246]

In the case of the Freedom Press anarchists, the NCCL was put on the back foot by the speed and effectiveness with which anarchists mobilized in defence of their comrades. Nonetheless, sluggish though it was, the NCCL did in the end take up the case – at any rate, they took up what they considered to be the real issue, the continued existence of war regulation 39A.

---

[241]For discussion see Brian Dyson, *Liberty in Britain 1934–1994: A Diamond Jubilee History of the National Council for Civil Liberties* (London: Civil Liberties Trust, 1994), pp. 23–7; and Chris Moores, *Civil Liberties and Human Rights in Twentieth-Century Britain* (Cambridge: Cambridge University Press, 2017), pp. 80–1, 82–92.

[242]Morgan, K., 'Pritt, Denis Nowell (1887–1972), Lawyer and Political Activist', *Oxford Dictionary of National Biography*. Retrieved 24 January 2020, from https://www.oxforddnb.com/view/10.1093/ref:odnb/9780198614128.001.0001/odnb-9780198614128-e-31570.

[243]Orwell, 'London Letter', 24 July 1944, Fall 1944, CW, XVI, p. 300.

[244]Janet Clark, 'Sincere and Reasonable Men? The Origins of the National Council for Civil Liberties', *Twentieth Century British History*, 20 (2009), pp. 513–37.

[245]*Catholic Herald*, 26 November 1943, clipping in Hull History Centre, Liberty Archive, DCL/41/3.

[246]Orwell, 'The Freedom of the Press', 1945, CW, XVII, pp. 258–9; his tone is interestingly different in Orwell, 'As I Please', 46, 27 October 1944, CW, XVI, pp. 441–2. These passages are discussed at length elsewhere in this chapter.

Herbert Read, as chair of the Freedom Press Defence Committee, wrote to the NCCL secretary, Elizabeth Allen on 14 March 1945. He provided her with a lengthy account of the case. He informed the NCCL that 'the widest issues of freedom of expression are involved', and asked 'if you would inform us of the action you propose to take on this matter'.[247] The NCCL Executive Committee could not at first reach a view on the case, as Allen informed Read on 21 March. He was unimpressed, and wrote on 13 April:

> I am instructed by this Committee to remind you that this is a case involving fundamental civil liberties and that your Executive is in possession of very full details as to the case; we feel that you should have been able to formulate some decisions as to whether this case does or does not represent, in the view of your Executive, an attack upon the freedom of speech and publication.

The NCCL Executive held a full discussion on 20 April with representatives from the Freedom Press Defence Committee in attendance. Elizabeth Allen informed Read that the NCCL Executive had resolved that they were 'of opinion that the prosecution of the four Anarchists is an attempted abuse of Regulation 39A and protests strongly at the action of the authorities which constitutes and infringement of freedom and the right of expression'. Read and the Freedom Press Defence Committee were not satisfied, writing on 26 April to ask how the resolution, which 'bears no weight in itself', would be implemented. How would the NCCL make the matter public and what practical actions would they take? Allen replied on 18 May, following further discussion in the Executive, which had received a full trial report from J.W. Borders, whom they had sent to observe the trial. The NCCL clearly took the view that the trial itself was conducted fairly and that the real issue was Defence Regulation 39A. Their chosen action was to try to send a deputation to the Home Secretary on Regulation 39A. The NCCL also contributed £20 to the costs that the Freedom Press Defence Committee incurred in defending the editors. Throughout this time, Elizabeth Allen was also fending off inquiries from individuals (including E.M. Forster, who had been lobbied directly by Read) and affiliated institutions wondering why the NCCL had not taken a stand on a case that was of such concern and prominence. Some threatened to disaffiliate. Possibly the long-standing concerns about the NCCL's impartiality in defending civil freedoms underpinned the hostility that some expressed at this time.

The NCCL's difficulties seem to have as much to do with the speed and effectiveness of the Freedom Press Defence Committee as they do with the

---

[247]The letter and other documents cited in this paragraph are in Hull History Centre, Liberty Archive, DCL/2/4.

NCCL's weaknesses. It certainly comes across in the records as cautious and bureaucratic, but not as hostile to the anarchists. The case quickly attracted some high-profile support for the cause of free expression generally and for the Freedom (Press) Defence Committee in particular. An open letter of support was published in *The Manchester Guardian* and elsewhere on 3 March, and its signatories included T.S. Eliot, E.M. Forster, John Middleton Murry, Herbert Read, Stephen Spender and Julian Symons – representing a broad range of political positions. Perhaps as a result of this breadth, the letter's defence of the anarchist editors was in terms of the classic liberal defence of free speech.

> We submit that such actions [the raid on the *War Commentary* offices and the arrest of the editors] are prejudicial to the liberty of speech and writing. If they are allowed to pass without protest, they may become precedents for future persecutions of individuals or of organisations devoted to the spreading of opinions disliked by the authorities. Once started, a process of this nature may well result in an intellectual tyranny of an extreme kind.[248]

The Freedom Defence Committee eventually listed amongst its sponsors these people (minus Eliot), with many more, including Vera Brittain, Benjamin Britten, Michael Foot, Julian Huxley, Henry Moore, Peter Pears, Bertrand Russell, Osbert Sitwell, Graham Sutherland and Michael Tippett.

Herbert Read, who led the campaign, appealed also to English traditions. Before the trial, he gave a speech in which he declared: 'I do not speak to you now as an anarchist: I speak to you as an Englishman, as one proud to follow in the tradition of Milton and Shelley – the tradition of all those poets and philosophers who have given us the proud right to claim freedom of speech and the liberty of unlicensed printing.' A second speech that followed the three convictions was, in part, a powerful defence of revolutionary anarchism, but, he conceded, 'you may not agree with it – you may not agree with Buddhism or Christianity, with communism or conservatism, but we do not, in this country, imprison people for being Buddhists or Christians, conservatives or communists. Why, then, in the name of all that is just and equitable, are these three anarchists deprived of their liberty?' The liberal tradition of free speech was again invoked.

> There is no longer in this land any such a thing as the liberty of unlicensed printing for which Milton made his immortal and unanswerable plea: there is no longer any such thing as freedom of expression which ten generations of Englishmen have jealously guarded. These words are

---

[248] *War Commentary*, 10 March 1945, p. 4.

now a mockery, and either we have been duped slaves to accept such a breach of our traditional rights, or we resolve never to rest until they are restored.[249]

Orwell similarly used Milton as a symbol of freedom of expression in two important essays, 'The Freedom of the Press' (the intended preface to *Animal Farm* that was only published posthumously) and 'The Prevention of Literature', published in *Polemic* in January 1946.[250]

Orwell, who was listed as a sponsor of the original Freedom Press Defence Committee,[251] was one of nine signatories to a letter, published in *Tribune* on 4 May 1945, protesting at the sentencing. The letter prudently acknowledged the right of the government to try the men, but noted that the pretence of the prosecution 'that the freedom of the Press was in no way involved is simply legal hair-splitting'. The prosecution was particularly inappropriate at a time when the war was clearly drawing to a close, leaving no grounds of national security on which to justify the trial. It was necessary for 'the whole body of Socialist opinion in this country to identify itself with these editors'. Orwell put his name to a letter that ended with a resounding defence of the anarchist tradition.

> The thing these men did which brought them standing, where thieves and murderers are wont to stand, inside the dock at the Old Bailey, spring from their love of justice and their concern for the victims and the poor. On trial with them were the teachings of Jesus, the philosophy of Peter Kropotkin, the politics of Tom Paine, the poetry of William Blake and the paintings of Van Gogh. No man who accepts these can remain true to them while rejecting the right of these three men to do the things they did.[252]

Through the Freedom Defence Committee, and in other ways, Orwell took up a range of causes, not all of them directly related to freedom of thought or expression but in defence of various forms of personal freedom. He was also generous in supporting the Freedom Defence Committee financially, donating two guineas in 1945, and in the first half of 1946 a further £10 (the second largest personal donation).[253] He responded to the

---

[249]Herbert Read, *A One-Man Manifesto and Other Writings for Freedom Press*, ed. David Goodway (London: Freedom Press, 1994), pp. 98, 103.

[250]Orwell, 'The Freedom of the Press', August 1945, published 1972, CW, XVII, p. 259; Orwell, 'The Prevention of Literature', January 1946, CW, XVIII, p. 370. See also Orwell, 'Review of *Milton: Man and Thinker* by Denis Saurat', 20 August 1944, CW, XVI, pp. 338–40.

[251]There is a blank letterhead for the Freedom Press Defence Committee in UCL Orwell/I/5a (papers of Vernon Richards).

[252]'Anarchist Trial', 4 May 1945, CW, XVII, pp. 135–6.

[253]CW, XVII, p. 358.

Committee's appeal for funds in 1947 by donating another £30, coming second only to Victor Gollancz with this contribution.[254]

The other causes with which Orwell was personally involved were diverse. He spoke at a public meeting in the Conway Hall on 7 November 1945 in support of the Freedom Defence Committee's campaign to secure an amnesty for political and military prisoners detained under wartime legislation. Orwell himself spoke about those who had been thought guilty of fraternization.[255] He lent his support to the case of John Olday (who was, among other things, a cartoonist for *War Commentary*[256]) and to that of Philip Sansom, one of the three imprisoned *War Commentary* editors. In both cases attempts were being made to continue harassing them after they had served an initial term of imprisonment. Olday was charged with a second offence, and Sansom was instructed to attend, within an hour of his release time, a medical to determine his fitness for military service. He did not do so and was charged with failure to attend. In both cases the Freedom Defence Committee's campaign succeeded: Olday's sentence was suspended, and the Home Secretary ordered Sansom's release.[257] Orwell was also approached by Gunner Nicholls who wanted to marry a German woman and bring her back to England. He brought the case to Woodcock's attention, who was able to ascertain that, once demobilized, the soldier could marry his German wife.[258]

Bigger issues were tackled too. Orwell spoke on 26 March 1946 at a public meeting campaigning to release 226 Spanish republicans held in a Prisoner of War camp in Lancashire, and to allow those who wished to do so to remain in England. The campaign was successful by August.[259] He also signed a letter from the Freedom Defence Committee to President Truman seeking an amnesty for US conscientious objectors.[260] More difficult was the case of physicist Alan Nunn May, charged under the Official Secrets Act with providing information to the Russians. Orwell had misgivings (as did others), considering Nunn May to be guilty as charged, but signed a petition of support 'because the less spy-hunting is indulged the better'. Orwell was willing to campaign to get him out of prison sooner, with little success. Nunn

---

[254]"Freedom Defence Committee Appeal', 1947, CW, XIX, p. 5.

[255]'The Amnesty Campaign', 7 November 1945, CW, XVII, pp. 357–8.

[256]A selection of his cartoons is in Marie-Louise Berneri, *Neither East Nor West: Selected Writings 1939–1948* (London: Freedom Press, 1988).

[257]Orwell to George Woodcock, 9 September 1945, CW, XVII, pp. 288–9 (Orwell supported Olday while recognizing that he was in fact guilty on both counts, of stealing an identity card and of desertion); 'The "Cat-and-Mouse" Case: Campaign for Philip Sansom', CW, XVIII, pp. 48–9, Orwell was signatory to a group letter, first published on 18 January 1946.

[258]Orwell to George Woodcock, 14 March 1946 & 20 March 1946, CW, XVIII, pp. 149–50, 158. See also material in UCL, Orwell Archive, Orwell I/5a.

[259]'Spanish Anti-Fascists', CW, XVIII, p. 169.

[260]'Freedom Defence Committee Letter to President Truman', 18 May 1946, CW, XVIII, p. 311.

May was not released until 1952.[261] Orwell was perhaps happier to support the Polish refugee Franciszek Kilánski, who had been repatriated from Scotland to Poland, and then charged with being a spy. Woodock, alerted to the case by Orwell, took up the whole issue of the political persecution of repatriated Polish exiles on behalf of the Freedom Defence Committee.[262]

During these years, when the Freedom Defence Committee was active, Orwell showed a willingness to give some support to the civil liberties of those whose views he loathed, Communists and Fascists. He wrote to Woodcock on 23 March 1948, asking whether the Freedom Defence Committee was going to do anything about the ban on Communists and Fascists in the civil service. He acknowledged that it was a difficult issue, and his analysis is worth quoting at length. It says a lot about Orwell's approach.

> It's not easy to have a clear position, because, if one admits the right of governments to govern, one must admit their right to choose suitable agents, & I think *any* organisation, e.g. a political party, has a right to protect itself against infiltration methods. But at the same time, the *way* in which the government seems to be going to work is vaguely disquieting, & the whole phenomenon seems to me part of the general breakdown of the democratic outlook. Only a week or two ago the Communists themselves were shouting for unconstitutional methods to be used against Fascists, now the same methods are to be used against themselves, & in another year or two a pro-Communist government might be using them against us. Meanwhile the general apathy about freedom of speech etc. constantly grows, & that matters much more than what may be in the statute books.[263]

The Freedom Defence Committee took the matter up, and Orwell signed its petition on the matter. Not surprisingly, because the line it took followed his own very closely. It refused to criticize the government for dismissing or transferring undesirable employees, but urged that there needed to be safeguards to protect the innocent. Those accused of Communist or Fascist allegiances should have the right to have a trade union representative speak on their behalf, allegations 'should be ... substantiated by corroborative evidence', and the accused civil servant should be allowed to cross-examine those giving evidence against him.[264]

---

[261]Orwell to Vernon Richards, 6 August 1946, CW, XVII, pp. 367–8; Orwell to George Woodcock, 9 August 1947, CW, XIX, pp. 188–9. See also material in UCL Orwell Archive, Orwell I/5a.

[262]Orwell to George Woodcock, 28 February 1947, CW, XIX, p. 54; Orwell to George Woodcock, 7 March 1947, CW, XIX, p. 71.

[263]Orwell to George Woodcock, 23 March 1948, CW, XIX, p. 301.

[264]'Civil Service Purge', 21 August 1948, CW, XIX, p. 421.

The version of this petition published by *Peace News* was introduced by a short statement that made much of the fact that the Freedom Defence Committee was prepared to defend the rights of both Communists and Fascists, '[u]nlike the National Council for Civil Liberties, which has called for the suppression of all Fascists and unlimited freedom for all Communists'.[265] In fact, the civil service purge was aimed at Communists primarily, but there is no doubt that both the Committee and Orwell himself were prepared to defend the freedoms of Fascists. Earlier in 1948, Orwell had raised the case of England's very own Fascist, Sir Oswald Mosley. 'I hope the F.D.C. is doing something about these constant demands to outlaw Mosley & Co.,' he wrote to Woodcock. Again, he is worth quoting at length on the subject:

> Tribune's attitude has been shameful, & when the other week Zilliacus [Labour MP and Communist fellow-traveller] wrote in demanding what amounts to Fascist legislation & creation of 2nd-class citizens, nobody seems to have replied. The whole thing is simply a thinly-disguised desire to persecute someone who can't hit back, as obviously the Mosley lot don't matter a damn & can't get a real mass following. I think it's a case for a pamphlet, & I only wish I felt well enough to write one. The central thing one has comes [sic] to terms with the argument, always advanced by those advocating repressive legislation, that 'you cannot allow democracy to be used to overthrow democracy – you cannot allow freedom to those who merely use it in order to destroy freedom'. This of course is true, & both Fascists and Communists do aim at making use of democracy in order to destroy it. But if you carry this to its conclusion, there can be no case for allowing any political or intellectual freedom whatever. Evidently therefore it is a matter of distinguishing between a real & a merely theoretical threat to democracy, & no one should be persecuted for expressing his opinions, however anti-social, & no political organisation suppressed, unless it can be shown that there is *a substantial threat to the stability of the state.*[266]

This nicely captures Orwell's mixture of principle and pragmatism, his recognition that, while freedom could not be unlimited, there was a strong presumption in favour of tolerating opinions and theories, however extreme, however unpalatable. It was only when those ideas threatened to do real harm, that is they ceased to be just theories or opinions, that some level of restraint might be needed.

---

[265]'Civil Service Purge', 21 August 1948, CW, XIX, p. 421.
[266]Orwell to George Woodcock, 4 January 1948, CW, XIX, p. 524.

Orwell's first comment on the question of Mosley's continued detention was in October 1944, and this makes it a little clearer just where the limits to freedom of expression might lie. He took issue with Middleton Murry's claim that 'the agitation against Mosley's release from internment ... [was] a sign of the growth of ... the totalitarian habit of mind'. Orwell agreed that 'on the face it' the protests 'were a very bad sign. In effect people were agitating against Habeas Corpus.' But he did not see the matter in black and white, and conceded that, early in the war, the case for Mosley's detention had been strong.

> In 1940 it was a perfectly proper action to intern Mosley, and in my opinion it would have been quite proper to shoot him if the Germans had set foot in Britain. When it is a question of national existence, no government can stand on the letter of the law: otherwise a potential quisling has only to avoid committing any indictable offence, and he can remain at liberty, ready to go over to the enemy and act as their gauleiter as soon as they arrive. But by 1943 [when Mosley was released] the situation was totally different. The chance of a serious German invasion had passed, and Mosley ... was merely a ridiculous failed politician with varicose veins. To continue imprisoning him without trial was an infringement of every principle we are supposedly fighting for.

The popular hostility to Mosley's release was, in Orwell's view, based on the feeling that he was treated leniently because he was rich and privileged. Indeed, 'the failure of any genuinely totalitarian outlook to gain ground among the ordinary people of this country is one of the most surprising and encouraging phenomena of the war'.[267]

The statement is typical of Orwell's willingness to embrace even a brutal response to an emergency, one aspect of his often deliberately provocative presentation of his *persona*. But it was not Mosely's views that Orwell feared; it was the risk that he would betray his country to an invading enemy. Compare the major statement on free speech originally intended as an introduction to *Animal Farm*, 'The Freedom of the Press', which puts the matter in a slightly different context. Orwell pointed there to the existence of 'the renegade Liberal' who has a 'tendency to argue that one can only defend democracy by totalitarian methods'. Those who opposed democracy must be crushed because they 'objectively' aided your enemies. But, Orwell warned, the renegade liberals 'don't see that if you encourage totalitarian methods, the time may come when they will be used against you instead of for you. Make a habit of imprisoning Fascists without trial, and perhaps the process won't stop at Fascists.' He pointed to the suppression of the

---

[267]Orwell, 'As I Please', 46, 27 October 1944, CW, XVI, pp. 441–2.

Communist paper the *Daily Worker* (1941–2), and argued that those who felt 'that it was a paper of doubtful loyalty and ought not to be tolerated in war time' had very likely picked up the attitude from the Communists themselves. The lesson – and the warning – was clear:

> Tolerance and decency are deeply rooted in England, but they are not indestructible, and they have to be kept alive partly by conscious effort. The result of preaching totalitarian doctrines is to weaken the instinct by means of which free peoples know what is or is not dangerous. The case of Mosley illustrates this. In 1940 it was perfectly right to intern Mosley, whether or not he had committed any technical crime. We were fighting for our lives and could not allow a possible quisling to go free. To keep him shut up, without trial, in 1943 was an outrage. The general failure to see this was a bad symptom ... [H]ow much of the present slide towards Fascist ways of thought is traceable to the 'anti-Fascism' of the past ten years and the unscrupulousness it has entailed?[268]

Orwell's defence of civil liberties clearly allowed for some strictly temporary deviations from principle. At the time, Woodcock accused him of 'opportunism'. As examples,

> he contends seriously that we must have conscription during the war, but that once the war has ended we must resist it as an infringement of civil liberties, During the war we must jail "fascists", but afterwards we must let them carry on their propaganda at will. In other words we can have freedom when it is convenient, but at moments of crisis freedom is to be stored away for the return of better days.[269]

Orwell took exception to this claim by Woodcock, and phoned him. '"I have my reasons for arguing like that," he said, but he never explained them.'[270] Whatever the reasons, Woodcock's assertion does not seem fair. Orwell recognized that when the very existence of state and society was threatened by an emergency, then emergency measure might be required. But he expected the normal principles to be reapplied as soon as possible, *even in war*, as with Mosley in 1943. He supported the detention of Mosley *only* when invasion seemed *imminent*, and there was an immediate risk that an invading Fascist army would find friends who would betray their country.

The Freedom Defence Committee survived until early 1949, but was clearly ailing by the end. As early as January 1947 it needed an immediate

---

[268] Orwell, 'The Freedom of the Press', 1945, CW, XVII, pp. 258–9. Are there echoes of this today in the illiberalism of some antifa intellectuals?

[269] George Woodcock, 'George Orwell, 19th Century Liberal', *Politics*, December 1946, p. 387.

[270] Woodcock, *Crystal Spirit*, p. 28.

cash injection of £250 and a regular income of £500, and issued a public appeal through the press.[271] This was successful. Another appeal for funds (to which Orwell was a signatory) was published in *Tribune* and elsewhere in September 1948. Survival required that the Committee should have an annual income of £1,000 p.a., but it had been falling short and had a deficit of £145. An immediate cash injection of £500 was needed.[272] Read also wrote directly to key supporters late in 1948 to try to keep the Freedom Defence Committee going, but the response, even though mostly positive, must have been dispiriting. Victor Gollancz was encouraging, but unwilling to give much financial support. Fenner Brockway, likewise, hoped the Committee would continue but was unable to contribute to its funds. Read reported to Gollancz that he could not find anyone to take on the leadership of the organization. E.M. Forster wrote on 6 December 1948: 'The situation is disastrous. Neither you nor Orwell are able to do much work for the F.D.C., I do not wish to start active work on it myself, and you have not succeeded in attracting any new blood.' His conclusion: 'you must wind the organisation up.'[273] Orwell himself wrote to Read on 26 February 1949 from the Cotswold Sanitorium. A meeting had, it seems, been called to decide the future of the Committee. Orwell, of course, could not attend or be in any way active, but he would support as best he could. 'If it is decided to continue the organisation, I am good for £10, not more I am afraid. This disease is an expensive hobby.'[274] The Freedom Defence Committee folded.

For a while, in 1948, Orwell had considered writing an essay for *The Observer* about the Freedom Defence Committee, but decided that he didn't know enough and suggested that George Woodcock might take it on instead. He even advised to Woodcock what he might put in the article, notably 'some remarks on the threat to individual liberty contained in the modern centralised state' (no doubt a congenial topic for the anarchist Woodcock).[275] In the end, neither of them wrote the article. Orwell did, however, publish in the *Freedom Defence Committee Bulletin* (no. 2, February–March 1946) a shortened version of his *Tribune* essay 'Freedom in the Park'. The essay was a response to the arrest for obstruction of five men for selling newspapers on the street outside Hyde Park. One of the papers was *Freedom* (the title to which the Freedom Press's *War Commentary* reverted after the war); all were pacifist or left-wing. Orwell began by musing about the fact that, while selling newspapers on the street could indeed constitute obstruction, it was

---

[271]'Freedom Defence Committee to the Public', 29 January 1947, CW, XIX, pp. 33–4.
[272]'Appeal by Freedom Defence Committee', 7 September 1948, CW, XIX, pp. 430–1.
[273]This account is based on the papers in UCL Orwell/I/5b.
[274]Orwell to Herbert Read, 26 February 1949, CW, XX, p. 48.
[275]Orwell to George Woodcock, 24 May 1948, CW, XIX, pp. 341–2; also Orwell to Woodcock, 24 April 1948, CW, XIX, p. 324, when Orwell had said that he would write the article, and that he might be able to use it 'to give a quiet kick' to the NCCL.

odd that it was always the seller of the (Communist) *Daily Worker* and never the seller of the *Daily Telegraph* (right-wing then as now) who was arrested. The British police, he thought, 'have been unfriendly to Left-wing activities' and side with 'the defenders of private property', and before the war had been scandalous in their willingness to work with Mosley's blackshirts to keep 'order' at demonstrations. Orwell wondered, now that there was a new Labour government, whether there was any scope for weeding out of the police and service those who might not be sympathetic to the government's aims. But the real issue was the interference with sellers of newspapers or pamphlets, especially outside Hyde Park, a special sanctuary for free speech. 'I have listened there,' he said, 'to Indian nationalists, Temperance reformers, Communists, Trotskyists, the S.P.G.B. [Socialist Party of Great Britain], the Catholic Evidence Society, Freethinkers, vegetarians, Mormons, the Salvation army, the Church Army, and a large variety of plain lunatics'. Though Hyde Park was, 'a special area ... where outlawed opinions are permitted to walk', few other countries had anything like it. Hyde Park was symbolic in a country that valued free speech. The degree of freedom possessed by the British press could be exaggerated, as we have heard him say before. 'Technically there is great freedom, but the fact that most of the press is owned by a few people operates in much the same way as a State censorship. On the other hand freedom of speech is real.' Real but fragile:

> The point is that the relative freedom which we enjoy depends on public opinion. The law is no protection. Governments make laws, but whether they are carried out, and how the police behave, depends on the general temper of the country. If large numbers of people are interested in freedom of speech, there will be freedom of speech, even if the law forbids it; if public opinion is sluggish, inconvenient minorities will be persecuted, even if laws exist to protect them. The decline in the desire for intellectual liberty has not been so sharp as I would have predicted six years ago ... but still there has been a decline. The notion that certain opinions cannot safely be allowed a hearing is growing. It is given currency by intellectuals who confuse the issue by not distinguishing between democratic opposition and open rebellion, and it is reflect in our growing indifference to tyranny and injustice abroad. And even those who declare themselves to be in favour of freedom of opinion generally drop their claim when it is their own adversaries who are being persecuted.[276]

This helps us to understand why Orwell defend the intellectual freedoms of anarchists, Communists and Fascists alike, and why he thought that the work of the Freedom Defence Committee was important. Public opinion

---

[276]Orwell, 'Freedom of the Park', 7 December 1945, CW, XVII, pp. 416–19.

must be encouraged to value intellectual liberty, and a body that defended such liberty impartially (unlike, it was alleged, the NCCL) was essential. Socialism with a liberal face remained Orwell's vision for the future, but it was the liberalism part of this mixture that seemed the less likely to survive. Socialism would come but would it preserve or destroy the freedoms of the individual? Orwell's activism was not confined to the work of the Freedom Defence Committee, and just before he began working in earnest on *Nineteen Eighty-Four* he was engaged in a project with more expansive ambitions to fight the cause of freedom than the Freedom Defence Committee had possessed.

## 6. Activist for Intellectual Freedom: (II) The League for the Dignity and Rights of Man

Let us step back a little, back to the Welsh winter of 1945–6 when Orwell and his son Richard spent Christmas with Arthur Koestler in his cottage of Bwlch Ocyn. Also present were Mamaine Paget, Koestler's partner and future wife, and her twin sister, Celia Kirwan.[277] Orwell and Koestler hatched a plan to establish an international organization to defend human rights. Its intended name varied but it is usually referred to as the League for the Dignity and Rights of Man. Not long before he left for Wales, Orwell had finished writing one of his most important essays on freedom of speech, 'The Prevention of Literature'. 'To defend your right of free speech,' the essay proclaimed, 'you have to fight against economic pressure and against strong sections of public opinion, but not, as yet, against a secret police force'.[278] Would that continue to be true? 'As yet' did not sound too hopeful. In the wake of his difficulties publishing *Animal Farm* and his experience defending anarchists and others through the Freedom Defence Committee, Orwell had come to see by 1945 that fundamental problem to be faced was how to preserve liberal rights and freedoms in a world in which totalitarianism threatened to carry the day. Economic collectivism and planning seemed inevitable: could it lead to anything except totalitarianism? Though the Freedom Defence Committee was doing its bit on a narrow front, the defence of freedom required an international organization – and one free of Stalinist influences. It was such an organization that Orwell and Koestler set out to create in 1946.

---

[277]I have used the names of the twins in the form closest to that used in the late 1940s (see below for the complications regarding Mamaine): Celia is sometimes referred to by her birth name, Paget, and sometimes by her second married name, Goodman.

[278]Orwell, 'The Prevention of Literature', January 1946 (but written by November 1945), CW, XVII, p. 379.

The Christmas break got off to a frosty start. Orwell (with Richard) had met Celia Kirwan on the platform at Paddington and they travelled to North Wales together. Koestler was later to recall that he and Orwell 'became very close ... not intimate, because I don't think anyone could be intimate with George'. His account of collecting Orwell from the train in Wales gives a hint of what Koestler might have meant by this.

My wife and I had a house in North Wales, in Snowdonia.[279] It was pretty tough living, and he came up for a week, or something. He arrived on Friday and we fetched him in the car in Llandudno, – or was it a Saturday?[280] Because just before leaving, the mail arrived with the TRIBUNE, in which George had written a review of a very bad play which I had written – I wish I hadn't. And it was what you call 'a stinking review'. He didn't say the play was bad; he hoped that next time K. would do better. It was just totally condemnatory. So I met – and we got into the car with Richard, his adopted son, [and Celia, presumably] and we drove up, and it was very jolly; I was happy to have him there, and I had a feeling that he was – he liked the harsh North Wales country, and I had a feeling he was also quite happy. And then over a drink I told him, 'George, but why on earth have you been so beastly?' And he said, 'What do you mean, – beastly, 'I don't know – it's a bad book isn't it? Don't you agree?' I said, 'Yes, I do agree, but I mean you could have cut out just one gentle sentence into it[']. A total blank. He couldn't understand, and he couldn't understand that it might hurt somebody's feelings. And indeed, as with all his closest friends, it was actually, as you'll probably agree, the mark of his friendship to treat a friend as he treated himself.[281]

---

[279]Mamaine did not marry Koestler until 15 April 1950 but apparently took the name Koestler by deed-poll on 15 October 1946: Koestler to Mrs Cunningham, 5 December 1949, Edinburgh University Library, Koestler Papers, MS 2376/3/246.

[280]Orwell apparently arrived on 23 December, which was a Sunday: Koestler to Tom Hopkinson, 8 December 1945, Edinburgh University Archives, Koestler Papers, 2374/1/172. It is possible that arrangements changed after this letter was sent.

[281]Interview transcript for BBC programme, 1960, UCL Orwell/Q/8. There is an alternative version of the story from an interview with Ian Angus in Audrey Coppard & Bernard Crick (eds), *Orwell Remembered* (London: Ariel Books / BBC, 1984), p. 168, and another quoted earlier in this book (Introduction). The play was *Twilight Bar*. Orwell described it as 'an unworthy squib' with 'mediocre dialogue': Orwell, 'Review of *Hui Clos* by Jean-Paul Sartre; *The Banbury Nose* by Peter Ustinov; *Twilight Bar* by Arthur Koestler', 30 November 1945, CW, XVII, pp. 406–9. The interview with Ian Angus adds to the account of the meeting that on his way home Orwell admitted that perhaps he might have softened the review. Koestler's portrait of Orwell's severity builds on the obituary he had written for *The Observer*, 29 January 1950, in Jeffrey Meyers (ed.), *George Orwell: The Critical Heritage* (London: Routledge & Kegan Paul, 1975), pp. 296–9.

Though Koestler complained that Richard 'is turning the house upside down', the visit seems to have been a success.[282] Koestler recalled that 'I have never seen [Orwell] so enthusiastic as when we discussed the projected League'.[283]

By the time he returned to London, Orwell had agreed to work with Koestler to establish a human rights league. The first step was to produce a statement of intent, which Orwell drafted and sent to Koestler on 2 January. 'It is a rough one and not well expressed, but it contains more or less what I mean and I think it is roughly along these lines that one ought to present the matter to anyone who is hearing about it for the first time.'[284] Koestler liked the draft. [285] From this point on, the story becomes complicated, and by the middle of 1946 the plans for the League had come to nothing and were quietly abandoned. One question to consider is why the idea went nowhere. A second is what the fate of Orwell's draft statement was. No version of it appears in Peter Davison's edition of Orwell's *Complete Works*, but it was seemingly rediscovered and published by David Smith in 2018.[286]

Let's begin with the question of why the attempt to found the League failed. Both Orwell and Koestler quickly began to sound out people whom they expected to be sympathetic. Orwell started with Tom Hopkinson and Barbara Ward. 'They were both a little timid, chiefly I think because they realise that an organisation of this type would in practice be anti-Russian, and they are going through an acute phase of anti-Americanism. However they are anxious to hear more and are certainly not hostile to the idea.' The thing to do 'would be to show them copies of the draft manifesto, or whatever it is, when drawn up'.[287] Orwell alerted Dwight Macdonald in New York to the plans, and told him that he would soon hear from Koestler.[288] Koestler seems to have broached the league idea to Michael Foot, reporting to Mamaine that he had spent an evening with him during a trip to London

---

[282]Koestler to Tom Hopkinson, 27 December 1945, Edinburgh University Library, Koestler Papers, 2374/1/191.

[283]Arthur & Cynthia Koestler, *Stranger on the Square*, ed. Harold Harris (London: Hutchinson, 1984), p. 41. Orwell wrote a brief account of his trip to Wales, though it does not mention the League: Orwell to Geoffrey Gorer, 22 January 1946, CW, XVIII, p. 52.

[284]Orwell to Arthur Koestler, 2 January 1946, CW, CVIII, p. 7.

[285]Arthur Koestler to Orwell, 9 January 1946, copy in UCL Orwell/I/4 (unnumbered); summary in CW, XVIII, p. 8. The copy in the Orwell archive is presumably from Edinburgh University Library, Koestler Papers, 2345/2, but I have not been able to find the original.

[286]David Smith (with illustrations by Mike Mosher), *George Orwell Illustrated* (Chicago, IL: Haymarket Books, 2018), pp. 230–4. The background to his discovery of the draft (which he refers to as 'Orwell's Manifesto') is described in Smith, 'References for *George Orwell Illustrated*', pp. 1–8, unpublished pdf available at https://www.researchgate.net/profile/David_ Smith366.

[287]Orwell to Arthur Koestler, 10 January 1946, CW, CVIII, pp. 27–8.

[288]Orwell to Dwight Macdonald, 3 January 1946, CW, XVIII, p. 12.

and that 'he has become very anti-bolshie and full of enthusiasm for the League idea'.[289] Orwell followed up. He showed a version of the draft manifesto to Foot, who suggested a couple of amendments.[290] There was talk of contacting Edward Fulton, proprietor of the *Picture Post*.[291] Ignazio Silone visited London for a few days in January 1946, and Orwell took him and his wife out to dinner. Koestler has asked Orwell to get Silone's views of the League proposal, which he did.[292] By chance, Silone travelled back to Europe on the same boat as Mamaine Paget, who was embarking on a month's visit to Paris.[293] Mamaine was able to further the discussion on the 'boat & train':[294]

> I talked to Silone about your & George's project, which he seemed to approve of. George hadn't told him very much about it so I enlarged a bit & emphasized that it was not to become a tool of any particular faction. He said that it would be most important to employ people with experience of that kind of thing, and to be quite certain of one's cases, otherwise it would soon get discredited. I didn't, however, say anything about Russia or Russian-occupied territory, which perhaps I should have; but I gather that S[ilone] is not in favour of any bloc or League which w[oul]d, in the present circ[umstance]s, appear aggressive towards Russia. He says he thinks 'qu'il ne faut surtout pas isoler la Russie', & that e.g. a Western Bloc would have that effect because it w[oul]d be interpreted by the Russians as aggressive. He wasn't very forthcoming about this however & I therefore didn't pursue the subject. I think he would be prepared to give his name but not to do any work. I told him that the idea was a recent one of yours which hadn't been worked out in detail but that you would send him a fuller description later.[295]

Koestler was equally energetic in spreading the word. Early in January, Mamaine Paget recorded 'an awful spell of highbrow social life with Polanyi,

---

[289]Arthur Koestler to Mamaine Paget, 5 February 1946, Edinburgh University Library, Koestler Papers, 2303/2/61.

[290]Orwell to Arthur Koestler, 11 February 1946, CW, XVIII, p. 105.

[291]Orwell to Arthur Koestler, 10 January 1946, CW, CVIII, p. 28. He later told Dwight Macdonald that he had had several conversations with Silone: Orwell to Dwight Macdonald, 7 February 1946, CW, XVIII, p. 93.

[292]Orwell to Geoffrey Gorer, 22 January 1946, CW, XVIII, p. 52; Arthur Koestler to Orwell, 9 January 1946, CW, XVIII, p. 8.

[293]Mamaine Paget's Diary, 23 January 1946; Celia Goodman (ed.), *Living with Koestler: Mamaine Koestler's Letters 1945–51* (London: Weidenfeld & Nicolson, 1985), p. 26.

[294]Mamaine Paget's Diary, 23 January 1946; Goodman (ed.), *Living with Koestler*, p. 26.

[295]Mamaine Paget to Arthur Koestler, 25 January 1946, Edinburgh University Library, Koestler Papers, 2303/2/50.

the Crawshays and Bertrand Russell'.[296] Michael Polanyi, Professor of Physical Chemistry at the University of Manchester, and Rupert Crawshay-Williams, a philosopher who lived near Koestler and Paget, were very likely sounded out on the idea. Russell definitely was. Mamaine told her sister that discussing politics with him 'came as a great relief to my weary brain' after the scientific and philosophical discussions that she had been subjected to. She had recorded in her diary: 'K. discussed with Russell his project for a new League, which he had also discussed with George and Tom Hop[kinson]. Russell seemed to agree with K's ideas though he didn't want to be involved and said he thought the first step should be a conference of say 12 people, all with special qualifications, who should discuss what to do to prevent atomic war.'[297] This lunch had taken place no later than the 9th, when Koestler wrote to Orwell with his own report of it. Russell's mind was clearly focused on how to avoid atomic war, and he had little time for an 'ethical movement' of the sort proposed by Koestler and Orwell. He would, he said, read a paper at a conference but not act as its convenor. Koestler recognized that this was not quite what he and Orwell were after, but thought that perhaps 'an organisation on our lines' might be a by-product of the conference that Russell wanted. He even suggested a couple of possible names for the League: 'Magna Carta League' or 'Renaissance – A League for the Defense and Development of Democracy'.[298] Russell himself told Orwell that he thought Koestler's proposal 'premature' and would prefer that 'a small group of us, who have a generally similar outlook, should meet to discuss the possible programme for the world'. He was keen to meet the author of *Animal Farm*, and they agreed to have lunch together in London on 12 February.[299]

The overture to Russell and what followed from it constitute one of the two major reasons for the failure of the League proposal. From the start, Russell pounced on an opportunity to promote his own concerns which were quite separate from those that Koestler and Orwell had discussed during their Welsh Christmas. On 21 January, Russell sent Koestler, via Rupert Crawshay-Williams, a twelve-page typescript, 'The Atomic Bomb and the Prevention of War'. The essay 'isn't for publication ... but a text for discussion'. 'Very depressing,' Crawshay-Williams thought it was:

---

[296]Mamaine Paget to Celia Kirwan, 11 January 1946, in Goodman (ed.), *Living with Koestler*, p. 25.

[297]Mamaine Paget's Diary, 10 January 1946. I am grateful to Mrs Ariane Bankes, Celia Goodman's daughter, who supplied me with unpublished extracted entries from the diary.

[298]Arthur Koestler to Orwell, 9 January 1946, copy in UCL Orwell/I/4 (unnumbered); summary in CW, XVIII, p. 8 (missing from Edinburgh University Library, Koestler Papers, 2345/2?).

[299]Bertrand Russell to Orwell, 18 January 1946, UCL Orwell/H/2/67, summary in CW, XVIII, p. 105; Orwell to Arthur Koestler, 11 February 1946, CW, XVIII, p. 105.

But given his premises (which can't very well be refused) the problem is horrid and, as he says, 'the difficulty is to persuade the human race to acquiesce in its own survival'. Much easier to persuade them to acquiesce in religious revival or antidisestablishmentarianism (the long word to end long words).[300]

Over the next couple of months, Koestler tried to move things in the direction Russell had indicated. He arranged for the small conference to be funded by Rodney Phillips. Phillips was also financing a new journal edited by Humphrey Slater, *Polemic*, with which Orwell was closely associated. (We will return to this association a little later.) The conference was intended to take place near Koestler's house in Wales on 19–23 April. Eight rooms were booked at a local hotel. Koestler told Manès Sperber that the 'People present will be Bertrand Russell, George Orwell, Michael Foot, an American journalist, somebody from the Church of England, a lawyer, Slater (Polemic) and two or three other people including I hope yourself'. He added: 'If you could persuade Malraux to come it would be grand.'[301] Koestler communicated with Phillips through Celia Kirwan, who had become an editorial assistant on *Polemic*, perhaps in the wake of Phillips' request for Mamaine to become the journal's business manager in May 1945.[302] But the plans for the conference quickly fell through, the second major reason for the loss of momentum behind the League, and this left Koestler even more inclined to work with Russell instead. On 19 March, Koestler was still writing to Orwell that rooms were booked for Easter and that he was 'corresponding with Rodney about technical arrangements'.[303] A few days later, though, it was all off.

The withdrawal of support by Phillips and Slater did not immediately kill Koestler's or Orwell's hopes for the League, but in time it proved to have been a blow from which there was no recovery. Koestler had indeed written to Phillips on the 14th, telling him that he had booked eight rooms, which could accommodate six to ten people. Slater would stay with Crawshay-Williams. Phillips it seems was recruiting the lawyer ('Sammy Cook or Rubinstein'), but was also prompted to remind Orwell to contact

---

[300]Rupert Crawshay-Williams to Arthur Koestler, 21 January 1946, Edinburgh University Library, Koestler Papers 2345/2/70. Russell's typescript is attached. Copies of both are in UCL Orwell/I/4/9. Russell used an intermediary because he did not have Koestler's address. As we shall see, Russell's essay was to be published in 1946.

[301]Arthur Koestler to Manès Sperber ('Munjo'), 14 March 1946.

[302]Mamaine Paget to Arthur Koestler, 10 May 1945, Edinburgh University Library, Koestler Papers, MS 2303/2/31.

[303]Arthur Koestler to Orwell, 19 March 1946, Edinburgh University Library, Koestler Papers, 2345/2/34.

Mallory Brown 'or a substitute American'. Koestler himself would contact Sperber and Canon Denman.[304] Perhaps the somewhat high-handed tone of this provoked a reaction. In any case, Humphrey Slater wrote 'a most serious letter' to Koestler on 19 March. Captivated though he was by Koestler's enthusiasm to establish 'a league against tyranny', and in spite of being thoroughly 'in favour of the project', Slater wrote to say that he and Phillips were withdrawing their support. He didn't manage actually to say this in his 'pompous and damping' letter, even though it was written 'for us all to understand exactly what is going on in each others'[sic] minds'. He and Rodney had decided that 'we ought not to be involved in the initial stages of your project'; for himself, Slater added 'I do not think that I have any right to come to the Easter conference at all'.[305] Celia Kirwan had also written to her sister about the matter, and perhaps this was more direct. Certainly, Koestler was in no doubt: 'The Easter conference was based on the organisatorial and financial support of Rodney and as this is withdrawn we can't hold it.'[306] Slater was motivated chiefly by the wish to maintain the intellectual independence and integrity of *Polemic*. He was convinced 'that there is a necessity in England for a theoretical magazine dealing with ideas on a more general level than that of politics and the particular sciences, and therefore that it is most necessary for Polemic not to be associated in the minds of the public with a practical organisation for a very directly and immediately political purpose'. He had heard from Francis Henson (an American in London to gather support for the International Rescue and Relief Committee) 'that it was intended that Polemic would become the official organ of the league to be initiated at the Easter conference in Wales'. This would not do; even worse fears arose from a conversation with the philosopher A.J. (Freddy) Ayer, a friend of Orwell's and a key member of the *Polemic* circle. Ayer had told Slater that he 'would consider, quite definitely, that he had been misled if Polemic were to get the reputation of being anything other than the independently theoretical magazine he and I originally projected, and he might not want to go on being associated with it'. The same would very likely be true of others.

Humphrey Slater, once a Communist and Head of Operations for the International Brigade in the Spanish Civil War, was in transition (like Koestler) to becoming a powerful voice of anti-Communism. During the

---

[304]Arthur Koestler to Rodney Phillips, 14 March 1946, Edinburgh University Library, Koestler Papers, 2345/2/69; also copy in UCL Orwell/I/4/11.
[305]Humphrey Slater to Arthur Koestler, 19 March 1946, Edinburgh University Library, 2345/2/108-9; copy in UCL Orwell/I/4/12.
[306]Arthur Koestler to Celia Kirwan, 21 March 1946, Edinburgh University Library, Koestler Papers, 2301/2/4; copy in UCL Orwell/I/4/13.

mid-1940s, alongside editing *Polemic*, he was also becoming one of the first novelists of the Cold War.[307] Movingly, he ended his letter to Koestler thus:

> It has taken me two or three wars and twenty years of reading and writing and talking and making love, two marriages, and the fathering of a number of children to come to the conclusion that the most interesting and useful thing that I personally can do is not to engage in practical politics, but to work in the theoretical field towards the consolidation of a humane world outlook synthesising the aesthetic and scientific discoveries of the day. One only has a limited amount (like the money in one's bank) of initiative and enthusiasm to expend, and for me I know the only sensible thing is to concentrate absolutely upon getting Polemic established and writing the novel I have begun. [*The Heretics* was published by June 1946, and Slater was presumably working on his subsequent novel, *The Conspirator*, to be published in 1948. In August, Orwell said to Celia Kirwan that he was pleased that Humphrey was getting on with the new book, and commiserated with him on Norman Collins' 'snooty' review of *The Heretics*. Collin's had commented: 'we are left with the sad spectacle of the Novel of Ideas as the lame child of letters'.][308]

Koestler was furious: 'Humphrey is an ass.' He denied having heard of 'that American' (Henson), though Orwell had in fact written to him at length about Henson and the IRRC only a few days before (and Koestler had replied on the 19th). He proposed a link between the IRRC and the League, and told Koestler that Henson was interested in the Easter conference.[309] It may well have been from Orwell that Henson got the idea that *Polemic* would be the 'official organ' of the League. Koestler, at any rate, claimed that the 'only connection with Polemic would have been a purely personal one, namely that until the league could find permanent quarters, Rodney agreed that it should have a secretary and typewriter working on *Polemic*'s premises and that Rodney as an individual would look after the finances and organisation of the league until Hulton or Gollancz took over.' Orwell and Michael Foot had been present at the lunch at which all of this was agreed, and Koestler asked Celia to let them know that the conference was off and to ask Orwell to cancel the invitation to Mallory Browne, if it had been issued.[310]

---

[307]Anton Fedyashin, 'The First Cold War Spy Novel: The Origins and Afterlife of Humphrey Slater's *Conspirator*', *Journal of Cold War Studies*, 19 (2017), pp. 134–59.
[308]Humphrey Slater to Arthur Koestler, 19 March 1946, Edinburgh University Library, 2345/2/108-9; copy in UCL Orwell/I/4/12; Orwell to Celia Kirwan, 17 August 1946, CW, XVIII, p. 376; Norman Collins, 'New Member', *The Observer*, 28 July 1946, p. 3.
[309]Orwell to Arthur Koestler, 16 March 1946, CW, XVIII, pp. 154–5; Arthur Koestler to Orwell, 19 March 1946, Edinburgh University Library, Koestler Papers, 2345/2/34.
[310]Arthur Koestler to Celia Kirwan, 21 March 1946, Edinburgh University Library, Koestler Papers, 2301/2/4; copy in UCL Orwell/I/4/13.

Orwell had indeed just attempted to rope in Mallory Browne, London editor of the *Christian Science Monitor*, who thought that he would be able to attend the Easter conference.[311] No one had yet told Orwell that plans for the conference had collapsed. Koestler wrote on the 23rd, 'I assume that Celia has meanwhile informed you of the latest developments on the Humphrey-Rodney front. The withdrawal of their support means that I had to cancel the rooms which I booked and wire Sperber not to come as otherwise you and I would have had to fork out about £100 ... As I wrote Celia, we must now really either get Hulton or Gollancz if we want to get on with it.'[312] Orwell was not immediately deterred by this setback, mentioning in his reply John Baker, an Oxford scientist, as 'evidently one of those people we should circularise when we have a draft proposal ready', and indicating that a publishing campaign seemed to be forming, with *Polemic* at its heart:

> He [Baker] could probably also be useful in telling us about other scientists who are not totalitarian-minded, which is important, because as a body they are much more subject to totalitarian habits of thought than writers, and have more popular prestige. Humphrey [Slater] got [C.H.] Waddington, who is a borderline case, to do an article for Polemic, which I think was a good move, as it will appear in the same number as our opening volley against the Modern Quarterly. Unfortunately it was a very bad article.[313]

Koestler, on the other hand, seems to have been, in part, grateful to be off the hook. He had told Celia Kirwan that he received Slater's letter with a mixture of 'anger and relief'. He didn't enjoy cancelling the hotel rooms at a busy time of the year but there was 'relief to have the whole thing off my hands'.[314] To Sperber he wrote that the conference 'has been postponed, probably for several months', adding that since people involved were 'quarreling between themselves ... this probably means that the time is not quite ripe yet'.[315] He was free to seek a closer relationship with Russell.

At some point, possibly to accompany his letters calling off the conference,[316] Koestler produced a little note headed 'S.O.S LEAGUE

---

[311]Orwell to Arthur Koestler, 22 March 1946, CW, XVIII, p. 164.

[312]Arthur Koestler to Orwell, 23 March 1946, Edinburgh University Library, Koestler Papers, 2345/2/37.

[313]Orwell to Arthur Koestler, 31 March 1946, CW, XVIII, pp. 213–14.

[314]Arthur Koestler to Celia Kirwan, 21 March 1946, Edinburgh University Library, Koestler Papers, 2301/2/4; copy in UCL Orwell/I/4/13.

[315]Arthur Koestler to Manès Sperber, 22 March 1946, copy in UCL Orwell/I/4/14, from Edinburgh University Library, Koestler Papers, original not located, though it should be in 2374/1.

[316]The copy in the Orwell Archive is filed immediately following the letter a copy of Koestler's letter to Sperber of 22 March 1946, as UCL Orwell/I/4/14; another copy is filed as Orwell/I/4/1.

for the Preservation of the Freedom and Dignity of Man'. It included a quotation from Russell: 'The difficulty to-day is to persuade the human race to acquiesce in its own survival.' The quotation was from the typescript that Russell had sent Koestler in January, 'The Atomic Bomb and the Prevention of War'. The essay was to be published in *Polemic* no. 4 (July–August 1946).[317] Koestler and Mamaine Paget had Ayer and Celia Kirwan to stay in April. They all dined with the Russells on the 8th, and a few days later Mamaine recorded: 'Sunday – very hot and fine, so we took our lunch & went up Snowdon ... K. has hatched a new plot to save the world from the Russians; Russell agreed to it so we (K & I) drafted a petition about it.'[318] Mamaine sent a draft of the Petition to Russell on 16 April.[319]

The ideas in the petition did not come to Koestler in a vision on the top of Snowdon. Indeed, the very wording of the petition derived from an article that he had published in March in the *New York Times Magazine* – 'Challenge to Russia: Lift the Iron Curtain!'[320] Both the article and the petition were addressed to achieving 'genuine world co-operation'. 'World peace can only become a reality if suspicions are abolished,' Koestler declared. What did he mean? The core idea was the advocacy of 'psychological disarmament', which would bring an end to the 'appeasement of [Russian] suspicion'. Most of the key words in this echoed the terms of Russell's essay on 'The Atomic Bomb and the Prevention of War' but 'psychological disarmament' was his own original contribution to the discussion. The concept formed a bridge between Russell's concerns and the interest in intellectual freedom that Koestler shared with Orwell. Psychological disarmament was the attempt to undo 'the extent to which a government obstructs the free exchange of information and ideas with the outside world'. A country that 'builds a Chinese Wall of censorship from behind which it fires propaganda salvoes, is

---

[317]Bertrand Russell, 'The Atomic Bomb and the Prevention of War', *Polemic*, no. 4 (July–August 1946), pp. 15–22. The quotation used by Koestler is on p. 22: the word 'to-day' has been deleted in the published version.

[318]Mamaine Paget's Diary, 14 April 1946; also Goodman (ed.), *Living with Koestler*, p. 29.

[319]Mamaine Paget to Bertrand Russell, 16 April 1946, Edinburgh University Library, Koestler Papers, 2345/2/83; copy in UCL Orwell/I/4/15; a xerox copy of the Petition is misleadingly appended in the Koestler papers to Orwell's letter of 2 January 1946, which accompanied his initial draft of the manifesto (Edinburgh University Library, Koestler Papers, MS 2345/2/4 [copy in UCL Orwell/I/4/17], and Koestler Papers 2345/2/10-12). Koestler himself was later to conflate these documents and events and to portray the Petition as Orwell's first draft of the Manifesto: Koestler, *Stranger on the Square*, pp. 42–3. This cannot be true. David Cesarani follows in taking the Petition as Orwell's first draft of the Manifesto (Cesarani, *Arthur Koestler: The Homeless Mind* (London: William Heinemann, 1998), pp. 252–3).

[320]Arthur Koestler, 'Challenge to Russia: Lift the Iron Curtain!', *New York Times Magazine*, 10 March 1946, pp. 7, 43–5; reprinted in modified form as 'A Way to Fight Suspicion', in Koestler, *The Trail of the Dinosaur and Other Essays* (London: Collins, 1955), pp. 17–24.

committing psychological aggression'. (In the version of the essay reprinted in *The Trail of the Dinosaur*, 'the Chinese Wall' becomes 'a Maginot line'.) The petition therefore called upon the Soviet Union and Britain to take steps to ensure the free exchange of uncensored ideas and news between their peoples, and to permit their citizens to travel freely. This was free speech on its way to globalization.

Koestler immediately discussed the petition with Storm Jameson. She thought that 'if it is for publication in the newspapers it must be written without anti-Soviet bias, and at present the bias stands out a mile', adding that 'I do not believe that it is yet time for a hundred leading clercs to appear in public holding their noses against the stink of censorship rising from Russia'. The first overture should be an 'as if' gesture, an open appeal from the intellectuals of one country to another, even though 'we know perfectly well that Soviet clercs have no right to their souls'.[321] Koestler replied that he and Russell were making changes to the draft, but that the time for 'as if' gestures was past and a frontal reply to the 'full blast accusations' of the 'Soviet clercs' was needed.[322] She was unpersuaded. The way to persuade those in the West who sympathize with Russia was 'to get them thoroughly snubbed by having an honest appeal for friendship and free speech ... thrown back in their innocent faces ...' The petition was too blatantly designed to provoke its own rejection.[323] Koestler sent a revised version to both Russell and Victor Gollancz. Unfortunately, he muddled the accompanying letters, sending the one intended for Russell to Gollancz, and *vice versa*. Russell replied: 'I was somewhat surprised to find that you told Gollancz you were sending him a draft which I had approved, while in fact the draft by no means satisfied the objections which I had asked my wife to communicate to you.' He had phoned Gollancz to tell him as much. There was a further source of contention. 'I was amazed to learn from my wife that you had refused to accept her as my plenipotentiary, after having yourself suggested that she should represent me, and had accused her of not accurately reporting my opinions as to the draft.' Russell concluded 'that co-operation is impossible if such incidents are to be expected', and requested an apology to both himself and his wife.[324]

---

[321]Storm Jameson to Arthur Koestler, Easter Sunday [21 April] 1946, Edinburgh University Library, Koestler Papers 2345/2/111; copy in UCL, Orwell/I/4/18.

[322]Arthur Koestler to Storm Jameson, 23 April 1946, Edinburgh University Library, Koestler Papers, 2345/2/112; copy in UCL Orwell/I/4/19, which also includes notes of the changes Koestler would make to the petition.

[323]Storm Jameson to Arthur Koestler, 27 April 1946, Edinburgh University Library, Koestler Papers 2374/3/79.

[324]Bertrand Russell to Arthur Koestler, 3 May 1946, Edinburgh University Library, Koestler Papers 2345/2/87; copy in UCL, Orwell/I/4/23.

Russell's wife Patricia, known as Peter, adds a further complication. She had already written a blistering letter to Koestler after their meeting on the evening of the 22nd, complaining of his combativeness and bad manners.[325] It is also possible that Koestler attempted to rape Peter Russell at around this time, though presumably not on this occasion when Mamaine was present, and attested that after 'a blazing row', Peter 'left in a huff after five minutes'.[326] The story of the attempted rape may not be true, though it would not have been out of character for Koestler, whose propensity to sexual violence is well attested.[327] Some years later Mamaine wrote to Koestler that: 'I have just discovered the reason why Russell does not like you. Three guesses. It is, of course, mainly because Peter told him that you had made love to her!!' She had been told this by a Cambridge acquaintance of Russell's. Mamaine commented: 'I asked him how it was possible that, knowing Peter, Russell should believe such a story.'[328] Sadly, to anyone who knew Koester, it was readily believable. Whatever may be the case regarding Koestler's behaviour to Peter Russell, he replied in an attempt to mollify Russell, apologizing 'if I unintentionally hurt Peter's or your feelings', denying that he had misled Gollancz, and reaffirming his 'conviction that the so-called intellectuals have to try to influence the politicians by concerted action, as a chorus not as solo voices'. Interestingly, he adds that '[d]uring the last months I have made three or four drafts to find a platform for such concerted action. I have altered each draft after discussion with Orwell and other people whose opinion I valued, and when, after your article on the atomic bomb, you advocated a crusade, I made another draft on the lines we discussed.' In his view they had been close to an agreed text, with only details left to agree. Unfortunately, though, Peter had objected to using the term 'psychological disarmament', which Koestler saw as 'the fundament of the whole draft'.[329]

---

[325]Peter Russell to Arthur Koestler, 29 April 1946, Edinburgh University Library, Koestler Papers 2374/3/84-6.

[326]Mamaine Koestler to Celia Goodman, 23 April 1946, in Goodman (ed.), *Living with Koestler*, pp. 30–1.

[327]It is described as 'probably apocryphal' in Michael Scammell, *Koestler: The Indispensable Intellectual* (London: Faber & Faber, 2010), p. 268. David Cesarani's biography of Koestler had exposed his appalling behaviour to women, most notoriously the rape of Jill Craigie, Michael Foot's wife. Scammell attempts to moderate the severity of Cesarani's verdict, but not convincingly. For a useful overview of the controversy see Edward Saunders, *Arthur Koestler* (London: Reaktion Books, 2017), ch. 7, pp. 161–8.

[328]Mamaine Paget to Arthur Koestler, 9 October 1950, Edinburgh University Library, Koestler Papers 2303.

[329]Arthur Koestler to Bertrand Russell, 6 May 1946, Edinburgh University Library, Koestler Papers 2345/2/90; copy in UCL Orwell/I/4/24.

Russell withdrew from the project. The issues were not personal, he said, but 'entirely of a public order'. While he did not object to the term, 'psychological disarmament' as such, he did not think that it 'could be made part of a bargain against territorial concessions', as the petition seemed to propose. It also suffered from 'a failure to make plain that this [psychological disarmament] must be demanded of all powers and not only, if chiefly, of Russia'. This was the same concern that Storm Jameson had raised. Russell had decided to revert to his earlier view 'that men who are writers do better work as individuals than by collaborating in groups', and advised Koestler to make the petition a statement of his own, which others might support, in whole or part, in their own way.[330] Koestler acknowledged that their collaboration was at an end. He would, he told Russell, 'talk to a few people about this and similar possibilities', and would let Russell know if anything of interest came from the discussions. 'Don't both to answer this', he concluded.[331] By early August, the row with the Russells had abated, and they all resumed social contact, temporarily.[332] Russell, as priapic as Koestler but without the violence, was to reciprocate by making a pass at Mamaine.[333]

Koestler's reference to Orwell in the letter of 6 May suggests that he saw the two projects – the one to create a League for the Dignity and Rights of Man, with a manifesto drafted by Orwell, and the other with the petition for psychological disarmament – as closely linked. The petition was abandoned, though Koestler did send it to Victor Gollancz along with the letter that had accidentally gone to Russell, in early June. This was at the same time as his final push on the League. As well as the Petition, he sent Gollancz the manifesto, which he described as 'a broadsheet about the necessity of reviving the League for the Rights of Man in a new form'.[334] By this time, multiple copies of the draft manifesto had been produced, and Koestler distributed them. He sent a few copies to Orwell on the same day that he wrote to Gollancz: 'Enclosed a few copies of our draft which I had at last roneod. I am sending it to Gollancz and Hulton ... Whether they will be interested I don't

[330]Bertrand Russell to Arthur Koestler, 13 May 1946, Edinburgh University Library, Koestler Papers 2345/2/94; copy in UCL Orwell I/4/25.

[331]Arthur Koestler to Bertrand Russell, 16 May 1946, Edinburgh University Library, Koestler Papers 2345/2/97.

[332]Mamaine Paget to Celia Kirwan, 4 August 1946, in Goodman (ed.), *Living with Koestler*, p. 33.

[333]Scammell, *Koestler*, pp. 268–9.

[334]Arthur Koestler to Victor Gollancz, 12 June 1946, Edinburgh University Library, Koestler Papers 2345/1/66; copy in UCL Orwell/I/4/28. It is this correspondence that makes it obvious that Koestler's memory was at fault when he later identified the Petition as Orwell's first draft of the manifesto. The Koestler-Gollancz exchanges are also in Victor Gollancz's papers: University of Warwick, Modern Records Centre, MSS.157/3/CL/5/1 to MSS.157/3/CL/5/8.

know.'[335] A few copies were also sent to Manès Sperber. Koestler made clear to his old friend that he was no longer taking any practical interest in the League idea. 'Personally, being far from London and engrossed in my new book, I cannot take any organising initiative about it, but it might be useful to have the draft discussed, and maybe sooner or later somebody will be found who will provide the organising push.'[336] Sperber seemed sympathetic, but thought the proposal could have been more original in form and more precise.[337] Koestler sounded a little more optimistic in a second letter of early August, asking Sperber 'for any suggestions, precisions, etc.', and indicating that 'the organisatorial side is in the hands of Gollancz who in principle wants to start it but is too busy for the moment with other things. I hope however that the thing will actually get going during the winter.'[338]

Hopeful he may have been, but Koestler had effectively abandoned the project. Gollancz was, indeed, his last hope for practical support. In response to the draft, he declared himself 'tremendously in favour of your new league for the rights of Man' and thought it 'should be pressed on with immediately'. He did wonder whether it might not 'cut across the Freedom Defence Committee – the thing with which Herbert Read and George Orwell are associated'. It was, he told Koestler, 'founded as a counterblast to the communism of the National Council of Civil Liberties', but it was 'very much a hole-and-corner and <u>coterie</u> affair: and is rather closely identified, I think, with philosophic anarchism'.[339] Koestler saw his opportunity. He reassured Gollancz that there 'would be no competition with the Freedom Defence League'. In fact, 'Orwell himself feels that it is a narrow thing and that some form of affiliation of the Freedom Defence League to this broader organisation could be achieved'. A number of other groups were waiting to affiliate too. He also pointed out that as he lived in Wales and Orwell was in the Orkneys, neither of them could take the idea of the League forward.

---

[335]Arthur Koestler to Orwell, 12 June 1946, Edinburgh University Library, Koestler Papers 2374/1/342. The draft was roneod by the Duchess of Atholl, who had attempted to interest Koestler (and Orwell) in her own plan for a 'British League for European Freedom'. Koestler had responded by sending her 'a rough draft which George Orwell and I wrote together'. The project was now 'postponed'. He asked the Duchess to roneo fifty copies in her office, as he had sent her his only copy (or, failing that, to return it). Arthur Koestler to the Duchess of Atholl, 28 April 1946, Edinburgh University Library, Koestler Papers 2374/1/308. Koestler had earlier hoped that Rodney Philips would produce copies. Koestler thanked the Duchess of Atholl for the work in a letter of 5 June 1946, Edinburgh University Library, Koestler Papers, 2345/1/8.
[336]Arthur Koestler to Manès Sperber, 17 June 1946, Edinburgh University Library, Koestler Papers 2374/1/349.
[337]Manès Sperber to Arthur Koestler, 26 July 1946, Edinburgh University Library, Koestler Papers 2374/3/222.
[338]Arthur Koestler to Manès Sperber, 2 August 1946, Edinburgh University Library, Koestler Papers 2374/1/390.
[339]Victor Gollancz to Arthur Koestler, 18 June 1946, Edinburgh University Library, Koestler Papers 2345/1/68; copy in UCL Orwell/I/4/29.

(In fact, Orwell was in Jura writing the first draft of *Nineteen Eighty-Four*, and Jura was one of the Inner Hebrides not the Orkney Islands.) Perhaps Gollancz might do so? 'I know nobody with your drive and experience who could take the initial steps.'[340] Gollancz did not rise to the flattery, and it seems that no further correspondence on the matter survives. Koestler did not forget the League altogether. One of the roneod copies of the draft was to be sent to Ruth Fischer on 26 August 1949, as the two of them with Melvin Lasky developed plans that led to the Congress for Cultural Freedom meeting in 1950. It was the plan for a league 'which some years ago I wanted to found with Russell and Orwell. It is out of date and was written for a different purpose, but one or the other formulation might be of some use.'[341] This was the copy of the manifesto that David Smith discovered in Ruth Fischer's papers now housed in Harvard's Houghton Library.

Let us look more closely at this manifesto. There are two versions of the draft manifesto in the Orwell and Koestler archives. One of them is obviously the final roneod copy that Koestler distributed to Orwell, Gollancz and Sperber in early June, and then sent to Ruth Fischer more than three years later. But what is the other version? Is it likely to be closer to Orwell's original draft? To answer these questions, it is worth re-capping what we know about the different drafts of the manifesto. Orwell sent his original draft to Koestler on 2 January 1946. Koestler shared this with Michael Polanyi, who promptly lost it.[342] Orwell notified Koestler of two changes suggested by Michael Foot on 11 February and enclosed another copy, and then on 27 February sent a revised draft with Foot's changes integrated. It does not sound as if this draft made any other significant changes: 'Here is another copy of the draft, with the two amendments suggested by Michael Foot. Will you be able to get the duplicating done?'[343] On 14 March Koestler told Sperber that 'I cannot send you yet the draft for the organisation as a number of people are still working on it'.[344] The same day he asked Rodney Philips to 'send me as many as possible copies of the draft as soon as it is typed out'. But then the arrangements with Philips and Slater collapsed. On 28 April Koestler asked the Duchess of Atholl to have copies roneod, which was completed no later than 5 June. Copies were at last made available for Orwell and others by 12 June.

---

[340]Arthur Koestler to Victor Gollancz, 20 June 1946, Edinburgh University Library, Koestler Papers, 2345/1/70; copy in UCL Orwell/I/4/30.
[341]Arthur Koestler to Ruth Fischer, 28 August 1949, Edinburgh University Library, Koestler Papers, 2376/3/141, quoted in Smith typescript, p. 6, though misdated to 26 August.
[342]Michael Polanyi to Arthur Koestler (postcard), 19 February 1946, Edinburgh University Library, Koestler Papers 2344/7/60; Michael Polanyi to Arthur Koestler (telegram), 19 February 1946, Edinburgh University Library, Koestler Papers, 2344/7/61.
[343]Orwell to Arthur Koestler, 27 February 1946, CW, XVIII, p. 133.
[344]Arthur Koestler to Manès Sperber, 14 March 1946, Edinburgh University Library, Koestler Papers, 2374/1/216.

From this we can be sure that there were *at least* three drafts of a manifesto:

1  Orwell's first draft (2 January).
2  Orwell's revised draft (27 February).
3  The final draft, worked on by a 'number of people', which seems to have been produced at some point between 14 March and 28 April.

The two drafts that survive in the archives are quite different, though clearly related to one another (both, for example, talk of the need to 'redefine the term "democracy"').[345] The second of them is obviously version 3 in the list above. The earlier draft that survives in the archives cannot be Orwell's original (version 1). The two changes that Foot suggested were to replace 'the masses' with 'great numbers of people', and 'to delete the suggestion about becoming victims of aggression'.[346] Neither the phrase 'the masses' nor 'great numbers of people' occurs in either surviving version, but the earlier does refer to 'the majority of people'. The earlier version also contains the phrase 'victims of infringements' of the League's principles, and this passage could be a reworking of one on victims of aggression. So is this draft version 2? Possibly, but we need not assume that the three versions of which we know were the only three versions prepared. There is at least one passage in the earlier draft that sounds more like Koestler than Orwell. ('The ideal state is the one which fulfils this function with the maximum of efficiency and the minimum of interference. Such maxima-minima problems are well known in the serie of differential equations (e.g. the construction of containers of maximum volume and minimum surface).') The scientifically educated Koestler, who had also worked for a time as a science journalist, seems the more likely originator of this than Orwell. On the other hand, Orwell might have included it on the basis of a discussion with Koestler that stuck in his mind (or in his notes). This draft also refers to Orwell in the third person, which again may suggest that he was not the author, but equally may reflect the nature of a document that he was not writing in his own persona. However, the draft could be something that Koestler wrote after the Christmas 1945 meeting, parts of which were then incorporated

---

[345]The two versions are (a) 'Draft', UCL, Orwell/I/4/16, fols 1–3 (5 pp.) – this is presumably a copy from the Koestler papers but I have not been able to locate the original; and (b) untitled paper, Edinburgh University Library, Koestler Papers, 2345/2/53-68 (eight roneoed copies, each 2 pp.) – this is the circulated version; some copies of it have handwritten emendations, one of them being that suggested by Gollancz; copies in UCL Orwell/I/4/7 and Orwell/I/4/20; copies of handwritten emendations are at Orwell/I/4/16, fols 4–7. Version (b) is the one sent to Ruth Fischer and printed in Smith, *George Orwell Illustrated*, pp. 230–4. There is also a copy in Victor Gollancz's papers: University of Warwick, Modern Records Centre, MSS.157/3/CL/5/6.
[346]Orwell to Arthur Koestler, 11 February 1946, CW, XVIII, p. 105.

into Orwell's draft to produce version 3. As seen above, Koestler did refer at one point to having produced 'three or four drafts' of a platform document.

It may help to take a closer look at what the two surviving drafts say, and then to return to the question of authorship.

The earlier draft opens with a comparison of the situation after each of the two world wars. After the first, the victors (America, England and France) were in reasonable accord that the defeated nations (Germany and Russia) were unlikely to be dangerous for some time. But after the Second World War there were economic tensions between America and England, and significant conflict between those Western powers and the third victor, Russia. It was this last conflict – Russia versus the West – that mattered most, and was evident in 'the two diametrically opposed interpretations of the word "democracy" which thus loses all practical meaning'. The first step, then, was to redefine 'democracy'. It was no longer enough simply to repeat the principles of nineteenth-century liberalism (or 'Western humanism'). 'Above all it is not enough to repeat the tenet of the French Revolution that "all men are born equal" if the economic structure of society remains such as to make such equality utter nonsense. Political democracy must remain a farce as long as economic equality from the cradle persists and handicaps the free display of individual faculties.' This passage should be noted: the later version of the manifesto weakens the insistence that economic inequality would necessarily make democracy and freedom impossible.

It was possible to identify four possible 'social systems' using two axes, 'dictatorship versus parliamentarianism' and 'national planning versus laisser faire'. The four combinations were:

i.   autocracy plus laisser faire. This combination has become practically obsolete since the French Revolution.

ii.  Autocracy plus national planning. This combination is realized in Russia and was probably the potential target of Hitlerite Germany.

iii. Democracy plus laisser faire (the United States and pre-Labour Britain).

iv.  Democracy plus national planning. Nowhere.

(One wonders where post-Labour Britain was supposed to fit: did it hold out hope that the elusive fourth combination might be within reach?) This was the context in which the new League would be formed.

The aim of the League would be 'to fight for the preservation of political democracy and its rejuvenation'. (A handwritten amendment suggests replacing 'political democracy' with 'Western Humanism'). 'The programme of the Rights of Man has to be restated in the light of developments since the French Revolution. The tenet that "all men are born equal" has to be developed into the tenet that all men should be born with equal opportunities to develop their individual potentialities. Not "uniformism" and "levelling down" but equality of chance as the basis of individual diversity.' Presumably, given what has already been said, this equality of opportunity requires economic equality. The 'main function of the State' was to ensure that this 'equality of chance' was maintained. It would achieve this by protecting individuals against 'exploitation' and against 'the misappropriation ... of his creative faculties and achievements'. These functions were to be performed, as we have already heard, 'with the maximum of efficiency and the minimum of interference'.

This is scarcely a coherent political position. The suggestion of minimal state interference leaves it unclear how the problems of economic inequality might be tackled. As democracy is said to be impossible in circumstances of inequality, then this surely must be the primary problem addressed before the state can even begin to be in a position to maintain equality of chance. The four combinations identified, though crude, might have been better used. The implication would seem to be that the fourth – democracy plus national planning – should be the objective. But the statement of aims disappoints.

The remainder of this version of the manifesto is concerned with how the League might be organized and positioned. Most existing organizations were either 'organisations of vague and dilletantic men of good-will without clarified fundamental ideas, or they were made up of theorists' and did nothing practical. 'The first type of organisation diffuses its activities and is further exposed to the danger of being captured by political cliques (as for instance the League for the Rights of Man and various Popular Front bodies were captured by the Communists) and as certain pacifist bodies became the instruments of Nazi policy).' This does sound like Orwell! The second group – the theorists – 'live in the clouds and their lack of practical activities condemns them to sterility'. It included Maritain and 'various groups for "the clarification of fundamentals" (Mannheim))'. The new League would combine 'theoretical soundness and clarity' with a 'maximum of noise'. It would support those who were the 'victims of infringements against the principles outlined above' wherever they might be, 'whether in the British Colonial Empire or in Russian occupied territory'. It is another weakness of the document that it is not obvious what these 'principles' that might be infringed actually are. It would follow the methods of the (old) League for the Rights of Man and other bodies, namely 'public protest' and 'the direct personal influence of its members on the press and the political platforms', combined with 'theoretical clarification' in a quarterly journal. A fortnightly bulletin would keep members abreast of activities, and there might be summer schools and the like. The League could form a sort of umbrella for other committees, 'for instance Save Europe Now, Defence of Freedom, etc.'. A handwritten emendation corrects the latter to Freedom Defence Committee, the body of which Orwell was vice-chairman. The manifesto concluded with this:

The committee of founders should theoretically include men of renown [corrected to 'standing'] and integrity who subscribe to the basic platform of the movement. Practically it will be wise to start with men whose names have not been too much worn out by similar past activities. Theoretically the committee should range from Voigt on the Right to Orwell and Read on the Left, but as each of these names has a certain political hall-mark the composition of the Committee will be a question of balancing these marks against each other.

The final version of the manifesto radically re-worked the earlier draft. Both versions share in their prefatory remarks an insistence on the inadequacy of ideas inherited from nineteenth-century liberalism. The final draft makes this thought its opening sentence: 'the Nineteenth Century conception of liberty and democracy ... [is] insufficient'. This version, though, immediately weakens the insistence of the earlier draft on the priority to be attached to equality. 'Without equality of opportunity and a reasonable degree of equality in income, democratic rights have little value.' So much was uncontentious, though there is a proposed amendment of this (from Gollancz?) that weakens it further by replacing 'little value' with 'only a limited value'. Nonetheless the implications of the point are tempered by this:

> But the tendency, especially since the Russian revolution, has been to over-emphasise this fact and to talk as though the economic aspect were the only one, while habeas corpus, freedom of speech and of the press, the right to political opposition and absence of police terrorism were merely phrases designed to side-track the attention of the poor from economic inequality. But Communists and Fascists have reiterated that liberty without social security is valueless, and it has been forgotten that without liberty there can be no security.

This removes some of the inconsistency in the earlier draft, but at the price of reducing the distance between the manifesto's position and that of traditional liberalism, in spite of the declared inadequacy of the latter.

The next paragraph has no precedent in the earlier draft, and serves to make the manifesto more partisan and more explicitly anti-Soviet. It condemns the development in the West (and 'perhaps especially in those countries which have no direct experience of totalitarianism') of 'a certain contempt for democratic traditions and a habit of sanctioning tyrannous practices abroad or at home, which would have raised an outcry a few years ago'. Even in Britain, 'the majority of people are largely uninterested in and even unaware of their own democratic rights, while a considerable section of the intelligentsia has set itself almost consciously to break down the desire for liberty and to hold totalitarian methods up to admiration'. The problem was global. 'Over considerable portions of the earth not merely democracy but the last traces of legality in our sense of the word have simply vanished.' But no one seems troubled by this. Nowadays, 'the normal reaction is either apathy or a certain admiration for what it has become usual to call political realism'. (This may well be a swipe at James Burnham: Orwell's review of his book, *The Machiavellians*, commented: 'Any theory which is obviously dishonest and immoral ("realistic" is the favourite word at this moment) will find adherents who accept it just for that reason'.[347]) As a result, liberal newspapers become advocates for 'totalitarian democracy' and civil rights organizations become subverted, 'pursuing objects [*sic*] which are almost the exact opposite of those for which they were originally founded'. Two such organizations were named, the League for the Rights of Man and the National Council for Civil Liberties. We will return to the former of these, but the fear that the NCCL had been perverted to Stalinist ends was clearly something that drove Orwell's active involvement in the defence of liberal freedoms, as we have seen already.

After this, the manifesto became overtly anti-Soviet. After the defeat of Hitler it was 'the one great power with a totalitarian structure'. Furthermore, 'it is chiefly in the form of uncritical admiration for the U.S.S.R. that totalitarian ideas establish themselves in western countries', and alongside this 'the gradual decay of democratic sentiment, of human decency and the desire for liberty goes on'. The barriers to autocracy and the will to withstand aggression were being weakened.

This was the time to establish a new body that would undertake the work that the League for the Rights of Man and others had failed to do. It would need to undertake two things, namely 'theoretical clarification' (a phrase drawn from the previous version) and 'practical action'. The first of these was essentially 'to re-define the term "Democracy"', an idea brought forward directly from the earlier draft. The discussion is often in identical language to that of the earlier version. Once again, we hear that it will not be sufficient to restate the principles of nineteenth-century liberalism. 'The programme of the Rights of Man has to be restated in the light of developments since the French Revolution. In particular a synthesis has to be found between political freedom on the one hand and economic planning and control on the other.' This restates the core message of the first draft, though the 'synthesis' proposed here is a rather blander expression of it, but the same core functions for the state were identified and now assembled into a four-point list.

(1) To guarantee the newborn citizen his equality of chance.

(2) To protect him against economic exploitation by individuals or groups.

---

[347]Orwell, 'Review of *The Machiavellians* by James Burnham', CW, XVI, p. 72.

(3) To protect him against the fettering or misappropriation of his creative faculties and achievements.

(4) To fulfil all of these tasks with maximum efficiency and a minimum of interference.

The chosen instrument for this clarification was again to be a 'quarterly and later monthly' magazine, which would facilitate a global discussion of the issues. The main aim of the League was to achieve 'the international co-ordination' of the theoretical and practical work of the interested individuals and groups.

The means by which the League would carry out its more practical work were very similar to those advanced in the earlier draft, committees, public meetings and the like. It tidied up a key statement in the earlier draft: 'The League has to make itself the advocate of infringements against the Rights and dignity of Man, whether they occur in the British Empire or in Russian occupied territory.' This version is perhaps no less vague than its predecessor, but does at least avoid the dangling reference to principles already established. In terms of its 'committee of Founders', the final version accepted one of the handwritten amendments on the earlier draft. Its members would be 'men of standing and integrity'. This draft included an extended defence of its impartiality: 'The League should be open to men and women of all parties, races and creeds who subscribe to the principles outlined above, and closed to all those who, for whatever ideological motives, condone infringements of these principles if carried out in the name of "higher interests" and thus become the instruments of totalitarian methods.' This, of course, reinforced its anti-Communist orientation. In a faint echo of the concerns raised in the Koestler-Russell Petition, the manifesto noted that '[w]e have initiated this action driven by the sense of urgency in the age of the atomic bomb' and the need for the co-ordination of the 'energies' of the like-minded.

The manifesto concluded with the declaration that it was a 'rough draft' and that its authors would welcome 'your reactions and suggestions'. Up to a point, at least: 'There is only one type of reaction that we are not anxious to hear: the answer that it is too late, that the evil has gone too far and can no longer be stopped by the methods visualised here. "Too late" is the motto of escape into destruction.'

Close analysis makes it clear that the final (June 1946) draft of the Manifesto, the one printed by Smith, is a heavily re-written version of the other surviving draft. Most of the material on 'theoretical clarification' and most of the more organizational content are obviously re-written from the earlier draft, with much of the wording the same. The material on the redefinition of democracy is notably very similar in both versions. Their biggest difference is that each has a quite different historical preamble, and the earlier draft a more resounding defence of the importance of equality. The later draft is obviously more polished, and it fills, or better disguises, some of the *lacunae* in the earlier version.

We can return to our question. Is this earlier draft a version of Orwell's 2 January original (which he described as 'a rough one and not well expressed'), notwithstanding the things that might be said against that view? It remains possible that it is a version of which there is no trace in the surviving record, but I am inclined to think that this is a post-Foot (27 February) version of Orwell's original, possibly drafted on the basis of notes taken during the Christmas visit to Koestler in Wales (and thus reflecting some of his input or conversation), and then possibly redrafted fully by Koestler. The reasons for thinking this are contextual. We can see reverberations of the work he put into this draft in other things Orwell wrote during the first couple of months of 1946. In particular, it seems to relate to the work he was doing for the series of four essays published in the *Manchester Evening News* (24 January–14 February 1946) under the title 'The Intellectual Revolt'. Orwell wrote this series at the same time as working on the draft.

The opening article in the sequence starts with the statement that 'laissez-faire capitalism is finished'. Its analysis charts the move from 'an individualistic society' to 'planned economies'. In mapping the 'intellectual revolt' against this tendency, Orwell identifies four groups. They are not, of course, a simple match for the four forms of society identified in the preamble to the first version of the manifesto, but the categorization works, *mutatis mutandis*, in similar ways, though without the rigid grid of the manifesto. The 'pessimists' oppose central planning; the 'Left-wing Socialists' wish to combine 'central planning' with 'individual liberty'; The 'Christian Reformers' wanted 'revolutionary social change' combined with Christian doctrine; and the 'pacifists' wished to do away with 'the centralised State and from … government by coercion'. This is some distance from the terms of the manifesto (autocracy, democracy, laissez faire), but not perhaps from the underpinning thoughts.[348] Furthermore, some of the figures discussed by Orwell as representative of particular positions are also referred to in 'The Intellectual Revolt'. F.A. Voigt had given the 'best expression' of the pessimist view;[349] Maritain was identified as a leading Christian reformer of Socialist tendencies;[350] and Herbert Read, whom Orwell knew well from their work together on the Freedom Defence Committee, was prominent among the pacifists.[351] Even more interestingly, Karl Mannheim was mentioned in the draft manifesto. He was not referred to in 'The Intellectual Revolt', but when Orwell wrote to John Beavan, editor of the *Manchester Evening News*, to outline his thoughts for the articles and to announce that the first of them would be ready in the week ahead, he said, 'I haven't yet got hold of anything of Mannheim's, but from what I can find out about him he

---

[348] Orwell, 'The Intellectual Revolt', CW, XVIII, p. 57.
[349] Orwell, 'The Intellectual Revolt', CW, XVIII, pp. 57–8.
[350] Orwell, 'The Intellectual Revolt', CW, XVIII, pp. 64–5.
[351] Orwell, 'The Intellectual Revolt', CW, XVIII, pp. 68–9.

seems to fit into category 3' (the Christian reformers).[352] The essays seem to outline an intellectual framework within which the manifesto was drafted. It also discussed figures closely associated with the attempt to create a new League, notably Russell (classed among the pessimists), Michael Polanyi (discussed alongside Hayek as another opponent of planned societies), and, of course, Koestler himself (among the Socialists).[353]

There are other traces of the manifesto work to be found too. The earlier version of it takes a vague swipe at the 'the League for the Rights of Man and various Popular Front bodies [that] were captured by the Communists'. When he sent the very first draft to Koestler, Orwell commented that 'I have not yet found out much about the League of the Rights of Man'.[354] The next day he told Dwight Macdonald that 'Koestler is also very anxious to start something like what the League for the Rights of Man used to be before it was stalinised'.[355] A few days later Koestler received a more expansive account of Orwell's ignorance on the subject

> I haven't found out anything significant about the League for the Rights of Man. No one seems to have much about it in their files. All I can discover is that it is still in existence in France, and that it did exist in Germany up to Hitler, so it must have been an international organisation. There is something about it in Well's 'Crux Ansata' (which I can't get hold of), so it is possible that it drew up the Declaration of the Rights of Man which Wells is always burbling about. But I am certain that some years before the war it had become a Stalinist organisation, as I distinctly remember that it refused to intervene in favour of the Trotskyists in Spain: nor so far as I remember did it do anything about the Moscow trials. But one ought to verify all this.[356]

There is little sign that this muddle of half-remembered opinion was ever verified, though Koestler did ask Rodney Philips, in preparing for the abortive April conference, to find a lawyer who 'could look up in the National Library the statute of the old League of the Rights of Man and bring along a draft for the constitution of the league'.[357] It is only the earlier surviving

---

[352]Orwell to John Beavan, 17 January 1946, CW, XVIII, p. 41.

[353]Orwell, 'The Intellectual Revolt', CW, XVIII, pp. 58–61.

[354]Orwell to Arthur Koestler, 2 January 1946, CW, XVIII, p. 7.

[355]Orwell to Dwight Macdonald, 3 January 1946, CW, XVIII, p. 12.

[356]Orwell to Arthur Koestler, 10 January 1946, CW, XVIII, p. 28.

[357]Arthur Koestler to Rodney Philips, 14 March 1946, Edinburgh University Library, Koestler Papers 2345/2/69; UCL Orwell/I/4/11. In addition the Koestler Papers (2345/1), with copies in UCL Orwell/I/4/4-6 contain copies of both the 'Déclaration' and the 'Programme d'Action' of the 'Ligue Internationale pour La Défense des Libertés Humaines'; as well as a 4 pp. pamphlet announcing the launch of Emmanuel Mounier's journal Esprit, which is mentioned in the first version of the manifesto.

draft that contained Orwell's slur against the pre-war League, though both versions mentioned it as a body whose methods they would emulate. Orwell was probably thinking of the *Ligue des droits de l'Homme*, founded in 1898 by defenders of Dreyfus (though there are other possible contenders).[358] The *Ligue* formed, in conjunction with similar bodies in other European countries, including Germany and Belgium, the *Fédération internationale des Ligues des droits de l'Homme* (FIDH) in 1922, of which Orwell might also have been aware. Most likely he knew of the *Ligue* through the writing of H.G. Wells (though not the book that Orwell mentioned in his letter to Koestler). Wells drafted and promoted a new Declaration of the Rights of Man, and compared it to the Ligue's *Complément* of 1936.[359] Wells's work became, in essence, what is known as the Sankey Declaration (1940), and has been thought to be an important precursor of the UN's Universal Declaration of Human Rights (1948).[360] Wells suggested that '[t]he ultimate pattern of world government to which human affairs move seems to be a combination of the collectivist ideal, the state socialism of Russia, *plus* a rigorous insistence on the Declaration of Rights we have set out here'. The sentiment – the need to combine collectivism and individual liberties – would seem to be one that Orwell would approve, though he was scornful of Wells's naive promotion of a world state. 'Mr Wells has never once suggested how the World State is to be brought into being.' But, in fact, he didn't think much of Wells's rights of man either.

> In formulating the 'Rights of Man', he does not even drop a hint as to how such a document could be disseminated in, say, Russia or China. Hitler he dismisses as simply a lunatic: that settles Hitler. He does not seriously inquire *why* millions of people are ready to lay down their lives for a lunatic, and what this probably betokens for human society.

In Orwell's view, Wells's work was rooted in 'the slogans of 1900 [repeated] as though they were self-evident truths'. It offered nothing to a world in which the totalitarian temptation had proven to be one that many could not resist. Furthermore, 'his declaration of the "Rights of Man" is a purely Western document. Almost any Indian, for instance, would reject it at a

---

[358]The Ligue's website has a good deal of historical information: https://www.ldh-france. org/. Other contenders include the International League for the Rights of Man, founded in New York in 1942: see Jan Eckel, 'The International League for the Rights of Man, Amnesty International, and the Changing Fate of Human Rights Activism from the 1940s through the 1970s', *Humanity: An International Journal of Human Rights, Humanitarianism, and Development*, 4 (2013), pp. 183–214.

[359]H.G. Wells, *The Rights of Man, or What Are We Fighting For?* (London: Penguin, 2015; reprint of 1940 Penguin Special), esp. ch. 10.

[360]For example, D. Gert Hensel, '10 December 1948: H.G. Wells and the Drafting of a Universal Declaration of Human Rights', *Peace Research* 35 (2003), pp. 93–102.

glance.' Some, Orwell noted, already had. Wells's programme was based on the hope of a world state, which he saw as inevitable (or rather the only thing that could prevent the ultimate triumph of barbarism); but, Orwell suggested, 'he is not ready to admit that even among scientists and thinkers generally the intellectual basis for world unity does not exist'.[361]

It is not apparent that the Orwell-Koestler manifesto itself addresses any of these problems, but the wider intellectual project of which the proposed League was a part did. The Koestler-Russell petition for 'psychological disarmament' might be thought to address some of the ways in which the world had changed since Wells's heyday in 1900. But there is also something more to be said about the *Polemic* circle, which included Russell, Ayer and Orwell. The surviving correspondence makes it clear that these people met and talked, and a form of liberal anti-totalitarianism coalesced around the journal, one with a strong interest in freedom of thought. Phillips and Slater, of course, thought that Orwell and Koestler intended *Polemic* to become the League's house journal. It is hard to say whether the fear was founded, and Koestler rejected it out-of-hand. But there are other signs that their fears had some justification. Orwell, writing to Koestler about the journal, spoke proprietorially about how it would contain 'our opening volley against the Modern Quarterly'.[362] He was referring to the editorial he wrote for the third issue (May 1946). He published five long and important essays in *Polemic* between May 1945 and March 1947 (the first and the last issue). The magazine gave him privileged treatment. One of his essays, 'The Prevention of Literature', excited a long attack from the Communist poet Randall Swingler. *Polemic* printed Swingler's reply (September–October 1946), but accompanied it with extensive and hostile marginal annotations from Orwell. The annotations were well over half the length of Swingler's essay. Orwell's was the journal's most prolific contributor (ahead of Russell and A.J. Ayer) and joined the editorial board not long before it went out of business.[363] Writing to his former Eton Classics tutor (by this time a Fellow of Trinity College, Cambridge), A.S.F. Gow – known to old Etonians as 'Granny Gow' – Orwell expressed high hopes of *Polemic*. 'You mentioned Freddie Ayer,' he told Gow. 'I didn't know you knew him. He is a great friend of mine. This new magazine, "Polemic", has only made two appearances so far, but I have great hopes that it will develop into something good. Bertrand Russell is of course the chief star in the constellation.'[364]

---

[361]Orwell, 'Review of '42 to '44: A Contemporary Memoir upon Human Behaviour during the Crisis of the World Revolution by H.G. Wells', 21 May 1944, CW, XVI, pp. 197–9.
[362]Orwell to Arthur Koestler, 31 March 1946, CW, XVIII, pp. 213–14.
[363]Peter Marks, George Orwell the Essayist: Literature, Politics and the Periodical Culture (London: Bloomsbury, 2011), pp. 14–15, 140–54, 173–5.
[364]Orwell to Andrew S.F. Gow, 13 April 1946, CW, XVIII, p. 242.

Orwell's Editorial for the May 1946 issue of *Polemic* might be read as another manifesto for his and Koestler's campaign for intellectual freedom – 'our opening volley'. It was a response to an attack on *Polemic* in the *Modern Quarterly*'s December 1945 editorial. The *Modern Quarterly* was a Marxist journal closely associated with the Communist Party of Great Britain. A number of prominent intellectuals wrote for it, and one of them, the distinguished physicist J.D. Bernal, bore the brunt of Orwell's counter-attack. *The Modern Quarterly* editorial charged *Polemic* with 'persistent attempts to confuse moral issues, to break down the distinction between right and wrong'. Orwell seized with glee upon Bernal's essay 'Belief and Action' in the same issue, which, in Orwell's summary, claimed that 'almost any moral standard can and should be scrapped when political expediency demands it'. How, he wondered, could such a slithery approach to the distinction between good and bad be compatible with accusing others of breaking down the very same distinction? Bernal's language was mercilessly picked apart by Orwell, to reveal the real meaning of what he said. 'A thing that is especially noticeable in Professor Bernal's article is the English, at once pompous and slovenly, in which it is written. It is not pedantic to draw attention to this, because the connection between totalitarian habits of mind and the corruption of language is an important subject which has not been sufficiently studied.' When this was published in *Polemic*, Orwell's great essay 'Politics and the English Language' had just appeared in *Horizon*. Bernal's language served to 'blur the moral squalor of what is being said'. Thus Orwell pointed out:

> To say, party loyalty means doing dirt on you own conscience', would be too crude: to say '(virtues) based on excessive concern with individual rectitude need reorienting in the direction of social responsibility', comes to much the same thing, but far less courage is required in saying it.

Orwell was scornful of *Modern Quarterly*'s claim to present a diversity of views rather than to promote a Communist orthodoxy. Its attack on *Polemic* was intended to cover up the Communist betrayal of liberal values, no doubt because the able defence those values received in *Polemic* made the editors of the *Modern Quarterly* 'a little nervous about the reactions of their more tender-minded readers'.

> The reason for the *Modern Quarterly*'s hostility to *Polemic* is not difficult to guess. *Polemic* is attacked because it upholds certain moral and intellectual values whose survival is dangerous from the totalitarian point of view. These are what is loosely called the liberal values – using the word 'liberal' in its old sense of 'liberty-loving'. Its aim, before all else, is to defend the freedom of thought and speech that has been painfully won during the past four hundred years.

In a final flourish, Orwell decoded Bernal's message as a preference for Fascism over liberalism and the 'rights of man'. 'So we arrive at the old, true, and unpalatable conclusion that a communist and a fascist are somewhat nearer to one another than either is to a democrat.' *Polemic* was resolute 'in *defending* a conception of right and wrong, and of intellectual decency, which has been responsible for all true progress for centuries past, and without which the very continuance of civilised life is by no means certain'.[365] '[A]bove all else ... freedom of thought and speech': this is what drove Orwell's writing and actions in the years after 1944, ultimately driving him to the almost obsessive focus with which he wrote *Nineteen Eight-Four* and perhaps to a death that came earlier than it need have done.

Yet, Orwell was not just a liberal individualist. The value of the earlier draft of the manifesto – if it is indeed closer to Orwell's first thoughts – lies in its strong insistence that freedom could not exist without equality. It is worth repeating the core passage: 'Above all it is not enough to repeat the tenet of the French Revolution that "all men are born equal" if the economic structure of society remains such as to make such equality utter nonsense. Political democracy must remain a farce as long as economic equality from the cradle persists and handicaps the free display of individual faculties.' There has been much speculation about how Orwell's thinking might have evolved after 1950, had he lived longer. Orwell's admirers were outraged by the contention of Norman Podhoretz that he would, in all probability, have joined the numerous ranks of those who moved from Socialism to Neo-Conservatism.[366] We can never know for sure, but Orwell's commitment to the principle that equality was needed so that freedom and democracy could be more than a farce – a commitment that he never abandoned – does not sound like the view of a man ready to begin the Right-ward march. Ex-Communists were particularly prone to this, and, of course, Orwell was never a Communist. He became a Socialist with a full awareness of the excesses (vegetarian, pacifist or Communist) that tempted those on the Left. He had never worshipped the God that failed. He had no reason to re-think his Socialism. But he was equally committed to defeating the Soviet myth in order to defend intellectual freedom. This commitment led him, in the last year of his life, to actions for which he has been reviled, co-operating with the British Foreign Office and their Information Research Department in the early phases of what was to become the cultural Cold War.

---

[365]Orwell, 'Editorial', *Polemic*, 3 May 1946, CW, XVIII, pp. 263–8.
[366]Norman Podhoretz, 'If Orwell Were Alive Today' [1983], reprinted in Thomas L. Jeffers (ed.), *The Norman Podhoretz Reader* (New York: Free Press, 2004), pp. 214–27; also Hilton Kramer, 'An Orwell for the Nineties?', *The New Criterion*, 10:3 (November 1991), pp. 4–8.

# 7. Propaganda Again: Orwell, His List and the Information Research Department (IRD)

Orwell's work to create a League in defence of liberalism provides a context for understanding one of his most controversial actions, the provision of a list of names of suspected Communists and fellow-travellers to the Information Research Department (IRD). Controversial is an understatement: when Orwell's action became known in 1996 he was reviled by many on the Left, for whom the revelation of 'the List' confirmed their long-standing loathing of Orwell. The publication of Orwell's *Complete Works* in 1998 (containing correspondence relating to the List and an incomplete version of the notebook from which the List derived) fuelled further controversy, as did publication of the list itself from a copy found in Celia Kirwan's paper after her death and the subsequent release by the Foreign Office of the actual document in 2003.[367] (Curiously, the existence of the notebook listing Crypto-Communists and Soviet fellow-travellers from which Orwell produced his list had been public knowledge since Crick's biography appeared in 1980, and was even more extensively covered by Shelden in 1991; and even the list itself was obliquely referred to in print by Alok Rai in 1988).[368] Orwell's critics seized upon the List with jubilant outrage. At the milder end of this was the historian Christopher Hill's comment: 'I always knew he was two-faced,' says Professor Hill. 'There was something fishy about Orwell. I am pained and sorry to hear of it and it confirms my worst suspicions about the man. It is consistent with the general tone of his stories and his journalism, which was always very ambiguous. Animal Farm is precisely an attack on communism.'[369] At the other end of the spectrum lay Alexander Cockburn: 'The man of conscience turns out to be a whiner, and of course a snitch, an informer to the secret police, *Animal Farm's*

---

[367]The initial publication was in *The Guardian*, 21 June 2003: Timothy Garton Ash, 'Love, Death and Treachery', *The Guardian*, 21 June 2003, Review, pp. 4–7 (not online). See also John Ezard, 'Blair's Babe' https://www.theguardian.com/uk/2003/jun/21/books.artsandhumanities (accessed 20 May 2020); and the letter to *The Guardian* (5 July 2003) from Ariane Bankes, the daughter of Celia Kirwan (later Goodman), who had arranged for publication of the list after discovering it in her mother's papers: https://www.theguardian.com/theguardian/2003/jul/05/guardianletters2 (accessed 20 May 2020).

[368]Crick, *George Orwell*, pp. 556 & 653–4, n. 49; Michael Shelden, *Orwell: The Authorised Biography* (London: William Heinemann, 1991, reprinted Politico's, 2006), pp. 467–9; Alok Rai, *Orwell and the Politics of Despair* (Cambridge: Cambridge University Press, 1988), p. 156.

[369]Ross Wynne-Jones, 'Orwell's Little List Leaves the Left Gasping for More', *Independent on Sunday*, 14 July 1996, https://www.independent.co.uk/news/orwells-little-list-leaves-the-left-gasping-for-more-1328633.html (accessed 5 February 2020).

resident weasel.'[370] Even the more dispassionately academic accounts of the events express disapproval ('a gross miscalculation ... his actions should be condemned'[371]), as do scholars undeniably very sympathetic to Orwell ('a serious mistake', 'the list itself was pretty unsavoury; certainly something he should have been ashamed of'[372]).

What had Orwell done?

On 29 March 1949 Orwell was visited in the Cranham sanatorium by Celia Kirwan. Celia (born Celia Paget) was the twin sister of Arthur Koestler's girlfriend and future wife Mamaine. Orwell first met Celia in December 1945, on the platform at Paddington Station. They were to travel together (with Orwell's young son, Richard) to North Wales for the Christmas and New Year break that both of them spent with the Koestlers near Blaenau Ffestiniog, and which resulted in the plan to found the League for the Dignity and Rights of Man.[373] Soon after, Orwell proposed marriage to Celia. She declined, as did three other women who received similar offers in the troubled months following the devastatingly unexpected death of Orwell's first wife, Eileen, on 29 March 1945. Nonetheless, Orwell and Celia remained friends and she came to see him at the Cranham sanatorium on 29 March 1949. By this time Celia was working for the Information Research Department (IRD), established the year before by the Labour Government as a department of the Foreign Office. Its purpose was to combat Soviet propaganda, particularly by circulating and commissioning magazines, articles and books. Like a number of other early Cold War institutions (notably the CIA-sponsored Congress for Cultural Freedom, in which Koestler was initially to be a key player), the IRD's preferred line seems to have been to support liberal or Leftish anti-Communism. Celia visited Orwell to discuss the work of the IRD. He 'expressed his wholehearted and enthusiastic approval of our aims'. He would not, however, write for the IRD, partly because illness made it impossible and partly because 'he does not like to write "on commission", as he feels he does not do his best work that way'. Celia still had hopes, though, and was going to send Orwell copies of some articles 'on the theme of Soviet repression of the arts, in the hope that

---

[370]Alexander Cockburn, 'The Fable of the Weasel', Foreword to John Reed, *Snowball's Chance* (Brooklyn, NY: Melville House, 2012), p viii. An earlier version of this essay is Cockburn, 'St. George's List', *The Nation*, 7 December 1998, which was preceded by 'The Rapist and the Snitch', *The Nation*, 23 November 1998, which, in case you're in any doubt, is about Koestler and Orwell.

[371]James Smith, *British Writers and MI5 Surveillance, 1930–1960* (Cambridge: Cambridge University Press, 2013), p. 145.

[372]John Newsinger, *Hope Lies in the Proles: George Orwell and the Left* (London: Verso, 2018), pp. 112, 125.

[373]Crick, *George Orwell*, pp. 483–4.

he may become inspired when he is better to take them up again'. Instead, though, Orwell suggested some names of writers who might be suitable for the writing of anti-Soviet material. These included C.D. Darlington, a scientist, as Orwell thought a full account of the Lysenko affair should be produced, and Franz Borkenau, whom he had long admired. Orwell also suggested Victor Gollancz as a publisher to work with: his 'books always sell well, and they are well displayed and given the widest publicity'. Orwell's India experience with the Burma police and through his BBC work led Celia to ask him about the best way of spreading anti-Communism there: 'he did not think that there was a great deal of scope for propaganda in India and Pakistan.' There, Communism was identified with hostility to the 'ruling class'. Encouraging trade and educational exchange would be more effective tools.[374]

There the matter stood, until Orwell found the energy to write to Celia on 6 April. He suggested a few more names (including the scholar of Russian literature Gleb Struve), and also mentioned American anti-Stalinist magazines like *Commentary* and *Partisan Review* (for both of which he wrote) as sources of names of people with the right sort of views and approach. Diverting to his own agenda rather than that of the IRD, Orwell also suggested that the British intelligentsia might benefit from seeing some of the scurrilously anti-British propaganda films made by the Russians, presumably to shake them from their blind support for Stalin. He warned, though, about making too much of Russian anti-semitism in propaganda. Ever alert to the corruptions of hypocrisy, and aware of Zionist hostility to Britain at the time, Orwell stated 'I do not think we do ourselves any good by denouncing anti-semitism in other nations'.[375]

This letter also contained the first reference to the list:

> I could also, if it is of any value, give you a list of journalists & writers who in my opinion are crypto-Communists, fellow-travellers or inclined that way & should not be trusted as propagandists. But for that I shall have to send for a notebook which I have at home & if I do give you such a list it is strictly confidential, as I imagine that it is libellous to describe somebody as a fellow-traveller.[376]

It is worth noting that Orwell offered this list, he was not asked for it. He wrote on the same day to Richard Rees asking him to locate and send him the notebook listing crypto-Communists and fellow-travellers (a 'quarto notebook with a pale-bluish cardboard cover, which I *think* was in my

---

[374]'Orwell and the Information Research Department', CW, XX, pp. 319–20. The quotations are from Celia Kirwan's file note of the meeting, compiled a day later on 30 March.
[375]Orwell to Celia Kirwan, 6 April 1949, CW, XX, pp. 322–3.
[376]Orwell to Celia Kirwan, 6 April 1949, CW, XX, p. 322.

bedroom, but might have been in the sitting room'), 'which I want to bring up to date'.[377] Orwell wrote to Rees again on 17 April, by which time he had the notebook. It seems that Rees had delivered it along with some thoughts of his own on the names that it contained,[378] to which Orwell responded in his letter. According to Rees's later account, the notebook originated in 'a sort of game we played – discussing who was a paid agent of what and estimating to what lengths of treachery our favourite bêtes noires would be prepared to go'.[379] On this occasion, resuming the game, Rees seems to have questioned some of the inclusions, and to have dissuaded Orwell from including some of them on the final list of thirty-eight that he was to give Celia Kirwan. Those discussed with Rees who did not make the final cut were Harold Laski, G.D.H. Cole, Niebuhr (though Orwell seems to have been confused as to which of the brothers Niebuhr he meant in the first place), Lester Hutchinson, John Platt-Mills (MP) and Ian Mikardo. More surprisingly dropped in the transition between notebook and list were Konni Zilliacus and D.N. Pritt, both Labour MPs. Orwell had publicly expressed his views of Zilliacus and the issue of fellow-travellers in *Partisan Review*,[380] and he told Rees that 'I feel completely certain' about Pritt being a fellow-traveller (Pritt had also been associated with the NCCL, one of the reasons why that body was suspected of being a Communist front). The one name discussed with Rees that made it to the final list was Kingsley Martin (editor of *The New Statesman*), of whom Orwell said that he was 'far too dishonest to be outright a crypto or fellow-traveller, but his main influence is pro-Russian and is certainly intended to be so, and I feel reasonably sure he would quislingise in the case of a Russian occupation, if he had not managed to get away on the last plane'.[381] This is outrageous, but the comment in the final list toned it down a bit: he was still 'too dishonest' to be reliable even as a traitor, but the rest of the verdict was truncated to: 'reliably pro-Russian on all major issues'.[382]

Orwell's willingness to act on Rees's doubts (even when he didn't altogether share them) suggests that there was a degree of circumspection in the compilation of the list that was given to Celia Kirwan on 2 May 1949. Furthermore the tone of the list proper is very different from the notebook

[377]Orwell to Richard Rees, 6 April 1949, CW, XX, p. 81.
[378]The notebook contents are in CW, XX, pp. 240–59. This excludes the names of people still living at the time of publication, and these can be found in Davison (ed.), *Lost Orwell*, pp. 149–51.
[379]Quoted in Sheldon, *Orwell: The Authorised Biography*, p. 468.
[380]Orwell, 'London Letter', *Partisan Review*, Summer 1946, CW, XVIII, pp. 286–7 and ensuing exchanges with Zilliacus and others in *Tribune*, 'Communists and Democrats', pp. 289–98; also Orwell, 'In Defence of Comrade Zilliacus', written August–September 1947 for *Tribune*, but unpublished at the time, CW, XIX, pp. 179–83.
[381]Orwell to Richard Rees, 17 April 1949, CW, XX, pp. 88–9.
[382]Davison (ed.), *Lost Orwell*, p. 145.

from which it derived, though there remains to this day much confusion between the two.[383] No one in the list was labelled 'homosexual' (Tom Driberg who appeared in both notebook and list was labelled 'homosexual' only in the former, as was Stephen Spender who did not make the list at all). Many of the crankier comments of the notebook were missing from the list (usually along with the names to which they were attached). He did, though, label Isaac Deutscher as a 'Polish Jew' who had been 'Trotskyist, and changed views chiefly because of Jewish issue'; he referred to Cedric Dover as 'Eurasian. Main Emphasis anti-white (especially anti-U.S.A.) but reliably pro-Russian on all major issues'. And George Padmore was said to be 'Negro. Dissident Communist (expelled from C.P. about 1936) but reliably pro-Russian'. Missing from the list, though, were Paul Robeson ('Very anti-white' in the notebook), Richard Crossman ('Zionist, appears sincere about this'), G.D.H. Cole ('diabetic'), Hugh McDiarmid ('Main emphasis Scottish nationalism. Very anti-English'). By and large, the list confined itself to an assessment of how pro-Soviet and how honest people were. One might wonder why E.H. Carr, a distinguished historian, was included just so that Orwell could comment 'Appeaser only' – presumably therefore neither crypto nor fellow travelling. Even so, it is noticeable that two people were given the condescending label 'Silly sympathiser' and both were women (Marjorie Kohn and Naomi Mitchison); men are just 'stupid' (John Anderson) or even 'very stupid' (Sean O'Casey, only in the notebook); or possibly they may be a 'sentimental sympathiser' (John Beavan in the list and Spender in the notebook). Orwell's use in the list of labels like Jew, German, Hungarian, Eurasian or Negro is harder to read. It may well be a sign of (possibly unconscious) prejudice; on the other hand, the labels may simply be *aides memoire*, distasteful as they may seem to our sensibilities.[384]

Laconic in nature, the list is a hard document to interpret. Whatever we make of it, Celia Kirwan was instructed to ask Orwell for the list. Adam Watson noted on 23 April that he was keen to see it: 'Mrs Kirwan should certainly ask Mr Orwell for the list of crypto-communists. She would "treat it with every confidence" and send it back after a day or two. I hope the list gives reasons in each case.'[385] Celia wrote to Orwell on 30 April to ask that

---

[383]To give but one recent example, Duncan White has castigated Orwell for his 'striking betrayal' of Stephen Spender, which is attributed to Orwell's 'callousness' or 'paranoia': but Spender's name was not on the list that Orwell gave Celia Kirwan (though he was included in the notebook) – Duncan White, *Cold Warriors: Writers Who Waged the Literary Cold War* (London: Little, Brown, 2019), p. 226.

[384]The notebook entries are (mostly) in 'Orwell's List of Crypto-Communists and Fellow-Travellers', CW, XX, pp. 240–59, supplemented by the entries for those who had been still alive in 1998 in Davison (ed.), *Lost Orwell*, pp. 149–51. The list is in TNA FO 1110/189, and is printed as 'List of Names of Crypto-Communists and Fellow-Travellers Sent to Information Research Department 2 May 1949', in Davison (ed.), *Lost Orwell*, pp. 140–9.

[385]TNA FO 1110/189.

he send it, promising that 'we would treat it with the utmost discretion'.[386] Orwell sent it to Celia on 2 May with a covering letter:

> I enclose a list with about 35 names [actually 38]. It isn't very sensational and I don't suppose it will tell your friends anything they don't know. At the same time it isn't a bad idea to have the people who are probably unreliable listed. If it had been done earlier it would have stopped people like Peter Smollett worming their way into important propaganda jobs where they were probably able to do us a lot of harm. Even as it stands I imagine that this list is very libellous, or slanderous, or whatever the term is, so will you please see that it is returned to me without fail.[387]

We don't know whether the list that Orwell sent was returned, but it seems that the version that survives in the Foreign Office archive is a typed copy not Orwell's original.[388] It is interesting that the one name mentioned in the covering letter was that of Peter Smollett. Smollett, who worked during the war as head of the Russia desk at the Ministry of Information, *was* a Soviet agent. Furthermore, he appears to have been the person in the Ministry who in 1944 advised Jonathan Cape not to publish *Animal Farm*. The historian Christopher Hill, quick to denounce Orwell for the list (as we have seen), was a colleague of Smollett's and has himself been accused of being a Soviet mole by Anthony Glees – though mole would seem an odd word for someone whose sympathies were hardly hidden.[389]

A great deal of huffing-and-puffing has taken place over Orwell's list, some of it quoted above. Both his supporters and his distractors seem capable of getting things out of proportion.[390] Part of the problem is that Orwell's actions inevitably suggest to us parallels with that other man who

---

[386]Timothy Garton Ash, 'Orwell's List', *New York Review of Books*, 25 September 2003, is the best and fullest account of the events; also Phillip Deery, 'Confronting the Cominform: George Orwell and the Cold War Offensive of the Information Research Department, 1948–50', *Labour History*, No 73 (November 1997), p. 221.

[387]Orwell to Celia Kirwan, 2 May 1949, CW, XX, p. 103.

[388]Davison (ed.), *Lost Orwell*, p. 140.

[389]Orwell, CW, XVI, p. 266; Crick, *George Orwell*, pp. 455–6; Peter Davison (ed.), *Orwell and Politics* (London: Penguin, 2001), pp. 227–8; Owen Bowcott, 'Outcry as Historian Labelled a Soviet Spy', *The Guardian*, 6 March 2003, https://www.theguardian.com/uk/2003/mar/06/books.politics (accessed 15 February 2020).

[390]A good survey of initial reactions in the context of broader revelations about the IRS is Andrew Defty, *Britain, America and Anti-Communist Propaganda 1945–53: The Information Research Department* (London: Routledge, 2004), Introduction. The stoutest defence comes from Christopher Hitchens, 'Orwell on Trial', *Vanity Fair* (https://www.vanityfair.com/news/1996/10/christopher-hitchens); and (rather better), Hitchens, *Orwell's Victory* (London: Allen Lane / Penguin, 2002), ch. 7; also Robert Conquest, 'In Celia's Office', *Times Literary Supplement*, 21 August 1998. Conquest, arch cold-warrior, worked for the IRD and for a time shared an office with Celia Kirwan.

came bearing a list, Joseph McCarthy.[391] But, as Celia Kirwan later said of
the people whom Orwell named: 'The only thing that was going to happen
to them was that they wouldn't be asked to write for the Information
Research Department.'[392] There is no evidence that the people named were
ever blacklisted for any other purpose; nor were their careers harmed; the
names were never passed on to any other agency such as the secret service
(MI5), and so did not result in any surveillance activity.[393] Exception has
sometimes been taken to a comment made by Scott Lucas (in the most
hostile biography written of Orwell): 'Far from being a one-off indiscretion,
Orwell's list is the culmination of his response to the left from the 1930s
onwards.'[394] Perhaps 'culmination' goes too far in suggesting that this is
somehow where Orwell's anti-Communism was headed from the start,
but surely Lucas is right to suggest that the compilation of the list and its
submission to the IRD fit neatly into Orwell's patterns of behaviour and
belief exhibited over many years. His conversion to Socialism in Spain was
at more or less the same time a conversion to anti-Communism. Unlike
Koestler, say, he had never been a Communist; the God that failed had
never been the object of Orwell's worship. But his anti-Communism, which
he saw as necessary to the preservation of a truly Socialist vision, was
integral to his political outlook from 1937 onwards. He had never hidden

---

[391]For a recent argument from the Right that Orwell's and McCarthy's actions were
fundamentally different, see Ron Capshaw, 'Was George Orwell a McCarthyite?', *The
Liberty Conservative*, posted 4 March 2017, https://libertyconservative.com/george-orwell-
mccarthyite/ (accessed 15 February 2020).
[392]Quoted in Garton Ash, 'Orwell's List'.
[393]It has been suggested that Orwell, himself the subject of Special Branch and SIS surveillance,
should have known better than to have had anything to do with the IRD. But the evidence
suggests a certain naivety on his part. He said in print, 'quite possibly there is a secret police
in England, but the point is that we don't feel afraid of it': George Orwell, 'Culture and
Democracy', November 1941, CW, XI, p. 68. In 1942 he was a referee for Georges Kopp's
security clearance, and the candid comments he made reinforce this impression. The report on
his comments ends: 'BLAIR states that he regarded KOPP as a loyal man, possessed of anti-Nazi
sentiments, but otherwise not deeply interested in politics though mildly Left wing. He was
physically courageous and resolute and, generally speaking, an adventurer. He had a tendency,
however, to embellish things, and although deserving of confidence in his personal conduct, one
hesitated to accept anything he said without additional corroboration' (Letter / memorandum
from Courtenay Young [SIS], 3 July 1943, Special Operations Executive, Personnel File for
Georges Kopp, TNA HS9/858/8). The surveillance files on Orwell have been digitized: SIS
surveillance, TNA KV2/2699; Special Branch surveillance MEPO 38/69. For these files, see
Smith, *British Writers and MI5 Surveillance, 1930–1960*; also Richard Lance Keeble, '*Nineteen
Eighty-Four* and the Spooks', in Keeble, *George Orwell, the Secret State and the Making of
Nineteen Eighty-Four* (Bury St Edmunds: Abramis, 2020), ch. 2; Newsinger, *Hope Lies in the
Proles*, ch. 6; Darcy Moore, 'Orwell and the Secret Intelligence Service', *George Orwell Studies*,
6:2 (2022), pp. 9–26.
[394]Scott Lucas, *Orwell* (London: Haus, 2003), p. 110 – actually Lucas's account of the whole
episode (pp. 105–10) is reasonably balanced and fair – though the pages that follow are less so.

the fact, and persisted with the publication of *Animal Farm*, his most anti-Communist work, against the odds and just as the Soviet Union was about to lead the final defeat of Nazi Germany. Orwell was happy for *Animal Farm* to be seen and used as propaganda, but he was not a believer in disinformation or falsehood. He wanted intellectual honesty and decency in propaganda, as in all things,[395] and had found the compromises of the BBC years deeply uncomfortable. His list was part of that effort – find the honest and intelligent anti-Communists, he suggested, if you want propaganda of intellectual integrity. There is no suggestion that this was a list of people to be persecuted in any way. Even Orwell's admirers are made uncomfortable by what he did in 1949, but, however we may judge Orwell, the list was no aberration.

The list also points us back to Orwell's individualism. He had written about the problem of crypto-Communism and fellow-travelling in 1947, pointing out that one should never assume that such people would hold the same views permanently and regardless of changing circumstances. '[T]he disillusioned "fellow-traveler" is a common figure.' Orwell acknowledged, though, the difficulties in dealing with suspected disloyalty:

> The important thing to do with these people – and it is extremely difficult since one has only inferential evidence – is to sort them out and determine which of them is honest and which is not. There is, for instance, a whole group of MP's in the British Parliament (Pritt, Zilliacus, etc.) who are commonly nicknamed 'the cryptos'. They have undoubtedly done a great deal of mischief, especially in confusing public opinion about the nature of the puppet regimes in Eastern Europe; but one ought not hurriedly to assume that they are all equally dishonest or even that they all hold the same opinions. Probably some of them are actuated by nothing worse than stupidity.[396]

Orwell's notebook was a tool to avoid hasty judgement. In it he weighed and sifted, individual by individual, the evidence for their likely loyalty to Communism and their honesty. The original notebook, with its crossing outs, multiple inks and interpolations, makes its character visible.[397] The content was often crass, and to our eyes the labelling of people is offensive if not racist and anti-Semitic (though few of Orwell's contemporaries would have seen it that way). Still, it was an attempt – a private attempt – not to jump to conclusions and to consider each individual case on its merits. The

---

[395] This point is made in the comparison of Orwell and Koestler in Smith, *British Writers and MI5 Surveillance*, ch. 4, p. 151.

[396] Orwell, 'Burnham's View of the Contemporary World Struggle', 29 March 1947, CW, XIX, p. 101.

[397] UCL Orwell/D/4.

frequent annotations of 'appeaser only' or 'sympathiser only' seem designed to keep people *out* of the crypto or fellow-traveller box not to put them in it. The list was a distillation, the results of Orwell's weighing and sifting. We might not approve of his action in passing it to the IRD, but Orwell seems to have tried (as with his BBC broadcast work) to behave with intellectual integrity as he saw it. He had made no secret of the fact that in his view Soviet Communism was anti-revolutionary, and that there was no hope for Socialism without the destruction of the Soviet myth – the myth that Stalin's Russia embodied the hope of Socialist revolution for all humankind. That destruction was work for the intelligent and the honest.

In the early years of the Cold War, Orwell showed an interest in supporting the anti-Soviet propaganda effort that went beyond providing the IRS with a list of names. In particular, he was keen to see *Animal Farm* translated into languages that would extend the impact of its anti-Soviet propaganda to places where it mattered.[398] The displaced persons camps of post-war Europe provided a ready audience of readers hostile to the Russian occupation of their homelands. A Polish translation was published by the League of Poles Abroad in 1946, and Orwell told his agent, 'I do not want any money out of it myself'; he would take nothing from 'these wretched exiles'.[399] He was similarly willing to waive any fee for an Estonian translation.[400] This was, indeed, a settled policy, as he said in relation to a Serbian translation: 'in the case of ... Russian-occupied countries where translations can only be done by refugees, I do not want any payment'.[401] The policy applied only to *Animal Farm*, for which, Orwell said, he would take no fee 'from Poles or any other Slavs, but I don't see why they should not pay a small fee ... if they decide to do one of the other books'.[402] He welcomed on these terms approaches for Serbian and Hungarian translations. The approach from the Serbs had suggested 'that about 5000 copies might be smuggled into Jugoslavia'. Neither this nor the Hungarian translation eventuated.[403] A Czech translation was made and published but suppressed by the

---

[398]See Ksenya Kiebuzinski, 'Not Lost in Translation: Orwell's *Animal Farm* among Refugees and beyond the Iron Curtain', *The Halcyon: The* Newsletter *of the Friends of the Thomas Fisher Rare Book Library*, 59 (June 2017), pp. 3–6; Masha Karp, 'Orwell in Translation', *European Studies Blog*, 21 November 2017, https://blogs.bl.uk/european/2017/11/orwell-in-translation.html (accessed 8 May 2020).

[399]Orwell to Leonard Moore, 9 January 1946, CW, XVIII, p. 24. The initial approach from the Poles and Orwell's willingness to waive his financial rights were noted earlier in Orwell to Gleb Struve, 1 September 1945, CW, XVII, pp. 274–5; and Orwell to Leonard Moore', 8 September 1945, CW, XVII, p. 286. See Krystyna Wieszczek, 'Orwell and the Poles: The Case of *Animal Farm* in Poland', *Orwell Society Journal*, 8 (May 2016), pp. 8–10.

[400]Orwell to Leonard Moore, 5 September 1946, CW, XVIII, p. 387.

[401]Orwell to Leonard Moore, 21 September 1946, CW, XVIII, p. 403.

[402]Orwell to Leonard Moore, 8 June 1948, CW, XIX, pp. 391–2.

[403]Orwell to Leonard Moore, 9 January 1947 & 15 July 1948, CW, XIX, pp. 11, 403.

authorities.[404] The best-known translation made in Orwell's lifetime is the one into Ukrainian published in 1947, for which Orwell wrote a preface. Ihor Szewczenko [Ševčenko] wrote, following an initial overture from Teresa Jeleńska who was responsible for the Polish translation, to get Orwell's permission for its publication. Szewczenko told Orwell that he had translated and read passages from the book to Soviet refugees. This audience, he told Orwell, 'approved of almost all of your interpretations' and found that 'the mood of the book seems to correspond with their own actual state of mind'. Of particular value, Szewczenko thought, was a book supporting 'a search for "human dignity" and "liberty"' that was not right-wing. They craved a 'warning voice' that came 'from the Socialist quarters, to which they stood intellectually nearer'.[405] Orwell must have been delighted to see the book recognized as the work of an anti-Stalinist Socialist. After completing the translation, Szewczenko requested a preface from Orwell, who agreed to provide one, pleased to learn from Szewzcenko that there existed within the Soviet Union a left-wing opposition to the corruption of the Revolution.[406] The preface was dispatched on 21 March.[407] His Ukrainian readers were thus able to read Orwell's declaration that *Animal Farm* was rooted in his conviction 'that the destruction of the Soviet myth was essential if we wanted a revival of the Socialist movement'.[408] About 5,000 copies of the translation were printed, but up to a half of them were confiscated by the American authorities in post-war Munich and handed over to the Soviet repatriation commission.[409]

One of the two approaches for a Hungarian translation came not from a refugee group or a dissident intellectual but from the Central Office for Information (COI), peacetime successor to the Ministry of Information. Orwell referred them to Leonard Moore, and nothing further is known of this particular project.[410] But Orwell does not seem to have been at all reluctant to co-operate with the COI. More interesting, though, is the story of the Russian translation. *Animal Farm* was translated into Russian by Mary Kriger and Gleb Struve. Struve had expressed an interest in seeing the work translated when he first read it. It would benefit Russians abroad to be

[404]'Orwell's Notes on His Books and Essays', CW, XX, p. 227; Orwell to Leonard Moore, 17 December 1947, CW, XIX, p. 234.
[405]Ihor Szewczenko to Orwell, 11 April 1946, CW, VIII, p. 236.
[406]Szewczenko to Orwell, 7 March 1947; Orwell to Szewczenko, 13 March 1947, CW, XIX, pp. 72–4.
[407]Orwell to Szewczenko, 21 March 1947, CW, XIX, p. 85.
[408]Orwell, 'Preface to the Ukrainian Edition of *Animal Farm*', March 1947, CW, XIX, p. 88; Orwell, *Animal Farm* (CW, VIII), p. 113.
[409]Orwell to Arthur Koestler, 20 September 1947, CW, XIX, pp. 206–7; Orwell to Gleb Struve, 22 November 1948, XIX, p. 472; 'Orwell's Notes on His Books and Essays', CW, XX, p. 227. Each account gives different numbers.
[410]Central Office of Information to Secker & Warburg, 23 January 1947, CW, XIX, p. 23.

able to read the truth about what their country had become. Orwell replied with enthusiasm, hoping that Struve himself would do the translation. 'If translations into the Slav languages were made,' he added, 'I shouldn't want any money out of them myself', though he was keen to ensure that the translators were rewarded.[411] So when the translation was nearly complete, Orwell reaffirmed that he was happy to see it published on his usual terms ('I don't want any money from D.Ps [displaced persons]'), though he did ask for 'a copy or two' if the translation appeared in book form.[412] Initially, the translation appeared in the journal *Possev*, founded in 1945 by Russian refugees in Germany. The journal bore the motto 'God is not in power, but in truth'.[413] Orwell's book was carried across several issues during 1949. On 24 June, P. Puachev wrote to him on behalf of *Possev* to say that the final instalment would soon appear, and enclosing 'a set of "Possev", beginning with the introductory article preceding the appearance of your work'. The book, Puachev remarked, 'made a very great impression on the Russian reading public and we have received many responses, and in particular requests that this strong satire should be made known on the other side of "the iron curtain"'. To achieve this, publication in book form seemed desirable. This would require a subsidy of 2,000 German Marks.[414] The letter was originally in Russian, and Orwell had immediately turned to Celia Kirwan and the IRD to have it translated. Once he knew what was in the letter, Orwell wrote to Ruth Fischer. She was a German former-Communist anti-Stalinist resident in America since 1941. Orwell had previously written to express his admiration for her 1948 book *Stalin and German Communism*,[415] but now, aware that she was visiting Germany, he was interested in what she could tell him about *Possev* and the people behind it. 'I suppose the editors of this paper are bona fide people, and also not whites?'[416] Typically, Orwell was concerned not to be associated with groups on the Right. A second letter, this time in English, was dispatched to Orwell on 16 July, reiterating the request.[417] Orwell asked his literary agent to check whether he was owed anything by the American-backed German magazine

[411]Gleb Struve to Orwell, 28 August 1945, UCL Orwell/H/2/85; Orwell to Gleb Struve, 1 September 1945, CW, XVII, pp. 274–5.
[412]Orwell to Gleb Struve, 22 November 1948, CW, XIX, p. 472. Orwell maintained a collection of translations of *Animal Farm*: see Orwell to Leonard Moore, 30 July 1949 and 12 August 1949, CW, XX, pp. 155, 157.
[413]The fullest information I can find on *Possev* is in the Russian-language Wikipedia, https://ru.wikipedia.org/wiki/Посев_(журнал) (accessed 12 July 2022).
[414]I have quoted from the typescript translation in the IRD archives: TNA FO 1110/221. The IRD archive also contains the original letter in Russian and the translator's handwritten version of his translation.
[415]Orwell to Ruth Fischer, 21 April 1949, CW, XX, pp. 93–4.
[416]Orwell to Ruth Fischer, 15 July 1949, CW, XX, p. 146.
[417]UCL Orwell/H/2/52, letter was from Vladimir Gorachek; CW, XX, p. 149.

*Der Monat*, which had published both a translation of *Animal Farm* and a reprint of one of Orwell's essays.[418] If he was owed money in Deutschmarks, this could be used to support the *Possev* publication of *Animal Farm* in book-form without the money leaving Germany. Orwell also revealed to Moore that 'I am trying to pull a wire at the Foreign Office to see if they will subscribe a bit. I'm afraid it's not likely. They will throw millions down the drain on useless radio propaganda, but not finance books.' For whatever reason, he continued to have suspicions: 'we shall have to make sure that these "Possev" people are O.K. and not just working a swindle.' Nonetheless, he asked Moore to let their London agents know that he was trying to raise the necessary funds.[419] Immediately after writing this, he heard that *Der Monat* wanted to serialize *Nineteen Eighty-Four*, and thought that payment for this might also be a source of finance for *Possev*. If necessary: 'Of course I'm not going to pay this myself if I can help it, but I haven't very great hopes of the government coming to my aid.'[420]

There can be no doubt, then, that Orwell was very keen to see the Russian translation of *Animal Farm* appear in book form, preferably financed by the IRD. All along, though, he seems to have doubted that the funds would be made available by the Foreign Office. So he told Gleb Struve that 'I shall see to it that the book appears in book form, even if I have to finance it myself'.[421] His doubts about the chances of Foreign Office funding turned out to be correct. 'I have heard from the F.O., who of course won't help to finance the Russian translation of A.F. However, they confirm that the "Possev" people are well known to them and are reliable.' The IRD translator of the first letter that Orwell had received from *Possev* had informed Celia Kirwan:

> This seems to me a sincere and business-like letter in a very good cause. If 'Animal Farm' does get through to the USSR as 'Possev' claims it would, I am sure it would be most effective and eagerly sought after.
>
> We do, of course, know the 'Possev' people who do a good job. Some of the refugees from the Soviet occupation forces have, I believe commented

---

[418]The magazine was edited by Melvin Lasky, and was soon to become one of the key publications sponsored by the Congress for Cultural Freedom: see Michael Hochgeschwender, '*Der Monat* and the Congress for Cultural Freedom: The High Tide of the Intellectual Cold War, 1948–1971', in Giles Scott-Smith & Charlotte Lerg (eds), *Campaigning Culture and the Global Cold War: The Journals of the Congress for Cultural Freedom* (London: Palgrave Macmillan, 2017), pp. 71–89.

[419]Orwell to Leonard Moore, 20 July 1949, CW, XX, pp. 148–9.

[420]Orwell to Leonard Moore, 21 July 1948, CW, XX, pp. 149–50. Moore was separately negotiating for a different Russian edition of *Animal Farm*, though this seems to have come to nothing: see Orwell to Leonard Moore, 24 July 1949, CW, XX, p. 151; and Orwell to Gleb Struve, 27 July 1949, CW, XX, pp. 152–3.

[421]Orwell to Gleb Struve, 27 July 1949, CW, XX, p. 153.

favourably about its effect among the Soviet occupation forces, but their organisation is thought to be weak.[422]

This, no doubt, is the information Celia passed on to Orwell, along with the Foreign Office's refusal to contribute to the costs. Orwell proceeded to use the payments from *Der Monat* to subsidize publication and the book appeared in 1950.[423] His suspicions of the *Possev* people turned out to have some foundation. He had asked Ruth Fischer whether they were 'Whites'. They were indeed a strongly Christian group, and when the Russian translation appeared in 1950 it was censored. The character of Moses, the Raven, was largely expunged from the book. Moses 'was Mr Jones's especial pet', who used lies to keep the animals subservient. He preached of 'Sugarcandy Mountain, to which all animals went when they died'. There 'it was Sunday seven days a week, clover was in season all the year round, and lump sugar and linseed cake grew on the hedges'.[424] The *Possev* exiles were happy to publish a satire on the degeneration of revolution but not one that treated Christianity as a soporific for the oppressed.[425]

Though the IRD were not willing to fund the publication in book-form of a Russian *Animal Farm*, they were generally as keen as Orwell to see the book translated. On 4 November 1949 Celia Kirwan, on instruction from Adam Watson, wrote to Charles Thayer (the Director of the 'Voice of America' broadcasts) about translations both of *Animal Farm* and of *Nineteen Eighty-Four*, informing him of the impending Russian translation 'by an impoverished but respectable group of Russian refugees' ('but for various reasons we should like to keep this particular translation confidential for the moment'). She was clearly in communication with Orwell about all of this, noting in the letter that 'as far as Mr. Orwell remembers, "1984" is being translated into Italian, Swedish, Dutch, Danish, German and French. He has no idea in most cases whether the translations are satisfactory or not: the same applies to the translations of "Animal Farm"'. Of the latter a full list was enclosed with the letter. Against some of them, it was noted 'Mr. Orwell has given permission for translation into all these languages' – this applied to Korean, Hebrew, Bengali and Guajarati.[426] That Orwell was working happily with the IRD through Celia Kirwan is equally clear from

---

[422]TNA FO 1110/221.

[423]Orwell to Leonard Moore, 28 July 1949, CW, XX, p. 153; Orwell to Melvin Lasky, 21 September 1949, CW, XX, pp. 172–3.

[424]Orwell, *Animal Farm* (CW, VIII), pp. 10–11.

[425]Masha Karp, 'Orwell in Translation', *European Studies Blog*, 21 November 2017, https:// blogs.bl.uk/european/2017/11/orwell-in-translation.html (accessed 8 May 2020); Masha Karp, 'The Raven Vanishes', *The Orwell Society Journal*, no. 9 (December 2016), pp. 16–19.

[426]TNA FO 1110/221 contains Celia Kirwan's handwritten draft of the letter, with amendments, and the typescript. It is not clear what prompted the letter to Thayer.

the effort to produce an Arabic version of *Animal Farm* to be published in Cairo. On 4 April 1949 Ernest Main of the Information Office in the British Embassy, Cairo, wrote to the IRD expressing his enthusiasm for the 'relevance' of *Animal Farm* and suggesting translations. 'The idea is particularly good for Arabic in view of the fact that both pigs and dogs are unclean animals to Moslems.' Main made separate enquiries about the Egyptian copyright for the book. Adam Watson noted on the file (14 April) that there already were many translations. 'Has it ever been done in Arabic?' he pondered. 'In any case the more the merrier.' He added, 'Whatever does transpire, Mrs Kirwan might keep Mr Orwell in the picture.'[427] This was, of course, in the midst of the exchanges that led Orwell to supply the IRD with his list of crypto-Communists and fellow travellers. Celia Kirwan was the accepted go-between with Orwell, who was perfectly easy in working with the IRD to utilize his own work for the anti-Stalinist cause. He had no qualms about entering into a fight that soon became the cultural Cold War.[428] Celia Kirwan remained close to Orwell in the brief time left before he died. She must have been one of the very last people to speak to him, telling Koestler that 'she rang George up on Friday – as you know he died that night – and he sounded rather better than usual, & said that in fact he did feel better, & was rather excited to be going to Montana [Switzerland] – that was fixed for next Wednesday. I arranged to go & see him tomorrow after work. I know we shall both go on missing George for ever.'[429]

With Orwell dead, there was no one able to protect his intellectual integrity. As his writings were transformed into Cold War weapons, they were translated, transformed – and traduced.[430] That included his final book, *Nineteen Eighty-Four*, a final effort, not of despair but of desperation, to preserve freedom by the pen, a weapon that, notwithstanding his other activist endeavours, he wielded more effectively than any other.

---

[427]TNA FO 1110/221.

[428]In an extensive literature see especially Peter Coleman, *The Liberal Conspiracy: The Congress for Cultural Freedom and the Struggle for the Mind of Postwar Europe* (New York: Free Press, 1989); Frances Stonor Saunders, *Who Paid the Piper? The CIA and the Cultural Cold War* (London: Granta, 1999); Hugh Wilford, *The CIA, the British Left and the Cold War: Calling the Tune?* (London: Frank Cass / Routledge, 2003); and Hugh Wilford, *The Mighty Wurlitzer: How the CIA Played America* (Cambridge, MA: Harvard University Press, 2009).

[429]Celia Kirwan to Arthur Koestler, 21 January 1950, Edinburgh University Library, Koestler Papers, 2301/2/15.

[430]John Rodden, *The Politics of Literary Reputation: The Making and Claiming of 'St George' Orwell* (New York: Oxford University Press, 1989), ch. 5; Tony Shaw, '"Some Writers Are More Equal than Others": George Orwell, The State and Cold War Privilege', *Cold War History*, 4 (2003), pp. 143–70; Daniel J. Leab, *Orwell Subverted: The CIA and the Filming of Animal Farm* (University Park, PA: Pennsylvania State University Press, 2007); and Andrew N. Rubin, *Archives of Authority: Empire, Culture and the Cold War* (Princeton, NJ: Princeton University Press, 2012), ch. 2.

# 8. Freedom and Truth: *Nineteen Eighty-Four*

Late in May 1946 George Orwell left London, heading north to Barnhill, a farmstead on the island of Jura. There over several visits he would devote his time and his diminishing energies to writing a book that he had begun thinking about in earnest in 1943. The book had the working title *The Last Man in Europe*, and Orwell remained undecided between sticking to this title and adopting the one that it would eventually bear, *Nineteen Eighty-Four*, even as he was completing the typescript in October 1948.[431] In May 1946 Orwell was still working with Arthur Koestler to establish a new League for the Rights of Man. He was an activist for civil liberties, including intellectual freedoms, and seeking by word and deed to destroy the Soviet myth and preserve civilized liberal traditions. As he began writing his new novel on Jura,[432] Orwell constructed on the page a society in which those traditions had been destroyed beyond all hope of repair. It was not, though, a work of despair; it was a work of warning. This was what the world would become unless the sort of work that he and Koestler were doing was successful. If others did not see this and did not join in the defence of freedom, then there would come a point at which freedom was irrecoverably lost. That was the condition of Oceania's Airstrip One (the equivalent of Britain situated in an American empire) in *Nineteen Eighty-Four*. Orwell's own activism was undermined by his determination to finish his novel, though he no doubt believed that his pen was likely to be mightier than any other sword he could yield, as well as by his deteriorating health. But to the end, he thought the fight for freedom was one worth pursuing, however muted his hopes for its ultimate success might on occasion have been.

The intellectual framework for *Nineteen Eighty-Four* was largely in place as early as 1944. In a remarkable letter to Noel Willmett, Orwell delivered a sort of political *credo* that brought together many of the themes that he would explore in essays over the next few years, but did so in a way that unmistakably connected them to his final novel, still in an early stage of gestation. Willmett had asked Orwell whether he really believed that totalitarianism was (still) on the ascendant. This is a crucial question: would the imminent defeat of Hitler make the world safe for freedom or would the totalitarian threat

---

[431]Orwell to Fredric Warburg, 22 October 1948, CW, XIX, pp. 456–7. There is an early outline of the book, which *may* date from late 1943: see Appendix 2, 'Notes for ... "The Last Man in Europe"', CW, XV, pp. 356–61 (on the dating) & 367–9 (the notes). Also Crick, *George Orwell*, pp. 387–9, and in orig. ed. only, pp. 582–5. Orwell told a friend that the title was not 'definitively fixed' as late as February 1949: Orwell to Julian Symons, 4 February 1949, CW, XX, p. 35.

[432]Or, perhaps, continued writing: Orwell seems to have written a few pages of *Nineteen Eighty-Four* in June and July of 1945: Note by Fredric Warburg, 25 June 1945, CW, XVII, p. 178; Orwell to Leonard Moore, 3 July 1945, CW, XVII, pp. 207–8.

remain or even strengthen? *Nineteen Eighty-Four* was rooted in the second of these assessments of the post-war world. Hitler and Fascism might go, but this would only strengthen Stalin, 'the Anglo-American millionaires' (a reminder that there were aspects of Capitalist oligarchy that Orwell aligned with totalitarianism, another reason that Socialism and freedom needed one another), and 'all sorts of petty fuhrers', like de Gaulle. A fertile source of these petty fuhrers was 'national movements', each of which seemed bound to generate 'some superhuman fuhrer'. In addition to the obvious names, Orwell listed Salazar, Franco, Gandhi and De Valera. The trend was towards 'centralised economies' (Orwell sometimes used 'Socialism' to cover this trend towards collectivist planned economies, hence his view that Socialism in some form was inevitable), which were undemocratic and 'establish[ed] a caste system'. Along with it went 'emotional nationalism', which produced 'a tendency to disbelieve in the existence of objective truth because all the facts have to fit in with the words and prophecies of some infallible fuhrer'. Even now, 'history has in a sense ceased to exist' because there 'is no such thing as a history of our own times which could be universally accepted'. We should be wary of this point, of course: has there ever been a universally accepted history, outside of societies in which one is enforced? The sciences were a bit better off, in Orwell's view. Hitler could, if victorious, establish the belief that the Jews started the war, but 'he can't say that two and two are five' because military technology requires accuracy in such matters. *Nineteen Eighty-Four* would go one better. Doublethink – 'the power of holding two contradictory beliefs ... and accepting both of them' – allowed one to believe, when required to do so, that two and two did make five, while (some) could also believe that this didn't apply in specific domains of science and technology.[433] This, too, was prefigured in the letter: 'if the sort of world that I am afraid of arrives, a world of two or three great superstates which are unable to conquer one another, two and two could become five if the fuhrer wished it'. That is to say, in some political circumstances, reality could be safely denied.[434]

Orwell believed until he died that this is the way things were going. He wrote *Nineteen Eighty-Four* so that others would share his fear. But as the letter to Willmett and other writing makes clear, this was not a despairing defiance of the inevitable. He had shown 'the direction in which we are actually moving', but added that 'of course, the process is reversible'. England – or rather the English *people* (Orwell underlined the word) – had withstood the trend and he retained faith in their 'capacity to centralise their economy without destroying freedom'. But there were still obstacles

---

[433]Orwell, *Nineteen-Eighty-Four* [CW, IX] (London: Secker & Warburg, 1987), pp. 201–2, 222–3, 277–9 (Penguin ed. pp. 222–3, 243–5, 304–5). Orwell did not use the 2+2=5 example to explain doublethink, but the application is obvious.
[434]Orwell to Noel Willmett, 18 May 1944, CW, XVI, pp. 190–1.

to achieving this. These included 'the general indifference to the decay of democracy'. (Again, we may see *Nineteen Eighty-Four* as an attempt to end this indifference.) An even greater problem was 'the fact that the intellectuals are more totalitarian in outlook that the common people'. Certainly, England's intellectuals resisted Hitler's blandishments – but only to accept Stalin's instead. 'Most of them are perfectly ready for dictatorial methods, secret police, systematic falsification of history etc. so long as it is on "our" side.' The Inner Party – above all O'Brien – in *Nineteen Eighty-Four* is a satirical representation of the totalitarian intelligentsia. One has to hope that the common people won't go the same way. Ensuring this 'will be at the cost of a struggle'. In words that could be the rationale for writing *Nineteen Eighty-Four*, Orwell noted that 'if one simply proclaims that all is for the best and doesn't point to the sinister symptoms, one is merely helping to bring totalitarianism nearer'.[435]

In this struggle it was important to maintain what Orwell called elsewhere decency. He had alluded earlier in the letter to the central problem that he and Koestler were wrestling with: the dangerous attractions of the 'theory that the end justifies the means'. But avoiding means that corrupted ends did not imply an unworldly purity. He knew that the war against Fascism was imperfect, not least because those fighting it had failed to cast the mote from their own eyes, but nonetheless 'it is a choice of evils'. British imperialism was appalling, but Orwell would support it against Nazism or the imperialism of Japan 'as the lesser evil'. Even the USSR was worth supporting against the Nazis because it 'retains enough of the original ideas of the Revolution to make it a more hopeful phenomenon than Nazi Germany'. Even amongst totalitarianisms, there was still the choice of the lesser evil.[436]

Orwell's greatest fear from the mid-1940s onwards was that the triumph of Socialism, in some sense inevitable, would be in totalitarian and not in liberal form. The world of *Nineteen Eighty-Four* was one in which that fear had been realized. Each of the three super-states into which the world would be divided in 1984 was dominated by a collectivist ideology; each obliterated individualism. Eurasia was controlled by 'Neo-Bolshevism', Stalinism perpetuated; Eastasia had given collectivism an orientalist flavour, with an ideology 'usually translated as Death-Worship, but perhaps better rendered as Obliteration of the Self', while Oceania lay under the spell of Ingsoc.[437] Ingsoc was, of course, a contraction of English Socialism, which has led the unwary to suppose that Orwell had become anti-Socialist. But Ingsoc was Socialism that had fallen for the Soviet myth, the very thing that Orwell was seeking to rescue Socialism from. 'Ingsoc had developed ~~directly~~

---

[435]Orwell to Noel Willmett, 18 May 1944, CW, XVI, p. 191.
[436]Orwell to Noel Willmett, 18 May 1944, CW, XVI, p. 191.
[437]Orwell, *Nineteen Eighty-Four*, p. 205 (Penguin ed. p. 226).

out of the amalgamation of the Socialist & Communist movements.'[438] In that merger, Liberal Socialism – the true and original variety – had been obliterated. As Goldstein put it in *Nineteen Eighty-Four*, 'the Party rejects and vilifies every principle for which the Socialist movement originally stood, and it chooses to do this in the name of Socialism'.[439]

This Orwell had long feared. He built his dismal analysis of the post-war world from both his observations of the Tehran Conference of 1943, when Roosevelt, Churchill and Stalin met to divide the world amongst themselves, and his reading of James Burnham. Orwell's reading of Burnham, which is first evident in his writing in January 1944, was reflected in the letter to Willmett, with its reference to superstates. Two of Burnham's core ideas helped to shape the foundation for *Nineteen Eighty-Four*. One was the idea that modern societies were becoming neither Socialist nor democratic: they were evolving into managerialist oligarchies, totalitarian in nature, in which power rested with a managerial elite of 'business executives, technicians, bureaucrats, and soldiers', or, in a later summary, 'managers, scientists and bureaucrats'.[440] The second idea was that the world was evolving towards a condition that Orwell was the first to christen a Cold War: 'the earth is being parcelled off into three great empires, each self-contained and cut off from contact with the outer world, and each ruled, under one disguise or another, by a self-elected oligarchy'; each of these states would be 'at once *unconquerable* and in a permanent state of "cold war" with its neighbours'.[441] This was the world of *Nineteen Eighty-Four* – a world of seemingly permanent totalitarian stasis. Three superstates lived in a state of constant but low-level war; none could defeat either of the others, but the state of war helped them to control their own citizens. And these superstates – at least this was true of Oceania – had eliminated all internal causes of dissent and challenge. The Party's rule was total. They had perfectly implanted the principle that power existed for its own sake. Politics, as in Burnham's view, was never anything but 'the naked struggle for power' in which human equality and fraternity are no more than 'empty phrases'.[442] The irrationalism of this – the idea that power had no purpose but itself – was something of which Orwell was keenly aware as marking out the totalitarian world from previous tyrannies or despotisms. *Nineteen Eighty-Four* was the portrait of a society based nakedly on this

[438]Orwell, *Nineteen Eighty-Four: The Facsimile of the Extant Manuscript*, ed. Peter Davison (London: Secker & Warburg, 1984), p. 210.

[439]Orwell, *Nineteen Eighty-Four*, p. 225 (Penguin ed. p. 246).

[440]Orwell, 'Second Thoughts on James Burnham', 3 May 1946, CW, XVIII, p. 269; Orwell, 'Burnham's View of the Contemporary World Struggle', 29 March 1947, CW, XIX, p. 98.

[441]Orwell, 'You and the Atom Bomb', 19 October 1945, CW, XVII, pp. 320–1; also Orwell, 'As I Please' 57, 2 February 1945, CW, XVII, p. 39.

[442]Orwell, 'Review of *The Machiavellians*', CW, XVI, p. 73.

principle. Winston Smith, like Orwell, found it hard to imagine this sort of world. He supposed that perhaps the Party realized that 'the choice for mankind lay between freedom and happiness, and that, for the great bulk of mankind, happiness was better. That the party was the eternal guardian of the weak, a dedicated sect doing evil that good may come.' People could not 'endure liberty or face the truth' and had to be ruled for their own good.[443] The freedom and happiness dialectic shows Winston thinking like many of the dystopian writers Orwell was aware of – Huxley especially. These were hedonist utopias, as Orwell called them, and they displayed a world in which freedom was indeed traded for happiness. But the reality of Airstrip One was much worse, as O'Brien brutally revealed. 'The Party seeks power entirely for its own sake. We are not interested in the good of others; we are interested solely in power. Not wealth or luxury or long life or happiness: only power, pure power.' Even Nazis and Communists might have deluded themselves that they had taken power for a purpose 'and that just around the corner there lay a paradise where human beings would be free and equal'. The Party suffered from no such delusion. 'Power is not a means, it is an end. One does not establish a dictatorship in order to safeguard a revolution; one makes the revolution in order to establish the dictatorship.'[444] *Animal Farm*, which had been a reflection on Koestler's means-ends conundrum, had wrestled with just this question; but unlike O'Brien it left open the possibility of a genuinely liberating revolution, one in which people liberated themselves and avoided establishing a new ruling elite. Orwell never lost hope that such a revolution was ultimately possible, but he had an uncanny degree of insight into both the politics and the psychology of those who used revolutions as a route to their own empowerment and thus betrayed the revolutionary aspiration to freedom. The lesson of *Animal Farm* still applied: free yourself because no one else can be trusted to do so.

Orwell differed from Burnham in one thing that is absolutely crucial to how we read the political implications of *Nineteen Eighty-Four*. Though he agreed that Burnham's vision of the future was, indeed, the way that the world was tending, there was nothing *inevitable* about the outcome. Whereas Burnham had predicted, at least as Orwell understood him, certain victory for Germany in the war and the defeat of the Soviet Union, neither had come to pass.[445] His predictions were always a simple continuation of the present state of affairs, implying a sort of power worship.[446] Capitalism

---

[443]Orwell, *Nineteen Eighty-Four*, pp. 274–5 (Penguin ed. pp. 300–1).

[444]Orwell, *Nineteen Eighty-Four*, pp. 275–6 (Penguin ed. pp. 301–2).

[445]Orwell, 'As I Please' 7, 14 January, 1944, CW, XVI, pp. 60–1 (Burnham challenged Orwell's reading of his work; Orwell typically gave no ground, pp. 62–4); Orwell, 'Review of *The Machiavellians* by James Burnham', 20 January 1944, CW, XVI, pp. 72–4.

[446]Orwell, 'Second Thoughts on James Burnham', CW, XVIII, pp. 273–4, 277–8.

and Socialism were both doomed, and the best one could hope for was a sort of tempered totalitarianism in which a free press and trade unions might persist as forms of 'trickery', ways of 'manufacturing consent' to use a later phrase.[447] Orwell aligned this vision with the predictions of the dystopian writers who had also caught his attention over the years (Jack London, H.G. Wells, Yevgeny Zamyatin and Aldous Huxley). All of these writers, too, wrote of a future that was not Capitalist but not Socialist either. Sometimes this future was called Socialist, but it was Socialist in name only. Managerialism and other contemporary forms of collectivism were a betrayal of the original ideals of Socialism.[448] This is a familiar Orwellian theme and lay behind his fight against the 'Soviet mythos'. But Orwell did not think we were doomed to end up in this sort of world. It could be averted. We could skip 1984.

But how? In essays that he produced while writing *Nineteen Eighty-Four*, Orwell developed an alternative view of a possible future: 'to make democratic Socialism work' through the establishment of 'a Socialist United States' of Europe. The idea of a 'unified Europe', insofar as it has any currency, 'is associated with Churchill', Orwell wrote, but it could instead serve as an alternative to Burnham's vision of the inevitable absorption of Britain into an American Empire (Airstrip One and Oceania). Orwell was not a reflex anti-American: alliance with the United States was a (considerably) lesser evil than being overrun by Soviet Communism. But it still wasn't the future that Orwell had hoped for.[449] His fullest exploration of the possibility of a Socialist Europe was in an essay he contributed to a *Partisan Review* series on the future of Socialism, 'Toward European Unity', published soon after his last significant piece of writing on Burnham. The series, launched by Sidney Hook in the Winter 1947 issue, was to have included contributions from Koestler and Victor Serge, among others, but not all of them appeared. The essays were intended to confront the 'disorientation and political impotence' felt on the Left. Socialism had for a century 'provided both an optimistic view of and confidence in the possibility of establishing a rational human order'. No longer. The dream had been perverted by Stalinism, and the masses in the advanced Capitalist world seemed unable to appreciate the merits of true Socialism. So bad was the situation that 'many intellectuals had abandoned socialism altogether, asserting that freedom is compatible only with the economic structure of capitalism'.[450] This is just what Orwell

---

[447]Orwell, 'The Intellectual Revolt', 14 January 1946, CW, XVIII, p. 59; Edward S. Herman & Noam Chomsky, *Manufacturing Consent: The Political Economy of the Mass Media* (New York: Pantheon, 1988).

[448]Orwell, 'Second Thoughts on James Burnham', CW, XVIII, pp. 270–2.

[449]Orwell, 'Burnham's View of the Contemporary World Struggle', CW, XIX, pp. 103–4.

[450]Sidney Hook, 'The Future of Socialism', *Partisan Review*, 14:1 (Winter, 1947), p. 23 (Editor's Note).

would not do. A Socialism compatible with freedom '*can* be established', he believed, while admitting that 'the actual outlook ... is very dark'.[451] Future possibilities included the United States using its atomic weapons to destroy Russia; the continuation of Cold War until such time as the Russians also obtained the atom bomb and nuclear holocaust was unleashed, or (the Burnham option) the division of the world into two or three superstates, 'with a semidivine caste at the top and outright slavery at the bottom'. The only way of averting these dangers and of creating 'a community where people are relatively free and happy and where the main motive in life is not the pursuit of money or power' was to make democratic Socialism work on a significant scale. The only place where this was conceivable was Western Europe. It would require the European states to federate as 'socialist republics without colonial dependencies'. This was 'the only worthwhile political objective today'. And, though fiendishly difficult to achieve, 'we ought not to feel that it is of its nature impossible'.[452] The obstacles would be numerous – Russian and American hostility, the Catholic Church, which might try to co-operate with Socialists but would always be an enemy of free thought, above all the requirement to end colonialism and stop exploiting other peoples, without which Socialism could not be established but which might reduce the standard of living for the European working classes.[453] Not surprisingly, then, Orwell concluded that 'the appearance of a United States of Europe seems to me a very unlikely event', not least because there was no person or party with any chance of gaining power that would have the 'imaginative grasp' to bring it about. Nonetheless, it was the best hope there was, though Orwell did concede the faint possibility that even in the world of superstates 'the liberal tradition will be strong enough within the Anglo-American section of the world to make life tolerable and even offer some hope of progress'.[454]

A liberal Oceania was not an impossibility, but it would not come about by hope alone. The question we might bring from this to *Nineteen Eighty-Four* is to ask how the novel contributed to this cause; more broadly, what are the practical politics that could lead to the creation of a democratic Socialist future for a united Europe? To put it another way: how is freedom, especially intellectual freedom, going to survive? It is the most intractable aspect of the book. Clearly it is a warning, but it does not really suggest any way forward, so how should the warning be acted upon? Orwell's answer seems to be the one constituted by his own activism and his own attempt to forge a liberal Socialist culture. He was sincere and consistent in praising

[451]Orwell, 'Toward European Unity', July–August 1947, CW, XIX, pp. 163, 167.
[452]Orwell, 'Toward European Unity', CW, XIX, pp. 163–4.
[453]Orwell, 'Toward European Unity', CW, XIX, pp. 164–6.
[454]Orwell, 'Toward European Unity', CW, XIX, pp. 166–7.

the values of the common people, but he never translated them into a plan for engagement with working-class politics. His focus was on the writer and intellectual.

Horrifying as it was, the totalitarianism of Airstrip One was still not the complete product. In an essay written as he began to work on the book in earnest, Orwell distinguished two forms of totalitarianism. There was 'the spy-haunted "police State", with its endless heresy-hunts and treason trials, all really designed to neutralise popular discontent by changing it into war hysteria'.[455] This was the world of *Nineteen Eighty-Four*. The condition of perpetual war, the Two Minutes Hate, the relentless denunciation of Goldstein's heresy and pursuit of those who followed it, the risk of prison and torture, the boot stamping on the human face – totalitarianism at its most brutally effective. It was not all that there was to Air Strip One: sex, though joyless and regimented, cheap gin, even the love of Big Brother, satisfied more positive – or at least more basic – human needs. And that's just the party members. The proles were kept docile with cheap entertainment, cheap drink (beer, though they had easy access as well to the gin that was in theory denied to them[456]), sports, lotteries and more abundant (and presumably more enjoyable) sex. Even so, this society could only still aspire to 'the highest stage of totalitarian organisation, the stage when conformity has become so general that there is no need for a police force'.[457] Oceania was moving this way. Perhaps the boot would not need to stamp on the human face *forever*. Oceania was progressing towards this highest stage of totalitarianism through the perfection of Newspeak. Syme, working on the definitive eleventh edition of the Newspeak dictionary, tells Winston that he is not inventing or adding words but 'destroying' them. 'We're cutting the language down to the bone.' This 'destruction of words' was a 'beautiful thing'. Its purpose was clear: 'the whole aim of Newspeak is to narrow the range of thought ... we shall make thoughtcrime literally impossible, because there will be no words in which to express it'.[458] Syme – too enthusiastic for his own good, it would turn out – declared: 'The Revolution will be complete when the language is perfect.' (Is this another echo of Zamyatin's *We*, the book of someone else who loathed orthodoxy, promoted of heresy and doubted that revolutions could ever be completed – there would always be another one?) When this had been achieved then totalitarianism would reach its highest stage:

---

[455]Orwell, 'Politics vs. Literature: An Examination of *Gulliver's Travels*', September–October 1946, CW, XVIII, p. 423.

[456]Orwell, *Nineteen Eighty-Four*, p. 92 (Penguin ed. p. 101).

[457]Orwell, 'Politics vs. Literature', CW, XVIII, p. 425.

[458]Orwell, *Nineteen Eighty-Four*, pp. 53–5 (Penguin ed. pp. 59–60).

How could you have a slogan like 'freedom is slavery' when the concept of freedom has been abolished? The whole climate of thought will be different. In fact there will *be* no thought, as we understand it now. Orthodoxy means not thinking – not needing to think. Orthodoxy is unconsciousness.[459]

Syme's ecstatic account of what Newspeak could achieve was given more academic form in 'The Principles of Newspeak', the appendix to *Nineteen Eighty-Four*. Once Newspeak was fully adopted, 'a heretical thought ... should be literally unthinkable'.[460] This was achieved not by inventing new words, but especially by 'eliminating undesirable words and by stripping such words as remained of their unorthodox meanings'. A telling example was the word 'free'. In Newspeak you could still say that a dog was free from lice and a field free from weeds. But the word 'could not be used in its old sense of "politically free" or "intellectually free", since political and intellectual freedom no longer existed even as concepts, and were therefore of necessity nameless'. The point was 'to *diminish* the range of thought'.[461] Language would be reduced to three types of words: The A vocabulary covered quotidian activity (eating, dressing, cooking, working and so on). It was so pared back, literal and grammatically simple that it could not be used for literary, political or philosophical purposes.[462] The B vocabulary contained 'words which had been deliberately constructed for political purposes'. For example *goodthink*, 'meaning, very roughly, "orthodoxy"'.[463] Though the word 'free' would continue to exist, with much reduced range of meaning, other words would disappear, among them '*honour, justice, morality, internationalism, democracy, science* and *religion*'. They were replaced by a few 'blanket words', which, 'in covering them, abolished them'. Another telling example: 'the concepts of liberty and equality ... were contained in the single word *crimethink*', while words relating to objectivity and rationality were in the obliterating embrace of *oldthink*. The C vocabulary, made up of scientific and technical terms, might contain more specific words, but it was not for use by the ordinary citizen. [464] The result was that though a sort of blasphemy or heresy was possible in Newspeak (*Big Brother is ungood*), it was of this crude sort and could appear to most people only as absurd. You could say *all mans are equal* but the statement was as self-evidently absurd as saying that *all mans are redhaired*. Equal only meant identical (equal in length or height

[459]Orwell, *Nineteen Eighty-Four*, pp. 55–6 (Penguin ed. p. 61).
[460]Orwell, *Nineteen Eighty-Four*, p. 312 (Penguin ed. p. 343).
[461]Orwell, *Nineteen Eighty-Four*, p. 313 (Penguin ed. p. 344).
[462]Orwell, *Nineteen Eighty-Four*, pp. 313–14 (Penguin ed. pp. 344–5).
[463]Orwell, *Nineteen Eighty-Four*, pp. 316–17 (Penguin ed. p. 347).
[464]Orwell, *Nineteen Eighty-Four*, pp. 319, 322–3 (Penguin ed. pp. 349, 352–3).

or strength) and its older political sense no longer existed. All men are equal was no more than a linguistic mistake.[465]

Though there were euphemisms among the B words (*joycamp* for a concentration camp), one of the striking features of Oceania was that there was so little effort to conceal the way in which society worked. There was nothing to hide: oppression was in the open. As one scholar has put it, *Nineteen Eighty-Four* was 'a description of a world in which hypocrisy has become impossible'. The governing slogans of this society – war is peace, freedom is slavery, ignorance is strength – couldn't be plainer.[466] So it should not surprise that in Newspeak *prolefeed* was the term for 'the rubbish entertainment and spurious news which the Party handed out to the masses'.[467]

Orwell connected all of this to the linguistic corruptions that he had identified in his essays of 1945 and 1946 as an enabler and a consequence of the totalitarian mind. 'Even in the early decades of the twentieth century,' he reminded his readers, 'telescoped words and phrases had been one of the characteristic features of political language ... most marked in totalitarian countries and totalitarian organisations': Nazi, Gestapo, Agitprop. Words needed to be neutralized, so that their more dangerous connotations were avoided and then the word 'can be uttered almost without taking thought'. The example Orwell gave was *Comintern*. Unlike the full phrase 'Communist International', this word did away with the risk that using it might 'call up a composite picture of universal human brotherhood, red flags, barricades, Karl Marx and the Paris Commune'.[468] Orwell's use of examples reminds us of two things. *Nineteen Eighty-Four* was a continuation of the polemic against Western Communist intellectuals and their corruption of political culture as much as it was aimed at the actually existing totalitarian regimes. And Orwell continued to value the ideals of universal brotherhood that were at the heart of Socialism, and even of the thought of Marx, and which Ingsoc obliterated. The attack on left-wing intellectuals adds an element of grim humour to Orwell's satire too: 'it was hoped to make articulate speech issue from the larynx without involving the higher brain centres at all. This aim was frankly admitted in the Newspeak word *duckspeak*, meaning "to quack like a duck"', a term of praise for speakers of orthodoxy. It was to deny *doubleplusgood duckspeakers* too accessible a platform that Orwell gave his notorious list to the Information Research Department.[469]

---

[465]Orwell, *Nineteen Eighty-Four*, pp. 323–4 (Penguin ed. pp. 353–4).
[466]David Runciman, *Political Hypocrisy: The Mask of Power, from Hobbes to Orwell and beyond* (Princeton, NJ: Princeton University Press, 2008), p. 186.
[467]Orwell, *Nineteen Eighty-Four*, pp. 319–20 (Penguin ed. pp. 350).
[468]Orwell, *Nineteen Eighty-Four*, pp. 320–1 (Penguin ed. pp. 350–1).
[469]Orwell, *Nineteen Eighty-Four*, p. 322 (Penguin ed. p. 352).

When Newspeak was brought to perfection, the final hold that the reality of the past might have on the present would disappear. Already, history was rewritten (repeatedly). That was Winston Smith's job. The triumph of Newspeak would also destroy the literature of the past. Some of it might survive in Newspeak translation, which would be simplified and ideologically transformed, though it is hard to imagine what some of the authors Orwell listed as undergoing translation might look like in Newspeak – Shakespeare, Milton, Swift, Dickens. (It seems that the Party at least had a similar taste in literature to Orwell's own.) But as Oldspeak faded from memory, the original works would become entirely unintelligible. They would, in any case, be obliterated.[470]

Orwell's account of Newspeak as the triumph of orthodoxy and the obliteration of freedom of thought, heresy, and all dissent is a bitter satire. Be careful what you wish for, he told the intellectual friends of totalitarianism. And especially the friends of Soviet Communism, better at cloaking their illiberalism than Fascists had ever been. Satire of this sort does not altogether rely on being plausible. Intended to reveal the hidden impetus behind things already happening, *Nineteen Eighty-Four* does not have to convince as a realizable dystopia. This is fortunate. The theory of language that underpins Orwell's account of Newspeak, and is also implied by parts of 'Politics and the English Language', is hardly tenable, resting as it does on a most implausible view of the power of linguistic fiat alone to reconstitute reality and determine thought.[471]

The bleak ending of *Nineteen Eighty-Four* was planned from the start. In his 1943 notes Orwell gave two summaries of the novel's final section. Take your pick between 'the final consciousness of failure' and 'recognition of own insanity'.[472] Whatever Orwell thought that he might have 'ballsed up' in writing the book, it wasn't the hopelessness of its ending.[473] The notes that Orwell made in 1948, as preparation it seems for the final revisions to his typescript, highlighted the starkness of the message. *Nineteen Eighty-Four* suggests two possibilities of political resistance, aside from Winston's attempts to maintain an inner life: hope lies in the proles (working-class revolt), and revolution (led) from the waist down (the subversive power of sexuality, the personal made political). Both of these possibilities are ruthlessly undermined in both the 1948 notes and the finished book. On the proles, Orwell's notes for revisions to Part 1, section 7, record: 'If there

---

[470]Orwell, *Nineteen Eighty-Four*, p. 325 (Penguin ed. p. 355).

[471]See the excellent discussion in Stefan Collini, 'When George Met Bill: Orwell, Empson, and the Language of Propaganda', *Modern Intellectual History* (2020), pp. 1–22.

[472]Orwell, 'Notes for ... "The Last Man in Europe"', CW, XV, p. 368.

[473]'I ballsed it up rather, partly owing to being so ill': Orwell to Julian Symons, 4 February 1949, CW, XX, p. 35.

is hope. And yet – why shd. they revolt? Perfectly satisfied.'[474] The same notebook also asks, with respect to Part 1, section 6, whether Winston's 'longing for a woman of his own' might imply the 'connection in his mind between sexuality & rebellion?'[475] His notes for the final section of the book dismiss the key rationale that the book advances for the connection, namely that sexual relationships create a private space of human communication that is beyond the surveillance of Big Brother. It is a space of shared inwardness. But this space was not inviolate. 'They can't get inside you – but they can,' Orwell would show. His notes picked out the key lessons of the final meeting of Julia and Winston: 'He had seen her (nobody cared now). By accident ... Arm around waist (didn't matter now) ... "I betrayed you".'[476]

If this is all so, then where in *Nineteen Eighty-Four* does the hope for freedom lie? Nowhere. The last man in Europe – the last humanist intellectual – would soon die and with him would die the hope of freedom. Even before death, he had been crushed by the totalitarianism that he resisted in vain. Winston Smith represented the last intellectual of the old order; the last person willing and able to dissent from the intellectual collectivism of Airstrip One.[477] In the statement that he gave to Fredric Warburg about the meaning of *Nineteen Eighty-Four*, Orwell denied that the book was an attack on Socialism or on the Labour government of Clement Attlee. But he did distinguish within the Labour party between an older generation 'nurtured in a Liberal tradition' and a more 'suspect' younger one, among whom 'the seeds of totalitarian thought are probably widespread'.[478] Winston, like Orwell himself, represented this older generation of liberal Socialists who defended the values of a European humanism rooted in the 'need for free intellectual interchange'.[479]

Ostensibly, then, there were two sources of resistance, and therefore of hope, in *Nineteen Eighty-Four* – the proles and sexual (more broadly,

---

[474]'Orwell's Second Literary Notebook', 1948, CW, XIX, p. 515.
[475]'Second ... Notebook', CW, XIX, p. 516.
[476]'Second ... Notebook', CW, XIX, p. 506.
[477]On Winston Smith as the last humanist, see especially Ian Watt, 'Winston Smith: The Last Humanist', in Peter Stansky (ed.), *On Nineteen Eighty-Four* (Stanford, CA: Stanford Alumni Association, 1983), ch. 13; also David Dwan, 'Orwell and Humanism', in Nathan Waddell (ed.), *The Cambridge Companion to Nineteen Eighty-Four* (Cambridge: Cambridge University Press, 2020), ch. 4. Patrick Reilly, '*Nineteen Eighty-Four*: The Failure of Humanism', *Critical Quarterly*, 24 (1982), pp. 19–30 suggests that the book demonstrates the limitations of secular humanism altogether, and leaves only a theistic response to totalitarianism possible.
[478]Orwell, 'Statement on *Nineteen Eighty-Four*', June 1949, CW, XX, pp. 134–5. Though cf. Warburg's notes on which this statement was based: Fredric Warburg, *All Authors Are Equal: The Publishing Life of Fredric Warburg 1936–1971* (London: Hutchinson, 1973), pp. 118–19.
[479]Watt, 'Winston Smith: The Last Humanist', pp. 110–11.

natural) drives. The book, as I have suggested, exposes both sources of hope as delusionary. During the novel, Winston several times tells us that hope lay with the proles. It is a thought that he first confided to his diary but cannot thereafter get out of his head. Hope '*must*' lie in the proles 'because only there, in those swarming disregarded masses, 85 per cent of the population of Oceania, could the force to destroy the party ever be generated'. It could never 'be overthrown from within'.[480] This sounds more like denial than hope. Nonetheless, 'the words kept coming back to him' – but as the 'statement of a mystical truth and a palpable absurdity'.[481] Still, 'You had to cling on to' the thought. 'When you put it in words it sounded reasonable: it was when you looked at the human beings passing you on the pavement that it became an act of faith.'[482] Winston believed that this was the message of Goldstein's book, which had been given to him to read by O'Brien. The book, *The Theory and Practice of Oligarchical Collectivism*, was an historical and critical analysis of Oceania, exposing the reality behind the Party's slogans – ignorance is strength, war is peace.[483] It was, or so Winston believed, the textbook for a resistance movement, the Brotherhood; O'Brien later claimed that the book was fraudulent and written by the Party itself. Winston's final musings on it, just before his arrest, were:

> If there was hope, it lay in the proles! Without reading to the end of *the book*, he knew that that must be Goldstein's final message. The future belonged to the proles. And could he be sure that when their time came the world they constructed would not be just as alien to him, Winston Smith, as the world of the Party? Yes, because at the least it would be a world of sanity. Where there is equality there can be sanity. Sooner or later it would happen, strength would change into consciousness ... In the end their awakening would come.[484]

But Winston's own experience of the proles fits better with O'Brien's verdict:

> The proletarians will never revolt, not in a thousand years or a million. They cannot. I do not have to tell you the reason: you know it already. If you have ever cherished any dreams of violent insurrection, you must abandon them. There is no way in which the Party can be overthrown. The rule of the Party is for ever.[485]

---

[480]Orwell, *Nineteen Eighty-Four*, p. 72 (Penguin ed. p. 80).

[481]Orwell, *Nineteen Eighty-Four*, p. 85 (Penguin ed. p. 95).

[482]Orwell, *Nineteen Eighty-Four*, p. 89 (Penguin ed. p. 99).

[483]Orwell, *Nineteen Eighty-Four*, pp. 191–2 (Penguin ed. pp. 213–14).

[484]Orwell, *Nineteen Eighty-Four*, p. 229 (Penguin ed. pp. 251–2).

[485]Orwell, *Nineteen Eighty-Four*, p. 274 (Penguin ed. p. 300).

Winston clearly does know this already. Orwell made this abundantly clear. One balmy April evening Winston Smith decided after work to go for a walk, all the while fretting that his preference for solitude or *ownlife* over another evening at the Community Centre would land him in trouble. He recalled the words he had written in his diary – 'if there is hope it lies in the proles'. But the portrait of the proles he encounters on his walk gives little justification for this hope. They 'swarmed' – an inhuman word – 'girls in full bloom, with crudely lipsticked mouths, and youths who chased the girls, and swollen waddling women who showed you what the girls would be like in ten years time, and old bent creature shuffling along on splayed feet, and ragged barefooted children who played in the puddles and then scattered at angry yells from their mothers'.[486] This was a world in which little changed, except that you got older. A rocket bomb hits. Someone is killed, but soon 'the sordid swarming life of the streets was going on as though nothing had happened'. The pubs were full and Winston saw a group of men arguing earnestly over a newspaper story. 'They were talking about the lottery ... the one public event to which the proles paid serious attention.' For many it was 'the principal if not the only reason for remaining alive'. 'It was their delight, their folly, their anodyne, their intellectual stimulant.'[487] No wonder that Winston needs to reaffirm his beliefs, though now in more desperate terms. 'But if there was hope it lay in the proles. You had to cling on to that. When you put it in words it sounded reasonable: it was when you looked at the human beings passing you on the pavement that it became an act of faith.'[488] Winston's walk took him to another pub where, amidst more discussion of the lottery and a game of darts, he talks to an old man, eighty or so. Here was someone who would have been alive before the Revolution, and able to compare life then with that of the present. 'Were things better then than they are now, or were they worse?', Winston might ask him. The conversation gets nowhere, as Winston probes the old man to find out whether the oppression by capitalists had been worse than his current life. Did he have more freedom in the past? 'A sense of hopelessness took hold of Winston. The old man's memory was nothing but a rubbish heap of details. One could question him all day without getting any real information. The Party histories might still be true, after a fashion: they might even be completely true.' The perspective of the Proles gave no leverage over the world: they lived for immediate pleasures. Winston tried one more time – would the old man prefer to live before or after the Revolution? The answer he got was purely personal. It was about ageing, the advantages of youth versus those of old age. The former are obvious enough. 'On the other

---

[486]Orwell, *Nineteen Eighty-Four*, pp. 85–6 (Penguin ed. pp. 94–5).
[487]Orwell, *Nineteen Eighty-Four*, pp. 86–9 (Penguin ed. pp. 97–8).
[488]Orwell, *Nineteen Eighty-Four*, p. 89 (Penguin ed. p. 99).

'and there's great advantages in being a old man. You ain't got the same worries. No truck with women, and that's a great thing. I ain't 'ad a woman for near on thirty year, if you'd credit it. Nor wanted to, what's more'.[489]

Winston's verdict on this experience confirmed O'Brien's cynicism rather than his own faith. Even those proles who should have been able to remember a better world, and perhaps to gain from that memory the hope of getting something better than what they had now, were unable to do so.

> Within twenty years at the most, he reflected, the huge and simple question, 'Was life better before the Revolution than it is now?' would have ceased once and for all to be answerable. But in effect it was unanswerable even now, since the few scattered survivors from the ancient world were incapable of comparing one age with another. They remembered a million useless things, a quarrel with a workmate, a hunt for a lost bicycle pump, the expression on a long-dead sister's face, the swirls of dust on a windy morning seventy years ago: but all the relevant facts were outside the range of their vision. They were like the ant, which can see small objects but not large ones. And when memory failed and written records were falsified – when that happened, the claim of the Party to have improved the conditions of human life had to be accepted, because there did not exist, and never could again exist, any standard against which it could be tested.[490]

In all but its ideological valency, this was the world of 'capitalist realism', a world in which an abusive social and economic order can persist simply because no alternative to it is imaginable.[491]

Throughout *Nineteen Eighty-Four*, Winston Smith remains ever alert to the possibilities of resistance. His job, of course, was to alter the evidential record of the past so that it confirmed to current orthodoxy. No record that could challenge the veracity of the orthodox or official view could ever be allowed to exist, even if this meant near perpetual alteration of the record. 'The mutability of the past is the central tenet of Ingsoc.'[492] He mused to Julia at one point that perhaps he might have hung on to a yellowing photograph clipped from the *Times* that proved the existence of three early leaders of the Revolution, Jones, Aaronson and Rutherford, since obliterated from the

[489]Orwell, *Nineteen Eighty-Four*, pp. 90–6 (Penguin ed. pp. 99–106).
[490]Orwell, *Nineteen Eighty-Four*, pp. 96–7 (Penguin ed. pp. 106–7).
[491]Mark Fisher, *Capitalist Realism: Is There No Alternative?* (Winchester: Zero Books, 2009). For a powerful account of the importance of remembering a different past in order to be able to conceive a different future see Steve Fraser, *The Age of Acquiescence: The Life and Death of American Resistance to Organized Wealth and Power* (New York: Basic Books, 2015).
[492]Orwell, *Nineteen Eighty-Four*, p. 222 (Penguin ed. p. 243).

historical record, like those old Bolsheviks who, once purged, were removed from photographs in which they had appeared alongside Lenin or Stalin.[493] He tells Julia:

> Already we know almost literally nothing about the Revolution and the years before the Revolution. Every record has been destroyed or falsified, every book has been re-written, every picture has been repainted, every statue and street and building has been re-named, every date has been altered. And that process is continuing day by day and minute by minute. History has stopped. Nothing exists except an endless present in which the Party is always right. I *know*, of course, that the past is falsified, but it would never be possible for me to prove it, even when I did the falsification myself. After the thing is done, no evidence ever remains. The only evidence is inside my own mind, and I don't know with any certainty that any other human being shares my memories. Just in that one instance, in my whole life, I did possess actual concrete evidence *after* the event – years after it.[494]

But Julia was not interested. Keeping it would have been dangerous, and what use would it have been anyway? 'Not much, perhaps,' Winston replied. 'But it was evidence. It might have planted a few doubts here and there … I don't imagine that we can alter anything in our own lifetime. But one can imagine little knots of resistance springing up here and there – small groups of people banding themselves together, and gradually growing and even leaving a few records behind, so that the next generation can carry on where we leave off.' Julia will have none of this. 'I am not interested in the next generation, dear. I'm interested in *us*.'[495]

'You're only a rebel from the waist downwards,' Winston tells her. Her resistance to the Party was for her own pleasure and lust; natural instinct not political or ethical principle was the drive. This second potential source of resistance to the iron rule of the Party is not as separate from the first as it might seem, for Julia's capacity to live in the moment is one that she shared with the proles.[496] Could desire, the instinct for pleasure, be the fuel

---

[493]See David King, *The Commissar Vanishes: The Falsification of Photographs and Art in Stalin's Russia* (London: Tate, new ed. 2014).

[494]Orwell, *Nineteen Eighty-Four*, pp. 161–2 (Penguin ed. pp. 177–8). Winston later learns from O'Brien that the evidence did survive – it made no difference: *Nineteen Eighty-Four*, pp. 258–9 (Penguin ed. pp. 282–3).

[495]Orwell, *Nineteen Eighty-Four*, pp. 162–3 (Penguin ed. p. 179).

[496]Evelyn Waugh perceived the link immediately: 'it was false. To me, that the form of his [Winston's] revolt should simply be fucking in the style of lady Chatterley – finding reality though a sort of mystical union with the Proles in the sexual act' (Waugh to Orwell, 17 July 1949, in George Orwell, *Nineteen Eighty-Four: A Novel*, ed. D.J. Taylor (London: Constable, 2021), p. 344).

of rebellion? For Julia it was. Her rebellion might have been apolitical, but it was still dangerous because it was rooted in drives that the Party could not control. Who could know what these drives might lead to?

Just before he and Julia are betrayed and arrested, they are looking out of the window at a fifty-year-old prole woman whose body was 'blown up to monstrous dimensions by childbearing, then hardened, roughened by work till it was coarse in the grain like an over-ripe turnip'. She was beautiful he thought, her body 'bore the same relation to the body of a girl as the rose-hip to the rose'. 'She's beautiful,' he told Julia, who replied 'She's a metre across the hips, easily'. That, said Winston, 'is her style of beauty'. Winston recognized that Julia was different in the sense that she could have no children, but had she been a prole her youth and beauty would follow the same course as that of the woman in the courtyard. 'The woman down there had no mind, she had only strong arms, a warm heart and a fertile belly.'[497] She represented the possibility of rebellion, from the neck down in this case: it is indicative of Orwell's deeply misogynistic assumptions that mindlessness is incarnated female.[498] Nonetheless, for this woman, Winston felt a 'mystical reverence'. He imagined women like her across the planet, 'people who had never learned to think but who were storing up in their hearts and bellies and muscles the power that would one day overturn the world. If there was hope, it lay in the proles!'[499] What made Julia potentially dangerous to the Party was that she too represented an uncontrollable carnality. The divorce of this carnality from fertility might in itself suggest its impotence.

But, in any case, Orwell went out of his way again to close off the suggestion that much hope really lay in this direction. If there is hope, Winston says again. A big if. In the sustained destruction of Winston's spirit and hopes that takes place in the final part of the book, O'Brien tells him that the Party has dedicated itself to the obliteration of bodily pleasure, especially the orgasm. The 'hedonistic Utopias' that people had imagined

---

[497]Orwell, *Nineteen Eighty-Four*, pp. 228–9 (Penguin ed. pp. 250–1).

[498]There is, not surprisingly, an extensive and valuable feminist literature on this topic, of which highlights might include: Elaine Hoffman Baruch, '"The Golden Country": Sex and Love in *1984*', in Irving Howe (ed.), *1984 Revisited: Totalitarianism in Our Century* (New York: Perennial / Harper & Row, 1983), ch. 3; Daphne Patai, *The Orwell Mystique: A Study in Male Ideology* (Amherst, MA: University of Massachusetts Press, 1984), ch. 8; Deirde Beddoe, 'Hindrances and Help-Meets: Women in the Writings of George Orwell', in Christopher Norris (ed.), *Inside the Myth – Orwell: Views from the Left* (London: Lawrence & Wishart, 1984), pp. 139–54; Blu Tirohl, '"We Are the Dead ... You Are the Dead": An Examination of Sexuality as a Weapon of Revolt in Orwell's *Nineteen Eighty-Four*', *Journal of Gender Studies*, 9:1 (2000), pp. 55–61; and Thomas Horan, 'Revolutions from the Waist Downwards: Desire as Rebellion in Yevgeny Zamyatin's *We*, George Orwell's *1984*, and Aldous Huxley's *Brave New World*', *Extrapolation*, 48:2 (2007), pp. 314–39.

[499]Orwell, *Nineteen Eighty-Four*, p. 229 (Penguin ed. p. 251).

(and which had long been the object of Orwell's scorn) sketched a future that was the opposite of the way things were tending. The links that bound parent and child, man and women, in sympathy were being broken.

> But in the future there will be no wives and no friends. Children will be taken from their mothers at birth, as one takes eggs from a hen. The sex instinct will be eradicated. Procreation will be an annual formality like the renewal of a ration card. We shall abolish the orgasm. Our neurologists are at work on it now. There will be no loyalty, except loyalty towards the Party. There will be no love, except the love of Big Brother. There will be no laughter, except the laugh of triumph over a defeated enemy. There will be no art, no literature, no science. When we are omnipotent we shall have no more need of science. There will be no distinction between beauty and ugliness. There will be no curiosity, no enjoyment of the process of life. All competing pleasures will be destroyed.

All that will be left is 'the intoxication of power', the 'boot stamping on a human face – forever'.[500] We might be tempted to view this as insane, in itself a sign that the society of *Nineteen Eighty-Four* could never be brought to the perfection that it might need if it were to ensure forever. Winston says as much. He *knows* that this ambition must fail. But O'Brien mocks.

> You are imagining that there is something called human nature which will be outraged by what we do and will turn against us. But we create human nature. Men are infinitely malleable. Or perhaps you have returned to your old idea that the proletarians or the slaves will arise and overthrow us. Put it out of your mind. They are helpless, like the animals.

O'Brien plausibly exploits Winston's own understanding of the proles (and Julia) as mindless and animalistic. This should not be understood as Orwell's own view. But within the closed world of the novel, it constitutes game, set and match.

O'Brien does not just assert these claims: he demonstrates them. The beatings, O'Brien's relentless exposure of his illusions, and the rats of Room 101, lead Winston to accept the false as true. Released, the last man in Europe is a man no more. He sits in the Chestnut Tree Café, tracing in the dust on his table 2+2=5.[501] Julia had once said, 'It's the one thing they can't do. They can

---

[500]Orwell, *Nineteen Eighty-Four*, p. 280 (Penguin ed. pp. 306–7).
[501]Orwell, *Nineteen Eighty-Four*, p. 303 (Penguin ed. p. 334). In the second impression of the English edition of the book (1950), and many printings thereafter the '5' was dropped from this and so Winston wrote only '2+2 = '. Some have speculated that this might have been deliberate and reflected a last-minute change of heart on Orwell's part, keeping alive the possibility that Winston's independence of mind had not been altogether destroyed. However,

make you say anything – *anything* – but they can't make you believe it. They can't get inside you.' Winston agreed. 'If you can *feel* that staying human is worth while, even when it can't have any result whatever, you've beaten them.'[502] The inner self, the emotions and the desires were inviolable. Therein, hope and humanity resided. But these final delusions – of the heart and body not the mind – were cruelly destroyed at the end. '"They can't get inside you," she had said. But they could get inside you.'[503] In his last meeting with Julia, Winston's 'flesh froze with horror' at the thought of having sex with her; she gave him a look of dislike. He noted her stiffening waist.[504] Was she going the way of the prole woman? Winston and Julia matter-of-factly admitted to betraying one another – and meaning it. Desire and emotion were eradicated. A little later Winston remembered a happy afternoon with his mother. But he cast it aside. 'It was a false memory. He was troubled by false memories occasionally. They did not matter so long as one knew them for what they were.'[505] As we have seen, Orwell from the start designed *Nineteen Eighty-Four* as a demonstration of the fact that they could get inside you. Rebellion from the waste down, the rebellion of desire and love, was in that case no more likely to succeed than the rebellion of the mind.

Margaret Atwood has famously claimed that the very last thing in *Nineteen Eighty-Four* is the place where hope resides. This was the appendix on 'The Principles of Newspeak', which we have already examined. As Atwood puts it, 'the essay on Newspeak is written in standard English, in the third person, and in the past tense, which can only mean that the regime had fallen, and that the language and individuality have survived'.[506] Did Orwell perhaps understand that the vision behind Newspeak was insane, and that the revolution could never be perfected? Perfect totalitarianism was impossible; imperfect totalitarianism would contain the seeds of its own destruction. This would be an attractive reading of the novel. It would render the book an endorsement of the ineradicable aspiration to freedom, and affirm the power of this aspiration to defeat totalitarianism in the long

---

a printer's error seems more likely. George Orwell, *Nineteen Eighty-Four*, Critical Introduction and Annotations by Bernard Crick (Oxford: Oxford University Press, 1984), pp. 448–9; Dennis Glover, 'Did George Orwell secretly rewrite the end of *Nineteen Eighty-Four* as he lay dying?', *Sydney Morning Herald*, 1 June 2017, https://www.smh.com.au/entertainment/books/did-george-orwell-secretly-rewrite-the-end-of-nineteen-eightyfour-as-he-lay-dying-20170613-gwqbom.html (accessed 31 May 2022). For an overview of the matter see Darcy Moore, '2+2= ', https://www.darcymoore.net/2020/03/07/22/ (accessed 31 May 2022).

[502]Orwell, *Nineteen Eighty-Four*, p. 174 (Penguin ed. p. 192).

[503]Orwell, *Nineteen Eighty-Four*, p. 303 (Penguin ed. p. 334).

[504]Orwell, *Nineteen Eighty-Four*, p. 303 (Penguin ed. pp. 334–8).

[505]Orwell, *Nineteen Eighty-Four*, pp. 304–7 (Penguin ed. pp. 340–1).

[506]Margaret Atwood, 'George Orwell: Some Personal Connections', in Atwood, *Curious Pursuits: Occasional Writing* (London: Virago, 2005), ch. 41, Kindle ed. 2009, loc. 5067. For a brilliant reading of the novel, more in keeping with Atwood's view than with mine, see Gregory Claeys, *Dystopia: A Natural History* (Oxford: Oxford UP, 2017), ch. 17.

run. But it is hard to square either with what Orwell wrote in *Nineteen Eighty-Four* or with the ideas that he held when writing it. If Orwell was, in Atwood's terms, signalling his 'faith in the resilience of the human spirit', then he chose to go about it in an odd way.[507] *Nineteen Eighty-Four* was designed from the start to close off all possibility of successful resistance to the control exercised by the Inner Party. The hope vested in the proles was a sign of *desperation*: clearly, if that was all the hope there was, nothing was going to change any time soon. That final appendix was indeed written in the past tense, but what is there to say that the regime had fallen? And even if it had, perhaps it had been replaced by one that had perfected the tyranny that had eluded Oceania. There is, of course, the fact that the appendix was itself written in Oldspeak, but perhaps the scholars of that new regime enjoyed the task of retrofitting such an appendix to Orwell's book, which would, of course, have been available, like Goldstein's, only to the selected few who could see it for what it was (and those whom they wished to destroy). The closing words of the book and the appendix – 'it was chiefly in order to allow time for the preliminary work of translation that the final adoption of Newspeak had been fixed for so late a date as 2050' – might suggest that the appendix was written after that date by Oceania's scholars, or by those of its perfected successor regime, looking back on how the final obliteration of all heterodoxy had been achieved, and with the confidence to write in an Oldspeak now no more threatening than ancient Greek.

\* \* \* \* \* \*

'Freedom is the freedom to say that two plus two make four,' Winston Smith confided to his diary. 'If that is granted, all else follows.'[508] Freedom, on this showing, is not so much having the right to say whatever you think than it is being able to speak the truth. Orwell's key objective during the later 1940s was to combat the totalitarian corruption of mind. Drawing upon decades of reading and conversation about Nazism and Stalinism, he was able to build a frightening picture of what a totalitarian tyranny could look like at its worst, but his immediate concern was the way in which those who sympathized with Stalin were betraying the legacy of a liberal and humanist Socialism. It was what was happening – what might happen – inside England and other capitalist democracies that was at the heart of his fear, more than what the continuing advances of Stalin might threaten from the outside. If England succumbed to totalitarianism, it would be English people that brought it about. And they would do so primarily by ceasing to respect the primacy of truth-seeking. The corruption of language and thought, the

---

[507]Atwood, 'George Orwell', Kindle loc. 5067.
[508]Orwell, *Nineteen Eighty-Four*, p. 84 (Penguin ed. p. 93).

destruction of memory, the manipulation of evidence would create a world in which truth was whatever those with power said it was. 'Whatever the Party holds to be truth, *is* truth', O'Brien proclaims.[509] We would all, I think, prefer Winston's view that 'being in a minority, even a minority of one, did not make you mad. There was truth and there was untruth, and if you clung to the truth even against the whole world, you were not mad.'[510] If that is what we want, we have to make it so.

*Nineteen Eighty-Four* capped half a decade that Orwell dedicated above all else to preserving intellectual freedom. In his work, three things are prominent. A commitment to **freedom of speech** and thought that was, if not absolute, then *maximalist*. People had the right to say what they thought, however unpopular. But this was not enough. There was also a requirement, particularly for writers and thinkers, with whom Orwell was most concerned, for **intellectual responsibility**, which amounted to the acceptance of a duty to seek and to speak the truth, as one saw it. It amounted to intellectual honesty and decency. Of course, people would not agree with one another. A free society would be one in a state of chronic intellectual conflict. What mattered was that all parties must share an honest search for the truth. The final feature of Orwell's work was **activism**, the recognition that the things that he valued would not be maintained without a fight. He forged an identity as an 'activist journalist', forging new forms of journalism in the process.[511] But, as this book has shown, he also dedicated as much time as writing and illness allowed to defending intellectual freedom through organizations like the Freedom Defence Committee, and developed with Arthur Koestler even greater ambitions to establish a League for the Dignity and Rights of Man. *Nineteen Eighty-Four* was a key part of this activism. Orwell began writing it in earnest just as the plans for the League were faltering. It constitutes an argument for activism in the defence of intellectual freedom. Orwell's faith in the 'common people' (see the epigraph to Part Two of the present book) was more a stick with which to chastise intellectuals than it was practical politics, though that does not make Orwell insincere. He really did believe in the good sense of ordinary people.[512] Winston Smith's faith in the proles also served to reveal the contrast with the Party's intellectuals, who unlike the common people had lost touch with their humanity. In a world empty even of the last man in Europe, though, the political agency of the proles itself was lost.

---

[509]Orwell, *Nineteen Eighty-Four*, p. 261 (Penguin ed. p. 285).

[510]Orwell, *Nineteen Eighty-Four*, p. 226 (Penguin ed. p. 247).

[511]Richard Lance Keeble, *Journalism beyond Orwell: A Collection of Essays* (London: Routledge, 2020), Part One.

[512]In addition to work cited (notably Newsinger), see Peter Goodall, 'Common Decency and the Common People in the Writing of George Orwell', *Durham University Journal*, 52:1 (1991), pp. 75–83.

*Nineteen Eighty-Four* is neither pessimistic nor optimistic; it is *urgent*. Whether the totalitarian world that it conjured into being would come to pass was entirely dependent on whether the book's readers could be brought to share its urgency. Sure, the totalitarianism of Oceania was not perfected. Perhaps it would be superseded by something even more monstrous; perhaps, as Margaret Atwood suggests, the book does at least gesture to the ultimate collapse of the Oceanic tyranny. Nothing lasts forever but that is little consolation to those who suffer in the meantime. The hope that infuses the book – a hope for a world that fosters the pleasures of sex and nature, of solitude and fellowship, of freedom and individuality, of truth-seeking – is a hope for the present. Whatever the odds, Orwell told his reader, you must act in hope to prevent the worst from happening now. Rebecca Solnit appositely quotes Octavia Butler: 'the very act of trying to look ahead to discern possibilities and offer warnings is in itself an act of hope'.[513] Winston Smith's diary was kept to honour the principle that 'it was not by making yourself heard but by staying sane that you carried on the human heritage'. In that spirit his diary apostrophized: 'To the future or to the past, to a time when thought is free, when men are different from one another and do not live alone – to a time when truth exists and what is done cannot be undone'.[514] The future, or only the past? That is up to us.

---

[513]Rebecca Solnit, *Orwell's Roses* (London: Granta, 2021), p. 259.
[514]Orwell, *Nineteen Eighty-Four*, p. 30 (Penguin ed. p. 32).

# INDEX

www.ingramcontent.com/pod-product-compliance
Ingram Content Group UK Ltd.
Pitfield, Milton Keynes, MK11 3LW, UK
UKHW031248020325
455689UK00008B/168